WOMEN-HEADED HOUSEHOLDS

Women-Headed Households

Diversity and Dynamics in the Developing World

Sylvia Chant
Reader in Geography
London School of Economics and Political Science
University of London

Consultant Editor: Jo Campling

First published in Great Britain 1997 by
MACMILLAN PRESS LTD
Houndmills, Basingstoke, Hampshire RG21 6XS and London
Companies and representatives throughout the world

A catalogue record for this book is available from the British Library.

ISBN 0–333–64067–5 hardcover
ISBN 0–333–64068–3 paperback

First published in the United States of America 1997 by
ST. MARTIN'S PRESS, INC.,
Scholarly and Reference Division,
175 Fifth Avenue, New York, N.Y. 10010

ISBN 0–312–17242–7

Library of Congress Cataloging-in-Publication Data
Chant, Sylvia H.
Women-headed households / Sylvia Chant.
p.   cm.
Includes bibliographical references and index.
ISBN 0–312–17242–7
1. Women heads of households.   I. Title.
HQ1381.C53   1997
305.42—dc20   96–38950
                                          CIP

This book is printed on paper suitable for recycling and made from fully managed and sustained forest sources.

10   9   8   7   6   5   4   3   2   1
06   05   04   03   02   01   00   99   98   97

Printed in Great Britain by
The Ipswich Book Company Ltd
Ipswich, Suffolk

Contents

List of Tables

List of Figures

Preface and Acknowledgements

I first became interested in women-headed households back in 1982 when I went to Mexico as a PhD student. From then on, the subject became ever more fascinating as my research extended to Costa Rica and, later, the Philippines. It was always my idea to conduct comparative research on gender and development and writing this book has provided the first major opportunity to draw together insights gathered in the course of various projects related to women and poverty during nearly one and a half decades. Had it not been for a year's sabbatical between October 1994 and October 1995 provided by a Nuffield Foundation Social Science Research Fellowship, the present endeavour may not have been possible, and I am extremely grateful to the Foundation for their assistance, as well as to the Geography Department at the LSE for supporting my leave. I am also indebted to Dr Jo Campling who encouraged me to write the book and who was a patient and supportive editor.

During my sabbatical year, I made return visits to all three countries, and am particularly grateful for the friendship and assistance provided during this time by Polly de Fraene, Prof Marielos Molina and Dr Carolyn Hall in Costa Rica, by Dr Mercedes González de la Rocha, Ezequiel Bajonero, Florence Martin and Patty Jeffs in Mexico, and Nonoy and Karen Gelito in the Philippines. I also spent a great deal of time in the homes of women in low-income communities in Liberia and Cañas, Costa Rica, in Puerto Vallarta and Querétaro, Mexico and in Boracay, the Philippines. Without their cooperation, my knowledge and understanding of the pains, pleasures and predicaments of female household headship would have been far less rich and vivid than they currently are. I am indebted to them for their openness and generosity with time and information, not to mention their hospitality.

Since the book is not just a product of one but several years' research, it is also appropriate to thank the organisations who funded the key projects which led up to the present one, notably the Nuffield Foundation, the Economic and Social Research Council, the Leverhulme Trust, the British Academy, and the Suntory-Toyota International Centre for Economics and Related Disciplines. I am also grateful for the assistance of Dr Cathy McIlwaine, Dr Sarah Bradshaw and Dr Nandini Dasupta in connection with fieldwork and data analysis for my project in Costa Rica in 1989, and to Emma Galvez, Tessie Sato and Nonoy Gelito for the project in the Philippines in 1993.

I received considerable help, advice and feedback on ideas and drafts of the text from Professor Nancy Folbre, University of Massachussetts, Dr Lynne Brydon, University of Birmingham, Dr Ros Gill, Goldsmiths College, University of London, Dr Patricia Jeffery, University of Edinburgh, Dr Simon Duncan, University of Bradford, Dr Penny Vera-Sanso, University of Kent at Canterbury, David Satterthwaite, International Institute for Environment and Development, Eleni Stamiris, Director of Women and Youth Affairs, Commonwealth Secretariat, and Dr Diane Perrons, Cecilia Tacoli and Hazel Johnstone at the London School of Economics. Above all, I owe major gratitude to Dr Cathy McIlwaine, Queen Mary and Westfield College, University of London, who found the time and patience to discuss ideas and to read and comment extensively on chapters at the early (and sometimes indecipherable!) stages. Thanks are also due to Mina Moshkiri of the LSE Drawing Office for artwork.

I would like to dedicate the book to Rebecca Chapman, and her three children Laurie, Ramsey and Hamish, for meeting their unforeseen and untimely entry to female household headship with consummate strength.

Sylvia Chant
May 1996

1 Introduction: Why Women-Headed Households?

'Single-parent family' is almost a euphemism in popular culture for 'problem family', for some kind of social pathology. Yet describing someone as a 'single-parent' or a 'single-mother' provides very little information except that the family is not headed by a legally married, cohabiting husband and wife. (Kamerman and Kahn, 1988:1)

Like a butterfly emerging from a chrysalis only to find itself caught in a collector's net, the lone parent has broken free from the creaking conventions of the nuclear family, only to become the captive of another less tangible set-up. (Cashmore, 1985:282)

When the father leaves the home, the household trembles; when the mother leaves it, the house crumbles. (Brazilian proverb cited in Stolcke, 1992:139)

If the topic of women is prone to controversy in the realm of social, political and moral (not to mention academic) debates, then that of female heads of household (especially those who are lone parents) seems to meet with greater controversy still.[1] In one sense this is surprising, since for many years (if not centuries), and in most parts of the world, the tie between mother and child has been strongly identified as the primary kin relationship, and parenting as women's fundamental and major responsibility in adult life. Indeed, persistent emphasis on the 'naturalness' of women's child-rearing role has arguably presented one of the biggest constraints to women's attainment of equal status with men in such spheres as the labour market, law and politics. Given that female household headship can tie women even more closely to responsibility for children, especially in societies where raising the young is the main, if not primary, task of biological parents, then why so much heated concern about a situation which in many respects epitomises a stereotypical ideal of womanhood? Moreover, to what extent does concern surrounding female headship rebound upon women who are not single parents, but living alone, with other women and/or in multi-generational 'complex' households?

Answers to this question are far from straightforward, and the present book is likely only to illuminate fragments of a complex (and increasingly polemical) area of enquiry. While data suggest that female-headed households are a diverse as well as a dynamic entity, debates about them are often framed within narrow parameters and based on limited empirical research. Discussions also seem to provoke emotive reactions and to veer unsteadily between fact and myth, particularity and generalisation. This is especially the case with lone-mother households, who have come to represent as much a 'public issue' as a 'personal trouble' (Hardey and Crow, 1991:18; see also Chandler, 1991:6) and who are commonly regarded as 'something of an affront to established beliefs about family life' (Collins, 1991:159). Having attracted considerably more attention than their relatively small numbers might notionally warrant, lone mothers in most parts of the world are viewed as an inauspicious and problematic group, notwithstanding that 'the definition of the "problem" varies depending on who is involved, who is carrying out the analysis, and current societal preoccupations with the concept of the single parent' (Kamerman and Kahn, 1988:1).[2]

In light of the above, the overriding aim of the present book is to provide an idea of the diversity and dynamics of female household headship in developing countries, and to disentangle, if not dispel, some of the stereotypes which surround the phenomenon. The book is concerned with examining what women-headed households are, how they arise, how they survive, and how these issues interrelate with various forms and aspects of gender inequality, particularly among the urban poor. An integral objective of the text is to explore how female heads of household and members of their households perceive their own status and circumstances, thereby offering something of a counter-balance to the somewhat 'public' discourses on the family produced by the state or élite groups (Moore, 1994b:6). To give the voices and opinions of female heads of households greater centrality, the empirical basis of the text draws, where possible, from studies based on interviews with households in developing countries and, in case study sections, from my own research among the poor in urban and/or urbanising areas of Mexico, Costa Rica and the Philippines.[3] Notwithstanding the numerous problems of validity, accuracy and representation attached to perceptual and attitudinal information gathered in one-to-one interviews and filtered though researcher aims and bias,[4] use of 'primary' material such as life histories and personal testimonies undoubtedly brings us closer to an appreciation of what female headship is actually like at the grassroots. As for the relevance of focusing upon Mexico, Costa Rica and the Philippines, these countries are sufficiently similar to indicate the kinds of development processes leading to what is widely regarded as a ubiquitous rise in women-headed units among the poor in the so-called 'Third World' (Bullock, 1994:17; Feldman, 1992:1; INSTRAW, 1992:236–7; Townsend and Momsen, 1987:53). At the same time, they are sufficiently different to highlight factors accounting for variations in their frequency, form, distribution, and economic and social viability. Having said this, another concern of the book is to locate these and other developing countries within the context of a wider global perspective, since women-headed households are clearly on the increase in advanced economies as well (see Freeman, 1993:97; Hobson, 1994:184; Pothukuchi, 1993:288; Shanthi, 1994:17). Yet while debates on female headship, and especially lone motherhood, are much more established in the context of industrialised nations, cross-country comparisons of female household headship within the developed world remain rare, let alone those which span the North–South divide. Although the present attempt to bring together perspectives on women-headed households from both hemispheres might be regarded as over-ambitious,[5] various factors render the exercise worthwhile. First, it allows us to assess the extent to which this 'minority' household form may actually be in the process of becoming a major presence at a world scale. Second, it permits exploration of similarities and differences in the formation and survival of female-headed households between and within the 'advanced' and 'developing' regions. Third, comparative perspectives facilitate greater evaluation of the relative importance of global, national and local factors in accounting for the emergence and experiences of female headship in different places. Fourth, there may be fruitful points of cross-fertilisation in terms of theory and policy. Fifth, a comparative overview of the frequencies and circumstances of women-headed households in different parts of the world may be positive for female heads of household themselves. In many countries, particularly developing nations, societal emphasis on the 'normality' of male-headed households renders women-headed units an anomalous, isolated and disadvantaged category. Knowing that they exist often in large numbers not only in their own countries, but at a global level, may provide a stepping-stone to resisting internalisation and/or acceptance of negative or discriminatory attitudes and practices. At the bottom line, a synthesis of facts, figures and ideas about the presence of women-headed households worldwide could sow seeds for international discussion and action. In this way, I hope the book will be seen as much as a resource for policy-makers, practitioners and activists working on gender in the richer and poorer halves of the globe, as a text for academic consumption.

ORGANISATION OF THE BOOK

Notwithstanding that a large part of the book looks at female household headship and development at the grassroots, the early and final chapters take a wider standpoint, the objective being to set out major characteristics and circumstances of women-headed households at a world scale and to locate key questions surrounding their formation and survival within a broader context. More specifically, the remainder of this chapter asks what female-headed households are and provides an outline of terms and types in different parts of the world. Chapter 2 summarises core debates on female household headship which have featured in the literature on gender and households in North and South, concentrating first on the place of female household headship in theory, and then on some of the key substantive issues (policy, poverty, intergenerational effects, and ideological and social marginality) which have emerged out of dominant discourses and which are taken up in the case study analyses. Chapter 3 reflects on macro-level data on women-headed households, offers ideas as to why there seems to be widespread growth of this group at a global level, and considers elements of their diversity and dynamics in different regions. Chapter 4 brings the focus onto the developing world and provides an overview of factors which have been identified as precipitating or constraining the emergence of women-headed households in different countries. The extent to which these factors are helpful in comparative analysis is examined in the specific contexts of Mexico, Costa Rica and the Philippines in Chapter 5, which also gives information on national patterns of female headship, and sets the scene for the second half of the book which moves from global, regional and national dimensions to the local level, and which brings women's own views into the arena.

Chapter 6, the first in-depth case study chapter, examines women's 'routes' into household headship and the factors they identify as being critical in the process.[6] Chapter 7 considers the extent to which women-headed households are 'disadvantaged', not only on the basis of material conditions, but in psycho-social terms as well. This discussion includes perspectives on 'insider' and 'outsider' images of female-headed households in low-income settlements, differential experiences of domestic and community life, perceived satisfaction with existing circumstances, and views on marriage and remarriage. Chapter 8 deals with the impacts of female headship on younger generations. Alongside material issues such as education and employment, space is dedicated to views on 'father absence' among children, to household trajectories over time, and to the ways in which experiences of growing up in female-headed households affect sons' and daughters' attitudes towards gender, marriage and their own futures. Since the bulk of female-headed households in the case study areas are extended or non-extended lone-parent units, all three case study chapters concentrate predominantly on this group of 'family-based' households, set against comparative information from female spouses in male-headed nuclear and extended households. Attempts are also made thoughout this part of the text to highlight key points of correspondence and divergence among the case study areas. Aside from providing a synthesis of the main conclusions of the book, Chapter 9 returns to more general questions (and priorities) for theory, research and policy on female-headed households.

WOMEN-HEADED HOUSEHOLDS: MANY TERMS, MANY MEANINGS

Most national and international data report a 'female-' or 'woman-headed' household as a unit where an adult woman (usually with children) resides without a male partner. In other words, a head of household is female in the absence of a co-resident legal or common-law spouse (or, in some cases, another adult male such as a father or brother) (UN, 1991:17; see also Rosenhouse, 1989:4). A male-headed household, alternatively, is a unit in which there is an 'intact' couple, or at least other adult females if not the man's spouse (Bruce and Lloyd, 1992:3). Quite apart from the basic asymmetry of these definitions (*ibid.*), both 'households' and 'headship' are problematic concepts.

Defining households

The vast majority of censuses in developing countries define households as spatial units, where members live in the same dwelling and share basic domestic and/or reproductive activities such as cooking and eating (see Mackintosh, 1979; Mishra, 1992; Robertson, 1984; also Brydon and Chant, 1989:8–11; Netting *et al.*, 1984:xi; Pothukuchi, 1993; Young, 1993:14).[7] Although this definition makes sense to my respondents in Mexico, Costa Rica and the Philippines and I will accordingly use it in the text, it is important to flag-up the potential pitfalls of deploying the definition uncritically.

One is that 'households' mean different things to different people in different places, and there is growing debate on the desirability (or otherwise) of generating definitions which might be universally applicable (see Guyer and Peters, 1987; Harris, 1981; Kabeer and Joekes, 1991; Roberts, P., 1991). As Thorner and Ranadive (1992:153) point out, households might just as readily be understood as kinship units or economic units, than as housing units (see also Kalpagam, 1992:78). The relative weight of these different emphases is unlikely to be the same everywhere, and they may also shift over time, especially among the urban poor in developing societies where residential units can 'metamorphose three or four times, not in a life cycle, but in a single year' (Fonseca, 1991:135; see also Moore, 1994b:8–10). In cases where seasonal male labour migration is common, for example, women and children may be left behind at certain times of year and depend entirely on remittances for household survival. More generally, it is vital to acknowledge that even household *reproduction* may not depend entirely (or even predominantly) on the efforts of those who live within the four walls of the spatially defined household, but on wider networks of kin, friends and neighbours (see Gardner, 1995; Lomnitz, 1977; Lomnitz and Pérez-Lizaur, 1991; Nelson, 1992; Peterson, 1993; Schmink, 1986; Willis, 1993; Yanagisako, 1984). In many African countries, for example, the fluidity of boundaries between households is such that a large share of 'domestic' functions is performed outside the residential unit (see Guyer and Peters, 1987:105–7; Lloyd and Gage-Brandon, 1993:117; Moore, 1994b:2; Robertson, 1976; Westwood, 1984). The fact that extra-domestic links might be particularly relevant to female-headed households is indicated by research on both developed (for example Hewitt and Leach, 1993:10; Stack, 1974; McAdoo, 1986; Young and Willmott, 1957) and developing countries (for example Anderson, 1986; Bolles, 1986; Bruce and Lloyd, 1992; González de la Rocha, 1988b; Lewis, 1993:25).[8]

Other problems with the conventional definition of households in macro data sources, is the notion that co-resident households function on the basis of shared participation in survival activities. This view corresponds with neoclassical assumptions embodied within New Household Economics about households being unified entities where income is pooled and labour allocated according to principles of comparative advantage (see Koopman, 1991:148). Yet literature adopting a New Institutional Economics perspective draws attention to the fact that the inputs to and benefits of household membership may be heavily circumscribed by shifting and intersecting inequalities revolving around gender, age and relations to other household members (see for example, Browner, 1989; García and de Oliveira, 1994:209; Kabeer, 1994: Chapter 5; Kabeer and Joekes, 1991; Murray, 1987; Sen, 1987, 1991). Accepting that relations of power and hierarchy are as much a feature of household life as cooperation, households may be more accurately depicted as an 'uneasy aggregate of individual survival strategies' (Bruce and Dwyer, 1988:8; see also Schmink, 1984), or as Moore (1994a:87) puts it: '... a locus of competing interests, rights, obligations and resources'.

A final factor in need of emphasis is that while households often consist of individuals related by blood or marriage, they are by no means always family-based entities, but may comprise unrelated persons such as colleagues, friends or lodgers, or indeed lone individuals (see Brydon and Chant, 1989:137–9; see also Moore, 1994b:2–3; Muncie and Sapsford, 1995:11; UNDAW, 1991:34; Winchester, 1990). Even accepting that most households are family-based, 'Household refers to the basic unit of co-residence and family to a set of normative relationships' (Roberts, 1994:10).[9,10] Thus when we talk of female heads of household, it is not necessarily the case that they are mothers, or, if they are, that their children reside with them. In other words, female-headed households are a diverse group, as outlined in greater depth below.

Defining household headship

If defining households in any universal or standardised way is difficult, then defining headship seems to be more difficult still (Baden and Milward, 1995:18; Chant, 1994c). The short answer to the matter of which criteria might be used to designate a 'household head' is that no-one seems to be clear, and consensus on interpretation has proved consistently elusive. Seminal work on this subject by Harris (1981) argues that the idea of one person in the household being responsible for other household members is a construct of patriarchal thought and practice, inscribed by assumptions about fathers being the natural source of authority within the family, the devolution of varying degrees of power to adult males by the state, the practices of census-takers and so on. The apparently ubiquitous presence of this notion throughout the world owes to the export of Eurocentric ideals of household headship during the colonisation process (Folbre, 1991:90). However, what household heads might actually do or represent in given societies (in relation to other household members) is rarely held up to scrutiny, and still less their function as perceived by people themselves (Stolcke, 1992:138n). Much of this may have to do with the fact that: 'Many of our ideas about heads of household are strongly gendered and to some extent imposed by the need among outsiders to find a readily manageable analytical category' (Lewis, 1993:25). Yet while it might well be the case that in patrilineal and/or patriarchal societes, adult men are vested with varying measures of control over and responsibility for wives and children,[11] constant reference to a singular household head, and especially one who is male, masks the complexity of household allocation systems and can act as a tool to reinforce male power in society at large (Illo, 1992:182). In addition, the characteristics of the household as a whole are routinely identified with those of the head of the household. In cases where male heads are farmers, for example, households are generally classified as 'farming households' regardless of whether other members are engaged in off-farm activities. In this way, women *within* households tend to become invisible, 'their characteristics and contributions being largely ignored' (INSTRAW, 1992:236; see also Folbre, 1991:94; Saradamoni, 1992; Thorner and Ranadive, 1992).

Although a few censuses use instrumental criteria for household headship in place of or in conjunction with self- or proxy-reporting, these are not without problems. The two main ones identified in a UN review of survey documents by Youssef and Hetler (1983) are breadwinning and decision-making: the head of household is either classified as the person earning the major income, or who has most influence over decisions on matters affecting the household as a whole. Recognising that these criteria are usually imputed to (male) heads anyway (see Bruce and Lloyd, 1992; Rosenhouse, 1989), the latter criterion is problematic since it does not specify which *types* of decision are referred to, nor how ranking might be executed when various (if not all) decisions might be taken jointly by spouses or shared with other people (and not just individuals who reside in the household, but outside it as well) (see for example, Gardner, 1995:103–4). As for breadwinning, the question arises as to whether this is a meaningful basis for headship when it may have little relevance for the welfare of other people in the unit. The member earning the biggest wage may not play a particularly active role in family life or contribute much of their income to household reproduction. Indeed, while it is increasingly apparent that many women are playing the major economic role in household survival, patriarchal traditions coupled with the prevalent practice of self- or proxy-reporting means men may be reported as heads irrespective of their earnings (or decision-making roles).[12] For example, women may not see themselves as household heads if the position is normally equated with men (see Gardner, 1995:103; Lewis, 1993:25 on Bangladesh), or, if they do, they may not declare themselves as such. In Jordan, for instance, men are seen as 'protectors' as much as 'providers', and in the absence of a father, the eldest son is likelier to be designated household head than his mother (Kawar, 1996: Chapter 5; see also Chant, 1991a:234 on Mexico). Such patterns may be reinforced by enumeration procedures. In the Bicol region of the Philippines, for example, when interviewers ask about household headship in local dialect, the translation of the term as *'padre de familia'* automatically biases the reporting of a male household member (Illo, 1992:184–5). Cleves Mosse (1993:47) notes more generally that in some countries census takers are 'instructed to name the oldest son, even if he is a young boy, in preference to the woman who is actually keeping the household together'. In short, it is no surprise that 'In most countries of the world today both family law and statistical convention reinforce men's authority as household heads' (Folbre, 1991:91). Moreover, it is important to recognise that household headship is often so integrally bound with masculinity that to earn respect *as men*, males have to exert authority *as* household heads. In the Peruvian Andes, for example, male household heads are expected to act as guardians of 'order and discipline' (Harvey, 1994:74; see also Saktanber, 1994:118 on Turkey).

To better reflect women's critical and under-acknowledged responsibilities in household life, a growing body of academic and policy literature has advocated basing headship more systematically on economic criteria, and to use the term 'woman-maintained' household for situations where women play the key role in household survival, even where a male is present (see Buvinic and Gupta, 1993; Buvinic *et al.*,1992).[13,14] Aside from potentially making the concept of headship more 'policy relevant' in that fewer assumptions are made about particular categories of person, and support might be more accurately targeted to those with major economic responsibility for dependants (see Rosenhouse, 1989:45), this body of literature makes it 'increasingly clear that "headedness" is a question of degree' (Lehmann, 1994b:6), and as Cleves Mosse (1993:45) asserts: 'Using the term "women-maintained" instead of the more usual "women-headed" emphasises the fact that, although many women take responsibility for supporting their families, they are seldom accorded the same recognition, rights and powers as male household heads' (see also Nash, 1980:12).

Indeed while women-maintained households are an important group in their own right, it is important, in my view, to maintain a clear delineation between them. This is especially so given that even if the 'culturally determined overemphasis of the man/husband/father figure' (Jelin, 1991:122), or blind identification of men as the main breadwinners or figures of authority in household units (Buvinic and Gupta, 1993:11) has led to previous exaggeration of the importance of male presence or absence in family life, to *downplay* men's importance may be equally inappropriate. One clear danger of conflating women-maintained with women-headed household is that women in the former might be assumed to have more autonomy than they actually do: yet just because women may have a major economic input into household survival, this does not necessarily translate into power or control, as is evident in many households where women earn more than their husbands (see for example, Blanc-Szanton, 1990b on Thailand; Chant and McIlwaine, 1995a on the Philippines; O'Connell, 1994:5 on the Caribbean; Thorner and Ranadive, 1992 on India). Another is that women who would otherwise be deemed heads are not, because they are economically inactive (Varley, 1996). Beyond this, a problem pertinent to the analysis of both women-headed and women-maintained units (and perhaps especially the latter), is that men outside the household who are not actually partners of the women concerned may have greater influence and/or play a much more important part in daily reproduction than suggested by existing nomenclature (see for example Fonseca, 1991 on Brazil; Stack, 1993 on black families in the USA; Thorbek,

1994: Chapter 6 on Sri Lanka; White, 1992:40 on Bangladesh). Indeed, many of the relationships women have with men outside their immediate households may not only be active, but extremely positive (see Pulsipher, 1993:120 on the Caribbean).

Disaggregating female headship

The above discussion suggests there is a clear need to develop more elaborate and comprehensive household typologies which encompass greater detail on inter- and intra-household flows of economic and social support, and that this might be particularly pertinent to female-headed households. Although an exercise of this nature would require considerably more information than we have at present, I attempt below to provide a preliminary outline of existing terms and definitions of the principal types of female headship documented for different parts of the world, and to introduce key criteria by which each type might be further differentiated. Since a key function of this typology is to act as reference for discussions on the case study countries, it should be treated as schematic and selective rather than exhaustive.

FEMALE-HEADED HOUSEHOLDS: A SELECTIVE TYPOLOGY

Lone-mother households

Lone-mother households are generally understood to describe units comprising a mother and her children and seem to be by far the biggest group of female heads at a world scale.[15] Other terms for this type of household include single mother, solo mother, mother-only, mother-led, or female-headed family with children.[16] Since most one-parent households in the advanced and developing economies are women, then single or lone parent is also generally seen as interchangeable with lone mother (see Kamerman and Kahn, 1988:5). However, the latter clearly indicates the dangers of stereotyping when an increasing number of single parents are male. Stereotypes are also problematic in respect of the characteristics imputed to female lone parents. In the advanced economies, for example, lone mothers are usually seen as young, poor and single, although 'the reality reveals a highly diversified group of women, with not precisely the same characteristics from country to country' (Kamerman and Kahn, 1988:72). These kinds of qualifications are echoed by Millar (1992a:152) for the UK, who argues that 'The "typical" lone mother is hard to find because the phrase covers so many people with so many diverse experiences' (see also Collins, 1991:156; Hobson, 1994:9). Since lone-mother households are headed by a potentially vast range of women, it is accordingly important to consider criteria by which the group might be further sub-divided.

Differentiating factors among lone mothers

Marital status

One important criterion of differentiation between female-headed households is marital status. This not only indicates the routes by which women enter lone parenthood, but may also help to illuminate the reasons for their varied material circumstances. For example, in some contexts, divorced and separated women may be better off than never-married women in that they may have greater legal claim to maintenance from the fathers of their children (see Folbre, 1994a:114), notwithstanding that even women who have been formally married may not be in a particularly privileged position. For example, Kodras and Jones (1991:160) cite a range of studies of the United States which indicate that women undergo a 30–70 per cent decline in economic status in the first year after divorce (see also Gelles, 1995:407). Acknowledging the inevitable difficulties of generalisation, marital status may also have a major effect on lone mothers' social standing and self-images, with widows often facing a more sympathetic reaction than divorcées, both socially and in terms of policy (Folbre, 1991:111; Hewitt and Leach, 1993:15; see also Chandler, 1991; Hobson, 1994:183; Lewis, 1993:33–4). At the same time, it is important to note that the term 'widow' may mean different things in different contexts. In Assyria, for example, widows were not women who had simply lost their husbands, but whose fathers-in-law were deceased and who had no sons (Buitelaar, 1995:1). Moreover, marital status rarely has the same implications among different groups of women *within* societies, let alone *between* them. For example, the position of divorcées vis-à-vis the law (in respect of support from ex-spouses, prospects of remarriage and so on) may depend on a wide range of factors such as class, age, and the circumstances of the marriage breakdown. As for widows, their situations may vary on account of whether former husbands were able to leave them with some form of income (through insurance policies for example), whether they themselves worked and were able to save money at earlier stages of their lives, and/or whether their children or other relatives have taken it upon themselves to care for them. While the latter is not especially likely in developed economies, widows usually do have some access to state financial support in the form of pensions and other allowances (see Hobson, 1994; Winchester, 1990:82). In Third World nations with skeletal social security systems, however, this is much rarer. In a survey of widows in rural North India, for example, less than 10 per cent reported receiving a pension (Chen and Drèze, 1992:39; see also Eswara Prasad, 1995; Gulati and Gulati, 1995). Indeed, in Bangladesh, Kabeer (1991:256) notes that for women without adult sons, the death of a husband can 'precipitate an abrupt descent into poverty' (see also Cain *et al.*,1979:432), and Lloyd and Gage-Brandon (1993:24–5) indicate that households headed by widows in Ghana are worse off than divorcées. While it is clearly difficult to generalise about any of these sub-groups on a cross-country basis, elementary disaggregation by marital status is clearly a step towards dismantling obfuscatory stereotypes.

Stage in the life course
Another important criterion of differentiation between lone-mother households is stage in the life course. This reminds us that households are dynamic entities subject to constant change as a result of internal and external forces, and highlights the irrelevance of thinking in static terms that a 'given percentage of the population lives and reproduces itself with a "nuclear", "extended" or "female-headed" pattern' (Fonseca, 1991:135; see also Hobson, 1994:176). The age of female heads may, in certain contexts, for example, influence how likely they are to remain unpartnered in the longer term. This, in turn, is prone to intermesh with marital status, with Graham (1993:39) pointing out that single mothers tend to be on their own for shorter periods of time than separated or divorced mothers. Even then, circumstances vary, when in some societies serial monogamy is common and regardless of their age, marital or fertility status, women may have a succession of partners over the life course (see Chant, 1991b on northwest Costa Rica; Wilder, 1995 on Malaysia).

Life course is also important from the point of view of resources, in that as households reach a stage at which sons and daughters are entering the labour force and/or are no longer in need of full-time parental care, then access to income may be greater, partly because female heads themselves are freer to work and partly because children may contribute to the household budget (see González de la Rocha, 1994a:268 on households during their 'expanding' and 'consolidating' phases; also Brydon and Legge, 1996:131–2; Safa, 1995:180). Indeed, Thomas's (1995:82) work on Chile shows that the average age of 'non-poor' female heads of multi-person households is 56.9 years compared with 46 years for those classified as 'destitute', and 51.9 years for those classified as 'poor'. In addition, the labour burden of female heads may be lessened when children, particularly daughters, are older and able to share domestic and childcare responsibilities (Benería, 1992:96). Beyond this, there may be fewer social contraints on the mobility and income-generating activities of older women, as in Bangladesh (see Lewis, 1993:35), notwith-standing that widows in this country are usually poor regardless of their labour force activity (Cain *et al.*,1979). Differentiation of lone-mother households on the basis of their own ages/stage in the life course and those of their co-resident offspring is none the less helpful, even if it is unlikely that the same parameters can be used from one developing country to another, let alone across the North–South divide. A baseline categorisation of a lone mother household used in most developed societies, for instance, is that where a woman lives with her dependent children (with the youngest child being below a certain age, usually 15 years), and/or other persons except a spouse or boyfriend (see Roll, 1992). However, as with any standardised definition, difficulties abound. For example, although this is used by Millar *et al.* (1992) in their study of lone-parent households in Ireland, they also point out that many children over 15 years are still at school and in this sense remain dependent. In addition, various social welfare allowances may be paid to lone parents with older children (sometimes up to 21 years) (*ibid.*:9). As far as developing societies are concerned, the definition is even more problematic since many children have already left school and are working by the age of 15; in this instance, they may well have become major supporters of their parents (Moore, 1994b:21–2). In short, life course cannot be used in any universal way: it needs to be considered in relation to the particular socio-economic and cultural characteristics of given societies and contextualised with reference to a wide spectrum of other factors.

Class
Class is clearly another important consideration. At one level, higher socio-economic status is likely to equip women with greater capacity, at least financially, to raise children alone or to live independently; at another, higher class position may make this more difficult in social terms. In Bangladesh, for example, notions of 'self-respect' and female propriety among middle-class women may inhibit their ability to engage in activities that would ensure their survival (Kabeer, 1991:243; see also Gardner, 1995:209–10). In India too, Drèze (1990:51) notes that 'social restrictions on the lifestyle of widows tend to become more rigid as one moves up the caste hierarchy'. While widows from the Untouchable caste can remarry and take a job, for instance, Brahmin widows are 'still under strong pressure to lead a life of seclusion, austerity and chastity dedicated to the memory of their husband'. As for separation or divorce, Kumari (1989:46–7) observes that 'this is socially permissible only in the case of intermediate and scheduled castes. Among upper castes, separation of husband and wife is not at all permitted.' Shanthi (1994:19) also notes that 'unmarried mothers against whom there is a social boycott are almost absent among middle and high income groups, while they are found in large numbers among people living below

the poverty line'. The question of whether lower class status gives greater flexibility in social terms, however, is something about which it is perhaps even less easy to generalise, since cross-class comparisons of female headship remain very rare.[17]

'Race'

The analysis of differences in lone parents on grounds of 'race' has been subject to greater investigation, especially in respect of minority groups in advanced economies. This is partly because lone motherhood may be more common among ethnic minority groups than 'host' populations. For example, in the USA in 1985, 56.7 per cent of all black families with children were headed by women, compared with only 17.8 per cent among whites (Kamerman and Kahn, 1988:10). Even though levels of lone motherhood among white families more than doubled between 1970 and 1985, the rate of increase among black families was almost as high (*ibid.*; see also Simms, 1986:141–2). Among other ethnic minorities in the USA, however, female-headed households are not so numerous: while 1987 data show that women-headed households were 43.3 per cent of the Puerto Rican population, they were only 25.5 per cent among Central and South Americans, 19.2 per cent among Mexicans, and 17.7 per cent among Cubans (Zinn, 1989:871). In the UK in the late 1980s, large inter-ethnic variations were also apparent: for example, 49 per cent of families of West Indian origin were lone-parent units, compared with 30 per cent of Africans, but only 6 per cent of Indian and 8 per cent of Pakistani families (Millar, 1992a:153). Such variations strongly indicate the dangers of generalisation. Similar reservations apply to assumptions that high frequencies of women-headed households are negative, which is often the case when ethnic minority groups lie at the bottom of the socio-economic hierarchy and female headship is taken both as symptomatic and constitutive of disadvantage. This applies in Colombia, for example, where images of 'abnormal' Afro-Caribbean family structures with 'irresponsible fathers' are commonly projected onto the marginalised black population by the dominant *mestizo* (Hispanic) majority (Wade, 1993:20) The fact is, however, that within ethnic minority groups themselves, high frequencies of female-headed households may be accompanied by different perceptions. As Hewitt and Leach (1993:9) point out for the UK: 'In the Afro-Caribbean community … female-headed households are commonplace and not regarded as second best' (see also Shanthi, 1994:20 on the USA). This is echoed by Graham (1993:51) who observes that for Afro-Caribbean women: 'Marriage is not the gateway to adulthood and the guardian of family honour that it is for many Asian households.'[18]

Acknowledging the call to reconceptualise racial diversity 'in a way that embraces the experiences of white families as well as racial ethnic families' (Zinn, 1990:68), it is also critical to view 'race' in conjunction with socio-economic status given that increasing numbers of studies have shown that it is not 'race' *per se* which influences headship, but a combination of factors stemming from various forms of marginalisation to which different ethnic minorities have historically been exposed, such as slavery, the use of black male labour in seasonal plantation agriculture, their recruitment as manual workers in developed economies, racial discrimination, and low wage levels (see Blumberg and García, 1977; Ellis, 1986; Massiah, 1986; Simms, 1986:142; Trotz, 1996).

De facto/de jure status
Another major axis of differentiation between female-headed households relates to whether they have *de facto* or *de jure* status. Although Youssef and Hetler (1983) developed a fairly elaborate typology around these terms, my preference is to use *de jure* female-headed unit to denote households where women live without a male partner on a more or less permanent basis and receive no economic support from one *except* in the form of child maintenance (see below), which in most parts of the developing world is negligible or non-existent anyway. This category would thus include single mothers, divorced and separated women and widows. *De facto* female heads, on the other hand, I restrict to women whose partners are absent due to labour migration, but who have ongoing contact, normally accompanied by the sending home of remittances. Women in this situation are thus heads of household on a temporary basis.

There are clearly a number of difficulties with this simplified distinction between *de facto* and *de jure* female headship. One is that although *de facto* female heads are 'temporary', they may actually spend longer on their own than some *de jure* women heads (especially where male partners have migrated overseas). Another complication is that contact between *de facto* heads and their spouses, while nominally ongoing, may be intermittent, and long periods may elapse between remittances. Beyond this, absent men may in some cases continue to exert major control over family life, and in others not (INSTRAW, 1992:237). Having said this, delineating between the two groups is likely to be important in psychological terms, in respect of decision-making, and in respect of financial resources. As Schlyter (1989:16) sums up, the situation of *de jure* and *de facto* female heads can be 'quite different in regard to economy, power and rights'.

In economic terms, for example, some *de facto* women heads may be better-off than *de jure* ones, especially those whose spouses find well-paid work and are reliable in sending remittances. In Malawi, for example, the households of *de facto* female heads whose husbands are working overseas are the richest in the community (Kennedy, 1994:33–4; see also Gardner, 1995:123–5 on Bangladesh; Watkins, 1994 on Pakistan). More commonly, however, *de facto* heads face greater poverty. Over and above the fact that many men may only be able to move simply within the same country and/or to inferior casual jobs, one key cause of privation is where the assets left behind by husbands are minimal. In Botswana, for example, where many rural women are *de facto* heads of household, half this group have less than one acre of land or no land at all, and a government survey carried out in the early 1980s revealed that 57 per cent had no cattle and 59 per cent no stock, compared with respective figures of 19 and 34 per cent among male-headed households (Johnson, 1992:25). Since women often lack oxen and/or the money to hire draught animals, around half again are unable to plough (*ibid.*). Added to this, however, another reason for the comparative poverty of *de facto* heads is that women may not be in a position to take employment or engage in agricultural production on account of their gender. While *de facto* headship might conceivably lead to greater participation by women in farming or to the acquisition of new skills, more often than not, women are constrained by limited rights to land and/or the power to work it (Cleves Mosse, 1993:46). For example, in most parts of India it is taboo for women to use a plough, meaning that they themselves are unable to cultivate (Drèze, 1990:85; Kumari, 1989:82–3; see also Radcliffe, 1986 on Peru). In Pakistan, Rahat (1986) further notes that women may be reluctant to work in the fields without the 'protection' of spouses since this is likely to attract gossip about their moral propriety. For this reason, other males within the family often take over the agricultural role of absent partners (see also Parnwell, 1993:107). In rural Bangladesh, Gardner (1995:119) observes increased reliance by women with migrant husbands on male relatives, and in Honduras too, women's sons are more than likely to perform agricultural tasks in female-headed units (Bradshaw, 1996a). In such circumstances, women without close male kin of appropriate ages are clearly disadvantaged, and as Elson (1992:41) suggests, 'Male migration reduces the expenses of the household – but all too frequently reduces household resources to an even greater extent ... Migration, in a growing number of cases, appears to be a polite word for desertion. It is a male survival strategy rather than a female survival strategy.'

Despite the poverty of many *de facto* female heads, some authors have noted an expansion in women's say in household negotiations and in community affairs as a result of male migration (Deere, 1990:310; Hugo, 1992:192). In the absence of easy communication with migrant spouses, women in northwest Costa Rica find themselves having to deal with short-term crises, to make decisions and to engage in dealings with the outside world (Chant, 1992:64–5). In rural Pakistan, illiterate women left behind by migrant husbands often force themselves to learn to read and write (often through their children) in order to correspond with spouses directly (and thereby avoid the use of relatives as intermediaries), and also take advantage of the opportunity to expand their personal influence over budgeting and saving (Rahat, 1986). At the same time, men's overall control of household life may remain unchallenged. For example, most Pakistani women 'still have to refer to the male head of household before major production decisions are taken, even when he is absent from the village for months or years on end' (Parnwell, 1993:107). In Bangladesh, many tasks such as financial arrangements and business concerns are handled by women's male kin (Gardner, 1995:119). In Central Java, Indonesia, too, female heads may not increase their participation in public life as a result of male absence (Hetler, 1990). In general then, 'rather than leading to a process of social change whereby women are being removed from the restrictions of their traditionally defined roles, their more prominent position in society tends only to be a temporary phenomenon, with women reverting to their traditional roles once the menfolk have returned from their migration' (Parnwell, 1993:107).

Another issue distinguishing *de facto* heads from their *de jure* counterparts, is the problem of maintaining relationships with partners over long distances. Long spells apart and erratic communication can be highly stressful, sowing seeds of mistrust and/or provoking men and women alike to engage in extra-marital liaisons (see Gledhill, 1995 on Mexico; Gordon, 1981; Murray, 1981 and Wilkinson, 1987 on Lesotho; Hugo, 1992 on Indonesia; Nelson, 1992 on Kenya). For example, Deere (1990:310) notes for the northern Peruvian highlands that men's out-migration can lead to the formation of second families on the coast and to the abandonment of women and children in the *sierra,* and/or to women themselves entering new relationships. Similar patterns are noted by Connell (1984:974) for the South Pacific where 'Migration itself has been noted to contribute to increased divorce rates. Male migrants may come to regard agricultural work as trivial and demeaning and hence the value of a rural life and a rural wife also declines. Both men and women may experience loneliness and psychological pressures that direct them to new partners', notwithstanding that 'Others may gain strength from their separation and prefer a single status.' The latter in many ways, can begin to challenge male authority and lead to new social patterns, such as rising numbers of 'unwed mothers' (see Larsson, 1989:44 on Botswana), or distancing by women from control by their husbands' relatives (see Rahat, 1986 on Pakistan). It may even result in women using their husbands' remittances to finance ventures with new partners, as documented by Parnwell

(1993:107–8) for northeast Thailand where many men move to the Gulf States as overseas contract workers.

> Several stories were circulating in north-east Thailand about cases where the wives of migrant workers had had affairs with other men during their husbands' long absence (typically two years). Their husbands had regularly and reliably remitted money back to their wives, who had squandered it on their lovers or had invested it in building a new home and a new life with their new partner. The first time the migrant may have been aware of these goings-on was when he returned to the home village to find neither spouse or savings.

While it is clearly difficult to generalise about *de facto* female heads, let alone the differences between them and their *de jure* counterparts, their situation might be construed as representing something of a 'halfway house', where key elements of husbands' power remain unless the relationship culminates in permanent separation or death. This may help to explain why in the minds of people themselves, the concept of *de facto* female headship may be of little relevance. As Hetler (1990:178) notes for her study of Jaten, Central Java: '*De facto* heads did not exist in the minds of villagers. "Head" is a legal and social concept and a person does not have to maintain continuous residence in the village to be a *de jure* head.' Since censuses are unlikely to document *de facto* headship either, then this group may well be invisibilised in national data too, which, given the difficulties faced by women 'left behind', may undermine alleviation by policy interventions aimed at assisting vulnerable sections of the population.

Child support

Another piece of information commonly absent from large-scale data sources is whether lone mothers are in receipt of child maintenance payments from the fathers of their children, let alone how much they actually receive. Yet this is clearly extremely important in respect of examining the economic condition of lone-parent households, and in contributing to understanding variations between them. My reading of the literature and my own case study material suggests that the enforcement (and receipt) of child support is extremely weak in developing societies, and while more likely in the advanced economies, there is no guarantee that fathers will pay, especially where couples have not been legally married. Indeed, problems over the absence of fathers' income were critical in stimulating the passing of the Child Support Act in the UK in 1992, and the history of the Child Support Agency (created in 1993), suggests that enforcement is no easy task, as discussed further in Chapter 2.

Agency, gender and lone parenthood

A final element of differentiation among lone-mother households which may well be important in influencing how they fare economically and socially and how they perceive themselves, is whether they have arisen out of some kind of so-called 'positive decision' on the part of women or whether women had little option in the matter. While a 'choice-constraint' dichotomy is by no means appropriate to situations where a wide range of personal, emotional, social, economic and other factors are at stake, and perhaps especially where children are involved (see Bradshaw, 1996a), there are also numerous methodological difficulties in determining the relative power of individual agency, in disentangling cause from effect, and in sifting out immediate reactions to precipitating events from *post hoc* rationalisations. Yet as Palriwala (1990:41) points out '... even where women are clearly oppressed, there are spheres where they may act and decide'. It is accordingly important to explore the extent to which women might have been architects of their existing status, or at least have not actively resisted becoming heads of their own households[19,20] especially when the literature often emphasises male instigation (Chant, 1985b:637).

Considering frequencies of the sex of persons taking the decision to head their own households, for example, may tell us something about the relative power and access to resources (actual and/or perceived) accruing to different groups of women and men in different socio-economic and cultural contexts, and how these might change over time. In the Middle East and South Asia, for example, where 'protection' by men of women's honour is paramount and where women have limited powers to act independently, female headship has historically resulted from male desertion, male-instigated divorce, or widowhood (see for example, Cain *et al.*, 1979; Caplan, 1985; Chen and Drèze, 1992; Drèze, 1990). Yet the increase of women-headed households in countries such as Bangladesh raises questions as to whether this owes mainly to a breakdown in the social protection conventionally offered to women through family systems, or whether this is a 'new form of social organisation in which women assume more assertive roles in patriarchal society' (Lewis, 1993:24). In other parts of the world, where mother–child units have traditionally had more autonomy (see Kandiyoti, 1991), it certainly seems that the weight of men's decisions in the formation of female-headed households may be less. For example, in Antigua, Powell (1986:92) found that as many as 35 per cent of currently single women had initiated the move out of their previous relationship, and in the West Indies more generally, Pulsipher (1993:113) notes that: 'While the tendency for women to have children by several mates is changing as education and employment options for women increase, some educated women with well-established careers may choose to have a child with an acquaintance, and marriage or even long-term involvement may never be a consideration', especially if a man is not a suitable lifelong companion or does not possess attractive economic assets. In sub-Saharan Africa too, it has been noted that 'the unmarried state often arises due to an individual and deliberate choice of freedom and emancipation' (Cutrufelli, 1983:71; also Moore, 1988:64). In Ghana, such decisions may well be underpinned by strong lineage support (Lloyd and Gage-Brandon, 1993:118), which is not to say that in various parts of the continent, men too might be reluctant to marry because they fear taking on economic respon-sibilities they cannot fulfil due to declining employment and incomes (Moore, 1994b:12). Indeed, in poor townships in South Africa, Muthwa (1993:4) talks about the prevalence of 'family breakdown' in contributing to high numbers of women-headed households, drawing attention to the crucial role played by men's growing inability to fulfil the expectation of providing for their families. Yet, while men themselves may feel unable to cope with a sense of failure and depart of their own accord (especially where there is no enforced child support to reduce their incentives to do so), women too may 'opt-out' of a relationship in order to avoid the problems of living with men who might become 'burdens' on family welfare. In Latin America, similar patterns are in evidence: while male desertion has often been stressed as a key factor leading to female headship (see Arizmendi, 1980; Bridges, 1980; García and de Oliveira, 1994:153 on Mexico), increases in female-instigated separation may represent an attempt amongst women to free themselves from some of the more repressive and restricting aspects of *machista* (male-dominated) culture (see Harris, 1982; also Chant, 1985b). Having said this, Jelin (1991:121) cautions that while the 'self-reliance that women exercise for daily survival may be linked to increasing autonomy and choices to greater equality and freedom, at least for middle- and upper-class women, ... for women less well-off economically, it may be the result of a more perverse process'. Indeed, in the absence of properly regulated child support, it may well be that women's freedom is heavily constrained as a result of material privation.

Although the question of agency is riddled with problems, the patterns which predominate in different settings may at least illuminate something of the underlying causes and correlates of female headship in given areas, and the case studies in the book are intended to draw us into this relatively underexplored issue by providing some of the personal interpretations of women in Mexico, Costa Rica and the Philippines as to how they came to be lone mothers and how they and the members of their households perceive themselves and their situations. Yet although lone mothers are the biggest group of female heads in all three areas, others are also found in the case study communities and elsewhere, as detailed below.

Female-headed extended households

Various studies, particularly of Latin America, the Caribbean and sub-Saharan Africa have revealed a greater likelihood of extension among female- than male-headed households, whereby female heads (unpartnered women with or without children) have other relatives living in their homes (see Benería and Roldan, 1987; Bolles, 1986:69; Chant, 1985a,b, 1991a; García and de Oliveira, 1994:152; González de la Rocha, 1988a, 1994a,b; Kanji, 1994:116; Rakodi, 1991:43; Safa and Antrobus, 1992:66–7; Tienda and Ortega, 1982; Willis, 1994). In Mexico in 1987, for example, data from the national household survey showed that 36.2 per cent of female-headed households were extended compared with only 21.5 per cent among men (Acosta Diaz, 1992:31). Similar patterns obtain in Costa Rica, where 1970 census data indicated extension in 34.5 per cent of female-headed households compared with 24.7 per cent among their male counterparts (Reuben Soto, 1986:23, Table 5). In their study of Durban, South Africa, Todes and Walker (1993:46) found that all women-headed units in the communities they studied lived as some form of extended arrangement, whereas this only applied to half the male-headed households.

Generally speaking, female heads of extended households are older than their counterparts in non-extended units, especially where extension is family-based. This is mainly due to the fact that the potential pool of kin who might join their households is wider since children are more likely to be forming partnerships and having children of their own, and also because the only households in which women are most likely to be heads are those in which they are the oldest members. Although few detailed studies have been conducted on the nature of household composition among female-headed extended units in different parts of the world, the evidence from Latin America and the Caribbean suggests that additional kin (excluding children's spouses or grandchildren) are more often female than male (see for example, Bolles, 1986 on Jamaica; Chant, 1985a and González de la Rocha, 1994b:13 on Mexico). This may arise because female relatives are more willing to take on a range of jobs around the home and/or present fewer problems of compatibility with female heads. An additional factor pointed-up by UNDAW (1991:35) with reference to Brazil, is that older women with few resources and/or who are incapacitated may have to move in with kin to be cared for. Yet in countries such as India where men have considerably greater economic and social power than women, married sons are likely to be more common in the households of unpartnered (usually widowed) women (see Chen and Drèze, 1992; Drèze, 1990; Kumari, 1989). In Ghana, alternatively, where women are more likely to be reliant on extra-household support, as many as 48 per cent of those heading households in the 15–59 year age group have no other adult, compared with only 2.6 per cent of male-headed households (Lloyd and Gage-Brandon, 1993:119).

The fact that household extension can provide female heads with greater scope to manage household survival, whether through conferring some relief from domestic labour and childcare and freeing women for employment, and/or increasing their access to other sources of income, is perhaps particularly necessary in situations where there is no welfare state to bolster the economic and labour capacities of female lone parents or indeed mothers in general (see Moore, 1994b). Yet even in the USA (where there is arguably some kind of governmental 'safety net'), a survey of black single parents in Baltimore showed that 32 per cent out of 318 respondents with custody of at least one child under 19 years lived in extended arrangements (McAdoo, 1986:159, Table 1). Indeed, 'The support and help provided by the intergenerational family units were the key ingredients to enable these black women to maintain positive mental health and to cope with the stresses and role overload they experienced as employed single mothers' (*ibid.*:164).

As with lone-mother households, it is clearly important to distinguish different types of female-headed extended units on the basis of where they live, whether they receive income or other forms of support from outside the household, their marital status, class, 'race', *de jure* or *de facto* status, and so on.

Lone female households

Another important sub-group of female heads are lone-female households. The pattern of women living alone is increasingly common among affluent/professional groups in the North (see Duncan, 1991a:103; Folbre, 1991:100; Gordon, 1994) and among the elderly in both hemispheres (see Rudd, 1989; Sykes, 1994 on advanced economies; Sethi, 1993; UNDAW, 1991; Varley, 1996 on developing countries), albeit for different reasons and with different characteristics in different places. For example, in advanced economies, women who live alone tend to be more common in urban than in rural areas and may be drawn from a range of ages and social groups (Chandler, 1991; Duncan, 1991a; Winchester, 1990). Factors exacerbating the tendency for elderly women to live alone in countries such as Australia include higher female life expectancy among women, lower age than husbands at marriage, increased government provision of support services, and the fact that smaller family sizes mean that there are fewer relatives with whom women can live in their later years (Rudd, 1989:14). As for younger women, Gordon's (1994) study of the UK, the USA and Finland indicates that increased access to education and income-generating opportunities (especially professional jobs) has led to postponement and/or avoidance of marriage or cohabitation as means of escaping domestic and career conflicts. In developing countries such as India, on the other hand, lone-female households are more likely to be found in older age groups and in villages from where sons and daughters have had to migrate to find work (Sethi, 1993). Lone-female households certainly seem to be more common than lone-male households, with 1979 data showing that while 26.5 per cent of all female-headed households in India were single person units, this only applied to 4.8 per cent of male heads (Visaria and Visaria, 1985:61, Table 4). A similar pattern is noted by González de la Rocha (1994b:12) for Guadalajara, Mexico where although only 8.5 per cent of female heads in her survey lived alone, this applied to virtually no men (0.3 per cent). In González's opinion, this could be interpreted as revealing 'greater male dependence on the social base created by households with adult women'.

Single-sex/female-only households

Aside from households consisting of one woman alone, there are also households where two or more women, who may or may not be related, live together, without men (see INSTRAW, 1992:236). In developing regions such as Southeast Asia, the growth of export-manufacturing industries has been associated with a trend for female factory workers to share lodgings with their colleagues in urban areas (Armstrong and McGee, 1985; Zosa-Feranil, 1984; see also Kabeer, 1995 on Bangladesh). The same can be observed in international tourism destinations, where some employers set up single-sex dormitories on work premises (Chant, 1996b). However, single-sex households are by no means unknown in other regions, such as West Africa, where a long history of matrilineal kinship and/or polygyny have been associated with a weakness in marital unions and a tendency for women to head their own households or to reside with female relatives. This is especially common among Ghanaian groups such as the Ga and the Asante (see Abu, 1983; Sanjek, 1983; Vellenga, 1983). Reasons commonly cited for separate residence among women include the desire to avoid direct exposure to sexual jealousy and a concern to maintain their economic autonomy (Abu, 1983; see also Etienne, 1983 on the Ivory Coast). Having said this, while women might live in different dwellings from their male partners, contact and interchange may be frequent (see also Hagan, 1983; Robertson, 1976; Westwood, 1984), which again raises questions about the value of a residentially- (as opposed to functionally-) based definition of household (see earlier). In addition, the fact that younger sons may live with their mothers means that some of these designated single-sex units would perhaps be better described as 'female-dominant/predominant' households.

Female-dominant/predominant households

Female-dominant/predominant households describe units where adult women, who may or may not be related, reside with one another and constitute the majority sex in the household (INSTRAW, 1992:236). The important thing about them is that although they may contain males (for example, children), the latter occupy a junior position, leaving women as the arbiters of authority, if not as major breadwinners as well (*ibid.*). This type of household has been noted amongst groups of workers in feminised occupations such as sex work (see Chant, 1996b on the Philippines; Oldenburg, 1992 on India).

Grandmother-headed households

Grandmother-headed households are distinguished by the fact that their households comprise a woman and her grandchildren (and possibly other relatives as well), but not the grandchildren's parents. Generally speaking, the children concerned are those of daughters who may have left their offspring with their mothers because they need to migrate for employment and/or cannot cope with the demands of childcare and a job simultaneously. This arrangement seems to be particularly common in East and West Africa (see Brydon, 1979; Lloyd and Gage-Brandon, 1993:120; Nelson, 1987), the Caribbean (see Clarke, 1957; Goody, 1975; Momsen, 1992; Smith, 1956, 1988), and in Southeast Asian countries such as Indonesia (Hetler, 1990:181). Grandmother-headed households are also known in Latin American countries such as Brazil where on remarriage a mother might be 'obliged by her new companion to disperse her children by previous liaisons' (Fonseca, 1991:143), although this might not necessarily involve a grandmother, but another relative or friend (*ibid.*).

Embedded female-headed units

Younger mothers without partners are often more likely to reside in other people's homes than to head their own households, meaning that the category of 'embedded' female head needs some discussion. Commonly used to denote lone mothers heading 'sub-families' within extended households, this group are variously referred to as 'concealed', 'embedded', 'disguised', 'submerged' or 'hidden' female heads (see Bradshaw, 1996a; Buvinic and Gupta, 1993; Moser, 1993b; Varley, 1994a). Even if these women do not head households in the strict sense of the term (see earlier) and for this reason 'female-headed sub-family' might be more appropriate, it is important to recognise their existence for a number of reasons. First, they tell us something about women's scope in different societies to live independently: in some circumstances women may not be able to afford to maintain children on their own, in others there may be strong social taboos which prevent them from so doing; in others there may be little institutional support in the form of childcare and women with children who need to work may have to rely on help from co-resident kin; in others it could reflect the deterioration in economic conditions for women following separation or divorce. As Graham (1993:60) points out for the UK, for example: 'Living with relatives and living in crisis accommodation are woven into the housing experiences of many lone mothers.'

A second, and related reason for acknowledging female-headed sub-families (if not to regard them as *bona fide* female-headed households) is that to some degree they indicate how many female heads there *potentially* are. Indeed, some authors talk about how their inclusion would double existing estimates of female headship. For example, in her study of clothing workers in Mexico's Yucatán peninsula, Peña Saint Martin (1992b) discovered that 50.8 per cent of female heads were 'hidden' in male-headed extended households, meaning that while only 26.5 per cent of *visible* heads were women, a more accurate figure would have been nearly half the sample (see also Brydon and Legge, 1996 on Ghana; Falú and Curutchet, 1991 on Argentina; Schlyter, 1989 on Zimbabwe; Todes and Walker, 1993:45 on South Africa). Having said this, embedded female-headed sub-families are not households *sensu strictu*, besides which if women raising children within a larger household are identified as a separate category, then it is probably also important to pluck out other sub-families, such as young couples, with or without children, living with in-laws and even single childless women who might actually be earning a salary sufficient to support themselves (see Varley, 1994a:127). Indeed, in their study of low-income settlements in Durban, where 22 per cent of households had one or more sub-families living with them, Todes and Walker (1993:49) found that although more consisted of an unmarried daughter and children, in quite a number of instances, the sub-families comprised an unmarried son and his offspring. Moreover, while there may be 'secondary groupings' identifiable as sub-families within larger households, 'this does not mean that they would (wish to) see themselves, or be seen by others, as a separate unit' (Varley, 1994a:128).

Marital status among embedded female heads is significant in that in some countries, such as the Philippines, unmarried daughters may be sheltered by parents or other relatives in order to minimise family shame, and/or gossip from neighbours, or to safeguard falling into socially-unacceptable occupations such as sex work (Chant and McIlwaine, 1995a; also Chapter 6). Athough Buvinic *et al.* (1992) claim that embedded female heads are often never-married women, and, more specifically, young adolescent mothers, Bradshaw's (1996a) work on Honduras suggests that this is by no means always the case. This is echoed by Graham (1993:44) for Britain, who refutes the idea that all single mothers are young and poor. Indeed, in India, for example, it is much more likely that older women (notably widows) will be embedded within the households of adult sons (see Chen and Drèze, 1992; Drèze, 1990).

While embedded female heads are undoubtedly a significant group, they do not form part of the mainstream analysis in the present text. This is mainly because the status of full household headship (whether on a short-[*de facto*] or long-term [*de jure*] basis – see earlier) and what this means for women, is itself so inadequately researched, and exploring its wide-ranging corollaries is my primary concern in the chapters which follow.

NOTES

1. A female-headed household is not necessarily a female *lone-parent* household, as discussed at length later in the chapter. In other words, female headship is a generic category within which female lone-parents are a specific sub-group. None the less, since the bulk of female-headed households worldwide are those which comprise a woman and her offspring, the terms are often used interchangeably.

2. With reference to the United States, Kamerman and Kahn (1988:1–3) point out that the 'single-parent family problem' is regarded variously as a problem of family breakdown and disorganisation, a problem of poverty, a problem of and for blacks, a problem of teenage unwed mothers, a problem of divorce, a problem of misguided welfare policies, a problem of societal change, a problem of the ghetto underclass and social dislocations, a problem of the feminisation of poverty, a problem of child poverty, a problem for children as they grow up, and a problem of deviancy.

3. My studies in Mexico have been based on interviews with an overall total of over 400 low-income households in the cities of Querétaro, León and Puerto Vallarta during 1982–83, 1986, 1992 and 1994. My work in Costa Rica has entailed interviews with an overall total of 350 households in the towns of Cañas, Liberia and Santa Cruz in 1989, 1992 and 1994. In the Philippines, a total of 240 households were interviewed in the Central and Western Visayas (mainly

in Cebu City, Lapu-Lapu City and Boracay) during 1993 and 1995, and nearly 80 workers from specific occupational groups in the same localities. Further methodological details are given in Chapter 6.

4. Much debate in feminist circles on research methods, objectives and epistemology is of critical relevance to the present book, one main issue being that it cannot be taken for granted that interviews produce 'truths'. The nature of interviews (location, content, mode of questioning and so on), connections between researcher and 'researched' (relations of power, language differences and so on), and characteristics and standpoints of the interviewer (colour, class, politics, research agenda, personal experiences, for example) all affect what is said, what is revealed, what information is used in the research account, and how it is presented. In this way, 'truths' are 'constructed', and cannot be read off dialogue as realities (see Maynard, 1994; Phoenix, 1994; Thompson, 1992). As Maynard and Purvis (1994:6) sum up: 'There is no such thing as "raw" or authentic experience which is unmediated by interpretation', and this applies as much to the researcher as the researched. Other considerations include the fact that female heads do not necessarily identify themselves solely in this manner, but have multiple positions and identities (affected by where they live, their marital status, stage in the life course and so on). Another issue is that my own entry points to the case study countries have taken place at different stages in my life (in respect of age, professional experience and status, marital circumstances and so on), although to some extent I tried to 'level' this out by revisiting all the countries in the space of six months during 1994–5. A final issue is that the in-depth semi-structured interviews from which I draw most of the qualitative material were carried out with relatively small numbers of respondents (see Chapter 6), so cannot be argued to be 'representative' as much as indicative.

5. Aside from the dearth of existing studies on female-headed households at a world scale, other factors which may contribute to some over-reaching in the present book are first, that I have no personal survey experience of female household headship in the advanced economies. Second, it is difficult in a volume of this size to give the developed world more than relatively scant treatment given the primary focus on developing regions. A further limitation is that my work within the developing world has concentrated on low-income urban groups, rather than taking a cross-class (or indeed rural–urban) perspective. It should also be noted that several countries are missing from the analysis (most notably, those in Eastern Europe and the former Soviet Union), mainly because of a lack of publications available in the UK on women-headed households in these areas.

6. The term 'route' into female headship has been used by Millar *et al.* (1992) in relation to Ireland, and by Bradshaw (1996a) in the context of her work on Honduras.

7. This definition is also common in statistical, policy and academic documentation in the developed world. For example the Irish Labour Force Survey classifies households as a person or group of persons (usually, though not necessarily, related) with common living arrangements. This involves sharing the same dwelling or part-dwelling, living at the address in question at least four nights a week, sharing household expenses such as light and heat, and consuming one meal together a day (Millar *et al.*, 1992:104). As Kalpagam (1992:78) points out with reference to India (where similar parameters obtain), this definition essentially refers to a 'housekeeping unit'. An alternative, broader definition

reached by an international group of scholars involved in the 'Households, Gender and Age' project initiated by the United Nations University in the early 1980s is that: 'The household, in all its different cultural connotations, is the primary social living unit. In it are encapsulated a cluster of activities of people who live together most of the time and provide mutual physical, socio-psychological, and developmental support and functions within the broader organisation and environment of the community' (Masini, 1991:4).

8.   While various authors have noted a greater likelihood of dependence among female heads on extra-household networks, Willis (1994) observes for low- and middle-income groups in Oaxaca City, Mexico, that women heads, particularly of non-extended units, make *less* use of networks than their counterparts in male-headed households, one reason being that their pool of contacts is smaller due to the absence of kin of male spouses. Another reason, noted by González de la Rocha (1994a:211) for Guadalajara, is that in the early stages of the domestic cycle in particular, lone mothers may not have the time to 'establish and extend relationships' because they are working for money at the same time as performing all the domestic chores. Indeed, the operation of extra-household networks, which is widely noted to be the responsibility of women, often requires considerable effort, (see Leonardo, 1993; Wilson, G., 1987). González de la Rocha (1994a:211) further suggests that the poverty of many female-headed households means that they may 'not have the material resources to get involved in social exchange'. This reinforces the observations of Lomnitz (1977) on the necessity for social and economic equality among members of exchange networks in Mexico, and is also noted by Chen and Drèze (1992:23) for India, where they claim that 'unreciprocated transfers between separate households are a rare occurrence'. It is also interesting to consider that widows in India may not have access to help either from their own or their dead husbands' families. Chen and Drèze (1992:22) for example, talk of findings which 'clearly invalidate the notion that a widow is typically reintegrated in the household of her in-laws, parents or other relatives', and that 'The consequences of this residential isolation might not be so severe if widows could count on getting regular support from their relatives through inter-household transfers. There is, however, little evidence of substantial support in that form ...' (see also Chapter 7).

9.   Citing the work of Laslett (1972), Wilk and Netting (1984:1) are also careful to draw attention to the fact that 'The very impetus to separate the concept household from family can be seen as an attempt to replace a culturally defined unit with one that is more based on observation and can be more readily compared across cultures.' They go on to indicate that 'This goal, while laudable, is unreachable as long as our criteria for finding, defining and counting households remain vague or inconsistent, grounded in yet more folk categories like "domestic functions" or based on our own intuitive ideas of what a household should look like.' See also Fonseca (1991) on the importance of distinguishing between household and family systems.

10. The US Bureau of the Census distinguishes household from family by classifying a household as a housing unit which may or may not contain related persons, and a family as consisting of two or more persons related by birth, marriage or adoption who reside together in a household (Gelles, 1995:119).

11. See Folbre (1991:90) for an interesting discussion of family law in various cultural and religious contexts, and the way in which the Roman doctrine of *Patria*

Potestas ('father as ruler'), though attenuated by Christian and Judeaic influences, displays many similarities with Islamic law and other traditional laws in assigning power to the eldest male in the household (see also Lerner, 1986; O'Connell, 1994:15).

12. Self- or proxy-reporting is sometimes associated with adoption of the term 'householder' or 'person of reference', as has been the case with census agencies in the United States, Canada, France, Italy and Switzerland amongst others. None the less, there is still a bias towards men, besides which it makes it more difficult to work out how many households are actually female-headed since less information about gender is provided (Folbre, 1991:94; see also INSTRAW, 1992:136–7). In Norway, for example, the householder is classified as the oldest person in the home, which gives no indication of gender (Folbre, 1991:94). Moreover, as for more arbitrary/less specific definitions of 'householders', 'Reliance on opinion (as in "the person recognised as such") makes responses highly sensitive to cultural context and enumerator behaviour' (*ibid.*:93; see also Kumari, 1989:25 *et seq.*). As Folbre (1991:113) goes on to point out, 'Mere adoption of the term "householder" in place of the more politically charged "household head" is no substitute for a coordinated international effort; census measures of household structure need to be defined in consistent terms that provide information about gender and age composition.'

13. The notion of 'women-maintained' households has historical precedence in the concept of matrifocality used to describe situations where women play the dominant role psychologically or economically in households, even where men reside with them (see Solien de Gonzales, 1965). The matrifocality concept originated mainly in the context of work on female-dominated families in the Caribbean in the 1950s and 1960s (see Clarke, 1957; Solien de Gonzales, 1960, 1969; Smith, 1956, 1988; Stolcke, 1992:138–9).

14. The term 'female-supported' has also been used to describe women-maintained households (see Mencher, 1989).

15. The term 'lone mother' is more common in the literature on advanced economies, but is gradually gaining ground in studies of the developing world.

16. Even then, different scholars attribute different meanings to these terms. For example, Hobson (1994:176) sees 'solo mothers' as distinct from 'lone mothers' or 'single parents' in that the former frequently live with kin (or sometimes with lovers) rather than on their own.

17. Notable exceptions include the work of González de la Rocha (1993, 1994b) and Willis (1993, 1994) on Mexico.

18. High frequencies are clearly not always accompanied by positive images within the same social or ethnic group. For example, although around half the women in the Sri Lankan slum studied by Thorbek (1994:118) were single or had been married several times, they often faced condemnation from neighbours.

19. In her analysis of single women, Gordon (1994:44–9) discusses the complexities of the term 'choice', preferring instead to use 'voluntary singles' for women who have come to view being without a partner as a satisfactory (or more appealing) alternative, and are not actively seeking to change their circumstances.

20. The point about non-resistance to heading a household is important in that women who are deserted by men may opt to move in with relatives (and become embedded sub-families) rather than retain or create an independent household.

2   Conceptual Context and Core Debates

INTRODUCTION

With reference to literature on women-headed households in both the advanced and developing economies, this chapter sets the scene for some of the more specific issues pursued in the course of the book, first by considering the place of women-headed households within wider family and feminist theories, and second by sketching out the parameters of research and debate on four key topics which have dominated the literature on female household headship and/or lone motherhood: policy, poverty, the intergenerational effects of lone parenthood, and ideological and social marginality.

CONCEPTUALISING WOMEN-HEADED HOUSEHOLDS: BACKGROUND AND CONTEXT

The place of female headship in 'mainstream' household theory

While noted in Chapter I that female-headed households are a subject of growing interest and research, there are few identifiable 'theories' on their evolution (or implications), nor do they have a prominent place in wider household theory. As Stichter (1990:50) has summed up: 'One major variation in family structure which has not been incorporated in most theories of the household is the mother–child or female-headed family.' Moreover, if female-headed *families* have been absent from theoretical discussions of household evolution, other types of female-headed unit (for example single person and non-family households) have received even less attention.

At one level these omissions undoubtedly relate to the generalised absence of gender in most mainstream research on the household (with the possible exception of anthropological work) until the mid-1970s. Another likely reason for the comparative neglect of women-headed households is the traditional emphasis in major theories of household evolution on size and composition (as opposed to headship), and, more specifically, the ways in which industrialisation and urbanisation have purportedly led to the displacement of large, extended households by smaller nuclear structures (usually based around a male breadwinner and a female home-maker) (see Goode, 1963:368–70, 1964:1083; Gugler and Flanagan, 1978; Wallerstein and Smith, 1992; Young, M.L., 1992).[1] Notwithstanding that the extended-to-nuclear trajectory has proved to be erroneous in numerous historical and contemporary contexts around the world (see Brydon and Chant, 1989:139–45; Flandrin, 1979; Laslett, 1972; Mitterauer and Sieder, 1982; Moore, 1994b:2; Wallerstein and Smith, 1992), the legacy of earlier discussions may have precluded exploration of alternative questions, other aspects of household form, and/or alternative types of household unit. Certainly, the focus on global evolutionary convergence in family structure and the accompanying quest for generalisation has traditionally meant that theory has often been 'deductive and grounded in evolutionary or functionalist principles more than in systematic observation' (Berquó and Xenos, 1992:9; also McDonald, 1992; Netting *et al.*, 1984:xv). This in turn has probably contributed to obscuring the fact that 'the concrete conditions of capitalist development do not in fact pare kinship relations down to a basic elementary family form but produce a range of modified extended family forms which are often female-centred' (Stivens, 1987:90). Indeed, where 'female-centredness' has been acknowledged, primarily in relation to families in the Caribbean, interpretations have traditionally combined ethnocentrism and antipathy in equal measure. As Pulsipher (1993:120) argues:

Being used to familial male dominance in their own cultures, many observers ... saw the pathological lack thereof in 'matrilocal' residential patterns and 'matrifocal' domestic relationships. Though few said so explicitly, many left their readers with the impression that the Caribbean family was in a state of disintegration.

Similar views apply where Afro-Caribbean households have been examined in relation to non-white populations within advanced economies, their 'alternative' forms and low ranking in the socio-economic order explained as a mutually-reinforcing outcome of 'cultural deviance'. As Zinn (1990:71) asserts with reference to the history of research on black women-headed households in the USA:

Mainstream (American) sociology ... supported popular ideology by legitimising the marginalisation of racial ethnic groups in the social hierarchy. As cultural holdovers in a modernising world, minority families were relegated to the sidelines with no relevance to the core of family theory.

The 'mainstream' American sociology to which Zinn refers was largely dominated by structural-functionalist approaches, which along with related neoliberal theories of social change and organisation such as Modernisation, not only confined residualist thinking to racial minorities, but to 'marginal' groups in general. In this light, it is no surprise that all types of women-headed household were subject to being branded as 'deviant' from the norm, 'dysfunctional' to society and indicative of 'system breakdown', not to mention 'moral decay' (see Chester, 1977; Dennis, 1993; Morgan, 1995; also Gelles, 1995:40–3 for a general review of structural-functionalist approaches to the family). Just as pathological discourses surrounding black family structures could be construed as a means of justifying and perpetuating white supremacy, cognate treatment of female household headship stood to minimise challenges both to patriarchal structures and to class divisions insofar as holding lone motherhood responsible for social and economic marginalisation deflected attention from broader societal processes responsible for inequality and disadvantage (see for example, MacDonald and MacDonald, 1979; Moore, 1994b:16–17; Segal, 1995:312; Zinn, 1990).

Female household headship and feminist theories

Although Marxist and Marxist-Feminist scholarship did not engage in head-on confrontation with these views of female household headship, it at least generated interest in the idea of mutual accommodations between patriarchy and capitalism, and to 'political economy' thinking that shifted the spotlight away from 'cultural deviance' as a factor explaining 'alternative' household forms, to mode of production and the state. That the emergence and endurance of female-headed households is linked to a given society's mode of production and political economy is central to the model of the mother–child household of Blumberg and García (1977) which, on the basis of work on the Americas, attempted to flag up the conditions which might lead to the formation of lone mother households in capitalist societies. Given that this seems to represent the only effort to synthesise ideas about the evolution of mother–child households into an explicit model, and that many of its points are relevant for comparative research (see Chapters 3 and 4), it is worth outlining the basic tenets of the schema in a little detail here.

Blumberg and García's 'political-economy' model of mother–child household formation
Blumberg and García's (1977) model sets out five basic conditions (or 'pre-requisites') likely to lead to the formation of households headed by lone mothers (see also Blumberg, 1978):

   Condition One is that 'the unit of labour, the unit of compensation and the unit of property accumulation be the *individual*, independent of sex' (Blumberg and García, 1977:109, their emphasis). In most patrilineal societies where assets are corporately held by households (and more particularly by male elders) and production is a collective family enterprise, it is unlikely that women could commandeer the resources necessary to determine their own living arrangements (see also Cain *et al.*, 1979; Kabeer, 1994:127; Momsen, 1991:26).

Condition Two is that 'females have *independent access to subsistence opportunities*' (Blumberg and García, 1977:109, their emphasis). This means women having access to cash via their own employment, through that of their children, through inheritance or state welfare, and/or by means of being legally able to head a separate residence and to control property.

Condition Three is that 'those subsistence opportunities open to females can somehow be reconciled with *child-care responsibilities*' (*ibid.*; Blumberg's and García's emphasis). This might be done through women drawing upon the help of relatives, friends or older children, waiting until children mature, organising paid assistance, or alternatively using state welfare (where available) in order to stay at home. Reconciliation of productive and reproductive responsibilities might also be achieved when economic opportunities are open to women that 'can be easily interrupted and resumed; are not dangerous; do not require fast and long spatial mobility; and do not involve a workplace from which children are excluded' (*ibid.*:123).

Condition Four for the emergence of female-headed households is that, 'the woman's subsistence opportunities from all sources in the absence of a male head must not be drastically less than those of the men in her class' (*ibid.*:109). Two factors are important here: first, if women's earnings are substantially lower than men's, they are less likely to be able to survive alone; second, where men's earning capacity is much greater than women's, so too is the incentive to find or retain a male partner (Blumberg and García, 1977:114–15; see also Edwards *et al.*, 1993:60). That female-headed households are generally most numerous among marginal economic groups (so-called 'surplus labour'), is explained by the fact that male contributions to household income are less significant than in households with higher socio-economic status.

The fifth condition, and more relevant to the *persistence* of the mother–child household, is that 'the political economy of the society produces and profits from a surplus labour population, and that the female-headed family unit successfully *reproduces* the surplus labour population to the benefit of those who control the political economy' (Blumberg and García, 1977:109–10, their emphasis), in short, the state, capitalists and other hegemonic groups (see also Wallerstein and Smith, 1992:17 *et seq.*).

While Blumberg's and Garcia's effort to identify factors affecting the formation of female-headed households is helpful insofar as it recognises that household headship is contingent upon economic and political structures, there are obvious weaknesses in respect of its exclusive focus on market economies, its omission of discussion about the variable 'costs' of children, its blunt instrumentalism, and its inability to explain non-economic forces. Indeed, given the more general shift from the idea that a society's mode of production is a major determinant of family systems and that family systems are constituted through compromises and negotiations between ideology and economic structure (McDonald, 1992:23; see also Guyer and Peters, 1987:198; Moore, 1994b:86), it is no surprise that the model has not been widely used by feminist researchers. Yet in many respects, criticisms that might be levelled at other aspects of Blumberg and García's framework, such as its neglect of social and cultural diversity, also apply to more explicitly feminist approaches such as radical feminist theory in which the formation of female-headed households has been construed as a means by which women escape 'domestic patriarchy' (see Duncan and Edwards, 1994; MacDonald and MacDonald, 1979; Weedon, 1987; also later section in this chapter on discourses on lone motherhood). While radical feminist thought brings the importance of ideology to the fore, however, it has the unfortunate tendency of converting concepts of 'female subordination', 'male dominance' and so on into reactive, monolithic categories that have little relevance in particular historical and cultural contexts.

Feminist post-modernist perspectives on women, gender and households

The idea that dynamic, interacting differences in gender, class, 'race', age, culture and so on are central rather than peripheral to thinking about households has been forcefully argued by feminist post-modernist scholars who are highly circumspect about attempts at generalisation, let alone models with universal pretentions. From the mid-1980s onwards, Segal (1995:312) observes that post-modern feminist theorists 'began to place such emphasis on diversity between women and on the instability, uncertainty and complexity of the category "woman", that they reject *any* attempts at universalising women's experience' (Segal's emphasis). This has inevitably led to some discreditation of efforts in earlier feminist research to synthesise ideas relating to gender and households into any form of over-arching theory.

Instead of theorising about patriarchy as a social system, for example, feminist scholarship has undergone what Dore (1995:5) calls a 'sea change' in coming to conceptualise women's subordination as 'fundamentally fragmented and varied' in accordance with contingencies of class, history and culture (see also Duncan, 1995; Kandiyoti, 1991). In short, although gendered access to resources and power based on sexual difference is widespread, we cannot explain it by a monolithic concept of patriarchy, but instead need to explore historically-specific constructions of patriarchies (and masculinities), in relation to different dimensions of gendered relationships in family life, law, the labour market and so on (see Collier, 1995; Edley and Wetherell, 1995; Harris, 1995; Hood [ed.], 1993). Another relevant thrust in feminist post-modernist work has been to refute assumptions about shared mothering experiences cross-culturally (see for example, Fraser and Nicholson [eds], 1990; Glenn *et al.* [eds], 1994). As Collins (1994:61) points out, previous feminist theorising about motherhood 'reflects a lack of connection between ideas and the contexts in which they emerge. While such decontextualisation aims to generate universal "theories" of human behaviour, it routinely distorts and omits huge categories of human experience.'

As for theorising about households, post-modern feminists have emphasised that these need to be treated as units which have specific symbolic significance in different societies (Yanagisako, 1984:330). Thus instead of seeing households as mere 'clusters of task-oriented activities' which serve as places to live, eat, work and reproduce, we must also recognise that they are 'sources of identity and social markers ... located in structures of cultural meaning and differential power' (Guyer and Peters, 1987:209; see also Harris, 1981; Roberts, P., 1991; Stolcke, 1992:138). However, while paying greater attention to diverse socio-cultural influences on household formation is eminently desirable, it also renders comparative analysis harder, since 'meanings' are not easily dealt with in a generalised or cross-cultural manner. Another difficulty here is that 'meanings' have a number of dimensions and correlates – political, economic, social, ideological, cultural – which requires the far from simple task of intermeshing insights from different disciplines with different interests, languages and theoretical starting points (see Folbre, 1991:113; Kabeer, 1994:97).). Problems also arise given that representations of meaning vary according to who is writing the scripts and for what types of audience. Even accepting Netting *et al.*'s (1984:xxvi) assertion that 'At the very least the household is more universal and more cross-culturally comparable than many more frequently studied institutions', and that increasing numbers of Southern writers are considering developing country research in relation to that on advanced economies (see Blumberg and García, 1977; Saradamoni [ed.], 1992; Shanthi, 1994), it is clear that research agendas and methodologies continue to be overwhelmingly determined within Northern academic institutions and, in this way, generate terms, ideas and perspectives that may be inappropriate for other parts of the world (see for example Mohanty, 1991; Momsen and Kinnaird [eds], 1993; Parpart, 1995; Parpart and Marchand, 1995; Spivak, 1988; Townsend *et al.*, 1994 for discussions on epistemological, political and other difficulties of Northern writing about gender in the South).

Towards a basis for theorising the formation and implications of female-headed households

While acknowledging the immense difficulties of conceptualising households, let alone female-headed households, there do seem to be some striking consistencies in the kinds of factors to which people attribute the existence of and/or increase in female household headship in different areas. Weaving together these observations and interpretations might accordingly provide a helpful basis for larger-scale theorisation. Moreover, there are also processes of a global dimension which do not necessarily eclipse the relevance of local findings. For example, Folbre's (1991) global review of female household headship identifies a number of common threads (principally demographic antecedents, the legacies of colonialism and economic development) which aid understanding not only of the worldwide presence of these households, but of regional variations in frequencies and forms.

In addition to comparative work, theory could also profit from being more inductive, engaging in greater scrutiny of what is going on at the grassroots, and locating itself more directly within in-depth field research among specific populations in particular contexts. This is one reason why a large section of the present book is devoted to case study discussions of female household headship in Mexico, Costa Rica and the Philippines and to factors people themselves cite as important in influencing their household forms at particular points in time.

The above is also important for considering experiences of female household headship and whether there are common features attached to the state in different countries, especially when women-headed households are often reported as experiencing common 'predicaments' such as poverty, social vulnerability and the transmission of intergenerational disadvantage. Issues such as these, which are examined in relation to the case study material later in the book, arise out of wider debates which are summarised with reference to the general literature in the latter half of this chapter. Prior to so doing, however, it is important to see where attention to these issues has come from and for what reasons. Here the work of Duncan and Edwards (1994, 1996) in synthesising discourses on lone motherhood from a combination of governmental, religious, political and academic sources provides a useful framework. Despite the fact that Duncans and Edwards' discussions relate primarily to the UK and Europe and to lone mothers, many aspects have significance for developing economies and to female heads of household more generally.

Duncans and Edwards' synthesis of discourses on lone motherhood

The four main discourses identified by Duncan and Edwards are: (1) lone motherhood as a social threat; (2) lone mothers as a social problem; (3) lone motherhood as 'lifestyle change', and (4) lone mothers as women escaping patriarchy.

(1) 'Lone motherhood as a social threat'

The 'social threat' discourse on lone motherhood is identified as linking into 'underclass' debates, whereby certain groups in society are viewed as having little stake in the social order and are, in turn, pinpointed as the 'source of crime, deviancy and social breakdown' (Duncan and Edwards, 1994:13; see also Chester, 1977; Hobson, 1994:176; Muncie and Sapsford, 1995:31–4; Murray, 1994). Duncan and Edwards point out that this discourse has been particularly strong in the USA in this century (especially with respect to black lone parents), and is currently resurfacing in Britain (having also been prominent in the Victorian era) (see also Lewis, 1989:596, 1995:47; Macaskill, 1993; Stolcke, 1992:137; Zinn, 1989; also Blumberg and García, 1977:101–2 on low-income Afro-Caribbean households).[2] As far as the developing world is concerned, strong parallels are found with the 'Culture of Poverty' thesis expounded by Oscar Lewis in the context of Latin America in the 1950s and 1960s, where social and economic privation was seen to result in the evolution of a 'subculture' characterised, amongst other things, by family breakdown, lack of parental authority, early initiation of children into a lifestyle of pathological degeneracy, and self-perpetuating cycles of familial neglect and conjugal dissolution.[3] Such perspectives are closely allied with right-wing and/or neoliberal theories of social change and organisation such as Modernisation and structural-functionalism which, aside from seeing women-headed households as 'deviant' (see earlier) have traditionally viewed the underclass as a permanent phenomenon, 'locked in by its own unique but maladaptive culture' (Zinn, 1989:857; see also Stack, 1974).

Taking on board Hobson's (1994:174) point that 'all welfare states take policy stands that assume a typical family and organise benefits to reflect these norms', policy implications arising from the 'social threat' standpoint include the drive to reduce or eliminate state benefits for lone mothers, since these potentially exacerbate the syndrome (Duncan and Edwards, 1994) As Millar *et al.* (1992:3) point out: 'there is often a desire not to be seen encouraging marital breakdown and unmarried parenthood' (see also Folbre, 1991:111; Kamerman and Kahn, 1988:27; Millar, 1992a:156; Zinn, 1989:863–4). The second set of policy implications fuelled by 'social threat' perspectives is, to 'supervise or penalise lone mothers, to enforce "good behaviour" and improve "good family models"' (Duncan and Edwards, 1994:15). This might include placing young single mothers in hostels, where their 'children's upbringing and their "shiftless" sexual relations can be supervised' (Edwards and Duncan, 1996a). The third and related objective is the desire to strengthen the institution of the two-parent family, headed by a legally-married couple in which the man is breadwinner and the woman homemaker (see also Boyden and Holden, 1991:16–17). Various of these measures (including the Child Support Act)[4] have taken place in the wake of the British Conservative Party's social security cutbacks in the 1990s. Aside from worry about the breakdown of the family and the rising costs of benefit payments,[5] recent UK policy changes relate to shifts in employment and the growing expectation that women should participate in the labour market, and to concern about benefit dependency's prospective creation of an 'underclass of individuals' (Millar, 1992a:156; see also Harris, 1993 on the USA, and Mädje and Neusüss, 1994:1429 on Germany). More insidiously, undermining the viability of female-headed households and/or blaming lone parents for their inability to stand alone takes the spotlight off the fact that most state welfare regimes fail to compensate any mother for her disproportionate burden of childcare and human capital reproduction (see Folbre, 1994a,b; Hobson, 1994; Moore, 1994a:95, 1994b).

(2) 'Lone mothers as a social problem'
In the second discourse identified by Duncan and Edwards, the emphasis lies less with the idea that lone mothers are a threat to society, and more with the notion that they are the victims of wider social and economic forces. This partly arises out of recognition that over 70 per cent of lone mothers have been married (rather than entering lone parenthood as single women), and that only 4.5 per cent of lone mothers on benefit are actually teenagers (Edwards and Duncan, 1996a). In other words, women are not necessarily 'choosing' to be lone mothers.

In accordance with what Duncan and Edwards align with a liberal/Fabian social policy perspective, one view of the 'social problem' school, is that because poverty is a major cause of the plight of lone mothers, their upward mobility through employment (and reduced dependency on the state) should be facilitated by adjustments in existing benefit and childcare systems. Improved facilities for childcare would be paid for by savings in benefits and higher income from taxes (Duncan and Edwards, 1994). This approach has much in common with anti-poverty policies in the developing world where women's problems in general, and those of lone parents in particular, are seen as being primarily material (rather than social or cultural) in nature (see Moser, 1993a:66–9).

A second strand of the 'social problem' discourse, is that the predicament of lone-mother households is not only exacerbated by lack of fathers' incomes, but by their absence as persons. In this respect, improving female lone parents' access to jobs is only a partial answer to household disadvantage; emphasis also lies on reinforcing 'traditional' (male-headed) families and 'back-to-basics' moral values (Duncan and Edwards, 1994). Yet, this fails to problematise the nature of child-rearing within two-parent families, or to acknowledge that it is often when parents remarry (and so attempt to recreate the 'traditional' family) that children (and step-children) fare worse (see also Burghes, 1994; Collins, 1991; Hewitt and Leach, 1993:11–12; Joseph Rowntree Foundation, 1994). Blanket idealisation of the nuclear unit also means that regardless of the quality of marital and family relationships, 'The morale of lone parents is being severely battered by government ministers who believe that parenting is only valuable if a mother does it and has a husband to pay for it' (Hewitt and Leach, 1993:25; see also Hardey and Crow, 1991:17).

(3) 'Lone mothers as lifestyle change'

In stark contrast to the negative views of both the social threat and social problem discourses, the third discourse identified by Duncan and Edwards heralds single parenthood as an outcome of conscious personal choices about how people live their lives in the wake of broader economic, cultural and social changes. It also invites deconstruction (and de-idealisation) of the two-parent household. From this vantage point, 'Current trends are not some epoch-shattering development, there was no golden age of family life' (Duncan and Edwards, 1994:20). In fact, it is just as plausible that a so-called 'golden age' could be ushered in by contemporary shifts in gender and family organisation, including the rise in lone mothers (see also Cashmore, 1985; Mädje and Neusüss, 1994). Whether or not these ideas are fanciful or romanticised (Duncan and Edwards, 1994), they at least signpost the notion that women might be agents and/or architects of social change, and that lone-parent households might be a solution to (rather than a cause or outcome of) 'social ills'. Indeed, some have argued that heading households might be a route to female emancipation (see Itzin, 1980; Mädje and Neusüss, 1994). None the less, there are obvious problems with what might be construed here as an almost naïve inversion of binary gender stereotypes. As Lehmann (1994b:6) points out: 'The literature on single mothers, necessarily suffused with a feminist drive, has succeeded in de-pathologising that phenomenon, but it is now time to insert it into a kinship theory, moving beyond the defense (or indeed the denigration) of a particular category of person. In particular this will involve transcending the polarised categories of single-headed and (presumably) jointly-headed households' (see also Lewin, 1994 on the difficulties of working with bipolar concepts of gender in the context of lesbian mothers).

Another downside of the 'lifestyle change' approach is its vulnerability to hijacking by 'New Right' beliefs in the sanctity of privacy and individual choice: if lone parents have opted for a life of independence, then they should be free to do so, but with little or no help from the state (Duncan and Edwards, 1994). In other words, lone mothers reliant in part or in full on government pay-outs risk being scapegoated as an 'undeserving' poor (Collier, 1995:227), regardless of the fact that they may have few other options. Indeed, lack of opportunities to combine careers or training with childcare were specified by a large number of lone mothers in a West Berlin study as justifying their right to welfare (Mädje and Neusüss, 1994:1423–4).

(4) 'Lone mothers as women escaping patriarchy'

The notion that lone parenthood might be liberating for women gains even greater currency in the fourth and final discourse identified by Duncan and Edwards. This idea of lone motherhood as a mode of resistance to patriarchy draws inspiration from radical feminism where the male-headed family is seen as a major cause of women's oppression (see earlier). Even if many women do not make a conscious choice to be lone mothers, the departure of men (whether through death, divorce or desertion), can have positive results both for them and their children (Duncan and Edwards, 1994, 1996). Potential gains include greater scope for decision-making, greater self-esteem, a sense of achievement in parenting under difficult circumstances, greater control over finances, greater personal freedom, reduced physical or emotional abuse, and the chance to move beyond the confines of the gendered divisions of labour common to heterosexual partnerships (see Itzin, 1980; Shaw, 1991:147–51; also Blanc-Szanton, 1990b; Bradshaw, 1996a; Brydon and Chant, 1989:150–1; Chant, 1985b; Chant and McIlwaine, 1995a: Chapter 7 for developing country examples). For example, Mädje and Neusüss (1994:1424–5) found that almost two-thirds of their sample of female lone parents in West Berlin considered it an advantage to be in the state of not having to 'care for a man', a sentiment that, interestingly, was not restricted to better-off households.[6]

The policy prescriptions arising out of this perspective are oriented towards enhancing women's independence from men and, in terms of examples, have taken the form of campaigning against the Child Support Act in the UK (see Note 4), and the formation of 'Single Mothers by Choice' in the USA.[7] Hardly surprisingly, such initiatives are regarded with extreme suspicion by those of the 'social threat' persuasion concerned to uphold patriarchal institutions and authority (Duncan and Edwards, 1994). Further evidence of polarised attitudes towards lone-parent households and female-headed units more generally comes through in some of the major substantive debates which have emerged out of these discourses, to which we now turn.

CORE DEBATES ON WOMEN-HEADED HOUSEHOLDS

Policy

While we have seen that female heads have perhaps received more than their fair share of policy attention (at least in terms of rhetoric) from governments in the advanced economies, the converse might be said to apply to developing countries where social welfare systems are minimal and female-headed households are often 'missed' in development plans and projects because the vast majority of people are assumed to live in nuclear structures headed by men (Buvinic *et al.*, 1978; Levy, 1992:95). As Kumari (1989:3) argues for India: 'female-headed households have not received the same attention of planners and policy makers as ... other underprivileged sections'. While uneven attention constitutes one complication in talking about policy across the North–South divide, another is that the absence of adequately resourced or comprehensive systems of social welfare in most developing societies means that the context of policy interventions is usually very different. Despite current moves to 'rationalise' state functions and to locate a greater range of welfare responsibilities within the domain of the family (Moore, 1994b), most policy discussions of female headship in the advanced economies revolve around the place of lone parents within relatively long-term state-subsidised national welfare programmes. In the developing world, by contrast, such discussions are commonly restricted to city-wide or community-level projects, often funded by grants or loans from external aid agencies and/or local non-governmental organisations (NGOs). None the less, a number of fundamental policy concerns are shared by both hemispheres and figure prominently in respective regional debates.

Targeting

One of the key issues in policy debates North and South is whether female heads of household should be targeted as a 'special category' and/or 'priority' for assistance, whether among households or among women. In the context of developing countries, this question has assumed particular importance because although policies to alleviate the social costs of structural adjustment policies are now beginning to target female household heads, this group have traditionally been excluded from development projects, either because their existence is not recognised or because the means of reaching and/or incorporating them are too costly or complicated (see Chant, 1996a; Moser, 1987). For example, women heads of household often find it difficult to obtain housing, despite this being a basic need, and a vital tool in strategising household arrangements (Schlyter, 1989:180; see also Chant and Ward, 1987). As Larsson (1993:111–12) asserts with reference to Botswana, for instance, 'a dwelling of one's own is important not only for unmarried women's *survival* in town, but also for supporting their *identity* as independent women and when fulfilling their role as mothers' (my emphasis). Housing is also important as a productive asset for female heads given that income-generating activities may have to be home-based if children are young or women have limited access to formal employment (Nimpuno-Parente, 1987; Sherriff, 1991). Yet access by female heads is often blocked because they lack the incomes necessary to gain access to formal government housing projects, and, within sponsored self-help projects (programmes involving large inputs of beneficiaries' labour in the building process), may not have the time or expertise to construct dwelling units as well or as rapidly as their male counterparts (Moser, 1987:25–8; see also Falú and Curutchet, 1991; Machado, 1987; Momsen, 1991:100–1; Rasanayagam, 1993:145). Similar constraints extend to any project requiring community participation (primary health care schemes, nutrition programmes, urban services initiatives), where female household heads may be unable to join in because they have no other source of income on which to rely and/or cannot spare time for 'voluntary' activities (Brydon and Chant, 1989:226–7; Rogers, 1980).

Yet while it is clearly important to acknowledge the existence of women-headed households in development planning, and this is now beginning to become something of a clarion call in gender policy circles (particularly in respect of lone mothers and widows – see Lewis, 1993:23; Varley, 1996), there is perhaps less consensus on whether it is desirable to *prioritise* female heads over other groups of women. It is not necessarily the case, for example, that female heads are poorer than their counterparts in male-headed units (Grosh, 1994:84; see also later section on poverty), besides which, an exclusive focus on this group 'leaves out large numbers of very poor women and children living in other kinds of household' (Gilbert, 1994:621). Similar considerations apply in the North where, although lone parenthood and poverty are frequently linked, Lewis (1989:595) argues that: 'It is not possible to abstract the problems faced by lone parent families from those faced by two-parent families, especially in regard to the efforts of any parent to combine paid work and family life.' Yet, as Lewis goes on to note, the bulk of British and US policy developments have treated lone-parent families as a separate category, which 'results in one kind of behaviour being deemed appropriate for women in two-parent families and another for lone mothers which has been premised on a set of dichotomous choices (mothers or workers, dependency or independence)' (*ibid*.:598; see also Duncan and Edwards, 1996). With reference to Germany as well as the USA, Hobson (1994:181) adds that this 'bifurcation in policy' produces extreme levels of poverty among mothers who are dependent on social transfers. Beyond this, female lone-parent households are often treated as 'deviant' cases, when if policies are to come anywhere near addressing the particular problems faced by lone parents, 'it is necessary to approach lone parents and their children as households and families in their own right, and not as a mutant form of the so-called "normal" two-parent family' (Hardey and Crow, 1991:2; see also Hewitt and Leach, 1993:8).

Underpinning many considerations about targeting is the idea that providing welfare assistance to female-headed households is wont to increase their numbers. As noted earlier, this concern is especially prevalent among right-wing groups in the North, but is also found in socialist countries of the South such as Cuba (Safa, 1995:166). Conservative religious bodies with political influence may also attempt to block programmes to support single mothers if these are thought likely to generate increases in promiscuity or divorce (see Grosh, 1994:84–5 on the Catholic Church's resistance to support for lone mothers in Honduras). The fact that women-headed households seem to be increasing in countries where there is little welfare provision of any description, however, may well indicate that state support has a relatively minimal part to play (see Chapters 3 and 4).

Nature of assistance

A related issue of critical importance in policy debates, especially in countries which provide some form of social welfare, is the nature of assistance given to female household heads. Here, most attention has been paid to lone mothers and centres around (1) the relative benefits of supporting full-time mothering or facilitating the labour force participation of lone parents, and (2) alleviating poverty or promoting equity. While choice of strategy depends very much on political orientation of individual country governments and the extent and manner in which the state acts to support social reproduction, Kamerman and Kahn (1988:xvi) identify four main policy alternatives to 'mother-alone' families for the USA and other industrialised countries:

> (1) anti-poverty strategies which give financial help to all poor families and, in the case of single mothers, allow them to remain in the home while raising their children;

(2) categorical single-mother strategies which give special cash benefits for single mothers to permit them to stay at home until their children are able to get to school on their own;

(3) family policy strategies with a special focus on young children whereby modest help is given to all families, but extra benefits accrue to people with very young childen, so that single mothers are helped as a by-product;

(4) family policy strategies in which there are attempts to integrate work and family life: here help is given to single mothers to act like other parents by facilitating their labour force participation.

Although this range of options is quite wide, in many states of the USA it seems as if lone mothers are increasingly required to 'earn' their benefits (Lewis, 989:596). An unfortunate corollary of this is that 'the undercurrent of hostility to the lone parent family, which has been a strong motivating force in American developments, means that workfare programmes tend to teeter between a desire to enable and a desire to punish' (*ibid*.: 597) – the punitive aspects being scant childcare services and restricted parenting leaves. In Kamerman's (1984:269) view, US policy strategy needs to take on board the idea that all mothers are employable, and to support them as workers by providing job opportunities and training backed up by housing allowances, enlarged subsidies for childcare, universal child benefits and so on (*ibid*.:270–1). Indeed, the United States differs from many other industrialised countries such as Canada, Australia, France, Finland and Sweden, in that it does not offer non-means tested universal family allowances for children (Kamerman, 1984:258).

Family policy in France, for example, is designed to help all families with children, with some of the most important elements as far as single mothers are concerned being the attempted equalisation of economic burdens of those with children and those without; the assurance of minimum living standards for all families with children; the attempt to make childcare compatible with employment (by guaranteeing nursery places), and the provision of special help to parents with young children (Kamerman and Kahn, 1988:86; Parker, 1995:43). Finland's family policy is also targeted at all families with children, and although single mothers receive some specific benefits, primary attention is given to families with young heads (under 30 years). The fact that there is a universal tax-free allowance for children and a special supplementary allowance for children under three means that women can choose to stay at home and receive a modest cash benefit *or* work and use subsidised childcare facilities (Kamerman and Kahn, 1988:93–5). Indeed, from 1990 onwards, the male or female parent has had the choice of staying at home until the child is three by means of monetary compensation and job guarantees, or using community childcare if they go out to work (UNDP, 1995:8). For this reason, it is perhaps no surprise that Finnish women have the highest rates of labour force participation in Europe.

Sweden, in many respects, has the most sophisticated approach insofar as it emphasises full employment and labour market policies in achieving social policy objectives, and unlike Britain or the United States, stresses the reduction of inequality (rather than poverty) alongside the promotion of gender equity (Kamerman and Kahn, 1988:95). The granting of benefits not only on the basis of labour force participation, but parenting as well, meaning that lone parents stand to gain (Hobson, 1994:183). More specifically, Sweden not only has a generous child support package, but provides one year leave for parents, 60 days per annum to care for sick children, and the right to work a six-hour day until the child is eight years old (Lewis, 1989:598). On top of this, lone parents are provided with income maintenance payments in the absence of help from fathers and are given priority in day-care places for their children (Hobson, 1994:183).

As for the few developing societies which have some kind of social assistance for female heads of household, programmes are usually much more limited in scope and coverage, and/or provide few opportunities for equality between male and female household heads. In Bangladesh, for example, the only help generally given to poor and 'destitute' women (the official term covering female heads of household) is through the Vulnerable Group Feeding Programme and Food for Work programmes, and, as Lewis (1993:33) points out: 'Such schemes are closer to welfare than to development in their orientation and bring with them the limitations of unsustainability along with the moral issue of using poverty as a cheap source of labour.' Even if female household heads in other contexts such as Puerto Rico do not have to work for benefits, assistance in the form of social security and food stamps is still of a predominantly welfare nature (see Safa, 1995:84) and does little to diminish women's huge responsibility for reproductive work.

Childcare

Leading on from the above, the absence or underprovision of childcare facilities is one of the most important factors inhibiting the freedom of lone mothers to escape residualist welfare schemes and to actively improve their position in society. Although some countries such as Canada have a long history of daycare provision (see Rose, 1993:197), in many other nations, even those with fairly substantial welfare regimes, childcare has been woefully neglected. For example, despite Norway's relatively generous system of state support for single mothers (encompassed within a framework of support for all families with children), lack of adequate and affordable childcare services has acted as a disincentive to work among lone parents and provided few prospects for upward mobility (Kamerman and Kahn, 1988:78–86). In Britain too, although the state managed to lay on nurseries during both World Wars when women were badly needed in the labour force (see Hardey and Glover, 1991:90–1), the underlying assumption that women's primary duty is to look after their children means that the policy response of most post-war governments has been to assist single mothers to remain at home via supplementary benefit payments for children under 17 (Kamerman and Kahn, 1988:74–8; see also Duncan and Edwards, 1996; Lewis, 1989:596; Parker, 1995:43). Although the 1980s saw a dramatic rise in the number of day-care places in the UK, the bulk of this was due to increased private provision (Monk, 1993:25), and in 1985, local authority nurseries were unable to provide places for even one per cent of children under four years (Hardey and Glover, 1991:95). Although tax relief on private childcare might act as something of a counterweight to deficiencies in state-provided services[8,9] many lone parents do not earn enough to pay tax (*ibid.*).

It is also important to acknowledge, of course, that not all lone mothers may wish to be employed (see Edwards and Duncan, 1996b; Folbre, 1994a,b). Although employment can mean less poverty and more independence, nearly two-thirds of respondents in a survey by Bradshaw and Millar (1991) said they did not want to work immediately, especially those with very young infants. Others also felt that their children had been damaged by family breakdown and needed extra care, and/or, in order to compensate for the 'loss' of the other parent, wished to remain at home (Millar, 1992a:161). The fact is, however, that lack of adequate childcare facilities may well have been a contributory factor in these decisions. As for developing societies, where formal childcare services are even rarer and social welfare payments scant or non-existent, women's options (whether as female heads or female spouses) are usually limited to the use of relatives and/or resorting to home-based income-generating activities that allow them to combine productive and reproductive work.

Children's rights and the role of fathers

Another issue relevant to policies regarding lone mothers, and which has provoked considerable debate in North and South alike, is that of children's rights. Bruce and Lloyd (1992), for example, assert that one of the most pressing concerns of the future will be how to assure that children are to get a fair share of the social and economic resources of both parents: 'Explicit costs and economic expectations must be assigned to those who bear children and penalties must be imposed on those who try to avoid their responsibilities' (*ibid.*:22). This echoes Folbre's (1991:112) argument that: 'Specification and enforcement of fathers' child support responsibilities would not only benefit children, but also would increase men's incentives to share responsibility for fertility decisions and decrease their incentives to default on family responsibilities.' None the less, the manner in which this might be done is problematic, as revealed by the experience of the UK Child Support Agency (see Note 4), besides which, even if men were to pay, their responsibilities for caring for children in other ways also need to be addressed (see Collier, 1995: 228 *et seq.*).

Distinguishing between different groups of female household heads
Related in several respects to the above, a final critical question in policy debates concerns the relevance of distinguishing between different types of female head. This practice is already apparent in that lone mothers are given a disproportionate share of attention in most parts of the world, but the desirability of so doing is contentious when, as Varley (1996) notes, 'in spite of the heterogeneity of women-headed households, the policy focus on single mothers implies that women are either someone's mother or someone's dependent', which, in turn, 'is in danger of reproducing old stereotypes whereby "woman" means "mother"'. Beyond this, widows have often been treated as more 'deserving' than, for example, never-married, divorced and separated women (see Folbre, 1991:111; Hobson, 1994:183; Lewis, 1989:596–7, 1995:3).

While in some respects, making distinctions can sharpen biases against particular groups, it may be helpful for certain kinds of programme to distinguish between different types of lone mother on the grounds of characteristics such as age and life experience. For example, in relation to skills or training schemes, older divorced women are likely to have a different set of needs to young unmarried women with limited employment experience prior to motherhood (Lewis, 1989:599). Moreover, programmes which lack explicit eligibility criteria may run into other kinds of difficulties. For example, the Honduran '*Bono Madre Jefe de Familia*' food coupon programme, targeted at primary school children from female-headed households, took the reasonably progressive standpoint that female headship should first and foremost be determined by the relative financial support mothers received from male partners. This arose through recognition that legally married women might actually receive less support than their counterparts in non-formalised unions, either because their husbands had left home or failed to cooperate economically. As such, marital status was not made an explicit eligibility criterion. However, the task of schoolteachers trying to work out which mothers 'deserved' help or not involved all sorts of roundabout questions about sensitive matters with children and neighbours, and frequently to arbitrary and inappropriate decisions (Grosh, 1994:84).

At the end of the day the relevance of general and specific targeting of female household heads may be better determined by extensive consultation with women at the grassroots, as discussed in greater detail in Chapter 9.

Poverty

Integral in several ways to policy discussions is the issue of poverty. Women-headed households are not only frequently seen an 'automatic outcome of poverty' (Fonseca, 1991:138), but female headship itself is construed to add greater hardship to being poor (Chant, 1994c). In this light it is perhaps no surprise that women-headed households are persistently identified as a disproportionate percentage of low-income populations, with Bullock (1994:17–18) being one of many to assert that 'Women-headed households are overrepresented among the poor of rural and urban, developing and industrialised societies' (see also Acosta-Belén and Bose, 1995:25; Graham, 1987; INSTRAW, 1992:237; Levy, 1992:96; Standing, 1989:1093; Staudt, 1991:63; UNDAW, 1991:45). Even if the dearth of gender-disaggregated income and poverty data makes it difficult to qualify the veracity of such a statement at a global level (see Sparr, 1994b:23) and that poverty is open to varied modes of conceptualisation and assessment,[10] there would seem to be some evidence to support the assertion in income terms for individual countries, notwithstanding that bias is built into the picture by the fact that lone-parent households are often the exclusive focus of calculations.[11,12] None the less, in the USA in 1985, for example, median family income was less than one-third among single mothers than in husband–wife households (Kamerman and Kahn, 1988:15), and mother-only households represented almost two-thirds of all poor families with children (*ibid.*:16). In the UK in 1989, lone-parent households had only 40 per cent of the income of two-parent households (Millar, 1992b). Moreover, between 1979 and 1988, the situation of UK lone-parent households deteriorated to the extent that while 29 per cent in 1979 had less than half the average income (measured net of tax and National Insurance, after housing costs, and taking into account family size), 59 per cent were in this invidious position by 1988 (Millar, 1992a:150). By 1990, 53 per cent of one-parent families had weekly incomes of £100 or less, compared with only 4 per cent of two-parent families, and for lone mothers specifically, the figure was 70 per cent (Monk, 1993:8). As for developing countries, detailed survey data for the Mexican city of Guadalajara collected by González de la Rocha (1994b:6–7) indicates that female-headed households are on average 18 per cent poorer than male-headed households, and Todes and Walker's (1993:48) study of low-income settlements in Durban, South Africa found that the average income of female household heads was only 56 per cent of men's. Beyond this, it is critically important to note that aside from income disparities, households headed by women (especially non-extended households) are likely to have fewer non-market resources insofar as male-headed two-parent households have a 'wife' who may perform these on a full-time basis.

By the same token, it is also important to note that comparing male- and female-headed households as units (and specifically two-parent against one-parent units) can obscure poverty among women in male-headed households and thereby overemphasise the particular difficulties of lone mothers (Millar, 1992a:149; Millar and Glendinning, 1989). Indeed, the tendency to categorise the poverty of female-headed lone-parent families separately seems to have been much more pervasive than research which has 'uncovered poverty for women within marriage and argues that, again, particularly for women and children, lone parenthood can often herald an improvement in their living standards' (Graham, 1987:57; see also Lewis, 1989:595). Mencher (1989:130) notes in relation to India, for example, that landless households in which men play a minimal economic role are as poor as female-headed households without males (see also Eswara Prasad, 1995), and Muthwa (1993:8) echoes with reference to South Africa that:

> within the household, there is much exploitation of women by men which goes unnoticed when we use poverty measures which simply treat households as units and ignore intra-household aspects of exploitation. When we measure poverty, for example, we need measures which illuminate unequal access to resources between men and women in the household.

Prior to considering the extremely important question of intra-household resource allocation, it also is critical to point out that despite the stress on links between poverty and female headship, even macro-data show that women-headed units are not always a higher percentage of poor households. For example, World Bank data suggest that while female-headed households are likely to be overrepresented among the poor in Asia and Latin America, this is less the case in Africa (Kennedy, 1994:35–6). Even then, for the six Central American countries considered in a regional poverty analysis by Menjívar and Trejos (1992), only Nicaragua and El Salvador had higher levels of female headship among the poor than the national average, notwithstanding that one-half to three-quarters of the national populations of most of the six nations fall into the category of 'poor'.[13] Research on several other countries also shows that women-headed households are found in all socio-economic strata, and are by no means confined to the lowest-income sections of the population (see Hackenberg *et al.*, 1981:20 on the Philippines; Kumari, 1989:31 on India; Lewis, 1993:23 on Bangladesh; Weekes-Vagliani, 1992:142 on the Côte d'Ivoire; Willis, 1994 on Mexico).

Indeed, notwithstanding that poverty and female headship are so often presented as mutually reinforcing, it is perhaps important to ask why the overall average incidence of female headship is actually lower in developing countries than in the developed world. Moreover, within the developed world itself, evidence from countries such as the USA suggests that the growth in the total number of female-headed households during the 1970s exceeded increases in the number of poor female-headed households (see Kodras and Jones, 1991:163). None the less, the majority opinion is still that households headed by women are more likely to face poverty than those headed by men, especially lone-mother units (see Buvinic and Gupta, 1993; Lewis, 1989:598).

Reasons for the comparative poverty of lone-mother households
Among the reasons offered for the comparative poverty of lone-mother households is that they have fewer wage earners than two-parent households (Haddad, 1991; Kamerman and Kahn, 1988:15; Safa and Antrobus, 1992:54 UNDAW, 1991:38; see also Note 11). The disadvantages linked to limited household labour supply are exacerbated by gender segmentation in labour markets and the inferior kinds of jobs which women obtain, especially those with children (see Browner, 1989:467; Hewitt and Leach, 1993:v; Kamerman and Kahn, 1988:15; Mann, 1994:191; Monk, 1993:16; Winchester, 1990). In Belo Horizonte, Brazil, for example, Merrick and Schmink (1983) note that 85 per cent of female heads are engaged in informal economic activities (which are usually unprotected by labour legislation and low paid), compared with only 25 per cent of male household heads. In the UK, Millar (1992a:154) observes that 'Many lone mothers are excluded from employment by lack of jobs, lack of childcare, and negative attitudes to working mothers.'

Declining employment opportunities, especially for full-time work, have added to these difficulties. While nearly 47 per cent of lone mothers were employed (22 per cent full-time) in the late 1970s, by 1986–88, only 39 per cent of lone mothers were in work, and a mere 17 per cent were full-time (Millar, 1992a:151; see also Duncan, 1994:1184; Graham, 1993:122–3). Although in 1990 49 per cent of lone mothers in the UK were economically active, the rate was 66 per cent among married mothers (Monk, 1993:23).

As indicated by Millar, women's disadvantage in employment is exacerbated by a lack of childcare facilities. In order to work around the demands of attending to children, women often have to do part-time, early morning and evening work, which lacks proper protection and fringe benefits (Hardey and Glover, 1991; see also Brownlee, 1989 on Australia). Indeed, the costs of childcare may be so prohibitive as to encourage dependence on welfare instead of going out to work (see Rose, 1993 on Canada; Monk, 1993:14 on the UK). That single mothers have many burdens upon their time and energy (Kamerman and Kahn, 1988:22–6; McAdoo, 1986:166) is perhaps particularly relevant in developing countries where birth rates are considerably higher,[14] where there is negligible state welfare, and where inadequate provision of shelter and services makes housework and childcare extremely time-consuming (Chant, 1984b, 1996a). This is not to deny, however, that childcare may not be particularly costly if women have kin upon whose help they can draw, and/or also that children themselves may make an important economic contribution to the household. Whatever the case, differential poverty between one- and two-parent households, especially those with young children, can in many respects be accounted for by the fact that they do not 'compete on a level playing field' (Hewitt and Leach, 1993:v), whether in terms of adult labour resources or access to jobs. This could well be a reason why in countries like the United States, lone mothers seem to be increasingly impoverished, regardless of their labour force participation (McAdoo, 1986:153).

Although in a handful of countries (for example, Sweden, France and Germany), child maintenance from fathers may be strictly enforced, in others lack of child support may also play a major role in contributing to the poverty of lone-parent households. In the UK, for example, Bradshaw and Millar found that only 29 per cent of lone mothers received maintenance (which as it is contributed a mere 7 per cent of their total income), and this varied with marital status. As few as 13 per cent of single mothers received any support, compared with 32 per cent of separated women and 40 per cent of divorcées (Millar, 1992a:15; see also Hardey and Glover, 1991:94). Data on employed black single mothers in Baltimore also showed that only 37 per cent received financial assistance from the fathers of their children, and then often on an irregular basis (McAdoo, 1986:158; see also Kodras and Jones, 1991:160). In Puerto Rico, a survey of female industrial workers revealed that none of the heads of household among them received support from the fathers of their children, although some did immediately after the break-up of their marriages (Safa, 1995:84). A crucial issue here may be that divorce rates are often highest among low-income groups where men face periodic unemployment (Gelles, 1995:397). In fact, one reason pointed up by Bane (1986) for poverty among black women-headed households in the USA is that couples who break up tend to be poorer than other households. This echoes Zinn's (1989:862) assertion that, 'A two-parent family is no guarantee against poverty for racial minorities.'

Although in some countries such as Sweden and Finland, the state may not only pick up the tab for father maintenance when men cannot pay, but provide generous welfare entitlements (linked both to labour force participation and to parenting) with which to bolster the position of lone mothers (see Hobson, 1994; Kamerman and Kahn, 1988:94), in most other contexts low levels of social security benefits also contribute to the privation of mother-headed households (Folbre, 1991:110 *et seq.*; also Baerga, 1992:141; Hobson, 1994:180; Mädge and Neusüss, 1994:1420). Rising reliance on state benefits among lone-parent households in the UK, for example, has resulted in falling incomes in the last two decades, mainly as a product of changes in the British social security system, notably the appearance of income support and the Child Support Agency (Millar, 1992a:151).[15] Edwards and Duncan (1996a) further point out that almost 70 per cent of lone mothers rely on state benefits for the bulk of their income, and 60 per cent have incomes below half the national average. In Germany, 12 per cent of all lone parents depend on social security compared with 1.2 per cent of two-parent households (Walther and Simbriger, 1996).

While women are conceivably worse off where they lack access to state benefits of any description, networks of kin, friends and neighbours may go some way to compensate. Notwithstanding the argument that female-headed households may be disadvantaged on this count because their heavy burdens of labour make it difficult to find the time to cultivate and/or maintain these networks (Chapter 1), research in Guadalajara, Mexico indicates that female-headed households receive substantial contributions to their monthly household income (in the region of $30 US) via remittances from absent family members, compared with negligible amounts (under $2 US) in male-headed households (González de la Rocha, 1994b:19). Women-headed households in Ghana are also significantly more likely to receive remittances than male-headed units (Brydon and Legge, 1996:49 & 169, Table 3.10; Lloyd and Gage-Brandon, 1993:121 & 123).

Qualifications about female household headship and poverty
Although lone mothers are clearly disadvantaged with respect to earnings, available labour for non-market work, and the hardship that usually accompanies being dependent on ex-partners and/or the state for financial support, a growing body of literature points out that blanket portrayals of disadvantage among female-headed households as a whole can be highly misleading (see Baden and Milward, 1995:16–21; Brydon and Chant, 1989:149–50; Heyzer, 1986:7; Joekes, 1985; Moore, 1988:63–4, 1994b:10; Sanjek, 1983:343; Thomas, 1995:84–5). Challenges raised to dominant assumptions linking female headship and poverty have come from three main

quarters: (a) feminist critiques of orthodox economic models of the (male-headed) household which have discredited the idea that households are unitary entities operating on altruistic principles; (b) alternative development writings which have stressed that poverty is more than incomes and consumption, and that notions of well-being, deprivation and vulnerability should be included in its assessment (see Baden and Milward, 1995; Kabeer, 1994: Chapter 5; Lewis, 1993; Sen, 1987, 1991; also Note 10), and (c) empirically-based studies of households in different parts of the world which show that even if female heads are lone mothers, they may have other kin in their households or access to sources of income and/or non-market assistance outside the domestic unit. Beyond this, while there is little doubt that women's earnings are lower than men's, it cannot be assumed that the labour market status of household heads provides an automatic indicator of household welfare (Brydon and Chant, 1989:149–51; Chant, 1985b; Evans, 1992:22), or that female heads are necessarily responsible for the maintenance of children (Varley, 1996). Indeed, overemphasis on a head's wage in determining levels of household finances is perhaps particularly inappropriate in developing countries where low-income households often have multiple earners who contribute to a common budget (see Chant, 1985a,b; González de la Rocha, 1994b:10; Mencher, 1989:130). In fact, relative to household size, female-headed households may have more earners than their male-headed counterparts who, for various reasons including pride, honour and/or jealousy, fail to make full use of their labour supply. Studies carried out in Mexico, for example, have noted that men may not only forbid their wives to work, but daughters as well, especially in jobs outside the home (Benería and Roldan, 1987:146; Chant, 1985a, 1994a; Fernández-Kelly, 1983; Willis, 1993:71). When this leaves households reliant on a single monetary source, the result may be higher dependency ratios (that is, greater numbers of non-earners per worker) and greater risks of destitution. Notwithstanding that female-headed households may *need* more workers (for example, low female wages may require supplementation by children's earnings), dependency burdens are often lower, and per capita incomes higher in female-headed households (Chant, 1991a: 204, Table 7.1; Selby, Murphy and Lorenzen, 1990:95; Varley, 1996: Table 5).[16] Having said this, Brydon and Legge (1996:181, Table 6.2) note for Tamale, Ghana that a much greater proportion of female household heads are reliant on the income of the head alone, and Larsson (1989:47) observes for Botswana that the mean income per adult equivalent is almost 25 per cent lower in female- than male-headed households (see also Buvinic and Gupta, 1993:4; Lloyd and Gage-Brandon, 1993:119). Millar *et al.* (1992:xiii) also report for Ireland that households headed by lone parents have the lowest per capita incomes of all household types in the country.

None the less, the need for country- and context-specific analyses is paramount when a general tendency to exaggerate the 'plight of female-headed households' can lead to many assumptions that do not hold for local realities (Scott, 1994:86; see also Fonseca, 1991:138).

Indeed, assumptions about the unity of household financial arrangements can also be obfuscatory, when economic differences between male- and female-headed units may be tempered by intra-household distributional factors (Folbre, 1991:110). For example, many studies show that male household heads do not contribute all their wage to household needs, but keep varying proportions for discretionary personal expenditure. This may include spending on items or activities that prejudice the well-being of other household members such as drugs, alcohol, tobacco and extra-marital affairs (see Appleton, 1991; Benería and Roldan, 1987:114; Chant, 1985a,b; Chant and McIlwaine, 1995a: Chapter 3; Dwyer and Bruce, [eds], 1988; Graham, 1987; Kabeer, 1994:104; Millar and Glendinning, 1989:367; Land, 1977; Pahl, 1995; Thorbek, 1987:111; Trenchard, 1987:164; Young, K., 1992:14). The 'secondary poverty' which this imposes upon wives and children may be considerable when in Honduras, for example, men on low wages may only dedicate an average of 68 per cent of their earnings to the collective household budget (Bradshaw, 1996b), and in Guadalajara, Mexico, the proportion may be as little as 50 per cent (González de la Rocha, 1994b:10). Moreover, given that male heads may command a greater share of resources (due to their superior bargaining power) than they actually bring to the household, it is no surprise that households may be better off after their departure (Folbre, 1991:108). Women on the other hand tend to be more household-oriented in their use of wages, with the overall result that women-headed households are not necessarily the 'poorest of the poor', just as 'being a member of a male-headed household does not guarantee high levels of well-being for women and children' (González de la Rocha, 1994b:9–10; see also Chant, 1985b, 1991a; Visaria and Visaria, 1985:63). Women may also have more debt to manage in male-headed households due to their partners' fecklessness with money (see Chapters 6 and 7).

On a final note on poverty, it is also important to stress that even if women *are* poorer as lone parents than they are as wives or partners in male-headed households, they may *feel* that they are better off. As Graham (1987:59) sums up with reference to developed countries: 'single parenthood can represent not only a different but a preferable kind of poverty for lone mothers' (see also UNDAW, 1991:41). This arises from the fact that whereas 'the origins of women's poverty in and beyond marriage may share a common root in women's economic dependency, the experience of it can be very different. For while one is mediated directly through a man, the other is indirect though supplementary benefit, maintenance and wage packets' (Graham, 1987:58–9). In other words, women's perceptions of poverty are likely to be contingent upon the degree to which they have personal power over resources and/or the extent to which the use of income is dictated by men or used as an instrument of male control. This is borne out by the work of González de la Rocha (1994a:210) in Guadalajara, Mexico, where although lone-parent units usually have lower incomes (both total and per capita) than other households, the women who head them 'are not under the same violent oppression and are not as powerless as female heads with partners'. This further underlines the point that 'poverty' is constituted by more than income alone, and is better conceived as a package of resources in which, amongst other things, the power to manage expenditure, to mobilise labour, and to obtain social and community support are vital elements (see Chambers, 1995; Lewis, 1993; also Note 10). Indeed, while not denying that the shadow of income disadvantage looms large in the lives of female-headed households, the case studies of Mexico, Costa Rica and the Philippines show that the material and psychological benefits of female control are often substantial (see Chapters 6 and 7).

Effects on children

The above observations are also relevant to growing debates on the inter-generational implications of female household headship, which tend to be threaded with assumptions similar to those underpinning poverty discussions. As Kennedy (1994:36) argues: 'Because the number of female-headed households has been increasing throughout the developing world, and because these households are poorer in many cases, there is a concern on the part of national policymakers and among donors that there may be a negative effect on children.' This concern is sometimes borne out in practice, especially where *prospective* female headship is linked with fear of destitution, and leads to pre-emptive actions which (albeit unintentionally) prejudice children's upbringing. For example, in India and Bangladesh, the likelihood that women will be widowed at a relatively early age, is one factor leading to high fertility, since the more sons they have, the better the mother's chance of surviving after her husband's death (see Cain *et al.*, 1979; Chen and Drèze, 1992; Drèze, 1990; Jeffery and Jeffery, 1996: Chapter 16; Kandiyoti, 1991:110). Yet if women are prematurely bereaved (or deserted), and children are still young, the hardships of household survival become greater, and the life chances of children (especially daughters) may be severely reduced. In Bangladesh, for instance, Lewis (1993:35) notes that female-headed households which are poor in material resources such as land and income find it problematic to secure favourable marriages for daughters. Having said this, such phenomena cannot be generalised, and as Moore (1994b:10) argues: 'The straightforward assumption that poverty is always associated with female-headed households is dangerous because it leaves the causes and nature of poverty unexamined and because it rests on a prior assumption that children will be consistently worse off in such households because they represent incomplete families.'

Material circumstances and implications
One problem commonly emphasised for children in female-headed households in both the advanced and developing economies, is that of poor living conditions. Lone motherhood has been associated with residence in marginal or substandard housing and poor health, both of which can prejudice the life chances of parents and dependants (Hardey and Crow, 1991:1; see also Duncan, 1991b:431; Graham, 1993: Chapter 3; Pothukuchi, 1993:288; Shanthi, 1994:20; Winchester, 1990:81 *et seq.*). In Canada, for example, nearly 80 per cent of partnered women are in owner-occupied housing, compared with 58 per cent of single fathers, and a mere 31 per cent of lone mothers (Brink, 1995). In the UK, only 29 per cent of lone parents have a mortgage compared with 70 per cent of other families (NCOPF, 1994b:5). Conversely (and while recognising that not all local authority housing is poor quality), 54 per cent of all lone mothers are council tenants as against only 18 per cent of two-parent families (Miller, 1992a:154). Peach and Byron (1993:421) note the intersecting effects of ethnicity here: in 1986–89, only 3 per cent of local authority tenants were white lone parents, but 33 per cent were black lone parents. More specifically, 62 per cent of female-headed Afro-Caribbean households in the UK are council house dwellers, and beyond this, are disproportionately concentrated in the least desirable properties (*ibid.*: see also Dhillon-Kashyap, 1994).[17] Such are the difficulties attached to low incomes and poor accommodation that it is perhaps no surprise that in the late 1980s, babies of single mothers in Britain were much more likely to die in their first year of life than those of married women, with infant mortality rates being 10.5 per 1000 and 7.7 per 1000 respectively (Graham, 1993:189).

As indicated in the policy section earlier, female household heads in developing countries may not even be able to obtain government-subsidised housing due to restricted eligibility criteria and low incomes. Thus although some female heads may be able to take on mortgages in formal site-and-service schemes, many have no other housing option but to rent in the lower tiers of the private or informal market, or to become quasi-owners in informal self-help settlements (see for example, Brydon and Legge, 1996: Chapter 3 on Ghana; Varley, 1993a on Mexico). This does not necessarily mean that women-headed households are disadvantaged *within* such areas however. Larsson's (1989:111) research on self-help housing in Botswana, for example, shows that despite being poorer than male-headed households, women somehow manage to invest the same amount of money and to build the same number of rooms. In self-help settlements in Querétaro, Mexico, too, housing is such a priority for female household heads that by scrimping and saving they often succeed in improving their homes to a greater degree than their male-headed counterparts (see Chant, 1987). In some cases, therefore, children may find themselves in physical environments which are as, if not more, comfortable than their counterparts in male-headed housholds.

Research on intra-household resource distribution also casts interesting light on assumptions about child disadvantage in that, as noted earlier, expenditure is often biased in favour of nutrition and education in female-headed households, whereas in male-headed households more money may be spent on 'non-merit' goods such as alcohol and tobacco (see also Engle, 1995; Hoddinott and Haddad, 1991; Koussoudji and Mueller, 1983). This is clearly likely to benefit children, with data from Kenya and Malawi indicating that pre-school children in female-headed households are less likely to be stunted or to have low weight-for-age levels than in male-headed households, and/or to be malnourished (Kennedy, 1994:36). Indeed, Kennedy (1994:37) asserts that 'as household income increases, there is not necessarily a direct one-on-one effect on the caloric adequacy of pre-schooler diets'. This is echoed by data from the Nothern Province of Zambia, where under-fives are less likely to be malnourished in female-headed households than those in slightly better-off two-parent households (Moore and Vaughan, 1994). Notwithstanding that in some two-parent households women may control substantial amounts of money, as González de la Rocha (1994b:23) points out for Mexico: 'negotiations and bargaining among individuals and collective interests are permeated by conflicts in the case of male-headed households and drive the household towards difficult and often violent crises. In female-headed households, conflict, although present, is solved in favour of the collective interest since women almost fully control incomes.'

Beyond this, there may be greater gender inequalities in resource distribution and consumption in male-headed households insofar as men and boys may receive more in the way of nutrition than women and girls (see González de la Rocha, 1994b:20). One reason why diets may be less gender-differentiated and/or more child-oriented in female-headed households is that women do not have to take into account the food needs or preferences of partners (O'Connell, 1994:68). Detailed work on the UK also shows that diets in the households of lone parents are often more varied than in couple-headed households, which is not to ignore the fact that female heads may eat less themselves in order to economise, and thereby juxtapose the power to exert 'personal preference' with the practice of 'self-sacrifice' ((Graham, 1987:69). Indeed, 'while controlling and managing food gave the lone mothers the freedom to improve their diet, their poverty meant that they often used this freedom to deny themselves' (*ibid.*).

Despite this and other evidence for women's tendency to think of their children first (see for example, Dwyer and Bruce [eds], 1988), we must be wary of subscribing to essentialist notions of female altruism and uncritically accepting the idea that material self-denial is some kind of 'natural' female attribute (see Land and Rose, 1986:85). Not only do some studies indicate that women are not always prone to self-sacrificial expenditure on other family members (see Wolf, 1990:64, 1991:134 on factory worker daughters in Central Java), but it is crucial to recognise that willingness to spend their own wages on others' well-being may owe to women's lack of power within households (Folbre, 1988; Kabeer and Joekes, 1991), just as women in many countries do not enter the labour force of their own volition, but as a response to family needs or directives (see Salaff, 1990 on Taiwan, Hong Kong and Singapore). This is illustrated by Blanc-Szanton (1990b:43) who points out for Thailand that although married women seem to pass over money to their husbands of their 'own free will' (mainly to finance the latter's recreational pursuits), this could more accurately be described as 'a form of culturally-condoned emotional blackmail', since if women fail to comply with their husbands' wishes, they threaten to take other 'wives'. As Kabeer (1994:107) observes more generally:

> when (a) the subordination of personal needs in favour of the well-being of others appears to be systematically the property of the less powerful category of individuals (women and/or children), while the beneficiaries appear to belong to another more powerful category (men), and when (b) the consequences of such behaviour are life-threatening levels of ill-health and malnutrition, then the notion of voluntaristic decision-making becomes patently absurd.

As summed up by Leonardo (1993:329) therefore, '"Altruism" and "self-interest" are cultural constructions that are not necessarily mutually exclusive, and we forget this to our peril.'

Social and psychological issues

Aside from debates on material and physical effects on children of lone parenthood, there is also quite heated discussion on psychological outcomes, with Shanthi (1994:27) claiming that 'the children of such households suffer social stigma and deprivation of education and better future prospects'. One dominant concern here is the issue of mothers working and not having time to give children due care and attention (Moser, 1992:108–9; Rogers, 1980:23–4). A related factor, especially noted for developing countries, is that daughters are negatively affected by mothers' employment insofar as they have to shoulder greater burdens of domestic labour and therefore miss homework or forgo their schooling (Dierckxsens, 1992; Moore, 1994b:23; Moser, 1989; Rodríguez, 1993). This obviously intermeshes with socio-economic status in that children in poor households are under greatest pressure to engage in paid labour too (see Lewis, 1993:35 on Bangladesh; Moghadam, 1995c on Egypt). Since educational sacrifice also shapes children's future prospects in the labour market, the knock-on effects add up to what Momsen (1991:26) describes as a 'poverty trap'. Yet as Boyden and Holden (1991:18) point out, there is still too little evidence to make a direct link between child deprivation and the employment of mothers. Moreover, employment among adult women is not confined to single mothers alone, especially given rising economic pressure on many households throughout the world in recent years (see Chapter 3). For the industrialised economies, Gelles (1995:402) also observes that since the fertility rate has lowered over time: 'today's working mother with one or two children is probably spending as much, or more, time with each of her children than the non-working mother who has five or six children at home'. Beyond this, where female heads do work, this may give daughters a wider and more positive set of female role models (see Chalita Ortiz, 1992:275 on Latin America).

Another issue commonly held to prejudice children's emotional well-being in female-headed households is their lack of daily interaction with fathers. As Collier (1995:201) points out: 'The presence of the father continues to be seen as a signifier of stability, "normality", and, crucially, the "healthy" adjustment of children.' The numerous studies which have considered the negative outcomes of father absence typically concentrate on delinquency, and among boys in particular, psychological and moral problems arising from the lack of a male role model (Collins, 1991:160–1; see also Edwards and Duncan, 1996a). Dennis's (1993:8) work on 'fatherless families', for example, has argued that this reduces the prospects of sons becoming 'responsible husbands and fathers' (see also Dennis and Erdos, 1992). However, it is also important to note that 'Such strictures on lone parents find only weak and ambiguous support in the available empirical evidence', and that even if children from lone-parent households are disproportionately likely to become delinquent, then this is much more the case of divorced than widowed parents (Collins, 1991:160–1). Moreover, given high levels of social security dependence among lone parents, 'it makes just as much sense to look to poverty as an explanation as to seek to blame lone parenthood' (*ibid.*). Indeed, it is probably not so much father-absence which is the problem, but the fact that 'the whole structure of masculine identity is in doubt' in the wake of increasing poverty and unemployment (Moore, 1994b:21; see also Collier, 1995; González de la Rocha, 1995a:392–3). Hewitt and Leach (1993:15) are also concerned to stress that 'father absence' can be just as much of a problem in two-parent households where fathers work long hours, and/or because of gendered divisions of labour and leisure entitlements, may not spend much time with their children.

Building on the idea that the dichotomy between legal constructions of the familial masculinity of the 'good father' and extra-domestic masculinities have drawn a veil over the 'socially destructive nature of masculinities *inside* the family' (Collier, 1995:215, his emphasis), another aspect of father *presence* which may have decidely negative consequences for children relates to the observation that 'isolated' male-headed nuclear families are those in which violence is most likely to occur (see Levinson, 1989:54–6 on the USA). As Boyden and Holden (1991:17) sum up: 'the nuclear family has its darker side. It may provide an environment in which children can be loved and cherished, but it is also in the home that physical or sexual abuse most often remains hidden. The domesticity fostered by the nuclear family removes power and independence from women and children, making them vulnerable to exploitation and mistreatment.' Indeed, evidence from Thailand and other developing countries suggests that increases in violence may be associated with a shift from three-generational to nuclear households (Hoffman *et al.*, 1994:143). Unhappy and/or inegalitarian relationships between spouses are a major catalyst of domestic violence (Bradley, 1994:18; Edley and Wetherell, 1995:120; Levinson, 1989:56), and it is also observed that men who beat their wives are also likely to beat their children (Hoffman *et al.*, 1994:143). While domestic violence is by no means absent from matrifocal household arrangements (see Prior, 1993:313), especially given the stresses attached to poverty, Graham (1987:59) asserts that: 'For a significant proportion of women, it is a poverty without violence.' Indeed, regardless of whether domestic violence actually occurs, there is evidence to suggest that married women stand a greater risk of poorer emotional and mental health than single women, whereas married men are happier, healthier and live longer (see Bernard, 1972; Chandler, 1991:70–1). In other words, children may not be at such a disadvantage if their mothers' personal happiness increases as a result of separation.

The matter of how female-headed households have formed is also likely to be significant in affecting children. As Burghes (1994) notes, a question mark hangs over the issue of whether children who live with lone mothers but who have not experienced the disruption of their parents' marriage are also disadvantaged, when there is always the 'bad marriage' and the 'good divorce' to bear in mind (see also Jacobsen, 1994:161). Having said this, research in the UK shows that children who have experienced a series of family disruptions are more likely to undergo stressful situations such as having less contact with non-resident parents and receiving limited support from extended family networks (Joseph Rowntree Foundation, 1994).

Methodological questions

Underlining many of the problems of determining the intergenerational effects of female headship are the methodological difficulties involved in linking process, response and outcome. In many analyses, for example, samples are unrepresentative (in other words they only focus on children showing extreme reactions), and where they are based on 'snapshots' there is no basis for knowing intervening or future change (Burghes, 1994:13–19). Detailed longitudinal studies might be more reliable, but may not look at other family types, besides which the problems with statistical associations and causalities remain. For example, in some cases, the moment at which marital disruption occurs may be significant, in others the nature of disruption may be important (for example, the children of widowed parents may not suffer to the same degree as when divorce has taken place) (*ibid.*:20–3). The number of disruptions may also be significant (see Joseph Rowntree Foundation, 1994).

Yet while Jacobsen (1994:191) asserts that we cannot really ascertain how well-off children would be had they remained in intact families, Burghes (1994:46) notes a distinct tendency in the literature to 'concentrate on negative outcomes from, as it is perceived, negative situations', notwithstanding that there may well be be 'unexpected' or 'good outcomes' from lone parenthood and family change, and negative outcomes in two-parent families. Indeed, 'Escaping from very stressful and conflictual family relationships or violence could bring psychological relief. It cannot be assumed that divorce will always be a negative experience or intact family life a positive one. Yet feelings of relief might still go hand in hand with increasing stress caused by practical and financial anxieties arising from the separation' (*ibid.*:40). Given these considerations, Burghes (1994:45) stresses the need for further research into the quality of family relationships, how they change as a result of family disruption, and how they impact upon people in relation to their socio-economic circumstances. Although my primary case study material concerning children's experiences in women-headed households in Mexico, Costa Rica and the Philippines is somewhat limited in terms of length and breadth, Chapter 8 suggests that children are not affected particularly negatively by the absence of fathers.

Ideological and social marginality

Another critically important, but possibly less developed area of debate around female household headship is that of its ideological and social dimensions, how these vary from one society to another, and how they shape images and self-images of women heads of household.

In most parts of the world, female heads, and especially lone parents, seem to occupy an ambivalent position in society. As Collins (1991:159) notes for advanced economies: 'The large majority of dependent children ... live with both biological parents, and the situation of the majority is readily graced with moral approval.' He goes on to argue that 'It serves the ideological requirements of dominant groups in society to depict lone parent families as nothing more than spoiled versions of nuclear families, and to create the belief that relationships within lone parent households are impaired replicas of those in "proper" families' (*ibid*.:159–60). This is somewhat surprising given that that 'the norm of the nuclear family and the belief in its superiority as an arrangement for child-rearing is a very recent and culturally specific invention' (Dallos and Sapsford, 1995:159). Moreover, the nuclear household is by no means always numerically dominant (see Brydon and Chant: Chapter 6; Moore, 1994b). None the less, emphasis on the value of couple-centred family life seems to be all-pervasive and the pressure on lone parents to conform means that they may be pushed into remarriage, even when step-parenthood carries its own set of negative connotations (Collins, 1991:162 & 165; see also Dallos and Sapsford, 1995:130; Hardey and Crow, 1991:1).

While Winchester (1990:82) contends that one-parent families face greater social marginalisation in some countries (for example, Ireland, Italy) than others (Britain, Australia), it is rare that lone parents escape any element of 'blame' or 'social stigma'. This is particularly true of female lone parents: whereas lone fathers are often deemed to have been deserted and receive more social support by friends and family, lone motherhood is often taken as a signal that women have failed in their primary role (*ibid*.). In the developing world too, Kumari (1989:79) notes for India that divorced women are always held responsible for marital breakdown. This carries serious penalties when divorce is treated not only as a 'sin against the social system', but an 'act against religion'.

Other major problems for female heads include the fact that they lack a series of positive images to aspire to, whatever their marital status. As Gordon (1994:92) points out for the case of divorced women, for example, 'there are few conceptual models for the benefits of life without marriage'. As for single parents, Chandler (1991:6) claims these have become 'a synonym for moral breakdown and social disorder'. And as for single women, these have 'defied definition because they are not formally connected to men (except their fathers) ... and they remain unassigned in the structure of cultural terrain. They are contested characters with ambivalent sexuality' (Gordon, 1994:3–4). Single women may also be the 'objects of social suspicion and butts of sexual innuendo' (Chandler, 1991:6), and Lewis (1993:32) notes for Bangladesh, that lack of a male 'guardian' casts serious aspersions on women's 'femininity' (see also Kabeer, 1995). Where marriage is a central institution, therefore, women who fall outside the category of 'wives' tend to give rise to tensions and 'cultural anxiety' (Buitelaar, 1995:8–11). This applies even to widows who in many parts of South Asia may not only be regarded as having defied male authority by outliving their husbands, but:

> The sexual experience of widows ... renders them suspicious. While as a sexually experienced and therefore 'real' woman, the widow is less ambivalent than the virgin, in her case it is predominantly her unleashed sexuality that makes her an anomaly. The symbolism that surrounds the ambiguous position of widows is imbued with fear of uncontrolled female sexuality. This makes a widow a powerful symbol of disorder and destructive potential. (*ibid.*)

The position that female heads (and again, especially lone parents) occupy in a social sense is important insofar as it affects their material condition and vice versa. Winchester (1990:82), for example, suggests that public and policy responses to lone mothering contribute to poverty. In turn, poverty affects women's social standing and gives them the double disadvantage of being social 'outsiders' as well as financially deprived (Monk, 1993:10). Similar patterns apply in the developing world, with Lewis (1993:34–5) noting for Bangladesh that economic resources intersect with social and cultural resources to dictate status and well-being, and that female-headed households are usually disadvantaged in all domains.

Having said this, some studies have shown that female headship may be positive not only in personal but wider terms. For example, in Jamaica and other parts of the West Indies, Caldwell and Caldwell (1992:62) note that female responsibility for running the household and bringing up the children gives women a substantial amount of autonomy,[18] and Safa (1980:5) argues in relation to Latin America that rising female headship among the poor is extremely important in the formation of class consciousness among women.

Aside from 'autonomy' and 'heightened consciouness', another apparent advantage of female headship, especially vis-à-vis lone motherhood, is its association with more fluid parenting roles and some relaxation of the burden of gender-assigned duties that conventionally befall women in male-headed units (Collins, 1991:71; Hardey and Crow, 1991:10). In her study of housework among single fathers and single mothers, for example, Fassinger (1993:211–12) concludes that greater equality in men's and women's behaviour arises through single parenthood, with men tending to do more, and women less. At the end of the day, however, the scope for women to capitalise on their domestic gains in any broader sense may be severely curtailed by their lack of power and secondary status in society in general (see for example, Chant, 1991b; Chant and McIlwaine, 1995a: Chapter 7; Dore, 1995). In fact, Elson (1992:41) goes as far to argue that: 'The growth of female-headed households is no sign of emancipation from male power; in a society in which women are subordinate the absence of a husband leaves most women worse off. The core of gender subordination lies in the fact that most women are unable to mobilise adequate resources (both material and in terms of their social identity) except through dependence on a man.' This is echoed by Jelin (1992:121–2) who observes that: 'the destruction of the traditional patterns of social organisation and division of labour among the genders implies an increasing burden for women. They have to take care of their families and are left to themselves. Thus their lot today is not freedom and autonomy, but rather hardship and solitude.' In this way, although there may be a bright side of female headship in terms of its scope for offering potential independence from men, this is usually 'shadowed by increased financial responsibility for dependents' (Folbre, 1994a:114). Men, on the other hand, are likely to benefit from living alone because in this way they might not merely reduce their family commitments, but evade them altogether (*ibid.*). As Shanthi (1994:21) concludes:

> though feminists and militant liberationists view female headedness as a new lifestyle and a boon against patriarchal oppression, it is a fact that female-headed families are poor compared to two parent famiies and experience sustained economic hardship. Trying to be family head, mother and also be an active member of the labour force continues to be a difficult challenge for most women.

These challenges, however, do not seem to be insurmountable, as explored in the context of Mexico, Costa Rica and the Philippines in Chapter 7, and in a more general theoretical and policy framework in the final chapter of the book.

NOTES

1. Two theoretical schools have provided rationalisations for the putative shift from extended to nuclear family composition and share a common focus in terms of the weight they accord to the nature of wider economic and social organisation. The main factor emphasised by 'Modernisation' theorists is the decline in family functions as societies become more 'developed' and, more particularly, as production (economic activity) and reproduction (schooling, health care and so on) become taken out of the the hands of family units (see Gugler and Flanagan, 1978; Hulme and Turner, 1990:83–4; Muncie and Sapsford, 1995:14–16). This leaves families with a fairly narrow remit of predominantly moral and social responsibilities (Pine, 1982). Marxist arguments share similarities but place greater emphasis on the way in which nuclear households are more able to respond to the labour migrations required by capitalist development, to guarantee a market for capitalist goods and to sit more easily with the ideology of economic individualism. All these processes are seen to be hastened by proletarianisation and rising landlessness (see Barrett, 1986; Leacock, 1972; McDonald, 1992; Seccombe, 1980). Another important factor in debates about household size, is declining fertility in response to the rising costs of children in urban-industrial societies (see Caldwell, 1976, 1977).

2. Hardey and Crow (1991:4) point out that lone parents 'have been subject to a long history of stigmatisation going back several centuries, for their "deviance" from the two-parent norm'. In particular, the focus has been on women who have had children without being married, and who are described by a series of 'negative labels' such as 'unmarried mothers', 'unwed mothers', 'fatherless families', 'incomplete families', which 'identify their subjects by what they are not (that is, parents in couples) rather than what they are' (*ibid.*). It was only in 1973, for example, that the National Council for One Parent Families in the UK changed its name from the National Council for the Unmarried Mother and Her Child (*ibid.*; see also Lewis, 1995:28).

3. 'Marginality' theories of the 1960s and 1970s share several features in common with 'Culture of Poverty' ideas, although there is less emphasis than in Lewis's work on the family *per se* (see Perlman, 1976:114–8).

4. The objective of the UK Child Support Act of 1992, was to ensure that a greater number of absent parents (usually fathers) would pay maintenance, and to increase the amounts paid. The Act specified that absent parents should be allowed to keep money for personal needs (set by income support rates) plus reasonable income, but beyond this, would be set an amount for maintenance (again according to income support rates), and pay half of his or her remaining income in child support (Millar, 1992a:156). The initiative has been criticised on several grounds, one being its tendency to reinforce women's dependence on the fathers of their children (Duncan and Edwards, 1994; Millar, 1992b), another being the loss of so-called 'passported' benefits (for example free school meals, medical prescriptions, subsidies for housing and council tax) as women replace social security with father support (NCOPF, 1994a:5).

5. In 1989, for example, 43 per cent of all expenditure by the UK Department of Social Security was accounted for by lone-parent households (see Hardey and Glover, 1991:93). The disquiet felt in Conservative Party circles about levels

of benefit spending is paralleled in studies by the right-wing think tank, the Institute of Economic Affairs, which has identified that government subsidies to lone parents are making single-parenthood more attractive than two-parent families and even accuses the Conservative Party of encouraging the breakdown of the so-called 'traditional' family (see 'Right Group says Tories Anti-Family', by David Brindle in the *Guardian*, 3 January 1995; also Morgan, 1995). Parker (1995:88) for example, claims that: 'Whether or not one takes a moral view about lone-parent familes, there is no doubt that under present arrangements they impose a costly burden on the rest of society – hence reason enough, from an economist's point of view, for changes that will strengthen the traditional two-parent family.'

6. Women on lower incomes might conceivably have felt in greater need of economic support from the fathers of their children.

7. 'Single Mothers by Choice' was founded in New York in 1981 to provide information and support for existing and prospective single mothers. Although the organisation does not describe itself as an advocacy group, it is undoubtedly helpful to those women who, for a wide range of reasons, opt to raise their children alone (Kamerman and Kahn, 1988:134–5).

8. At present, the only tax relief on childcare in Britain comes with workplace nurseries (Monk, 1993:33).

9. Leaving children with a childminder is another option, and, as Hardey and Glover (1991:97) point out, this can also provide employment for some lone parents. Another option is the use of relatives, although they may have to forgo their own employment in order to undertake childcare (see Monk, 1993:15), and, in the context of what Edwards and Duncan (1996b) term 'gendered moral rationalities', might resist this through disapproval of mothers not being at home with their children. Another option is private day-care, although this is usually prohibitively expensive (Monk, 1993:15). A related factor impacting upon women's caring responsibilities in societies where numbers of old people are growing substantially, is the lack of public service provision for the elderly and infirm (Duncan, 1991b:424).

10. Poverty has conventionally been defined on the basis of an absolute or relative lack of income (or consumption), and measured by means of quantitive data. Usually this has taken the form of a 'poverty line' based on household budget surveys (Wratten, 1995:29, Table 2). An alternative definition of poverty is the 'participatory social development definition', whereby via qualitative discussions, mapping and the collection of life history profiles at the grassroots, people's perceptions of poverty are given precedence. This approach sees poverty as multifaceted, as having different meanings for different groups (e.g. the young and elderly, women and men, different castes), and has flagged-up the relevance of concepts such as vulnerability and intra-household and community-level entitlements (*ibid*.: see also Baden and Milward, 1995; Chambers, 1995; Kabeer, 1991).

11. Quite apart from the fact that the bulk of lone parents are women and women's earnings tend to be lower than men's (as discussed later in the text), the fact that two-parent units potentially (and often actually) have two adult earners means that comparisons with lone-parent structures (who usually have only one adult earner) are prone to be unfavourable (see Baden and Milward, 1995:18).

12. Household income is clearly not solely made up of earnings. This is perhaps particularly relevant in respect of female-headed households where maintenance and welfare payments are likely to form part of their budgets. As Folbre (1991:107–8) sums-up: 'If the household is treated as an income pooling unit its full income can be conceptualised as the sum of five different contributions: market earnings (from wages or self-employment), property income, non-market household production, non-government transfers (e.g. from non-resident family members) and government transfers' (see also Beittel, 1992:224; Hobson, 1994:177 *et seq.*; Wallerstein and Smith, 1992:7). Beyond this, Folbre (1991:108) also points out that 'each individual's net contribution to household income is equal to the sum of his or her contributions minus his or her consumption of household income'.

13. The criteria for measuring poverty inevitably varies from country to country. None the less, broadly speaking, Costa Rica, El Salvador, Panama and Guatemala rely on the 'poverty line', which is based on income and defines the poor as those who are unable to afford a 'basic basket' of foodstuffs. Nicaragua and Honduras, on the other hand, use a 'basic needs' assessment, where poverty is equated with the non-satisfaction of necessities that extend beyond food to include access to basic goods and services as well (see Menjívar and Trejos, 1992:55–6, Table 7). See also Note 10.

14. As of 1992, the average crude birth rate in high-income economies (13 per 1000 population) was only half that of low- and middle-income economies (27 per 1000) (World Bank, 1994:212–13, Table 36). In terms of total fertility rates (i.e. the average number of children likely to be born to women surviving through their child-bearing years), the figure was only 1.7 for high-income economies, and 3.3 in low- and middle-income economies, ranging from 2.3 in East Asia and the Pacific (excluding China and Japan), to 3 in Latin America and the Caribbean, to 6.1 in sub-Saharan Africa (*ibid.*).

15. Income support replaced supplementary benefit in 1988 (Millar, 1992a:151). In contrast to supplementary benefit, income support does not take into account expenses such as childcare and travel costs (e.g. to work), even though, as under previous schemes, lone parents have a higher earnings disregard than other individuals (Hardey and Glover, 1991:93; Parker, 1995:28).

16. Per capita income figures are calculated by dividing total household income receipts by the number of household members, and are arguably more useful than total household income in comparing levels of wealth and poverty *between* households (see Chant, 1985a,b; González de la Rocha, 1994b). Indeed, when per capita figures are used, they often reveal few differences in the financial circumstances of male- and female-headed units (see for example, Chant, 1985b; Kennedy, 1994; Shanthi, 1994:23), notwithstanding that the consumption needs of individuals vary according to age (Lloyd and Gage-Brandon, 1993:121), and that it has also been argued that, in respect of expenditure, total (rather than per capita) figures are more appropriate because of household establishment costs (Buvinic, 1990, cited in Baden and Milward, 1995:59).

17. This is not to say that other groups of women escape disadvantage in the housing market. See for example, Douglas and Gilroy (1994) on young childless women, and Sykes (1994), Keigher (1993), and Yen and Keigher (1993) on elderly women.

18. The question of 'autonomy' can be looked at in a range of ways, and should always be qualified by the fact that individuals are rarely in the position of acting entirely by or for themselves. None the less, with regard to female autonomy, a useful set of criteria is provided by Mencher (1989:118) on the basis of Eleanor Leacock's definition which relates to the extent to which women hold comparable power over their own lives and activities as men. Mencher feels that this concept of autonomy is useful, since 'it does not equate uniformity with equality i.e., it does not assume that men and women do (or should do) the same things' (see also Chapter 7, this volume). More specifically, and in relation to her work on Kerala and Tamil Nadu, southern India, Mencher (1989:119) uses the following guidelines in evaluating autonomy among landless households:

(1) whether a woman is able to control her own earnings or has to give them over to her husband or other household member such as a mother-in-law;
(2) whether a woman can make personal purchases without consulting her husband;
(3) the degree to which she is involved in decisions on household matters such as housing, children's schooling and so on;
(4) the degree to which a woman can refuse her husband's requests for cash or jewellery;
(5) the extent to which a woman is exposed to domestic violence;
(6) the extent to which a woman can exert any control over her sexual relations.

Mencher also notes that areas of potential autonomy increase when households own land.

3 Women-Headed Households in Global Perspective

INTRODUCTION

This chapter is concerned with identifying frequencies and trends in the formation of female-headed households in different parts of the world and in highlighting reasons for what appears to be widespread growth at global and regional levels. Integral to this discussion are the problems which arise from data collection, enumeration and synthesis at national and international scales. As indicated in Chapter 1, while there are major (and possibly insurmountable) problems involved in developing universally-applicable categories of households and/or household heads (and many would advocate abandoning this search altogether), the lack of standardised definitions across space and through time inevitably places serious obstacles to the comparative analysis of female headship. My reflections on the macro-level dynamics of female headship are accordingly tentative. Similar reservations apply when I move on in the latter part of the chapter to take a broad look at the diversity in forms and characteristics of women-headed households at inter- and intra-regional levels.

WOMEN-HEADED HOUSEHOLDS: A GROWING MINORITY?

Many writings on both the northern and southern hemispheres have asserted that women-headed households are on the rise. According to Kamerman and Kahn (1988:71): 'all industrialised countries have experienced a significant increase in the number of female-headed families with children, and in the proportion of all families with children these families constitute' (see also Duncan and Edwards, 1996; Haskey, 1991; Kamerman, 1984:250; Millar *et al.*, 1992:2). For the developing world, reports are similar (Chalita Ortiz, 1992:273; Larsson, 1993:109; Nash, 1980:12; Sen, 1994:32–3; Stewart, 1992:23; Townsend and Momsen, 1987:53). While noting that there are 'considerable variations in the relative numbers of women-headed households', Moser and Levy (1986:4) assert that 'globally this is an increasing rather than declining phenomenon', and generalised figures for female headship have suggested for at least a decade that women-headed households are one-third of households worldwide (see also O'Connell, 1994:67).

Problems of data

While there is little dispute that women-headed households are a growing presence in many places, this is often difficult to verify empirically since relevant sources of data, where they exist, may not extend very far back in time, or if they do, have rarely followed consistent modes of enumeration and tabulation.[1] Moreover, it is important to emphasise that women-headed households are still a minority group, with properly weighted calculations by Varley (1996) from United Nations data pertaining to the years 1971–82 suggesting that the world average is nearer one-fifth of the total household population than one-third. Varley further shows that the highest proportion is in the developed world (24.5 per cent) followed by Africa (19.1 per cent), Latin America and the Caribbean (18.2 per cent) and finally Asia and the Pacific (13 per cent) (*ibid.*:Table 2). A previous attempt at such calculations by Folbre (1991:95–8, Table 3.1) using UN data for the early 1980s, yields slightly different figures on the basis of a more disaggregated regional breakdown: the highest percentage of women-headed households (26.6 per cent) is found in non-European English-speaking countries (Australia, New Zealand, Canada and the United States); the next highest (22 per cent) is Northwest Europe, then 19.5 per cent in Eastern Europe, and 16.9 per cent in Southern Europe. In the 'developing' world, most figures are lower, being 17.7 per cent in the Caribbean, 14.5 per cent in Latin America, 14 per cent in East Asia, 13.6 per cent in sub-Saharan Africa, and only 5.7 per cent in South Asia (*ibid.*). Although Folbre also uses weighted regional averages, it should be noted that most of her calculations are only based on two or three countries in each region.

One major problem with UN statistics is that these are mainly drawn from census data which, somewhat inevitably, vary in quality and definitional criteria from one country to another (see Folbre, 1991:92–8). This, coupled with the fact that censuses are undertaken in different years in different places, makes comparisons and/or regional syntheses extremely hard. As Oliveira (1992:207) adds, while census data are in some respects advantageous due to their wide coverage and where they have been systematically collected over time, the descriptive character of their observations means inevitably that there is 'difficulty of going deeper into the analysis of some important explanatory dimensions'. As indicated in Chapter 1, the criteria for household headship, where instrumental, are often ill-defined and measured, and in the case of self- or proxy-reporting are clearly prone to be conditioned by respondents' subscriptions to normative familial or social ideals in different societies.

Beyond this, female headship may be tabulated in conjunction with different types of variables and in different ways from country to country.

For example, while Mexican census data offer the possibility of seeing how many households headed by women are single-person units, family-based units and non-family units, this does not apply in the case of Costa Rica or the Philippines. Alternatively, while Costa Rican census data show the marital status of female heads, this is not so in Mexico or the Philippines (Chapter 5).

Even at a national level, there may be immense difficulties involved in enumerating female-headed households in general, as well as specific groups such as lone mothers. With reference to Ireland for example, Millar *et al.* (1992) point out a huge range of problems designating household headship when marital separation may extend over a lengthy period of time and children may move between parents. Another problem is that women may be embarrassed or ashamed to admit to being lone parents – especially if they are unmarried (*ibid.*; see also Chant, 1991a: 234 on Mexico; Lewis, 1993:25 on Bangladesh). Beyond this, Millar *et al.* (1992) highlight the problems of comparability between different statistical sources. For example, the Irish Census of Population counts all individuals present in a household on one particular night as household members, which may inflate numbers of lone parents since partners might be working nightshifts elsewhere. On the other hand, extracting numbers of lone parents from benefit records from the Department of Social Welfare is likely to deflate figures since not all lone mothers claim benefits. Finally, the Labour Force Survey in Ireland discounts lone parents who live with other people, which is again likely to depress overall levels of female headship (*ibid.*).

As for Britain, while the Census gives information on one-parent families in relation to all households, the General Household Survey often relates these only to families with children, or to those with dependent children only (Winchester, 1990:73).[2] Definitions of childhood (usually equated with dependency) also differ (although usually from country to country rather than within countries), with cut-off points varying between 12 and 18 years (see also Chapter 2).

Given the difficulties of imposing classification systems on countries where households have very different forms and meanings, detailed case studies which identify more closely the interface between people's own perceptions and classificatory systems offer a potential solution. Then, however, the problem becomes one of 'scaling-up'. Proportions of female-headed households not only vary widely at intra-national levels (see Bradshaw, 1996a; Chant, 1991a), but much research, especially on the developing world, is restricted to low-income groups (see Chapter 1).

Evidence for increases in female household headship

Bearing in mind the caveats of macro-level data, official statistical sources for many advanced economies suggest that female-headed households, especially of the lone mother variety, have increased quite dramatically in the last 20 or so years (Folbre, 1991; Hobson, 1994).

In terms of specific examples, more than 26 per cent of all households with children in the USA were single-parent families in 1985 (90 per cent of whom were headed by women), compared with only 12.9 per cent in 1970 (Kamerman and Kahn, 1988:7, Table 1.1). Female-headed single-parent families were only 8.5 per cent of all families with children in Norway in 1960, yet were 14.7 per cent by 1980 (*ibid.*: 79, Table 3.2). In Britain, 19 per cent of all households in 1991 were lone-parent units (92.1 per cent of which were headed by women), compared with 13 per cent in 1981 and only 8 per cent in 1971 (Burghes, 1994:7 and 50; Duncan and Edwards, 1994), and by 1992, the figure had risen to 21 per cent (NCOPF, 1994b:3). Census data for Ireland indicate that numbers of lone parents rose by 23 per cent between 1981 and 1986, and by this latter date were 8.6 per cent of all households with at least one child under 15 years. Moreover, the proportion of lone-parent units headed by women displayed an even greater overall rise (29 per cent), over the same period (equivalent to more than 5 per cent per annum), so that by 1986, they were 84.1 per cent of the total (compared with 79.9 per cent in 1981) (Millar *et al.*, 1992:19, Table 2.9). In Australia (as in Britain), one-parent households, over three-quarters of whom are headed by women, are the most rapidly growing household type (Winchester, 1990:74). Indeed, whereas according to the 1979 Australian census, female-headed lone-parent units were 10.8 per cent of all families (Kamerman, 1984:257, Table 3), by 1985 the Social Survey Review estimated the proportion at 14 per cent (Winchester, 1990:74).[3]

Increases are also reported for many developing countries in the post-war period, although data here (usually based on censuses or official national household surveys) tend to relate to women-headed households in general as opposed to lone parents *per se*, even if many happen to fall into this latter category. Moreover, although increases in some countries are substantial, comparatively speaking they do not seem to be quite as marked as in the advanced economies, possibly because women-headed households have been a large proportion of the population for some time. In Jamaica, for example, although 39 per cent of households were headed by women in 1975, the level was also high back in 1946 (28.6 per cent) (Wyss, 1990 cited in Folbre, 1991:82). In Botswana, too, female headship increased only marginally between 1980 and 1990, from 45.2 to 45.9 per cent (UNDP, 1995:64, Table

A2.5). Yet in other countries, baseline figures for earlier periods are lower and rises greater. In Guyana, for example, the increase was from 22.4 to 35 per cent between 1970 and 1987 (Patterson, 1994:122), in Puerto Rico from 16 to 23.2 per cent between 1970 and 1990 (Safa, 1995:17), and in Argentina from 16.5 to 19.2 per cent between 1970 and 1980 (Rojas Chaves, 1986:4). In Ghana, women-headed households (*de facto*, as well as *de jure*) increased from 22 to 29 per cent of the household population between 1960 and 1987 (Lloyd and Gage-Brandon, 1993:116), and to 32.2 per cent by 1990 (UNDP, 1995:65, Table A2.5; although see also Brydon and Legge, 1996:131). Rises are also evident from detailed micro-level surveys. For example, Moser (1992) observed an increase in female-headed units from 12 to 19 per cent of the population in a low-income community in Guayaquil, Ecuador between 1978 and 1988.[4] Among African households in the Witwatersrand, female-headed households grew from 14 to 29 per cent of the total household population between 1962 and 1985 (Beittel, 1992:217). Despite these post-war increases, however, it is also significant that where historical data are available, they not only indicate that female-headed households existed in the past, but that they may have been even more prevalent in some places during given periods. For example, while female-headed households in Brazil increased from 5.2 per cent in 1960 to 20.6 per cent in 1987 (Buvinic, 1990 cited in González de la Rocha, 1994b:1),[5] in São Paulo back in 1802, as many as 44.7 per cent of all urban households were headed by women, partly because the sex ratio was heavily feminine with only 75 men per 100 women (Kuznesof, 1980; see also Dore, 1995 on nineteenth-century Nicaragua; Gudmundson, 1986 on Costa Rica).[6] As for the advanced economies, Laslett (1984:371) notes that around 20 per cent of English households between the sixteenth and nineteenth centuries were headed by women, and that women played a significant role as *de jure* and *de facto* heads in Italy and Russia too (see also Moore, 1994b:4). Yet notwithstanding historical antecedents and the fact that women-headed households in some countries result from 'customary practice rather than family crisis' (Boyden and Holden, 1991:19; see also Baden and Milward, 1995:19), there is little doubt that lone-mother households are on the rise (O'Connell, 1994:4).

Other types of women-headed household which have been increasing in recent decades include older lone person households (see Chapter 1). However, while differences in types of female heads are also likely to be important in respect of factors accounting for their overall increase, census data are not particularly informative on sub-groups (see Folbre, 1991). Beyond this, it is also important to point out that in some countries female household headship in general has not risen, or at least not risen substantially. For example, in India, women-headed households were 10 per cent of the household population according to both the 1961 and 1971 censuses (Kumari, 1989:4) and more recent estimates suggest similar levels (Drèze, 1990:9). In the Philippines, too, official data indicate that women-headed units only rose from 9.8 to 11.3 per cent between the end of the 1960s and 1990 (Chant, 1995b). In fact, in some countries proportions have fallen in the last decade: for example, women-headed households fell from 14.2 to 13 per cent of the total in Indonesia between 1980 and 1990, from 21.6 to 21 per cent in Chile, and from 21.8 to 21.3 per cent in Venezuela (UNDP, 1995: 64–5, Table A2.5). Beyond this, we also have to bear in mind that anything up to a 15 per cent difference in the proportions of a particular household type at two points in time may be a purely 'chance' occurrence (due to random demographic events, natural disasters and so on) (Netting *et al.*, 1984:xxiii). Having said this, a substantial upward trend in many countries in both the North and South suggests that chance is not the main determinant and other factors are at play.

MACRO-LEVEL DYNAMICS IN FEMALE HOUSEHOLD HEADSHIP: PERSPECTIVES ON GLOBAL INCREASES

While there are clearly variations in levels of and increases in female headship between countries, and both intra- and inter-regional diversities are often pronounced (as discussed later in the chapter and in the context of the developing world more specifically in Chapters 4–6), it is interesting to consider which kinds of factors might help to account for upward trends at a world scale, especially as these might provide pointers to more specific influences on changing household forms in individual countries. As Kamerman and Kahn (1988:70) point out with reference to the rise in female headship in advanced economies:

> Similar social trends and definitions of issues tend to characterise all of the industrialised countries – population ageing; declining fertility; earlier retirement, especially among male workers; and increased female labour force participation, especially among women with young children. Similar social problems – for example, poverty, alcoholism, delinquency, child abuse, divorce, the tension between work and family life, changing gender roles, and changing family structures – are of concern and addressed in all countries to varying degrees.

Since many of these tendencies can also be observed in developing countries, it is helpful to speculate on the kinds of factors operating at a global level which might impact upon the apparent worldwide increase in women-headed households.

Global economic development and integration

Although it is unlikely that there is any consistent link between female household headship and economic development (Baden and Milward, 1995:17), besides which both take such different forms in different times and places that they are virtually impossible to speak of in any unitary manner, it is probably just as *unlikely* that economic development, broadly defined, has *no* role to play in accounting for increases in women-headed households (see UNDAW, 1991:38). One of the main ways in which economic development (particularly of a capitalist nature) might raise the likelihood of female headship is through eroding structures that have traditionally kept women tied to men in the context of corporate (and usually patriarchal) kin groups. Folbre (1991:99) notes, for example, that economic development 'diminishes the significance of the household as a unit of production and contributes to the revision and "modernisation" of traditional structures of patriarchal governance – the property rights, cultural norms, and implicit contracts that reinforce male authority' (see also Kabeer, 1994:127). The growth of labour markets and increased geographical mobility certainly seem not only to have led to greater economic power among women (see Folbre, 1994b:86) but to have lessened their dependence on men for access to livelihood (at least at the domestic level) (see Hobson, 1994:171; Monteón, 1995: 43). In these circumstances it is perhaps no surprise that many authors have drawn association between the rise in female headship and women's increased economic activity (Baerga, 1992:14; González de la Rocha, 1994b; Patterson, 1994:121; Safa, 1995:83; see also Blumberg, 1978).

The link between women possessing an independent source of income and being more likely to head their own households may be particularly important in the light of a late twentieth-century process which some have termed the 'global feminisation of labour' whereby in many parts of the world women are an increasing presence in the workforce (see Joekes, 1987; Moghadam, 1994, 1995f; Standing, 1989). While economic development has historically been linked with the failure of traditional forms of agricultural production to sustain survival and has therefore pushed men and women alike into various sectors of the wage economy, recent decades seem to have witnessed rising demand for female workers. This is particularly the case with the transfer of labour intensive production operations by multinational manufacturing firms to Third World locations, commonly to special 'export processing' or 'free trade zones'. Being cheaper to employ and assumed to possess a range of additional advantages such as greater productivity in detailed manual work, women have been recruited as factory operatives in preference to men as a means of paring production costs to minimal levels (see Elson and Pearson, 1981; Froebel *et al.*, 1980; Safa, 1981; also Chant and McIlwaine, 1995b; Fernández-Kelly, 1983; Sassen-Koob, 1984; Sklair, 1991). Beyond this, women are also a significant presence among informal workers sub-contracted by these firms (Benería and Roldan, 1987; Blumberg, 1995; Moghadam, 1995b). In addition, the increased concentration of economic activity in urban areas has led to a proliferation of service jobs which, again, has often favoured women in both the advanced and developing economies (Joekes, 1987; Moghadam, 1995a; Townsend and Momsen, 1987), and women's concentration in retail and services may have cushioned them from employment contraction in the last decade or so (Baden, 1993:14; de Barbieri and de Oliveira, 1989:23).

Although women's employment has by no means risen uniformly, and in fact, in sub-Saharan Africa women's share of the workforce seems to have dropped in the last two decades (from 39 per cent in 1970 to 37 per cent in 1990), in the developed economies, women were 39 per cent of the labour force in 1990 (compared with 35 per cent in 1970), and in many developing regions, rates have also risen (UN, 1991:83). For example, in Latin America and the Caribbean, women were only 24 per cent of the labour force in 1970, but 29 per cent by 1990, and in North Africa and the Middle East, the proportion rose from 12 to 17 per cent over the same period (*ibid.*). At the same time, it should also be noted that women who have entered the labour market under conditions of economic restructuring (see below) have done so at a time when employment circumstances have deteriorated (see Baden, 1992:9; Baden and Milward, 1995:31; Kodras and Jones, 1991:262; Moghadam, 1995a). Moreover, women's economic participation rates are everywhere considerably lower than men's. Even if male employment has fallen in recent years, in North Africa in 1990, only 16 per cent of women aged 15 years or more were economically active compared with 80 per cent of men, and in Latin America and the Caribbean, the rate was 80 per cent for men, as against 32 per cent for women (UN, 1991:86). Another important issue to bear in mind is that in one or two contexts, notably Britain, the employment of single mothers has dropped by around half since the mid-1970s, leading Duncan (1991b:423) to conclude that 'The much lauded "feminisation" of paid work does not extend to these women, quite the reverse – they are increasingly *excluded* from paid work' (Duncan's emphasis; see also Edwards and Duncan, 1996b; Land, 1995:109–12; NCOPF, 1994b:4).

Notwithstanding contradictory tendencies in respect of connections between the feminisation of paid labour and rises in female headship, a further factor in the globalisation of economic activity which would appear to be linked to increases in both phenomena is world recession and the influence exerted over increasing numbers of debt-burdened countries by global financial institutions, notably the International Monetary Fund (IMF) and the World Bank. In order to meet debt payments and to qualify for further loans, many nations in the developing world and Eastern Europe have been forced to adopt neoliberal stabilisation and structural adjustment programmes. These have involved increasing export performance, relaxing restrictions on imports, privatising parastatal enterprises, 'streamlining' government institutions, cutting back on social welfare, and 'unblocking' labour markets in the form of reducing workers' wages, security and fringe benefits (see Cornia *et al.* [eds], 1988; Elson, 1989; Sparr, 1994a; Standing and Tokman [eds], 1991). In most countries, restructuring has caused great hardship for low-income groups and increased poverty has been linked with rising levels of female headship in this strata, often encapsulated in the concept, the 'feminisation of poverty' (see for example, Brodie, 1994:49; Sen, 1994:32; Staudt, 1991:63).[7] Some authors have argued that men's relative loss of employment and/or regularity of employment has led to greater labour migration which has fragmented families and, in the process, increased propensity for breakdown (see for example Bullock, 1994:17; Connell, 1984:974; Cleves Mosse, 1993:45; Radcliffe, 1992:47; Shanthi, 1994:19). Additional factors (which could also have made men less willing to marry) include stress or loss of self-esteem where there is the expectation that they should fulfil the role of primary breadwinners within households (see for example Boyden and Holden, 1991:19–20; also González de la Rocha, 1995a:392–3; Moore, 1994b; Safa, 1995:183; Stichter, 1990:53). Another factor is frustration on the part of women at the prospect or actuality of having to support male partners on their meagre earnings (Bradshaw, 1996a on Honduras; Casinader *et al.*, 1987:317 on Sri Lanka). A number of studies have emphasised the role played in family breakdown by the rising burdens on women of working in and outside the home, and the injustice felt at men's limited help in housework and childcare (see Benería, 1991:177–8 on Mexico).[8] Others have noted the tensions provoked by transitions in family systems and the decline of extended family networks, which have led to lessened control over marriage, rising divorce and non-marriage, and the greater abandonment and destitution of women and children (Boyden and Holden, 1991:18; Kumari, 1989:31; Lewis, 1993:28; Weekes-Vagliani, 1992:142). As Shanthi (1994:17) points out for India: 'the very fact that those cultural values and practices which made automatic provision for absorption of widows by the nearest kith and kin are fast disappearing and have almost collapsed is a cause for concern', with increased poverty being attributed a major role in making it more difficult for women to return to the homes of parents or brothers in the event of widowhood or desertion (see also Cain *et al.*, 1979:408; Kabeer, 1991:257; Pryer, 1992:141 on Bangladesh; Youssef and Hetler, 1983 on Morocco; Stack and Burton, 1994:41–2 on the USA).

World population change

Demographic factors cannot easily be disentangled from economic aspects of world development, but they do merit some attention in their own right. As indicated previously, one of the major demographic impacts of economic growth and integration is labour migration, whether national or international. This has altered sex ratios in many areas and increased the likelihood of women heading households either on a short- or long-term basis. The worldwide shift to urbanisation is an integral part of this process[9] and localised changes in sex ratios can obviously impact on household headship at national levels, as discussed in detail in Chapter 4.

Another demographic factor linked with female household headship is ageing of populations throughout the world, with lone-female households becoming more common among the elderly (see Folbre, 1991:100). This interrelates with gender-differentiated life expectancy and age gaps in marriage, with women more likely to become heads of household through widowhood (see Rojas Chaves, 1986 on Latin America; Safa, 1995:180 on the Caribbean; also Bullock, 1994:17). The only exception here would be regions such as South Asia where women have an above average risk of mortality as infants and in their child-bearing years (see Harriss and Watson, 1987).

Fertility rates are also significant, in that declining birth rates in most parts of the world may make it more feasible for women to head households on their own when they have young dependent children, mainly because they may be less burdened by childcare and freer to move into paid work (see for example, Harris, 1993). Declining fertility is also likely to increase prospects of female headship at the other end of the age spectrum in that older widowed women will have fewer people who might take them in (see Folbre, 1991). On top of this, fertility decline seems to be associated with increased costs of raising children, and this is claimed to have led men to become less interested in fatherhood, at least in the USA (Folbre, 1994a:205).

World trends in women's movements and representation

A final factor at a world scale which might be construed as having had some impact on female household headship over the last quarter century is the growth in organised women's movements (see Kamerman and Kahn, 1988:260–7). Accepting the premise that, at some level, women's ability to head their own households is a matter of civil and human rights, general moves in the direction of strengthening women's positions in society and of attempting to reduce gender inequalities in economic, social and legal domains may have had a part to play in explaining rises. For example, UN initiatives for women at a world level (the Decade for Women, 1975–85, the Beijing Conference of 1995 and so on), have undoubtedly been important if not in globalising the women's agenda, at least in fostering interchange of ideas and in getting governments to consider their positions in relation to gender (see Pietilä and Vickers, 1994; Moghadam, 1995e). As del Rosario (1995:102) observes, the Decade prompted a number of governments to ratify international conventions concerning women, to revise aspects of their legal codes, to institute new legislation, or to establish departments or women's desks as 'ways of signalling their acknowledgement of the importance of women's issues'. So-called 'machineries' for policy formulation, programme implementation, the monitoring of women's status and women's projects have now been set up in around 140 countries.

Notwithstanding that international recommendations concerning women's rights are often not implemented (or implemented in full), a whole host of legal initiatives have been taken in individual countries as a direct or indirect result of global pressure, which undoubtedly raise visibility of female subordination, provoke questions about patriarchal privileges at both domestic and extra-domestic levels, and may, in a range of ways, contribute to conditions more favourable to women's rights as independent citizens, including scope to head their own households. Changes in divorce legislation constitute an important factor here, and accordingly merit some attention.

Rising divorce rates and female household headship

One major reason for rises in female headship in several countries in the post-war period, especially in the North, seems to be women's increased access to divorce and/or likelihood of petitioning for divorce (see Boyden and Holden, 1991:19; Cashmore, 1985:1–2; Gelles, 1995:392–6; Kamerman and Kahn, 1988:6–11). Between 1960 and 1980 for example, the United Nations estimated that the divorce rate tripled in the North, and between 25 and 50 per cent of marriages now end up dissolved (O'Connell, 1994:18). In the United States, the divorce rate rose from 9.2 per 1000 marriages in 1960 to 14.9 in 1970 to nearly 23 in 1980, although by 1989 the rate had dropped back slightly to 20.7 (Gelles, 1995:391).[10] In the UK, the number of divorces per 1000 marriages rose from 11.9 to 12.6 between 1980 and 1989, giving the country the second highest divorce rate in Europe after

Denmark (Muncie and Sapsford, 1995:21, Table 4). Indeed, Winchester's (1990:74–5) research on Britain and Australia points out that while illegitimacy and widowhood were the main reasons for female lone parenthood in the 1970s, divorce is now much more significant.

Rising levels of divorce are also noted for developing countries, albeit within a more recent span of time. For example, in Thailand, Hoffman *et al.* (1994:135) observe that 'various marital and family problems have escalated and the divorce rate has risen by 50 per cent over just the last decade' (see also Edwards *et al.*, 1993:61). By the early 1990s, 25 per cent of marriages were ending in divorce (Bell, 1995:4). As indicated in Chapter 1, male migration and long term *de facto* female headship in Thailand and elsewhere is often a precursor to permanent separation and divorce. None the less, other factors are clearly at play, one being greater consciousness and concern about women's rights. For example, Diagne (1993:46) notes that in several parts of Francophone Africa, steps have been taken to legalise divorce as a means of counteracting the practice of repudiation and to strengthen women's ability to defend their own and their children's interests.

Yet discerning where these changes are coming from is inevitably problematic, since analyses of the subject are often based on conjecture or statistical inferences rather than on systematic in-depth surveys with relevant parties. As Moore (1994b:19) points out: 'The reasons for increasing divorce rates have to be specified culturally and historically, and no single generalisation could cover all the kinship and marital systems of the world.' None the less, one 'technical' factor often cited relates to the relaxation of barriers to divorce and to a wider basis on which marriages can be dissolved. For example, a rising trend in divorce in the UK (amounting to a trebling in the last 30 years) is argued to have been given a major boost by the 1969 Divorce Law Reform Act, which, like the USA, removed the concept of a 'guilty party' and created a single ground for divorce: irretrievable breakdown (Muncie and Sapsford, 1995:20; see also Gelles, 1995:393–4 and Jacobsen, 1994:97–8 on the USA.[11]

Another factor linked to rising divorce rates is increased labour force participation among women, although, as indicated earlier, the causal links between these and other demographic changes (including female household headship) are by no means well established (see Edwards *et al.*, 1993; Gelles, 1995:394–5; Jacobsen, 1994:191).

Separation and non-marriage

Aside from divorce, separation also seems to have been increasing, especially in countries such as Ireland, where divorce did not become legal until 1995 (Millar *et al.*, 1992:21). This trend represents something of a break from the past since as Duncan and Edwards (1994:10) point out, lone motherhood has traditionally been viewed as a major threat to Catholic marriage, and a whole range of measures (including stringent eligibility for welfare benefits, semi-custodial institutions for 'fallen women' and the like), have acted both to discourage the phenomenon and to keep its visibility to a minimum. Given the opprobrium traditionally shown towards cohabitation in Ireland, rising separation has undoubtedly been significant in contributing to female headship insofar as while this represented increased 'inflow' into lone parenthood, the 'outflow' was restricted because lack of divorce meant people could not remarry (Millar *et al.*, 1992:21).[12]

Also important in accounting for increases in female headship are rising rates of non-marriage and changing responses to non-marriage, the latter particularly relating to more relaxed attitudes towards out-of-wedlock births. Remembering that out-of-wedlock births can take place within stable cohabiting partnerships (as is now common in Sweden for example), in places where cohabitation is rarer, such as Ireland, women have shown a rising tendency to keep children rather than give them up for adoption (Millar *et al.*, 1992:23). In Australia too, one-parent families with illegitimate children are increasingly likely to be independent and less concealed within complex households than they were in the past (Winchester, 1990:74–5). These kinds of trends also apply to the UK, where, back in the 1970s, many lived in multi-unit households, particularly those of their own parents (Edwards and Duncan, 1996b). This accompanies rising proportions of unmarried mothers among lone parents, notwithstanding that some might previously have been in a cohabiting relationship (Burghes, 1994:7, Table 1; Muncie and Sapsford, 1995:13). In 1991, for example, over half of lone parents in the UK were divorced or separated, one-third had never been married and only 6.3 per cent were widowed (Hewitt and Leach, 1993:8). This is in marked contrast to the situation in 1971, when only 15.8 per cent of lone parents were single and as many as 21 per cent were widowed (Burghes, 1994:7, Table 1). It is an even bigger change since the Second World War when widows predominated among female lone parents (Lewis, 1989:596; see also Hardey and Crow, 1991:7–8; Haskey, 1991). Indeed, between 1982 and 1992 alone, the proportion of births outside marriage in the UK rose from 14.4 to 31.2 per cent (NCOPF, 1994b:3). Both these figures are substantially higher than the rate for 1970 which was 8 per cent (Land, 1995:88). Data for the USA indicates similar trends: among black families in 1970, the biggest single group of female heads (53.6 per cent) were separated from their husbands and 16.6 per cent divorced; only 16.3 per cent were women who had never married and a mere 13.9 per cent were widows; by 1980, however, 30 per cent of black women heading households were never married, which brought them to the same level as separated women as the principal type of female head (Simms, 1986:142; see also Shanthi, 1994:21).

As for developing country contexts, Brydon (1987a:261) notes for Avatime, Ghana, that while it is still deemed socially important for women to become adults through child-bearing, they can now 'be regarded as such without the secular arrangement of marriage'. As such, 'Over the years, the proportion of female-headed units and sub-units has grown as women have become economically and socially independent, widows and divorcées remain unmarried, non-married women set-up households and "*kupome*" of their own.'[13] Among the reasons Brydon gives for the declining importance of 'wifehood' amongst Avatime women, are that changes in women's economic roles provoked by the spread of the cash economy have enhanced their freedom from family-based subsistence production, and *ipso facto* reduced pressure to conform with familial norms. This again underlines the importance of considering social factors in relation to their economic and demographic corollaries. In the context of South Africa, Moore (1994b:20) points out that in the wake of the decline in male migrant labour and employment, women are not marrying because marriage provides little security for them and their children, and in fact can add to vulnerability in view of men's demands on their labour, time and income (see also González de la Rocha, 1995b:22–3 on Mexico).

INTER- AND INTRA-REGIONAL DIVERSITY IN FEMALE HEADSHIP

Having offered an idea of trends in female headship at a world scale and general factors that might account for increases, it is clear that patterns, and the processes behind them, are far from uniform. It is accordingly important to consider some of the key differences in frequencies and forms of female-headed households in different world regions.

Comparative frequencies

While the opening section of this chapter showed that women-headed households are a larger proportion of the population in the developed than the developing world, differences *within* these regions are often extremely marked. For example, whereas 24.6 per cent of households in Australia were headed by women in 1980, in Japan the figure was 15.2 per cent (UNDP, 1995:63, Table A2.5). Moreover, within Europe *per se*, data from the early 1980s show that while an average of 22 per cent of households in

Northwest Europe were headed by women, this ranged from 20.9 per cent in France and 28.1 per cent in Austria, whereas in Southern Europe the average was only 16.9 per cent (Folbre, 1991:95–8, Table 3.1). Patterns of lone motherhood reveal similar variations. On the basis of data pertaining to the late 1980s, an average of 11 per cent of all families with dependent children throughout Europe were headed by a lone parent (with at least three-quarters and, more usually, over four-fifths being headed by women). Yet the rates were as low as 5–6 per cent in circum-Mediterranean countries such as Greece, Spain and Italy, and up to 15 and 16 per cent in Denmark and Sweden respectively (Millar *et al.*, 1992:25, Table 2.11). In 1991, lone-parent families were 17.4 per cent of all families with children in Germany and over 86 per cent were headed by women (Mädje and Neusüss, 1994:1419). In Britain in 1992, 20 per cent of families were headed by a lone mother (Duncan and Edwards, 1996).

With the 'developing world' being a much larger and diverse entity it is no surprise that ranges are even greater, and often extremely marked within continents. This is especially the case with sub-Saharan Africa, where, in 1980, women-headed households were only 5.1 per cent of all households in Burkina Faso and 12.7 per cent in Guinea, but 21 per cent in Benin, 25.2 per cent in Rwanda, 27.8 per cent in Zambia and 45.2 per cent in Botswana (UNDP, 1995:64–5, Table A2.5). As for Latin America, 1980 data show that women-headed households were 14.4 per cent of all households in Brazil, 18.1 per cent in Paraguay, 21 per cent in Uruguay, 21.5 per cent in Panama (UNDP, 1995:63–5, Table A2.5), and 28 per cent of households in Cuba (Rojas Chaves, 1986:2).

In the Caribbean, while around one-third of households in the region as a whole are headed by women, proportions in 1980 were estimated to be 45.6 per cent in St Kitts-Nevis, 45.3 per cent in Grenada, 43.9 per cent in Barbados and 42.4 per cent in St Vincent, yet only 25 per cent in Trinidad and Tobago where there is a large East Indian population (Momsen, 1987:344; UNDP, 1995:63–4, Table A2.5; see also Patterson, 1994:122; Powell, 1986:105,Table 8). In Guyana, too, where people of Indian descent are just over half the population, women-headed households in 1980 were only 26.4 per cent of households (UNDP, 1995:64). Indeed, East Indian women in the region in general are more likely to live in patriarchal extended households than their Afro-Caribbean counterparts (Ellis, 1986; Trotz, 1996).

In South Asia, rates of female headship are generally lower. In the early 1980s, for example, women-headed households were only 9.5 per cent of households in Bangladesh and as few as 1.8 per cent in Pakistan (Folbre, 1991:95–8, Table 3.1), although in Sri Lanka in 1981, 17.4 per cent were female-headed. This latter figure may be higher due to political turmoil and the out-migration of men, although the traditional Kandyan legal code of the majority Sinhala community may also have a role to play (see Rasanayagam, 1993:150). Women in Sri Lanka have traditionally enjoyed rights to own land (independently as well as through marriage), to obtain and dispose of income, to keep their natal family name, and to represent themselves in a court of law without a man's guardianship (World Bank, 1995:54). Rates for the Middle East and North Africa are also low, being 5 per cent in Kuwait in 1980, 7.3 per cent in Iran and 10.4 per cent in Tunisia (UNDP, 1995:63–4, Table A2.5). As for Southeast Asia, there are considerable variations in female headship between and also within countries. As of the turn of the 1980s, for example, women-headed households were as many as 24 per cent of households in Hong Kong, yet only 16 per cent in Thailand and Myanmar and as few as 11 per cent in the Philippines (see UN, 1991:28–9, Table 2). In Indonesia, women heads were 14 per cent of all households at a national level (*ibid.*), yet Mather's (1988) research revealed a level of only 12 per cent of female heads in Western Java, whereas the figure for a Central Javanese village studied by Hetler (1990) was 35 per cent although 60 per cent of these were *de facto* units.

While different frequencies between continents, let alone countries, cannot readily be explained without recourse to more in-depth holistic overviews of particular societies (as attempted in the case study discussions of Chapter 5 and onwards), some idea of routes into female headship is possible from examining differences in dominant characteristics of female heads in different contexts.

Dominant characteristics of female household heads in different world regions

The civil status of female heads of household is often an important indicator of the factors behind their emergence in different regions. As suggested by the figures given earlier in the chapter, the bulk of female heads in the advanced economies are currently divorced, separated or never-married, and reflect rising rates of marital breakdown and unmarried motherhood as primary causes (Shanthi, 1994:18; see also Folbre, 1991:99–100). In the developing world, on the other hand, the majority of female heads are widows, married women whose husbands are away working, and women separated on a long-term basis: in turn these patterns reflect the prevalence of widowhood, desertion and migration (Shanthi, 1994:18).

While the above characterisations might be important in general terms, there is inevitably diversity within regions. Considering lone-mother households, for example, in the United States in 1986, the vast bulk of single mothers with children (46 per cent) were divorced, the next largest group (29 per cent) were never-married and widows were only 7 per cent (Kamerman and Kahn, 1988:32–3). Yet in Ireland in the same year, unmarried mothers were only 16 per cent of the total of lone-parent households; widows and widowers 24 per cent and separated people 60 per cent (Millar *et al.*, 1992:160).

Within the developing world there are also considerable variations. Despite the fact that widowhood, desertion and migration are the main factors for the developing world as a whole, in Latin America and the Caribbean, unmarried parenthood is more common (Baden and Milward, 1995:17; Folbre, 1991:99–100). In the Caribbean, for example, two-thirds of births in the region as a whole take place outside an official marriage (Powell, 1986), which is not to say that some women might not cohabit with the fathers of their children. None the less, there is evidence to suggest that many Afro-Caribbean women choose to have short-term visiting relationships than full-time residential partnerships (see also Pulsipher, 1993; Trotz, 1996). Moreover, while non-marriage, along with divorce and separation, might be associated with female household headship in Latin America as a whole, studies of low-income communities in Lima, Peru suggest that numbers of female heads are relatively low and that a large proportion are widows (see Scott, 1994:89 for discussion and references). In sub-Saharan Africa, on the other hand, female-headed households more often arise either through women being being widowed or left behind by male migrants (Baden and Milward, 1995:17; Folbre, 1991:99–100; although see also Lloyd and Gage-Brandon, 1993:116 on Ghana). As for Asia, Momsen (1991:26) notes that widowhood is still a prime cause of female household headship,[14] and in North and Southern Africa and the Middle East, international migration (see Kawar, 1996 on Jordan). Of course, it is often the case that factors are interlinked. For example, Mencher's study of the Muslim-dominated district of Malappuram in Kerala, India, reveals that the rising degree of male migration to the Middle East seems to be associated with increased numbers of divorced women in agricultural communities (Mencher, 1989:129), and Baden and Milward (1995:17–18) note that while the relative importance of widowhood in leading to female headship is diminishing, this is being 'over-compensated' by increases in marital breakdown arising from divorce and desertion. None the less, divorcées in India and other South Asian countries are still quite rare. On the basis of a survey of over 200 households in four Bangladeshi villages, Lily (1987:97) found no divorced women heading households themselves in any of the communities. This might have to do with fact that divorcées (like widows) have often been absorbed within their paternal or fraternal households, or as dependants in the households of adult sons, partly for reasons of shame, and partly because it is so difficult for lone women to gain a livelihood. Indeed divorced *or* bereaved women who are not supported by sons, who have no children, and/or who lack access to land in rural areas, may face a very limited range of employment, often forcing them into socially undesirable occupations such as midwifery in order to survive (see Jeffery and Jeffery, 1993:22, 1996: Chapter 15). On top of this, community constraints, such as rumours of sexual misbehaviour are, in Bangladesh for example, a 'common means of discrediting women whose activities take them outside the socially prescribed limits of female roles' (Lewis, 1993:31). In this respect, the chances of women heads surviving as independent entities are relatively small (see also Cain *et al.*, 1979; Gardner, 1995).

Historical precedents such as the Hindu practice of 'sati' (self-immolation of widows on their husbands' funeral pyres) may have also reduced numbers of potential female heads in South Asian countries such as India. Sati is actually a rather wide-ranging phenomenon, not necessarily involving death *per se* (although immolation along with sons or other male relatives is not unknown), but taking the form of good virtue, abstinence and other self-sacrificial acts (see van den Bosch, 1995; Shanti, 1995; Singh Shekhawat, 1989). Though the act and its glorification are technically outlawed by the Commission of Sati (Prevention) Act, the practice clearly continues (Chen and Drèze, 1992:37).[15] As Prakash Singh and Singh (1989:55) point out: 'Even though a woman may not be physically compelled to become a sati, the mythology she has imbibed and the norms which she has internalised all seem to portray her subordinate status. She is not seen as an independent entity who can live unblemished as a widow or divorcée.' Indeed, one option for widows and deserted women in India in the past was to enter a Shelter Home run by social reformers where they did not have to disclose their identity (see Dabir, 1993); this would inevitably have reduced numbers of individual households headed by women.

CONCLUSION

In conclusion, women-headed households in many countries of the developed and developing world seem to be increasing, even if the data on which rises are calculated are often wanting and need to be interpreted with caution. Global factors which might have an impact on widespread increases include economic development, the internationalisation of production and global moves towards neo-liberal economic strategies (under the influence of First World financial institutions), world population change, and the growing exposure of gender inequities through national and global initiatives by and for women. The institutionalisation of women's concerns as a response to these pressures seems to have had some effect on relaxing divorce legislation and in making it slightly easier for women to remain outside marriage. At the same time, levels of female headship vary widely within and between regions, as we go on to explore with particular reference to the developing world in the following chapter.

NOTES

1. These problems apply both to developed and developing countries. In Ireland, for example, Millar *et al.* (1992:18) point out that 'It is difficult to get accurate data on trends in lone parenthood over time, because the appropriate data have not been collected', and in this particular case, records only go back as far as the 1981 Census. As regards female headship in the USA, Folbre and Abel (1989:545) indicate that there are serious problems with enumeration (and more specifically underestimation) of women's work and women's households prior to the 1950 Census. As for developing countries, the Philippine census has only contained tables showing the sex of household heads since 1990, even if other statistical sources do exist (see Illo, 1992). See also Kalpagam (1992) on the changing nature of data collection and tabulation in Indian censuses since 1951 (also Kumari, 1989:27 *et seq.*; Visaria and Visaria, 1985:51); and Oliveira (1992:208) on the incomparability of Brazilian census data since 1940 in respect of basic concepts such as 'marriage', 'the family', complex households and so on.

2. Another feature worth noting is that many statistical sources on the developed world use the term 'family' to describe household units, whereas those on developing countries tend to stick with the term household, leaving family to describe the broader institutions surrounding consanguineal and affinal links between persons (see Kumari, 1989:27; also Chapter 9).

3. Winchester (1990:74) also notes, however, that there might be some under-recording of female-headed families in the Australian census which could in part inflate the increase.

4. In many respects, of course, micro-level survey data is more likely to indicate rises in situations where there is little turnover of neighbourhood populations and where ageing among sample respondents is prone to lead to increased prospects of widowhood and/or male abandonment.

5. This accompanies a trend whereby the proportion of single women with at least one child rose from 3 per cent to 7.5 per cent between 1960 and 1980 (Jelin, 1992:121).

6. The gender imbalance in São Paulo's population seems to have been provoked by the development of plantation-based export agriculture which employed individual men rather than family units, and meant that male labour migration to the countryside left a relatively large 'surplus' of women in the city. It is also interesting to note, however, that even by 1836, when the sex ratio in São Paulo had become more balanced, the level of female headship remained high, being 39.3 per cent in this latter year (Kuznesof, 1980).

7. Baden and Milward (1995:1n) observe that the term 'feminisation of poverty' originated in the 1970s in the context of debates in the USA about single mothers and welfare (see also Kodras and Jones, 1991). It should also be acknowledged, however, that there is by no means unilateral agreement on whether contemporary structural adjustment in developing countries has led to increased impoverishment among women, *or* a rise in female household headship, let alone that these are linked (see Sparr, 1994b for discussion and references; also Gilbert, 1994:620; Peña Saint Martin, 1994:32 *et seq.*).

8. Studies on households in the North have also indicated that men's domestic labour contributions (usually limited) are scarcely changed by wives' employment status (see Edley and Wetherell, 1995:119; Folbre, 1994a: 205; Pahl, 1984; Wetherell, 1995:223–4).

9. Between 1970 and 1992, the proportion of the world's population living in urban areas increased from 35 to 42 per cent, with the urban population in low- and middle-income economies increasing from 25 to 26 per cent, and that in high-income economies growing from 74 to 78 per cent (World Bank, 1994:222–3, Table 31).

10. The tendency to rising divorce levels in the United States has been going on since the beginning of the twentieth century, and 30 years ago, was attributed by family theorist William Goode (1964:94) to be the result of lessened social opprobrium, and the greater likelihood that people would find a wider choice of (new) partners with increased settlement in urban areas.

11. As part and parcel of responses to concern about the 'breakdown' of the family in the UK, a House of Commons vote on a proposal within the Family Law Bill to reduce the waiting period for divorce to one year in April 1996 led to an amendment to 18 months (see headline article by Rebecca Smithers 'Ministers hand Major divorce defeat', the *Guardian*, 25 April 1996).

12. The 'routes' into lone parenthood identified by Millar *et al.* (1992:22, Fig 2.1) include births outside marriage, termination of marriage (whether through separation or widowhood), the end of cohabitation, partner in prison (long term) or partner in hospital care (long term). The routes out of lone parenthood are specified as marriage, remarriage, reconciliation, cohabitation, the maturation or death of children, or the death of the lone parent herself (see also Bradshaw, 1996a; Hardey and Crow, 1991:2).

13. A *'kepame'* (plural, *'kupome'*) in Avatime is a residential unit, and is not necessarily coterminous with production and consumption (see Brydon, 1987a:257–8; see also Chapter 1).

14. In Gujerat, India, for example, 81.4 per cent of female heads in rural areas in 1972–73 were widows, and 80.6 per cent in urban areas (Visaria and Visaria, 1985:69, Table 8).

15. Sati was originally outlawed in 1829 under British Law and in the wake of considerable opposition from orthodox Hindus. The 1829 regulation equated the act of sati with 'culpable homicide', and its glorification with abetment under the Indian Penal Code 306 (Dandvate, 1989:86). However, this law remained a 'dead letter' in the statute books outside Bengal until 1987, when the burning of an 18-year-old widow, Roop Kanwar in Rajasthan, provoked public outcry and drew attention to the need for further abolitionist legislation. Even then, Section 3 of the law stipulates that the victim of sati herself be punished for attempted suicide, regardless of the fact that sati is never a voluntary act (*ibid.*:87).

4 Women-Headed Households and Development

INTRODUCTION

This chapter brings the focus onto developing countries and synthesises a range of factors identified in household studies as precipitating or inhibiting the formation of female-headed households in the South. The factors are discussed under four main headings: demographic, economic, legal-institutional and socio-cultural, and are treated as far as possible as 'variables' or 'themes' in their own right. This thematic approach is helpful in a number of ways. First, female household heads exist everywhere and thinking *across* countries not only reminds us that we are dealing with a phenomenon of global as well as regional significance but helps to guard against tendencies to consign women-headed households to the category of 'one-off' or anomalous group. Second, it assists in avoiding the repetition involved in considering individual country studies in turn. Third, a thematic approach permits the inclusion of insights from studies where female headship is an element but not the central focus of analysis. Fourth, by showing where in the developing world different factors have been identified as important, we are still able to see which influences might be more consistently linked with female headship than others. Finally, a review of this nature may also act as a 'checklist' of factors or 'entry points' for more detailed comparative research on the subject. Indeed, while there is no doubt as to relevance of in-depth holistic analyses of individual countries for understanding diversity and dynamics in female headship in the developing world, observations synthesised from a range of studies give an idea of the kinds of factors that merit at least preliminary examination. Moreover, in opening up scope for slightly more systematic research, such an approach may also allow us to be more confident in our conclusions about the relative importance of different factors in different places. At the same time, it is inevitably critical to recognise that factors are not easily objectified, classified, and/or treated in isolation from other factors affecting female headship in particular localities. For example, age at marriage is not merely a demographic phenomenon (as I categorise it here), but is also governed by legal practices, kinship ideologies and so on. Beyond this, early marriage may lessen the prospects of female headship in some areas (for example, where divorce and separation are rare), but not in others. With this in mind, while the present chapter flags-up a range of issues for general consideration in the analysis of female headship, in-depth reviews of specific countries (and the constructions and meanings of particular phenomena in particular places) are equally vital components of comparative research, as illustrated by the case study discussions of Mexico, Costa Rica and the Philippines which follow.

DEMOGRAPHIC FACTORS AFFECTING FEMALE HOUSEHOLD HEADSHIP IN DEVELOPING COUNTRIES

Feminised sex ratios

Feminised sex ratios are one of the biggest demographic correlates of female household headship insofar as where women outnumber men in the population of a given locality, evidence shows they are more likely to head households. Sex ratios can become feminised at a range of scales, with gender-selective migration being one of the most important causes.

Gender-selective migration
Gender-selective migration from rural to urban areas is common throughout the developing world. By its association with sex ratios, it is significant not only in explaining the growing frequency of female-headed households, but their spatial distribution within nations (see Brydon and Chant, 1989: Chapter 5; Chant and Radcliffe, 1992). In African and South Asian countries, for example, rural–urban migration has historically been dominated by men, sex ratios are more feminised in the countryside and women-headed households are much more of a rural than urban phenomenon (see Cleves Mosse, 1993:45–6; Kennedy, 1994:36 on Africa; Visaria and Visaria, 1985:54 and 56–7, Table 1 on India). Up to half the households in the Botswanan countryside, for example, are headed by women (Johnson, 1992:25; Larsson, 1989:39). In Zimbabwe and Zambia too, women-headed households are more commonly found in rural than in urban areas. In both countries women-headed households are around one-third of households at a national level, yet in urban areas such as Harare and Lusaka, the proportion is only about half the national average (Schlyter, 1989:27; see also Scarnecchia, 1993:195–6). Male-dominated rural–urban migration in West Africa has led to similar patterns. For example, among Ewe households in Ghana, male migration resulted in 42 per cent of households being headed by women in rural areas in the mid-1970s (Trenchard, 1987:164), and comparable figures (40 per cent) are reported for rural households in Kenya (Stewart, 1992:23). Clearly many of these women are *de facto* heads, still attached to men and reliant to some degree on their remittances (see Chapter 1).

In Latin America, the Caribbean and many parts of Southeast Asia, by contrast, rural–urban migration streams have been dominated by women and in these regions female heads are more prevalent in towns (Brydon and Chant, 1989:146; Rogers, 1980:66; Townsend and Momsen, 1987:53). In Latin America, for example, women-headed households are rarely more than 10 per cent of the household population in rural communities, yet up to 25 per cent of households in many urban areas (Browner, 1989:467), and a primary survey of low-income communities in a range of rural and urban localities in Honduras showed that 40 per cent of urban households were female-headed, compared with only 16 per cent in the countryside (Bradshaw, 1996a). Female-headed households are also more common in the towns and cities of the Caribbean. In Jamaica, for example, women-headed households were 45 per cent of the population in the Kingston Metropolitan Area in 1985 compared with 39 per cent at a national level (see Safa and Antrobus, 1992:70; also Bolles, 1986). In Guyana, too, there are higher rates of female headship in towns (Trotz, 1996).

Other forms of gender-selective migration also have an impact on household headship. In the English-speaking Caribbean, for example, international migration prior to the 1950s was heavily dominated by men and is seen as critical in explaining high levels of female-headed households on many islands (Safa and Antrobus, 1992:70; also Massiah, 1986:179). Similarly, women-headed households have long been common in the 'frontline' states of southern Africa such as Botswana, Lesotho, Mozambique and Swaziland due to men moving to work in mines and farms in South Africa (see Cleves Mosse, 1993:46; Murray, 1981). The outflow of Mexican male migrants into the USA also appears to be contributing to the feminisation of household headship in northern Mexico.[1] Although there are clearly variations between regions and countries therefore, where external and internal migration results in the feminisation of sex ratios, there seem to be fairly consistent links with female household headship.

Gender differences in life expectancy

Sex ratios are not only determined by migration, but by factors such as gender-differentiated life expectancy. The latter offers further insights into variations in levels of female household headship in developing regions. Although in most parts of the world women have greater survival rates than men (due to comparative biological advantage), in some regions, notably South Asia, sex ratios are masculinised. In the early 1980s, for example, there were 1075 males per 1000 females in South Asia, compared with 980 per 1000 in Africa and 990 per 1000 in Southeast Asia (Harriss and Watson, 1987:86, Table 5). A trend to the masculinisation of sex ratios over time has been attributed to the low social and economic valuation of women, and to discrimination against them at the household level in terms of nutrition and medical care (*ibid.*; also Varma, 1993:120). The 'shortage' of women produced by these processes is undoubtedly important in helping to explain the generally low incidence of female headship in South Asia in general (see Chapter 3), bearing in mind that the factors involved interrelate in a range of ways in different parts of the region. For example, although in India there is a broad correspondence between the numbers of women in given states and levels of female headship, female headship is more variable than sex ratios (Visaria and Visaria, 1985:163). In fact larger proportions of female-headed households in southern parts of the country seem to owe not so much to greater numbers of women, but to their higher social status and capacity for independent survival compared with the north, notwithstanding the clear interconnections between these phenomena (*ibid.*; see also Chen and Drèze, 1992:10–11; Kumari, 1989:8). In Bangladesh, in fact, the likelihood of death among widows can be up to three times higher than for women who are still married, with widows residing alone or in households headed by people other than themselves or their sons standing the greatest risks of mortality (see Chen and Drèze, 1992:8–9).

War and disease
As for other factors impacting on sex ratios and household headship, Folbre (1991:100) notes the importance of armed conflict, with female headship tending to be particularly high in the aftermath of war or civil strife (see also Menjívar and Trejos, 1992). In Cambodia, for example, aid agency workers report that around 80 per cent of village household heads are female, most being widows (O'Connell, 1994:68), and among Sri Lankan refugees in India, households comprising three or four siblings may be headed by orphaned daughters as young as 15 or 16 years of age (Cleves Mosse, 1993:45). Other factors affecting sex ratios include diseases such as AIDS, which in sub-Saharan Africa has caused heavy mortalities among middle generations and placed many grandmothers in the position of heading households (Moore, 1994b:5). Clearly war and disease are more random in their geographical distribution than processes such as gender-differentiated life expectancy and gender-selective migration which evolve through particular constellations of social, economic and demographic circumstances in specific places over time.

Urbanisation

While urbanisation is by no means consistently linked with rises in female household headship, in certain regions, particularly Central and South

America, the process does seem to be associated with 'an overall increase in women who are bringing up children alone' (Boyden and Holden, 1991:19; also Baden and Milward, 1995:5; Moore, 1988:63). Indeed Tinker (1993:23) has gone as far as to claim that 'In the mega-cities of the world, women-headed households are becoming the norm, particularly among the urban poor.'[2]

The extent to which urbanisation itself is responsible for increases in female household headship cannot easily be established, although uneven sex ratios arising from gender-selective migration to towns and cities are clearly one factor in the equation. An important facet of urbanisation *per se*, however, is the weakening of social constraints on women. The latter may arise not only with the breakdown of household-based economies, the fragmentation of kin networks through migration, and the erosion of traditional family support mechanisms (see Chapter 3), but exposure to other social and cultural practices, whether through the media or personal contact with different social groups, and some degree of social anonymity (see Chant, 1996b, for example, on international tourism destinations in Mexico and the Philippines). This is not to say, however, that new forms of male control and female subordination do not evolve in urban settings (see Safa, 1995: 38).

The proliferation of industrial and service jobs with urbanisation which, in many areas, have a greater tendency to absorb women than agricultural activities, is another factor which clearly contributes to lessening women's economic dependence on men and increasing their prospects of household headship in towns (see Bradshaw, 1995a; Safa, 1995; also later section on economic factors affecting female headship). Urbanisation is also associated with increased access to education and to family planning programmes. Both of these can increase female headship, either because women postpone marriage and/or childbirth and set up households of their own, or have fewer children to care for and may be better able to shoulder the responsibilities of lone parenthood (see below).

Women's age at marriage

Leading on from the above, age at marriage is sometimes noted as an important demographic factor influencing levels of female headship. In various developing countries, increased migration, education and employment opportunities for women seem to be associated with postponement of marriage. In Jordan, for example, women's average age at marriage rose from 19 years in 1979 to 24 years in 1991 (Kawar, 1996), and in Tunisia from 19 to 26 years between 1956 and 1995 (World Bank, 1995:51).[3] Although women in many places are accustomed to living in the homes of their parents until they marry, later nuptiality puts greater pressure upon them to assume responsibility for their own welfare, if not to support their parents as well (see for example Chant and McIlwaine, 1995a; Trager, 1988 on the Philippines). Where this involves leaving home to find employment, women clearly have to evolve other types of household arrangement in destination areas, which may include living alone or with female workmates (see Chapter 1). Rising age at marriage is by no means generalised however. In the Seychelles, for example, women's average age at marriage dropped from 25.6 years to 23.8 years between 1970 and 1990, and in the Solomon Islands from 22.3 to 21.2 years over the same period (UNDP, 1995:63–4, Table A2.5). Moreover, although women's average age at marriage in Morocco in 1970 was 19.4 years (*ibid.*), research in the 1980s claimed that up to 50 per cent of rural girls marry before they reach puberty and most of the rest within the first two years after menarche, the main objective of early wedlock being to prevent illicit sexual encounters and to protect family honour through the chastity of daughters (Mernissi, 1985:101). Similar imperatives apply in Bangladesh, where although the average age of marriage in 1990 was 18 years (UNDP, 1995:65, Table A2.5), 52 per cent of girls marry before they reach 15 years of age (O'Connell, 1994:16). In areas where early marriage continues, therefore, rates of female headship may be low as women are likely to move straight from the households of their fathers to those of their husbands, notwithstanding that divorce, separation and/or widowhood may offset this at later stages of the life course.

Gender differences in age at marriage

As noted in Chapter 3, widowhood is prone to occur not only where women have greater life expectancy than men, but where there are significant age gaps between husbands and wives. Having said this, widowhood may not necessarily lead to female household headship in contexts such as India and Bangladesh where bereaved women are more likely to reside with adult male offspring as 'dependants' (see Chen and Drèze, 1992). Yet gender differences in nuptiality can result in higher levels of female household headship in other ways than widowhood *per se*. In many rural parts of Asia (especially South Asia), an average age differential of 10 years between husbands and wives, combined with annual population growth rates of around 3 per cent, means that numbers of *potential* wives can be as much as 35 per cent greater than that of potential husbands (Caldwell and Caldwell, 1992:57). Although this may encourage polygamy (see later), other outcomes such as spinsterdom and/or the practice of discouraging remarriage among women can lead to higher potential female headship (*ibid.*; see also Mencher, 1989:129; Wilson and Dyson, 1992 on India; Hetler, 1990 on Indonesia). None the less, as with most of the variables already considered, other factors come into the equation. Chen and Drèze (1992:10–11) point out, for example, that while higher proportions of women are widows in South India than in the nation as a whole, this is only partially explained by age differentials at marriage (which are only one year greater in South India compared with the all-India average, and two years greater than in the North West). Other important elements are lower rates of widow remarriage in the South, and higher survival chances *as* widows (see also Jeffery and Jeffery, 1996: Chapters 14 &15, and earlier section on sex ratios).

Fertility and birth control

As suggested in the context of global influences on female headship in Chapter 3, lower fertility may raise levels of female headship at both ends of the age spectrum in that younger women with few children may find it easier to bring them up single-handedly, and older women may have fewer relatives to take them in. However, while these factors have been identified for advanced economies, they have been given little attention in relation to female headship in the South. Similarly, although access to birth control is often associated with older age at motherhood and fertility decline, the relationships between these variables are by no means clear, let alone their links with female headship. One could hypothesise that limited access to birth control by single people (as often applies to state services in developing countries) might conceivably be linked with greater numbers of out-of-wedlock births and higher rates of lone motherhood. However, non-marital pregnancy may not necessarily lead to female headship if illegal abortion using clandestine methods is widely practised (see Khasiani, 1992:61 on Kenya), if there are strong social pressures on couples to marry (see Chant and McIlwaine, 1995a on the Philippines), or, in cases of male desertion, that women have the opportunity and/or are under obligation to remain with natal kin (see Buvinic *et al.*, 1992 on Chile).

ECONOMIC FACTORS AFFECTING FEMALE HOUSEHOLD HEADSHIP IN DEVELOPING COUNTRIES

Access to land and property

While women's access to land and property might just as readily be classified as a legal-institutional or socio-cultural/kinship factor, the fact that this is often stressed as a critical basis for material independence and security among women means that it is probably of equal, if not greater, relevance to treat it as an economic issue in relation to household headship (see also discussion of Blumberg and García's political economy model in Chapter 2). Historically, family/household headship and property ownership have been very much connected. In Imperial China, for example, women only became heads of household in the absence of a competent male, and even then were not free to dispose of family property in the same way as male household heads (McCreery, 1993:269). This also applies in other parts of the world, and often regardless of kinship and inheritance patterns.

While there are no hard and fast rules governing women's access to land and property in different kinship systems, Koopman (1991:162) observes that where patrilineal inheritance obtains (as in many parts of South Asia), women usually only gain access to land through husbands. Daughters, on the other hand, do not inherit land, and divorced women lose rights to their ex-husbands' land. Scope for heading households in these contexts may be very limited. In India, for example, it was only in 1938 that the Hindu Women's Right to Property Act formalised the right of Hindu widows and widowed daughters-in-law to a share in the property of a dead spouse (Parashar, 1992:79–80). Even now, Jeffery and Jeffery (1993:11) note for the village of Bijnor that access to land from parents is foreclosed when women leave home to marry, and in North India more generally, women rarely exercise rights over their husband's share of family land either (Chen and Drèze, 1992:16; see also Kumari, 1989:31). This frequently ties widows (and daughters) to dependence on their spouses' kin for maintenance, which is generally so limited that they are unable to live independently (Chen and Drèze, 1992:33; Drèze, 1990:4; Wilson and Dyson, 1992:33). Similar constraints on female headship apply in Bangladesh. According to Islamic rules of inheritance, daughters receive only half the paternal property given to sons, and a mere eighth of their husband's property where they have children (Lewis, 1993:27). Laying claim to such meagre assets may well not be deemed worthwhile if it involves disrupting other kin-ascribed entitlements that guarantee survival and security (Cain *et al.*, 1979; Gardner, 1995:29; Kabeer, 1991:245).

In other parts of the world, such as sub-Saharan Africa, Southeast Asia and Latin America, where women may have greater access to land in their own right (albeit in the form of usufruct over natal family lands), there may be more scope to instigate divorce and/or to survive alone. This has historically been the case in Cajamarca, Northern Peru, where even though control of land may have been ceded to husbands, women 'could withdraw from relationships that became too oppressive' (Deere, 1990:141). Having said this, women's assets could also enhance their attractiveness to new partners, or encourage husbands to stay with them on account of being able to retain sufficient land to farm. Whatever the case, the likelihood of female headship was much less among land-renting groups, where widows and abandoned women, especially those without sons, were prone to eviction by landlords unless they remarried promptly or managed to obtain domestic service posts on the estates (*ibid.*:140). In many respects, the latter situation prevails because of women's heavy concentration among landless and/or land-poor groups, not only in Peru, but also in Honduras (Bradshaw, 1996a) and Bolivia (Sage, 1993:246). Even in cases where agrarian reform has taken place, women's entitlements remain limited. In Honduras, for example, although some land has now passed into the hands of widows and single women, they have generally received low priority and been awarded plots of very poor quality (Yudelman, 1989:241–2). In Costa Rica, too, although land and colonisation laws have not, in principle, excluded women as beneficiaries, the vast bulk of titles have gone to men (*ibid.*:242; Lara *et al.*, 1995:106).

Beyond the question of access to land, access to the means of working the land is also a critical determinant of whether women (especially those with few male household members) are able to survive without a partner (see Bradshaw, 1995a, 1996a; Lewis, 1993:30). For this reason, although women in rural Java, Indonesia may become *de jure* (as opposed to *de facto*) heads in the event of the death of a migrant husband, the transition to full female headship may not be easy:

Although women are quite likely to become heads of household, and there is no particular shame attached to this, they often begin with an economic handicap, since they may lack control of productive assets. Although the law prevents eviction of widows, it is much less protective of whether or not they receive such assets as those of rice fields, dry fields, gardens, cattle and machinery. (Hetler, 1990:192)

Production systems

Related in many ways to the above, women in agricultural areas may stand more prospect of heading their own households not only if they have land, but if husbands and wives have separate spheres of production. For example, in Cameroon, Koopman (1991:152) observes that rural households do not operate as a single unit of production. Instead, male heads and their wives tend to conduct separate enterpises, earn individual incomes and manage separate budgets. In the event of death, desertion or divorce, therefore, women are in a stronger position to head their own households. This is also noted for the Gambia by Dey (1981), where women's access to land has traditionally involved men having to pay their wives to farm their plots.

As mentioned earlier, urban-industrial development may also precipitate female headship through weakening family-based production systems and increasing women's access to individualised waged employment (see Blumberg and García, 1977:109). Having said this, small-scale family workshops have by no means disappeared with the advent of large-scale industrialisation; in fact in many areas, sub-contracting seems to be on the increase among manufacturing firms. This clearly places women at a disadvantage in respect of earning the type of livelihood that would enable them to live independently or as heads of household, especially if men are in charge of family businesses (see Blumberg, 1995; Chant, 1991a; Chant and McIlwaine, 1995a: Chapter 3, 1995b; Moghadam, 1995a).

Female labour force participation

Female labour force participation has been heralded as one of the major correlates of female household headship. Aside from the general significance of the so-called 'feminisation of labour' at a global scale (Chapter 3), a large number of detailed studies (especially of Latin America and the Caribbean) have indicated that female headship is much greater in areas where female employment is high (see Baerga, 1992:141 and Safa, 1983 on Puerto Rico; Bradshaw, 1996a on Honduras; Chant, 1991a and Fernández-Kelly, 1983 on Mexico; Patterson, 1994:121 on Guyana). Not surprisingly, perhaps, a range of studies have also shown that female heads of household are more likely to have employment than their counterparts in male-headed families (see Blumberg and García, 1977; Chant, 1991a; García and de Oliveira, 1994:152; González de la Rocha, 1994a:184; Willis, 1993), even if differences are sometimes slight (see Safa and Antrobus, 1992:53 on Jamaica). Sometimes the latter varies by race, with Trotz's (1996) study of Guyana showing that while Indo-Guyanese female heads are much more likely to work than their counterparts in male-headed households, differences are negligible among Afro-Guyanese women (see also McIlwaine, 1993 on black and *mestizo* groups in the Atlantic region of Costa Rica). In some instances, female heads may also have lower participation rates if children or relatives are contributing to household income (Moser, 1992:105–6 on Ecuador).

At one level, that there is some relationship between employment and headship is self-evident. As argued by Blumberg (1978) it is obvious that female heads of household need access to income of some description if they are to survive as independent units. This may be as important psychologically as it is pragmatically. For single women, for example, the knowledge that they can support themselves may mean that they feel they can postpone marriage or put it off altogether (Chant and McIlwaine, 1995a on the Philippines; Kabeer, 1995 on Bangladesh; Kawar, 1996 on Jordan). For married women, also, having an input to household finances and/or knowing that they can get employment if necessary may put them in the position of perceiving that they (and their offspring) can survive alone if the need arises (see Bradshaw, 1996a on Honduras; Chant, 1991a: Chapter 5 on Mexico; Mencher, 1989:128 on India; Trotz, 1996 on Guyana). Yet precisely how female labour force participation and headship might be connected in a processual sense is not well established.[4] Although it is often the case that once women become heads they have to work, as indicated in Chapter 3, work itself may provoke the formation of female-headed households, whether through aggravating relations between husbands and wives, or making women feel that they would be better off without a man to support. At the bottom line, however, as Safa (1995:83) points out for Puerto Rico: 'It would appear that paid employment, while not precipitating marital breakdown, at least enables the woman to leave an unsatisfactory marriage by providing her with an alternative source of income' (see also Edwards *et al.*, 1993 on Thailand; Kabeer, 1995 on Bangladesh). The question of causality is inevitably complicated by the fact that both female employment and household headship are contingent on a wide range of other interrelated issues such as industrialisation, family change, declining family size and fertility control (Oliveira, 1992:209), not to mention type of employment.

In some countries, female household headship seems to be more strongly associated with particular occupational groups than others. In the Philippines, for example, certain branches of work (such as sex work or formal sector tourism employment) are linked with women living in female-headed or female-dominant households (Chant, 1995a; Chant and McIlwaine, 1995a; Chapter 6 this volume). In Mexico, too, Peña Saint Martin's (1994:248) research on garment workers in the Yucatán shows that women who perform industrial work in factories (rather than in their homes as pieceworkers) are more likely to head their own households than women with husbands. Yet in India, Thorner's and Ranadive's (1992:145) Bombay-based study of working-class women revealed no significant differences in lifestyles between women who 'were holding jobs outside their own homes, those who pursued gainful occupations inside their own homes or on the verandah, those who had previously worked for pay but had temporarily or definitively ceased, and those who had, up to that moment, devoted themselves exclusively to domestic duties for their own families'. This again underscores the necessity of viewing labour force participation in conjunction with other factors in specific contexts. All things considered, however, it is fair to propose that the formation of independent households among women may be restricted by *lack* of access to work.

Economic restructuring and poverty

While a close association has been drawn between rising labour force participation and growing numbers of female-headed households during the '"lost decade" of the 1980s' (see González de la Rocha, 1994b:1 on Latin America)[5] neoliberal economic restructuring has been associated with female household headship in other ways. As noted in Chapter 3, restructuring has often acted to fragment households, whether through migration or conflict arising from economic hardship. This has often put women in the position of assuming sole responsibility for children, which, in turn, has been seen as exacerbating their disadvantage. As Tinker (1990:5) asserts, for example, 'the global economic downturn has pressed most heavily on women-headed households, which are everywhere in the world, the poorest of the poor'. Yet, in talking of the general relationship between poverty and economic change in Latin America and the Caribbean, and the position of female heads within this, Stolcke (1992:138) observes that 'economic processes do not occur in a cultural vacuum'. Social and ideological constructions of gender have shaped the ways in which people have tried to deal with economic crisis and how they have been affected by its outcomes. In other words, there is nothing 'natural' or 'inevitable' about the feminisation of headship under poverty. As Stolcke (1992:139) goes on to stress: 'women assume household and child-care responsibilities under such harsh economic conditions not because the mother–child dyad is the ultimate (biologically) irreducible core of the family, but on account of prevailing cultural values and gender ideology'. This may, of course, be bolstered or underpinned by the actions of the state.

LEGAL-INSTITUTIONAL FACTORS AFFECTING FEMALE HOUSEHOLD HEADSHIP IN DEVELOPING COUNTRIES

State attitudes and interventions

Although governments in many parts of the world appear to be in the midst of a process of slimming down their bureaucracies and pulling back from intervention in public life, there is undoubtedly some validity in Blumberg's and García's (1977:107–8) proposition that the state is a critical force in respect of the formation and endurance of mother–child units (see Chapter 2). According to their model, where women-headed households do not serve the interests of the political economy, 'state rhetoric may condemn such families as "disorganised", or a threat to the polity' (*ibid*.:108). Alternatively, states may provide or withhold targeted support for female-headed households through social security systems and welfare programmes, and thus play a vital role (directly or indirectly) in determining frequencies of women-headed households (see also Parashar, 1992:17). It must also be recognised, however, that states may provoke the formation of female-headed households when their overriding objective is the converse. In Cuba, for example, Safa (1995) argues that government policies favouring greater gender equality, higher levels of female labour force participation, and the provision of support services such as day care have all made it easier for women to raise children on their own. At the same time, Safa also notes that 'The Cuban government is clearly not pleased with the high rate of marital dissolution to which its policies of greater economic equality for women have indirectly contributed' (*ibid*.:139), further claiming that lack of special welfare benefits to female heads could reveal an underlying urge to discourage their emergence (*ibid*.:141). Although states in many parts of the world can hardly be described as 'gender-neutral', let alone 'pro-female', and notwithstanding that many may be more concerned with the costs of childcare and human capital reproduction than with women's rights (Folbre, 1994a; Moore, 1994b), some governments may be more tolerant of female-headed households than others. As a result, and for a range of reasons, states may favour initiatives in the sphere of policy or legislation which create conditions under which female-headed units may emerge.

Family and divorce legislation

It is clearly under the tutelage of the state and other hegemonic groups (for example, political parties, powerful business interests, religious factions and so on) that family law is devised and implemented. The latter undoubtedly exerts a very direct influence on whether, how and to what degree female-headed households come to exist. This is aptly illustrated by the work of Parashar (1992:51–8) on The Enactment of the Dissolution of Muslim Marriage Act in India in 1939. Although it is explicitly stated in the Koran that women may dissolve their marriages in cases of 'necessity', the majority of Indian Muslims have traditionally followed Hanafi Law whereby women wanting to divorce must forfeit their religious affiliation. As Parashar points out: 'In the absence of any other alternative for release from a difficult marriage, many Muslim women chose to convert to another religion' (*ibid*.:151), or stayed put in unhappy marriages for fear of excommunication. Mounting worry amongst the 'Ulema' (religious clerics of the

Jamiat-ul-Uluma-i-Hind) about losing followers during the 1930s, led to the passing of the Dissolution Act which empowered Muslim judges to decree divorce at women's request in specified circumstances. Yet while ostensibly in the interests of women, the Act did nothing 'to curtail the almost unfettered right of the husband to divorce his wife at any time and extra-judicially' (*ibid*.:155).

Even where women are able to obtain divorce and/or remarry, the criteria for female divorce petitions are frequently more limited than those for men, and in this way may inhibit women's scope for decision-making over marital and household arrangements. For example, in Iran, women can only initiate divorce proceedings if they have a special stipulation to this effect in their marriage contracts (Afshar, 1987:75; also Mir-Hosseini, 1996:146). In Bangladesh, the Family Courts Ordinance of 1985 specifies that women wishing to file for divorce must take the case to court, whereas men are merely required to petition the local union chairman (Lewis, 1993:30). In El Salvador, husbands can divorce their wives on the grounds of infidelity alone, whereas women can only bring a case against their husbands when infidelity has involved concubinage (Thomson, 1986). The latter also applies in Turkey (Saktanber, 1994:125), and in some societies (for example, the patrilineal Ngoni of South Africa) women may not obtain a divorce from their husbands for any reason at all (Cutrufelli, 1983:51).

Custody of children

Child custody laws are also extremely important in affecting female headship in that women may be dissuaded from petitioning for divorce if rights tend to go to fathers and their families, as is the case in parts of Francophone Africa (Diagne, 1993:46; see also Mernissi, 1985 on Morocco), and in some former British colonies such as Bangladesh (Kabeer, 1995) and Nigeria, where Pittin (1989:108) observes that:

> Divorce and separation are common and with these comes the awful wrench as a woman is separated from the children she has borne and nursed, often to leave them to the untender ministrations of co-wives or affines not particularly committed to their welfare. Indeed, it is often the case that women force themselves to remain in an oppressive and unhappy marriage, rather than leave the children behind.

Pittin goes on to note that the likelihood of women retaining custody is greatest under statutory law, yet this is usually less powerful than Islamic law, which is observed by the Hausa in the northern part of the country, and results in women rarely being able to keep their children following divorce (*ibid*.:109). Among the Kpelle of Liberia, on the other hand, women are frequently granted custody of children, even when they are found guilty in divorce cases, and are also able to obtain major items of conjugal property (Bledsoe, 1980). This can clearly increase potential female headship. Similarly, among urban Baule women in the Ivory Coast, women's maternal rights (even among adoptive mothers) are stronger than those of fathers thereby guaranteeing them security in the face of possible difficulties within their husbands' households or in old age (Etienne, 1993).

Enforcement of legal provisions
While the enactment and nature of legislation are one thing, enforcement is another, however, and so too is critical in determining the role played by family law in female headship. For example, although a Maintenance of Children Act was passed in Ghana in 1965, it remains extremely difficult for women to make their ex-husbands attend court proceedings (Brydon and Chant, 1989:37). In China, the 1950 Marriage Law gave the freedom to divorce as well as to marry one's own choice of partner (free from parental persuasion), yet the divorce provision was unpopular and many local-level cadres were reluctant to divulge the information, let alone to act upon it (see Croll, 1983:82–5; Wolf, 1985:144 *et seq.*). In Zimbabwe, the Legal Age of Majority Act of 1982 gave women the right to own land and property, removed the automatic right of fathers to obtain custody of children, and an amendment to the Maintenance Act in the same year gave community courts the power to order maintenance for divorced wives and their offspring. None the less, women still face problems over obtaining conjugal property (Schlyter, 1989:31–3). In other instances, however, there may be more protection for women. For example, in Bangladesh, women deserted by their husbands are legally entitled to maintenance payments and these may well be upheld through religious and social systems (Lewis, 1993:30). In Iran, amendments to Sharia divorce provisions in 1992 now enable courts to decide maintenance on the basis of the domestic labour a woman has perfomed within the marriage, as long as she is not petitioning for the divorce (Mir-Hosseini, 1996:144). The likelihood of women heading their own households as a result, however, remains limited.

Welfare and benefit schemes

While the issue of state policies in the field of welfare and benefits has in many respects been dealt with in Chapter 2, we noted earlier in relation to Cuba the additional fact that even though the government does not provide special help for female-headed households, within a general context of state promotion of gender equality and some socialisation of the burden of reproduction, this may be irrelevant. As Safa (1995:166) observes for Cuban single mothers, they 'do not need to marry or even require men to provide for their children because they can count on the support of the state and the extended family. No special privileges are given to female heads of household, perhaps out of fear that their number will increase even further, but free health and education, day care and other state services have reduced the cost of bearing children.' By contrast, women-headed households in Puerto Rico receive assistance from various federal transfer programmes such as social security, public welfare and food stamps (*ibid*.:84), although general policies on gender equality are not so advanced. This further undermines the argument that targeted welfare policies encourage the formation of female-headed households, since proportions of female-headed households, however calculated, are higher in Cuba than in Puerto Rico (*ibid*.:17 & 138).

Women's movements

Where women in developing countries are highly mobilised around issues relating to women (and particularly what might be called 'feminist' issues),[6] this may place more pressure upon governments to revise or instigate laws and policies which give women more rights, independence and decision-making capacity (see also Chapter 3). At the same time where these movements are allowed to flourish or indeed are actively supported by the state, this may indicate some tolerance of and/or sympathy towards women's rights and greater public acceptance of women heading households. Although few studies have been carried out on the combined influences of women's movements and state support on levels of female headship in developing countries,[7] Chapters 5 and 6 attempt a preliminary analysis in the context of Mexico, Costa Rica and the Philippines.

SOCIO-CULTURAL FACTORS AFFECTING FEMALE HOUSEHOLD HEADSHIP IN DEVELOPING COUNTRIES

Culture

While culture is inevitably integral to many of the factors already itemised as having an influence on female headship, it is worth identifying it as an entity in itself given that it is often treated as an all-encompassing phenomenon. With reference to India, for instance, Kumari (1989:8) asserts that 'prevalent regional cultural practices and social systems influence the pattern, degree and behaviour of female-headed households'.

'Culture' is clearly a matrix of different elements, comprising kinship, religion, gender ideologies and so on, and the whole is often greater than the sum of its parts. Indeed, even in patrilineal societies, such as the Avatime of the Volta Region of Ghana, women's increased independence as mothers at the household level is tolerated because of the continuity between women and Avatime culture as whole, whereby women and their offspring are 'claimed' for the culture as a whole family. In this light: 'Social organisation and residential unit patterns are secondary phenomena, the human embroidery on a divine (cultural) canvas' (Brydon, 1987a:264).[8] Beyond this, within specific cultural matrices, some factors may be more important than others, as discussed below.

Religion

While the impact of religion on female headship is not only contingent upon its role within culture as a whole but on its interplay with other constitutive elements, this is not to say that it might not exert independent influences. Where religion is strongly opposed to divorce, for example, then fewer couples may separate, and where religious observance is relatively weak or there is not the same emphasis on conjugal endurance, rates may be higher.[9] We have seen in earlier sections, for example, how women in Hindu and Muslim societies often face major social (and religious) penalties as a result of breaking up their marriages. Moghadam (1995e) also points out in her discussion of the Fourth Women's World Conference in Beijing that many Muslim and Catholic countries share common ground in respect of their stress on the importance of motherhood and family, opposition to abortion, and the confinement of sexuality to marriage (see also Baden and Goetz, 1996). Yet in Latin America, even though the Catholic faith and its anti-divorce message are very strong, marital separation of both a formal and informal nature is common (see Chapters 5 and 6). This highlights the importance of other factors such as historical legacies, which in Latin America include widespread concubinage during the period of conquest and colonisation, and the evolution of patriarchal complexes such as '*machismo*' (see below).

Gender roles, relations and ideologies

Although gender is a multifaceted phenomenon, is difficult to talk about in general terms, and virtually impossible to treat in isolation from other factors, female household headship seems to be more prevalent in areas where women have wider roles within and beyond the household than in places where their activities and personal freedom are highly restricted. This may be partly to do with the fact that involvement in a wider set of activities (such as labour force participation, interaction with outside bodies and so on) provides some form of experience or 'training' for adopting various duties associated with household headship. Another possibility is that if women are accustomed to involvement and/or being seen in the 'public' domain, then female heads of household do not stand the same risk of being marked as 'different', which may be particularly important in societies where women's use of space is heavily circumscribed (see Lessinger, 1990; Vera-Sanso, 1994 on India; Mernissi, 1985 on Morocco; Cain *et al.*, 1979; Lewis, 1993; Pryer, 1992 on Bangladesh). Another factor is that wider roles may give women greater access to economic or social resources (earnings, help from kin and friends, job contacts, information, for example) that enable them to support households without male partners, as is widely noted in sub-Saharan Africa and the Caribbean (see Guyer and Peters, 1987; Moore, 1994b; Pulsipher, 1993). Indeed, the limitations on women's spheres of activity and power in 'patriarchal cultures' of South and Southeast Asia, has led Kandiyoti (1991:115) to conclude that women may adopt a stance of what she terms 'passive resistance' to a situation which has historically given them a guarantee of being cared for: in other words, their survival and protection is better assured by complying with the rules and regulations attached to living in male-dominated households than by asserting their independence. This also raises the issue of gender relations, since in situations where women are not accustomed to taking decisions for themselves and/or are subject to male veto, the prospect of being 'in control' may be a major cause for concern. On top of this, even if gender relations have a tendency to be conflictive, where women are restricted in what they do and where they go, they may have no option but to remain in male-headed households unless they are prepared to face extreme poverty or isolation from their families and communities (see also Cain *et al.*, 1979; Jeffery and Jeffery, 1996; Kabeer, 1995). It may also be the case that men (fathers and brothers, as well as husbands) may be reluctant to let women 'go it alone' if this casts aspersions on family honour. This, in turn, underlines the need to situate gender relations within the context of gender and familial ideologies, since although male power is often predicated on the control of women, this takes different forms in different places and is not necessarily linked with upholding family institutions. The latter is to some degree apparent in Latin America where although '*machismo*' is associated with substantial male primacy and authority within the family, this does not prevent men leaving wives and children to their own devices via desertion (Bridges, 1980; Thomson, 1986).

Machismo is a term where consensus on meaning is far from established, but it is used mainly in relation to Latin America and encapsulates an 'ideology of masculinity which emphasises male dominance and virility' (Scott, 1994:79). Its origins are usually traced to the Spanish conquest of the New World, to Roman Catholicism, to patrilineal kinship and legal systems, and to a 'separation between public and private spheres' (*ibid.*). *Machismo* can take the form of men 'proving their masculinity' by siring children with a number of women, or engaging in behaviour such as drinking, gambling and violence that results in marital conflict (Goode, 1964:112–13; O'Connell, 1994:65). At the same time, as noted in Chapter 1, it is not always men who take the decision to detach themselves from domestic strife, but women too (see Bradshaw, 1996a; Chant, 1985b; Harris, 1982). Women's bid to escape male tyranny in the household is especially likely in urban areas where women have greater opportunities for financial independence. This adds further weight to the point that female headship is more likely in contexts where women have some scope to move beyond domestic boundaries.

Kinship and residence

As indicated earlier in the context of land rights, kinship systems are vitally important in determining the likelihood of female headship, not only in respect of inheritance, but also in terms of residence rules and family/social norms, and in the more general influence they exert on people's actions, beliefs and status in society. As Stolcke (1992:140) notes: 'Mating patterns and family forms have to do with the construction of social identity, and notions regarding social identity's influence on family ideas and behaviour' (see also Lardinois, 1992:39).

As far as residence is concerned, in many parts of the world, this has become increasingly neolocal as societies have urbanised, even if a preference for propinquity to kin remains (Chant, 1991c; Lomnitz, 1977). Although the nuclear household and conjugal unit may be given precedence (see Safa, 1995: 38), distance from relatives can weaken the control of wider family over issues such as marriage and separation (see Chant, 1991a on Mexico; Chant and McIlwaine, 1995a on the Philippines), and, in some respects, favours female residential independence. In other places, notably Asia, residence rules tend to continue to conform with the patrilocal tradition. For example, the classic North Indian Hindu or Muslim patriarchal pattern of joint (extended) family whereby sons remain in the parental home with their wives and children, and married daughters become part of their affinal family, still holds in many areas. Even after the death of the parents, married as well as unmarried brothers may remain together (Thorner and Ranadive, 1992:150–1). Since joint families among Hindus tend to be patrilineal and patrilocal, it is highly unlikely that female-headed households will emerge, except where poverty weakens family ties or undermines traditional obligations to protect abandoned or widowed women (see Chapter 3).

Marriage practices, childbirth and social identity

Polygamy
An integral part of kinship systems and ideologies are marriage norms and practices which are widely noted as affecting female household headship. As discussed earlier, for example, normative ideals about age of marriage are likely to be significant in influencing the prospects of female independence in the period between their being daughters and becoming wives and mothers. Concern about women being under the protection of men may in some instances encourage polygamy, which not only tends to be associated with low numbers of women-headed households in certain areas (for example North Africa and the Middle East), but is a prime illustration of the more general way in which strategies to uphold male household headship are often deeply embedded within wider structures of female subordination. As Afshar (1987:75) observes for the case of Iran, for example, while polygamy exists allegedly 'to protect young women from moral degradation', it is actually much more to do with safeguarding men's power and privileges. None the less, women are repeatedly advised of the advantages to them of male protection, especially in times of war, where 'polygamy is the only viable solution for protecting young widows and female orphans who, in the absence of a welfare state, would clearly not be able to fend for themselves, domestic creatures that they have become' (*ibid.*:79). While in some contexts polygamy may ensure that women are never bereft of a male 'protector', however, in others, such as sub-Saharan Africa, it may be associated with greater rates of female headship. In Kenya, for example, where one-quarter of the population are in polygamous marriages, women engaging in liaisons with married men may find themselves unsupported if their lovers' existing wives turn a blind eye to their infidelity: as Khasiani (1993:67) notes: 'extra-marital affairs are culturally tolerated because they could lead to another newly married or inherited wife'. Moreover, the practice of polygyny in sub-Saharan Africa more generally has historically been linked with the relative autonomy of mother–child households (Kandiyoti, 1991:106), or at least separate living arrangements between spouses (see Lloyd and Gage-Brandon 1993:117 on Ghana).

Arranged marriages
Depending on context, arranged marriages may also have a wide range of outcomes. In some areas (for example, the Middle East, North Africa and

South Asia), the practice may reduce the likelihood of female headship through its association with family intervention in the lives of married couples and/or relatives living in close proximity or the same residence. Yet although women may be less likely to break away from husbands when they live in multi-generational households dominated by their husband's kin, it is interesting to note that the biggest single cause of divorce (accounting for 29 per cent of cases tried in a district of Beijing in 1980) was cited as tension between mothers-in-law and daughters-in-law (Croll, 1983:83, Table 6.10).

Consensual unions

The effects of the legal status of conjugal unions on female headship seem to be more generalised insofar as separation is more common where ties between couples are informal/non-legalised. Low rates of formal marriage are particularly prevalent in areas afflicted by high levels of poverty and scarce and irregular employment (especially among men), particularly in the Caribbean (see Barrow, 1986; Powell, 1986; Rodman, 1965, 1971; Safa, 1995:180; also Moore, 1994b). Indeed in Guyana (then British Guiana) in the 1950s, dissolved marriages seem to have been accepted even among groups of Indian descent, with Jayawardena (1960:97) claiming that there was 'no public censure attached to a woman who leaves her husband'. Similar patterns are found in Guanacaste, northwest Costa Rica, where the seasonal out-migration of low-income men is associated with high levels of informal and unstable unions (see Chapter 6).

Wifehood, motherhood and social status

Even where pressure to marry is not direct, however, and consensual unions are tolerated as an alternative, emphasis on the *status* that being married gives to women may be highly persuasive and reduce the likelihood that they will remain single and/or live alone. In India, for example, marriage (and childbirth within the context of marriage) gives women social standing and legitimacy, whereas for unmarried, divorced or deserted women, the story is very different (Srinivasan, 1987:267). From her study of four villages in the eastern region of Uttar Pradesh, India, for example, Kumari (1989:46–7) notes that: 'The case of unmarried women remaining single and forming a household is non-existent. This is because a girl in all circumstances is married, provided she is not severely crippled. In such a case, she will remain with relatives, maybe brothers or sisters, and does not live separately forming a household' (see also Cain *et al.*, 1979:408 on Bangladesh). Indeed, if it is difficult for women to live alone in certain contexts, it may be even more difficult for them to have children alone and/or assume the status of lone parents. In Cuernavaca, Mexico, for example, LeVine (1993:66–7) reports immense social pressure from kin for pregnant women to marry the fathers of their babies. Having said this, in some countries, even those in which women are normally encouraged to marry, the primary social expectation may be for them to have children, and childbirth may thus be a more important determinant of female status than marriage. In Vietnam, for example, Albee (1995) notes that women may remain unmarried and seek sexual intercourse with a man for the sole purpose of having a child. A similar pattern applies to the Minangkabao in western Sumatra, Indonesia, where Davis (1995:7) reports that children are the main purpose of marriage and 'if a young mother becomes a widow or divorcée, there is not necessarily any family pressure on her to marry again, neither is there social stigma attached to her situation'. In such circumstances, female household headship may be more likely (see also Trotz, 1996 on Guyana).

Morality and sexuality

Notwithstanding that sexuality is a 'culturally-embedded concept' and difficult to talk about in any objectified or disassociated way (Harvey and Gow, 1994:5 & 12), it is worth flagging up how norms of female morality and sexuality in particular places act to constrain female household headship at every stage of evolution.[10] In most parts of the Middle East and South Asia, for example, a high price is placed on female virginity before marriage, making it extremely rare for single women to live without a male guardian of one form or another, let alone become lone mothers and head their own households. In Jordan, for example, living alone (especially as a single woman) indicates either poor relationships with one's family or 'loose' morality (Kawar, 1996: Chapter 5). In Iraq, too, a woman's chastity is strictly guarded by male relatives for fear of loss of family honour (Al-Khayyat, 1990). In some rural areas of Turkey, the social significance of a bride's virginity is such that women may end up being forced to marry men who have abducted and raped them, if they hope to marry at all (Starr, 1993:284). Even in countries such as Mexico, where there is arguably less social opprobrium attached to pre-marital sex and illegitimacy, work on Cuernavaca reveals a mother's attempt to conceal the out-of-wedlock pregnancies of her daughters (both in their thirties) by keeping them at home and out of the sight of neighbours (LeVine, 1993:134).

Where women do have children but remain unmarried, 'shame' may also condition the types of household arrangement they adopt (or are forced to adopt). In the Philippines, for example, single mothers are wont to live concealed within the homes of parents or relatives, unless they move away from their families altogether in order to protect their name and reputation

(Chant, 1995a). In this manner, a significant proportion of potential female heads are absorbed as embedded units within other households (see also Chapter 6).

Even if older women, including widows, divorcées and deserted women, are more likely to head their own households, they may still find themselves having to behave in an extremely conservative manner in order to win approval and respect. Other members of the community may well treat them as 'outcasts' (for example, by minimising contact with them), and men may try to exploit their social and economic vulnerability. For example, Shanthi (1994:26) notes for the case of India, that low-income female heads who are forced to set up separate households due to lack of help from parents or in-laws often face problems of insecurity, loneliness and threats of sexual harrassment. Similar reasons make male absence from household life problematic for women in Sri Lanka, with Thorbek (1994:118) pointing out that: 'The way in which decent women can guard their own morality is ... by having a stable and lengthy relationship with a man. Thus, good relations between the couple acquire overwhelming importance for the women, as opposed to men, who are not stigmatised by a broken marriage.' Morrison (1995:4) points out for the case of the Bajou of Sabah, East Malaysia: 'Widows and divorcées are considered both vulnerable and dangerous by both men and women. Married women in particular see young divorcées as a threat to their marriages.' The latter stems from fears about divorcées' relative freedom of movement and their known sexual experience, and for these reasons early remarriage is strongly encouraged (*ibid.*).

CONCLUSION

In summing up the relative influence of different factors on female headship, it is important to point out that there is insufficient evidence from a broad enough range of countries (or even regions) to to allow us to rank these different variables into any kind of order. What can be said, is that some factors seem to have more general relevance than others, notably gender-selective migration, feminised sex ratios, female labour force participation, state policies and family law, and social norms of gender, marriage, motherhood and female sexuality. With this in mind, the following chapter explores the relative importance of these different issues in a more holistic manner in Mexico, Costa Rica and the Philippines.

NOTES

1. Another major factor contibuting to the tendency for women to head their own households in the Mexican border region is the expansion of export-manufacturing plants. These have absorbed large numbers of female workers and increased women's capacity to support themselves without a man's earnings (see Fernández-Kelly, 1983). It is also interesting that there is a greater tendency for couples in this area to get married by civil law alone – 61.2 per cent higher than the national average (see Quilodrán, 1992:103).

2. Links between feminised sex ratios and female headship are also noted for developed countries, where urban areas are likely to have greater numbers of women than men. In metropolitan areas of South Australia, for example, the sex ratio is more feminised than in non-metropolitan areas, especially among the 65-plus age group (see Rudd, 1989:117, Table 7.1; also Brink, 1995 on Canada). As for women-headed households, Winchester (1990:75) notes that the highest concentrations of one-parent units in the UK are in metropolitan areas. In 1981, when the national total was 14 per cent, 26.6 per cent of households in Inner London were headed by a lone parent, 19.9 per cent in Liverpool, 20.4 per cent in Glasgow and 18.8 per cent in Birmingham (Monk, 1993:12; see also Duncan, 1991a on these and other types of female-headed unit).

3. The global average age of women at marriage is presently 20 years (O'Connell, 1994:15).

4. See for example Edwards *et al.* (1993) on the limited state of knowledge of the ways in which women's employment may destabilise marriage.

5. The 1980s were called the 'lost decade' because most of the gains of the 1970s in respect of wage levels, subsidies and public expenditure were forfeited as a result of economic crisis (Escobar Latapí and González de la Rocha, 1995:61).

6. What 'feminist' issues are is clearly something which is difficult to define, not least because their meaning varies from country to country. At the bottom line, however, they might best be characterised as issues which require some modification of the existing gender status quo for women's benefit and/or which involve expanded rights for women as citizens. Here, Molyneux's (1986) distinction between women's practical and strategic gender interests is helpful, the former being defined as women's interests in the context of their roles within existing gender divisions of labour, the latter being oriented to changing gender roles and relations, and redressing gender inequalities (see also Chapter 9).

7. An important starting point is the work of Bradshaw (1996a) on Honduras, who explores some of the interrelationships between female political participation and household headship.

8. Avatime women have not always had this level of independence. After a year of mourning for their dead husbands, Avatime widows were traditionally given over to the care of a close relative of the husband, often via marriage, even if the man in question already had a wife. Indeed, not only could Avatime women in general remain unmarried, but 'widows had to be remarried, even if they were extremely old and past childbearing'. This, in turn, reflected the social imperatives of taking care of elderly women (and men) (Brydon, 1987a:255). Here then, 'female-headed households were anomalous and their existence

paradigmatically impossible, although they came into being transiently as a short-term effect of widowhood or divorce' (*ibid.*:256).

9. Although not specific to the developing world, Goode (1964:95) noted with reference to the USA in 1960 that people without religious affiliations had the highest divorce rates, and the next highest were found in mixed-faith marriages (see also Gelles, 1985:399).

10. Bradshaw (1996a) identifies three stages of formation in female-headed households: (1) potential formation, (2) actual formation, and (3) survival.

5 Mexico, Costa Rica and the Philippines: National Perspectives

INTRODUCTION

In giving overviews of female household headship in Mexico, Costa Rica and the Philippines this chapter serves two purposes. First, looking at specific societies not only allows us to witness the interplay of different sets of factors affecting the formation of female-headed households, but establishes a stronger basis for assessing their relative influence in restraining or promoting female headship in different contexts. Second, national outlines of the three countries provide essential background to the case study discussions of women-headed households in succeeding chapters.

According to official 1990 data, Costa Rica had the highest level of female headship of the three case study countries with 18 per cent of households being headed by women (DGEC, 1990: Table 4).[1] In the same year the proportion of female-headed households in Mexico was 17.3 per cent (INEGI, 1993:109, Table 62), and in the Philippines, only 11.3 per cent (NSO, 1992:97, Table 14). While sharing some common features in respect of their historical evolution[2] and contemporary development, each nation is characterised by social, cultural, economic, demographic and legal-institutional differences which offer insights into variations in the incidence and nature of female-headed households. Bearing in mind limitations of space and the fact that grassroots experiences of the formation and survival of female-headed households are potentially more revealing than generalised accounts, this chapter confines itself to brief synopses of each country's development profile, and to factors identified in Chapter 4 as most likely to have a bearing on female household headship. In the interests of clarity, a broadly consistent format is used for the presentation of data on female headship and its corollaries in each country, notwithstanding that it is difficult to include exactly the same information for all three places.[3]

FEMALE HOUSEHOLD HEADSHIP IN MEXICO: CHARACTERISTICS AND CONTEXT

National profile of female-headed households

Household headship is classified in the Mexican census as the person recognised as such by other household members (INEGI, 1993:105).

According to census figures, female-headed households in Mexico increased from a level of 13.6 per cent of all households in 1960, to 17.3 per cent in 1970, then dropped to 14.9 per cent in 1980 and rose again to 17.3 per cent in 1990. Although the fluctuation between 1970 and 1980 is not easily explained (and may well owe in part to the general inaccuracies of the 1980 census – see Chant, 1994b), in absolute terms, households headed by women tripled between 1960 and 1990 (to a total of 2.8 million), compared with a 2.3 factor increase for households in general. This rise seems to be on a par with (if not slightly greater than) Costa Rica and certainly larger than in the Philippines over a similar timespan (see later).

Although the vast bulk (84.5 per cent) of women-headed households in 1990 were family-based units (defined as those where one or more members are related to the household head and which constitute 94 per cent of all households in Mexico), and 15 per cent of all family households were headed by women (INEGI, 1993:105), women were as many as 48.9 per cent of single person households (*ibid.*). Indeed, a much greater proportion of female heads (13.8 per cent) live alone than men (5.4 per cent). Moreover, nearly two-thirds (59 per cent) of lone females are aged 60 or more, as against 33.4 per cent of their male counterparts, mirroring a more general pattern whereby greater proportions of female than male heads lie at the extreme ends of the age spectrum (see Table 5.1).

Table 5.1 *Mexico: percentage distribution of female and male household heads by age cohorts, 1990*

Age Group (years)	Female Heads %	Male Heads %
12–19	1.1	0.9
20–24	4.2	7.1
25–29	6.5	13.1
30–39	18.6	28.7
40–49	20.1	21.0
50–59	18.9	14.1
60+	30.5	15.0
Not known	0.1	0.1
Total	100.0	100.0

Source: INEGI (1993: Table 62 'Distribución de Hogares por Grupos de Edad y Sexo del Jefe o Persona que lo Integra Segun Tipo de Hogar').

Excluding lone female households, the mean size of women-headed units is 4.3, whereas men's is 5.2 (INEGI, 1993:111,Table 64). The largest average size of women-headed households (4.9) is in the 40–49 year cohort, when children are likely to be getting married and/or having offspring of their own (*ibid.*).

Excluding unspecified and single-person households, fewer than 1 per cent of all households in Mexico are made up of unrelated members (designated in the census as 'co-resident' households and described as units where two or more persons do not have family ties with the household head). None the less, co-resident households make up 1.7 per cent of women-headed multi-person households, compared with 0.3 per cent among male-headed units. The vast bulk of women in this position (43 per cent) are, again, in the 60-plus age group.

Table 5.2 *Mexico, Costa Rica and the Philippines: selected gender indicators*

		Mexico	Costa Rica	The Philippines
Adult illiteracy 1990[1]				
- Total		13%	7%	10%
- Female		15%	7%	11%
Secondary school enrolment 1991[2]				
- Total		55%	43%	74%
- Female		55%	45%	75%
Mean female years of schooling as proportion of male mean, 1992[3]		96%	97%	90%
Percentage of seats occupied by women in parliament, 1992[4]		7%	12%	11%
Total fertility rate[5*]				
- 1970		6.5	4.9	6.4
- 1992		3.2	3.1	4.1
Life expectancy (years)[6]				
1970	- male	60	65	56
	- female	64	69	59
1990	- male	67	74	63
	- female	74	79	67

Sources:
1. World Bank (1994: 162–3, Table 1); 2. World Bank (1994: 216–17, Table 29); 3. UNDP (1994:146–7, Table 9); 4. UNDP (1994:144–5, Table 8); 5. World Bank (1994:212–13, Table 26); 6. World Bank (1994:218–19, Table 29).
* Total fertility rate refers to the average number of children born to an average women living through her child-bearing years.

Data from the National Survey on Fertility and Health in 1987, which, like the census, bases headship on self- or proxy-reporting, indicate that 15.5 per cent of female heads are single, 24.7 per cent divorced and separated and 51.4 per cent widowed (Acosta Diaz, 1992:31). A further 8.4 per cent are reported as married or cohabiting, and in these cases women are likely to be playing the major economic role in the household (*ibid.*).

To sum up, women-headed households in Mexico are (in line with their male-headed counterparts) predominantly family-based units. They are significantly more common among older age groups than male heads which undoubtedly relates to the fact that just over half of them are widowed. The latter could in part be attributed to greater life expectancy among women which has risen both absolutely and compared with that of men's between 1970 and 1992 (see Table 5.2). As it is, the fact that well over one-third of Mexican female heads are single, separated or divorced, indicates that demographic factors are not the only influence on female headship. This should become clearer in the following sections.

Economic development, urbanisation and crisis

Mexico is arguably the most developed of the three case study countries, with an economy based on oil, manufacturing and tourism, and boasting a per capita GNP of $3470 US in 1992 (see Table 5.3). In the same year, 74 per cent of Mexico's 85 million inhabitants lived in urban areas (compared with 59 per cent in 1970), and only one-quarter of the urban population resided in the capital (World Bank, 1994:223). This reflects a steady diminution in the primacy of the Federal District and a trend towards the growth of 'secondary' urban centres. Major sectoral shifts in the economy have also occurred when in 1970, agriculture's contribution to GDP was 13 per cent, but had dropped to 8 per cent by 1992. Whereas that contributed by industry stayed virtually constant (at 28–29 per cent), the share represented by services rose from 63 to 69 per cent over the same period (*ibid.*:167). In employment terms, sectoral shifts are even more marked. As of 1990–92, agriculture employed only 23 per cent of the economically active population (UNDP, 1994:162), compared with 39 per cent in 1970; in industry the proportion was 29 per cent in 1990–92 (as against 23 per cent in 1970), and in services 48 per cent (compared with 32 per cent in 1970) (*ibid.*).

Mexico's path to economic modernisation in the post-war period has not been without difficulties, particularly since the 1980s when rising interest rates and the fall in world oil prices plunged the country into severe crisis. The annual average growth rate in agriculture fell from 3.2 per cent in 1970–80 to 0.6 per cent in 1980–92, that in manufacturing from 2 to 2.1 per cent, and in services from 6.3 to 1.5 per cent (World Bank, 1994: 165, Table 2). These trends were set against a massive rise in inflation, which increased from an annual average of 18.1 per cent in the 1970s, to 62.4 per cent between 1980 and 1992 (*ibid.*:163, Table 1). As for the external debt, this rose from $3.6 billion US in 1970 to $113.4 billion in 1992, culminating in a debt service burden equivalent to 44.4 per cent of the country's export earnings (Zorrilla-Vazquez, 1995:96).

Table 5.3 *Mexico, Costa Rica and the Philippines:*
selected economic and demographic characteristics, 1990s

	Mexico	Costa Rica	The Philippines
Population, mid 1992 (millions)[1]	85	3.2	64.3
GNP per capita 1992 (US dollars)[2]	3470	1960	770
Average annual growth rate per capita GNP 1980-92 (%)[3]	–0.2	0.8	–1.0
Total external debt 1992 (billion US)[4]	113.4	54.7	32.5
Urban population as proportion of total population (%)[5]			
-1970	40	59	33
-1992	48	74	44
Proportion of urban population in capital city 1990 (%)[6]	34	71	32
Proportion of total population in capital city 1990 (%)[7]	25	33	14
Average life expectancy at birth 1992 (years)[8]	70	76	65

Sources:
1. World Bank (1994:162–3, Table 1); 2. *ibid*.; 3. *ibid*.; 4. World Bank (1994:200–1 Table 20); 5. World Bank (1994:222–3, Table 31); 6. *ibid*.; 7. *ibid*.; 8. World Bank (1994:162–3, Table 1).

Under pressure from the IMF and World Bank, an Austerity Programme was implemented by President Miguel de la Madrid in 1983. The restructuring dating from this period and continuing into the 1990s under President Carlos Salinas de Gortari (1988–94)[4] included, amongst other things, massive cuts in government spending, especially in the social sector, the reduction or removal of food subsidies, curbs on wage and employment expansion, widespread privatisation of state and parastatal enterprises, and the modernisation of production as a means of increasing export performance (see Cordera Campos and González Tiburcio, 1991; Lustig, 1992; Roberts, B., 1991). The emphasis on exports led to active promotion of multinational export processing manufacturing (usually referred to as the 'maquiladora' sector, and traditionally located in the US–Mexico border area). Between 1981 and 1990, maquila production increased by 350 per cent (as against an average of 10 per cent in other industries), and export-manufacturing employment grew at an annual rate of 14.5 per cent (Baden, 1993:22). Currently, 50 per cent of manufactured exports consists of automotive terminal parts and electrical and electronic equipment, most of which is in multinational hands (Zorrilla-Vazquez, 1995:105). Multinational investment and export orientation alike looked set for further expansion with Mexico's accession to NAFTA (North American Free Trade Agreement) (see Browne, 1994; Zorrilla-Vazquez, 1995), although economic crisis from the beginning of President Ernesto Zedillo's term of office may slow the process.

While Zedillo had aimed, in principle, to concentrate more than his predecessor on matters of poverty alleviation and employment creation (EIU, 1994c), his ascent to the presidency in December 1994 was marked by a crisis of massive currency devaluation and capital flight. The rescue package arranged by US President Bill Clinton in early 1995 was conditional on Zedillo curbing domestic demand. Since then, wages have remained depressed, value added tax and energy prices have been subject to sharp increases (EIU, 1995a:8), and in April 1995 the government was forced to authorise a 26 per cent rise in the price of *tortillas*, the staple Mexican foodstuff (*ibid.*:16). These factors have exacerbated the problems attached to a halving in real wages between the early 1980s and early 1990s (CEPAL, 1994:3; Stewart, 1995:202), and a significant rise in the proportion of Mexican households designated as 'poor' (from 52.5 to 62.5 per cent between 1981 and 1988) (Escobar Latapí and González de la Rocha, 1995:61). On top of this, the restructuring of labour markets has engendered considerable informalisation of working conditions. Between 1980 and 1987 alone, informal employment grew by 80 per cent in absolute terms, and occupied as many as 33 per cent of the economically active population by this latter year compared with 24 per cent at the beginning of the decade (*ibid.*:63–4). These are the circumstances under which female employment in Mexico has risen, and which, in a variety of ways, appear to be linked with recent rises in female household headship (see González de la Rocha, 1994b:1).

Female labour force participation, rural–urban migration and sex ratios

According to the International Labour Organisation, women's share of the Mexican labour force grew from 24.2 per cent in 1977 to 30.1 per cent in

1991 (see Table 5.4), and National Household Demographic and Fertility Survey data show that while women's economic activity rates were 21.5 per cent in 1979, they were 27 per cent by 1989 (García, 1992). A more significant change still, however, is the increased labour force participation of married women: while in 1970 only 10 per cent of married women worked, this was 25.6 per cent by 1991 (CEPAL, 1994:15). The highest economic activity rate among Mexican women is now in the 35–39 year age group (43 per cent), when most have major family responsibilities. The fact that male employment rates have declined (from 70.1 to 68 per cent between 1970 and 1990 – INEGI, 1993:75), and that women's unemployment is currently only 2.2 per cent compared with 2.9 per cent among men (*ibid*.:100), indicates that some form of 'feminisation of labour' may have been occurring. Indeed, at a national level, women's share of manufacturing employment rose from 21.1 to 25.7 per cent between 1980 and 1986 (Roberts, B., 1991:130). While much of this owes to the expansion of the maquiladora sector in the border region, it is also due to employers' attempts to cut costs by increasing levels of sub-contracting, with women being a major presence among home- or workshop-based piece-rate workers (Benería and Roldan, 1987; Peña Saint Martin and Gamboa Cetina, 1991). Another reason for women's rising share of employment is that low-level 'feminised' jobs such as waitressing and domestic service have not been subject to such drastic cutbacks as 'male sectors' such as construction (de Barbieri and de Oliveira, 1989:23). Having said this, some encroachment of men into the more prestigious branches of female employment is apparent, particularly in maquiladoras where men's share of the workforce rose from 28 to 38 per cent between 1983 and 1988 (Roberts, B., 1991:131), and to 41 per cent by 1995 (González de la Rocha, 1995b:10). Moreover, for every 100 women who work or are seeking work, there are 326 men (INEGI, 1993:75), and women's average earnings are only three-quarters of their male counterparts (UNDP, 1995:40).

In terms of sectoral distribution by gender, male workers are quite evenly spread across the three main spheres of the economy, being 28.9 per cent of the labour force in the primary sector (agriculture, forestry, fishing) in 1990, 30 per cent in the secondary sector (encompassing manufacturing, construction, electricity and mining), and 38.6 per cent in the tertiary sector (commerce and services) (INEGI, 1993:95). Women, on the other hand, are overwhelmingly concentrated in the tertiary sector (70.3 per cent), with a further 20.8 per cent in the secondary sector, and only 3.4 per cent in agriculture (*ibid*.:81). Women's labour force participation has always been higher in urban than in rural areas, which not only helps to explain female-selective migration in Mexico, but, undoubtedly, something of the country's urban bias in female headship as well.

Table 5.4 *Female share of total employment in Mexico,
Costa Rica and the Philippines, 1977–92 (%)*

Year	Mexico	Costa Rica	The Philippines
1977	24.2	–*	30.1
1978	24.4	–	35.9
1979	25.4	–	–
1980	26.2	24.3	35.4
1981	27.2	25.9	35.5
1982	27.6	25.6	37.1
1983	28.5	25.2	38.3
1984	29.3	27.9	36.5
1985	29.4	25.8	37.2
1986	30.2	25.9	37.0
1987	30.2	26.9	36.3
1988	30.0	27.7	36.4
1989	29.5	28.0	36.3
1990	29.5	28.1	36.3
1991	30.1	29.3	36.3
1992	–	29.5	37.7

* – = no data.
Sources: ILO *Yearbook of Labour Statistics* 1986, 1988, 1989–90, 1992 and 1993.

As regards migrant selectivity, for every 100 women living in a place different from their place of birth in 1990, there were only 93 men (INEGI, 1993:33). This is most marked in heavily urbanised areas in the Federal District, where the ratio of male to female migrants is only 77.8 per 100, and Puebla where it is 83.1 per 100 (*ibid*.:36, Table 18). In turn, sex ratios are more feminised in larger urban centres, even if gender imbalances have narrowed at extreme ends of the settlement spectrum in the last two decades (Table 5.5). This may help to explain the fact that while female-headed family units have traditionally been most numerous in larger cities, especially those with 10,000 or more inhabitants, they have shown relatively greater increases in smaller communities since 1970. As for lone-female households, increases over the last 20 years have been especially marked in larger settlements: while in 1970 there were 129.5 single-male households for every 100 single-female households in urban areas of 50,000 or more inhabitants, there were only 98.8 by 1990 (INEGI, 1993:114). Considering regional distribution, the proportion of female heads of family-based or multi-person units ranges from as low as 11.5 per cent in rural states such as Quintana Roo, to 19.7 per cent in highly urbanised areas such as the Federal District (*ibid*.:113).

Table 5.5 *Mexico: mean sex ratios according to size of settlement, 1970 and 1990*

Size of settlement	Men per 100 women	
	1970	1990
Total	99.6	96.5
1–99	109.0	106.8
100–499	105.9	102.4
500–999	104.4	100.1
1000–2499	102.5	97.3
2500–4999	100.5	98.5
5000–9999	98.7	97.3
10,000–19,999	96.4	95.1
20,000–49,999	96.6	94.6
50,000–99,999	95.5	94.5
100,000–499,999	95.2	93.8
>500,000	92.6	94.5

Source: INEGI (1993:8, Cuadro 4).

Family norms, gender and social identity

Despite the growth in female-headed households of various types, and the undoubted significance of changing sex ratios for their shifting numbers and distributions, nuclear households comprising a married couple and their children continue to be the norm and ideal in both rural and urban areas (Chant, 1991a; García *et al.*, 1983b; González de la Rocha, 1995a; LeVine, 1993; Selby *et al.*, 1990; Willis, 1993). Notwithstanding that the total fertility rate in Mexico dropped from 6.5 to 3.2 between 1970 and 1992 (see Table 5.2), marriage and motherhood continue to be highly emphasised in young women's lives (Benería and Roldan, 1987; Chant, 1991a). As of 1990, excluding the 30 per cent of Mexican women over the age of 15 who were single, 73 per cent were married, 12 per cent were in a co-resident consensual union, 9.1 per cent were widowed, and only 3 per cent and 1.7 per cent respectively were separated or divorced (INEGI, 1993:28, Table 14).

Within male-headed nuclear units, scope for female power and economic independence has traditionally been constrained by women's assignation to a domestically-centred, mothering role, encapsulated in the popular expression 'men are for the streets and women are for the home' (de Barbieri, 1982; also Benería, 1991:172). Even with the pressures of economic crisis and restructuring, men are still noted as showing reluctance to let their wives and daughters work, and some women remain in the position of having to ask their husbands' permission in order to do so (Chant, 1993:348; González de la Rocha, 1994a:260; LeVine, 1993: Chapter 3; Willis, 1993:72, 1994:174;

see also Wilson, 1991:167 on daughters). Notwithstanding that men's pre-eminence in household authority and decision-making does not preclude the existence of solidarity, loyalty and mutual assistance within households, unequal power is often detrimental for women and children. As González de la Rocha (1994a:260) summarises:

> relations of domination and subordination ... follow gender and generation lines. Women and children are in a subordinated position within the household. Their work is subordinated to men's. Their actions are subordinated to men's will, and their rights are obscured and ignored. Gender relations are asymmetrical, where men exert control and command. Violence is used by men to reaffirm their control over women, and to remind them that their place as women is the home in a subordinated position. (see also García and de Oliveira, 1994)

Yet although such patterns may have restricted women's scope for independence, it is also important to acknowledge that gender inequalities within male-headed households, especially traits ascribed to the cultural complex of '*machismo*' (Chapter 4), may just as readily act to destabilise marriage and *ipso facto* precipitate female household headship (see Gledhill, 1995:137). In the Mexican context, *machismo* is often linked with sexual infidelity on the part of husbands and the establishment of families with women other than their wives (often referred to as the 'big house, little house'/'*casa grande, casa chica*' phenomenon). This, in turn, has been associated with male desertion, especially where poverty, low earnings and underemployment make it difficult for men to fulfil the demands of 'breadwinner' (see Arizmendi, 1980; Bridges, 1980; Chant, 1985b; García and de Oliveira, 1994:153). On top of this, women's experiences of '*macho*' behaviour may also lead them to initiate a split (see Benería, 1991:177–8; Chant, 1985b), or, in the event of bereavement, divorce or separation, to avoid remarriage or a new partnership. Some studies have suggested that the latter tendency may have intensified during the crisis period. On the basis of her work in Mexico City, for example, Benería (1991:177–8) postulates that the asymmetry between male and female inputs to household life has made it more likely for women to leave men. On the other hand, analyses such as those of González de la Rocha (1988b, 1994b:8) on Guadalajara indicate that women's earnings are still too low to allow them to resist resuming relationships with former partners or taking new ones as a 'coping strategy'. Indeed, despite the wide range of difficulties women face in male-headed households, LeVine (1993:203–4) claims that 'In the 1990s, as much as in the past, motherhood and raising a family remains the chosen destiny of the overwhelming majority of Mexican women. Though some young women, embittered by soured romances, talk about avoiding marriage and raising children alone, only a few actually go that route.' To some extent, this may be bolstered by the state's efforts to strengthen the institution of marriage and the two-parent family.

Gender legislation, family policy and social welfare

Although the principle of equality between men and women is written into the Mexican Constitution and Civil Code[5] (see Editorial Porrua, 1992:40), unlike in Costa Rica or the Philippines there are few pro-female pieces of legislation or major state apparatus defending and/or promoting women's interests, let alone those which might favour female household headship.

Although Mexico had a National Commission for Women between 1983 and 1992, established a Coordinating Committee for the 1995 Beijing Conference, and there is talk by President Zedillo of instituting a women's programme (see Craske, forthcoming), the sole government organisation with any kind of practical relevance for Mexican women is the DIF (*Desarrollo Integral de la Familia*/Integrated Family Development). As suggested by its title, DIF's aims are to strengthen the family through women. This finds clear expression in the introduction to a report on one of its sanitation projects in Querétaro State: 'The participation of women in family and social development is fundamental. Without them (women), communities lack the impetus to better their lives, and without their inputs, the household lacks warmth and the family feels vulnerable' (DIF, 1994:61). DIF arranges community-level health, nutrition and service projects, and vocational courses such as dressmaking to enhance women's domestic skills. Notwithstanding this conservative, welfarist approach, it should be noted that DIF's efforts to fortify the family are at least beginning to extend to men. For example, DIF lawyers help deserted women to pursue men for maintenance payments, and claim also to assist women to register legal complaints about co-resident husbands who fail to uphold their economic duties. Although such services are available, however, relatively few women take advantage of them. In the words of the deputy chief of the Puerto Vallarta branch of DIF, '*se quedan calladas*' ('they stay silent'), mainly because husband–wife relationships are expected to be difficult, and have traditionally been regarded as a private domain.[6] While DIF does recognise that female heads of household have particularly difficult problems, there are no specific programmes for them, although some priority is nominally given to lone mothers for subsidised nursery places.

The only other state initiative for women in Mexico, and again of a preponderantly welfarist ilk, is '*Mujeres en Solidaridad*' (Women in Solidarity). Founded in 1990, '*Mujeres en Solidaridad*' forms part of the wider

Solidarity programme (PRONASOL) started by President Salinas in 1988 and incorporated within a newly-formed Ministry of Social Development (*Secretaría de Desarrollo Social*/SEDESOL) in 1992. Solidarity was established to promote state and community cooperation at a time when Mexico's economic liberalisation project involved a move from 'ubiquitous state intervention' to 'strategic, targeted and compensatory intervention' (Dresser, 1991:7; see also Escobar Latapí and González de la Rocha, 1995:65–6; Ward, 1993). *'Mujeres en Solidaridad' per se* is interested in combating the extreme poverty of women, with a particular focus on low-income urban, rural and indigenous groups. Although the programme aims to get women to identify their own needs and to create and expand organisational structures to assure their democratic involvement in economic, political, social and cultural life at community and national levels, they are again expected to 'take development to their families' (PNS, 1991:8). To date, the two main types of projects are: (i) social and service schemes as such as infant centres, social centres, and water supply projects, which aim to help women in their daily work and through this to improve the quality of family and community life, and (ii) productive projects which are oriented to enhancing women's traditional skills and to improving incomes (*ibid.*:11). Examples of the latter include centres where women may enrol on courses in cosmetics and dressmaking, and cooperative flour mills (*molinas de nixtamal*), all of which may go some way to meeting women's 'practical gender needs' (that is, the needs they experience in their existing roles as wives and mothers), but are far from meeting 'strategic gender needs' which might involve addressing gender inequalities (see Moser, 1993a; also Molyneux, 1986). In this way, the underlying objectives and activities of *Mujeres en Solidaridad* offer a prime example of the 'efficiency' approach to women, where rather than 'development working for women', women's energies are garnered to fulfil the wider interests of development (*ibid.*; see also Blumberg, 1995). Although gender-sensitisation sessions have been held to encourage men to let their wives cooperate in community ventures, the fact that many women do not have husbands does not seem to be recognised as an issue and/or programmes have failed to acknowledge that female heads of household have little time for participation in meetings and cooperative labour ventures.[7]

The Mexican Civil Code
Notwithstanding the shortfalls of welfare programmes, various elements of Mexican legislation seem more progressive in respect of gender. Although the legal age of marriage for women remains young (14 years, compared with 16 for men), the Mexican Civil Code stresses egalitarian rights and duties within marriage (Editorial Porrua, 1992). For example, Article 162 obliges

both spouses to contribute to the marriage and to give mutual help, and Article 164 declares that the economic maintenance of the household and children should be shared (or taken on by one partner if the other is unable). Article 164 further asserts that the rights and obligations of marriage should always be equal for the spouses, regardless of their economic contribution to the household (*ibid.*:75–6).

Beyond this, divorce, which was made legal in 1917, is permissible on a wide number of grounds. Aside from mutual consent, these include adultery, prostitution of a wife by her husband, the birth of a third party's child after marriage, pressure to commit a criminal offence, corrupt behaviour towards the children, a chronic or incurable disease such as syphilis or tuberculosis, sterility, mental illness, separation without just cause for six months, and a crime of a non-political nature which carries a prison sentence of at least two years. It is also interesting to note that a further basis for divorce is the unjustified and persistent indulgence of either spouse in gambling, alcohol or drugs, when this threatens the ruin of the family, or constitutes a perpetual source of marital discord (Article 267) (Editorial Porrua, 1992:93–4). As for procedure, divorce by mutual consent cannot be requested until one year after marriage (Article 274), and in other circumstances, divorce can only be solicited by the spouse who did not cause the breakdown.

In many respects the Civil Code favours women who wish to break free of unhappy marriages given that their limited social and economic freedom makes them less likely to be 'at fault' than men and thereby in a position to initiate divorce petitions. Yet as LeVine (1993:95) observes: 'though nowadays there may be a good deal of talk about divorce, women who remain in seemingly untenable relationships still greatly outnumber those who get out'. Women's compliance with the injustices of male household headship seem to owe partly to Catholicism (90 per cent of the Mexican population profess to be Catholics – INEGI, 1993:50, Table 30), partly to the fact that women have not traditionally been encouraged to assert themselves, partly because of the social difficulties attached to lone motherhood, and partly because low wages may dissuade women from taking on sole economic responsibility for their households. All these factors might be different if women were better represented politically, or the Mexican women's movement was more established at grassroots levels.

Women's movements and organisation

Although women were active in the Mexican Revolution of 1910–17, and formed a broad-based movement for suffrage in the 1930s, until the late 1970s, the women's movement tended to be somewhat fragmented and predominantly middle class (see Burns, 1992:215). Although the early-to-mid-1980s saw some attempt at forging cross-class feminist solidarity (Espinosa Damián, 1987:33), this did not really come to fruition until the late 1980s when political interest and action swelled around internal dissent within the long-ruling Institutional Revolutionary Party (PRI/*Partido Revolucionario Institucional*), and the formation of a Revolutionary Democratic Front under the leadership of Cuahtémoc Cárdenas (later to become the *Partido Revolucionario Demócratico*/PRD). These events opened up new possibilities for political organisation and 'prompted Mexican women's groups to create structures which would enable them to join in the debate about social democ-ratisation' (Maier, 1994:40; also Craske, 1993). One of these was the Benita Galeana Women's Association which brought together a wide range of women including seamstresses, feminist groups, women from the Revolutionary Workers Party (PRT/*Partido Revolucionario de Trabajadores*), who were concerned as much (if not more) about class as they were about gender, and whose collective aims became formulated as the struggle for democracy, the fight against violence, and the protection of life (Maier, 1994:41). Although by 1991, the organisation had lost too many members to mobilise effectively, the intervening years saw the formation of more specialist organisations such as a National Network Against Violence (*Red Contra la Violencia*), and the Feminist Coordinating Committee (*Coordinadora Feminista*), whose respective areas of concern were violence and reproductive rights (including women's rights to abortion) (*ibid.*:44) (see below). Moreover, the National Women's Convention for Democracy (*Convención Nacional de Mujeres por la Democracia*), came into being in 1991 with the aim of getting political parties to raise women's demands in government through including female candidates on their muncipal and parliamentary electoral lists. Although only three women from the Convention were actually elected, the fact that most parties (especially those left of centre) were willing to discuss the issue and take these ideas on board was signalled as a positive starting point for future action (see Burns, 1992:220; Colimoro, 1994).

Despite this new life in the women's movement, gains to date seem relatively limited. Abortion still remains illegal, except in case of rape, health of the mother, and foetal abnormalities, and when Chiapas state decriminalised abortion in 1990, this was promptly overturned in the wake of widespread protest (see Burns, 1992; Maier, 1994). Inequalities also remain in terms of education and women's political representation (see Craske, forthcoming; also Table 5.2).

FEMALE HOUSEHOLD HEADSHIP IN COSTA RICA: CHARACTERISTICS AND CONTEXT

National profile of female-headed households

As in Mexico, heads of household are defined in the Costa Rican census as the persons designated as such by other household members, with the suffix that this is usually the person who earns the principal income and who has greatest responsibility for household decision-making (DGEC, 1987:xviii). While women-headed households have long made up around just under one-fifth of Costa Rican households,[8] in absolute terms, their numbers nearly tripled between 1973 and the early 1990s to reach 135,000 (CMF, 1994:2). Despite this increase, and that the vast bulk are lone parents, the National Child Welfare Agency (*Patronato Nacional de la Infancia*/PANI), claims that '*madre solterismo*' (single motherhood) has been little explored, and knowledge of the causes, implications and consequences are limited (PANI, 1982:14).

In terms of basic characteristics, however, it would seem that while male-headed nuclear households are preponderant at the start or the middle of the family lifecycle (Vega, 1992:32), the vast majority (90 per cent) of female household heads are aged 30 or more (DGEC, 1993b: Table 6). Although the bunching of female heads in the 60-plus age group is similar to Mexico (see Tables 5.1 and 5.6), there is also a substantial proportion in their middle years. This undoubtedly relates to the fact that widows are only 27 per cent of female heads, with a bigger proportion (32 per cent) being single, and 17 per cent separated (CMF, 1994:52). Single female heads are more common in urban (34 per cent) than in rural areas (30 per cent), and whereas divorced women are 11.6 per cent of the population of female heads in towns and cities, they are only 8.7 per cent in the countryside (*ibid.*). Such combinations of age, marital status and spatial distribution could also help to explain why women-headed households in Costa Rica are not poorer than their male-headed counterparts, with data for the late 1980s showing that women-headed households were 17.9 per cent of households nationally, but only 16 per cent among the poor (Menjívar and Trejos, 1992:83–4, Table 13; see also Pollack, 1989). This could partly be attributed to the fact that only around one-fifth of the total population of the country is classified as 'poor' (CMF, 1994:41), and that two-thirds of the poor are in rural areas where female headship is lower.

On balance, most women heads in Costa Rica are older than male household heads, with many in their middle years, and, unlike Mexico where one-half of female heads at a national level are widowed, the majority are single, separated or divorced. They have also been a significant proportion of the population for some time, which in some respects is odd given that Costa Rican is much less urbanised and industrialised than Mexico.

Table 5.6 *Costa Rica: percentage distribution of female and male household heads by age cohorts, 1993*

Age Group (years)	Female Heads %	Male Heads %
15–19	0.3	0.4
20–24	2.1	4.1
25–29	6.9	11.2
30–39	18.8	28.4
40–49	21.5	22.2
50–59	18.6	15.4
60–69	16.3	10.3
70+	14.9	7.5
Not known	0.6	0.5
Total	100.0	100.0

Source: DGEC (1993b: Table 6 'Población Total por Relación de Parentesco con el Jefe, Según Zona, Sexo y Grupos de Edad').

Economic development, urbanisation and crisis

Whereas female household headship in the Latin American region is generally linked with large-scale urbanisation and the concomitant expansion of employment opportunities for women, Costa Rica is still a small, fundamentally agrarian economy with a per capita GNP of only two-thirds that of Mexico ($1960 US in 1992). While Costa Rica has experienced quite substantial urban growth since the first quarter of this century, urban settlements in the country (with the exception of the Metropolitan Area of San José), are predominantly small: none have populations over 100,000, and many have as few as 2000 inhabitants (see Hall, 1985). Moreover, less than half the population (48 per cent) could be classified as urban as recently as 1992 (see Table 5.3).[9] More important still, perhaps, is that the workforce in many towns still rely heavily for employment in the rural hinterlands.

Although agriculture's share of GDP has fallen over the last two-and-a-half decades (from 24 per cent in 1965 to 19.3 per cent in 1992), in 1993, three of the country's main traditional exports (bananas, coffee and beef) generated as much as 41 per cent of export earnings (EIU, 1994a:3). Despite the fact that agriculture suffered stagnation in the 1970s, renewed growth in the 1980s (reaching an annual rate of 3.5 per cent), meant that by 1990 it was the fastest growing sector of the economy (Chinchilla, 1992:457; World

Bank, 1994:164–5, Table 2). Even though the modernisation and expansion of agriculture of 1980s cost jobs, wages and the livelihoods of small producers, agriculture was still the largest single employer of the Costa Rican workforce in 1993, occupying 29.4 per cent of the economically active population (DGEC, 1993:Table 8).

Industrial manufacturing (together with mining), on the other hand, while generating 22.1 per cent of GDP in 1992, employed only 18.1 per cent of the workforce in 1993 (DGEC, 1993a: Table 8). Industrial development in Costa Rica has long been hindered by the small size of the internal market and a paucity of raw materials (Hall, 1985; Sheahan, 1987). Greater scope for economic and employment growth is offered by the service sector, which in 1993 was the second largest employer of the Costa Rican workforce (23.4 per cent) (with commerce employing a further 17.8 per cent). Prominent in contributing to the rise in service employment is tourism, which has been actively promoted by the government since the mid-1980s and is attracting increasing flows of foreign tourist traffic and currency (see Chant, 1996b; Trejos, 1992:506–7). With total earnings of $622 million US in 1994, it is currently a larger source of hard currency than banana or coffee exports (EIU, 1995b:15). In general terms, however, economic expansion in all sectors over the last one-and-a-half decades has been held in check by recession and economic restructuring.

In the early 1980s Costa Rica experienced the deepest recession since 1930, marked by falling GNP, rising debt, unemployment and inflation (see Barry, 1991:27; Gindling, 1993:277–8). In 1985, the first phase of Structural Adjustment Lending (PAE/*Programa de Ajuste Estructural*) was in place, with IMF and World Bank pressures for the government to reduce public expenditure, to privatise public sector institutions, to liberalise trade, and to promote and diversify exports (Barry, 1991:27–8; Green, 1995:218–19; Ulate, 1992). These kinds of initiatives continued during PAE II in 1988, and are set to intensify under the third stage of the programme in the 1990s.[10] As in Mexico, rising prices, falling wages, formal sector retrenchment and pressures on household incomes were accompanied by an increase in female labour force participation, and a increase in women's share of total employment from 24.3 to 28 per cent between the beginning and end of the 1980s (see Table 5.4). By 1993, this was 29.9 per cent (DGEC, 1993a: Table 3). Again, the biggest increases in female employment were in the age groups where women are most likely to be bearing and raising children. While in 1980 only one woman for every three men worked in the 20–39 year cohort, by 1990 the figure was one in two (Dierckxsens, 1992:22). Although female unemployment remains higher than men's (see CMF, 1994:4),[11] women's increased labour force participation has been central to what Achío and

Krauskopf (1994:22) regard as one of the most 'notorious' effects of the crisis in Costa Rica – namely the number of women who now fulfil the role of household breadwinners and the lack of institutional support to alleviate their multiple burdens. Given women's long-standing dearth of employment opportunities in rural areas, however, this is more likely to be an urban phenomenon.

Female labour force participation, rural–urban migration and sex ratios

Limited employment for women in rural areas of Costa Rica certainly seems to be associated with the familiar 'urban bias' in female headship in Latin America. Among the major export commodities, only coffee uses significant amounts of female labour, and then only for a very short period of the farming year (the 3–4 week duration of the harvest). Otherwise, women's employment in rural areas tends to be limited to ancillary activities such as providing food and laundry services to male labourers (Chant, 1992:52), or 'helping out' on family farms on an unpaid basis in tasks such as weeding, sewing, clearing, spreading, fertiliser and harvesting (Cartín Leiva, 1994:153–4). In this light it is not surprising that in 1993 women were only registered as 6 per cent of the agricultural labour force despite representing 25 per cent of the rural workforce as a whole (DGEC, 1993a: Table 7).

This aside, it is not just lack of employment, but lack of reasonably-paid employment, which makes livelihood difficult for rural women. As many as 60 per cent of female workers in rural areas earn less than the minimum salary, and 34 per cent only a little over half this amount (CMF, 1994:59). With limited scope for rural women to support households of their own, and in light of the fact that women have much higher shares of urban employment (being 35.6 per cent of the urban workforce in 1993 – DGEC, 1993a: Table 7), it is not perhaps surprising that women-headed households have always been more frequent in urban settings (Carter and True, 1978). A total of 21.6 per cent of urban households in 1973 were headed by women and 22.7 per cent in 1984, for example, compared with respective figures of 12.4 and 12.9 per cent in the countryside (DGEC, 1974, 1987). Although the rural figure had increased to 15.9 per cent by 1993, it was still higher in towns (24.3 per cent) (DGEC, 1993b: Table 4). As of this latter year, 56.8 per cent of all female household heads in Costa Rica lived in urban areas compared with only 42.8 per cent of male heads (DGEC, 1993b: Table 2). Yet while women may have little economic basis for heading their own households in the Costa Rican countryside, one feature of the agrarian economy which *does* give rise to female headship, albeit of a temporary nature, is male out-migration. In Guanacaste province, in the northwest of the country, for example, the expansion of cattle-ranching and sugar cane has led to concentration of land holdings, loss of opportunities for small farmers and massive seasonal fluctuations in employment. This has given rise to a situation where the male population in the region is prone to move elsewhere over several months of the year, leaving women behind as *de facto* heads of household (see Chant, 1991c; also Chapter 6).

De jure female headship, on the other hand, is much more common in urban areas, and undoubtedly partly relates to the fact that female labour force participation in towns and cities has regularly been at least one-third higher than in the countryside (Ramírez Boza, 1987). Both factors, in turn, are reflected in a feminised urban sex ratio with only 91 men per 100 women in urban localities at a national level (Chant and Radcliffe, 1992:6, Table 1.2).[12] In the capital, San José, this is even more pronounced, with as few as 88 men per 100 women (Chant, 1992:55,Table 3.2). Links between feminised sex ratios, higher shares of female employment and higher levels of female household headship are apparent in that the Central Region of Costa Rica (comprising San José and urban parts of Alajuela, Cartago and Heredia) has the highest frequency of female heads (21.5 per cent of households are headed by women), and the largest share of female employment (32.4 per cent in 1993). In the Región Brunca (part of Puntarenas), on the other hand, where the sex ratios in the capital is 99 men per 100 women, the proportion of female-headed households is 16 per cent and the female share of employment only 23 per cent (DGEC, 1993a: Table 3).

Not only do female heads of household have greater likelihood of forming in urban areas because they are able to support themselves economically, but single, separated, divorced or widowed women from the countryside may also move to towns because they cannot sustain themselves from rural livelihoods without men (Albert, 1982; Chant, 1991b:63). Indeed, it is interesting that in 1984, 40 per cent of women heads of household in Costa Rican towns were economically active compared with only 23 per cent of their counterparts in the countryside (Chant, 1992:53). Although the gap has closed somewhat in the 1990s, it is still quite large: in 1993, for example, 48.2 per cent of female heads were economically active in urban areas compared with 39.4 per cent in rural districts (DGEC, 1993b: Table 4).

Having noted that urbanisation in the country has been associated with rising opportunities for female workforce participation, this is not to suggest that women in urban areas have unrestricted access to the labour market. Most poor women are found in stereotypical female jobs with little security or remuneration, including domestic service, petty commerce, and un- or semi-skilled assembly positions in agro-industries such as floriculture (see Achío and Mora, 1988; Bolaños and Rodríguez, 1988; Chant, 1994a; Quiróz *et al.*, 1984). Indeed services and commerce occupied over two-thirds of all women workers in 1993, compared with 22 per cent in industry and a mere 6 per cent in agriculture (DGEC, 1993a: Table 8). There is also a distinct concentration of women in the informal sector (41 per cent of all women workers in 1991 – CMF, 1994:58). Even when women do similar work to men, their pay tends to be lower (Carvajal and Geithman, 1985; Yudelman, 1989). Figures for the 1980s reveal that women workers in personal services received only 55 per cent of the earnings of their male counterparts (CMF, 1994:xvi), and the gap between male and female wages widened during the early crisis period (Gindling, 1993). Dependence (of an ideological and pragmatic nature) on male wages amongst the lowest-income strata is such that women may even put up with domestic violence simply to safeguard the material well-being of their children (see Ugalde, 1989). Again, however, evidence would suggest that this is more likely in rural areas, since divorce rates are four times higher in towns (Dierckxsens, 1992:25).[13]

Family norms, gender and social identity

Despite the rising incidence of divorce in Costa Rica (see later), as in Mexico the nuclear family based around a female homemaker married to a male breadwinner persists in being the normative ideal. According to one 1990 survey, this arrangement is favoured by three out of four people in the country as the most suitable for rearing children (Fernández, 1992:19). Women in Costa Rica are widely encouraged to marry and have children, with the legal age of marriage being 18 (without parental consent). Despite the fact that informal unions are fairly common at younger ages, 86.3 per cent of women aged 10 years or more who reside with a male partner (45 per cent of the female population), are formally married (DGEC, 1987: Table 6). Although average fertility rates fell from around seven children to three between the mid-1960s and the early 1990s (Achío and Krauskopf, 1994:22; see also Table 5.2), this varies by class and region, with poor women still giving birth to an average of 4.3 children in 1993 (CMF, 1994:3–4). The decline in birth rates is largely due to widespread availability of family planning, although abortion is only possible in extreme circumstances such as medical grounds, rape or incest (*ibid.*:41). Many have argued that the lives of Costa Rican women are heavily circumscribed by patriarchal family norms, where women gain social legitimacy primarily as wives and mothers, and are bound to the domestic domain as reproducers and consumers. Men, on the other hand, are regarded primarily as producers and breadwinners (Facio, 1989a; Romero *et al.*, 1983). In addition to gender divisions of labour within households, there are also divisions of power. For example, the National Child Welfare Agency observes that women are required to put the interests of their husbands and children first, and to seek approval for their decisions from men (PANI, 1990:4–5), and Cartín Leiva (1994:144) describes the Costa Rican rural family as one in which there is a 'strict patriarchal hierarchy' where the man is generally the head of the family, with considerable power over wives and children.

The identification of breadwinning and household headship as pre-eminently masculine attributes mirrors patterns in other parts of Latin America (Goldenburg, 1994:200). In Costa Rica this is further endorsed by Article 35 of the Family Code which stresses that the husband should be the main economic provider, even if wives contribute to household finances (Chant, 1991b:17; see also Vincenzi, 1991:262), and Article 11 which specifies marriage as entailing shared living, cooperation and mutual help, and as the '*base esencial*' (fundamental base) of the family (Vincenzi, 1991:255).

The extent to which cooperation and mutual help are actually a reality in nuclear households, however, is doubtful. In addition to divisions of power and labour, sexual double standards mean that married men have considerable sexual freedom, whereas women are expected to be totally faithful to their husbands and to show little awareness of their own sexuality (CEFEMINA, 1986; Chaverría *et al.*, 1987; Goldenburg, 1994:204–5). Another major source of conflict is domestic violence, with surveys suggesting that this affects at least 30–40 per cent of women in male-headed households (CMF, 1994:xvii). Indeed, a study by the National Child Welfare Agency of nearly 1500 women who visited the organisation in April and May 1989 on routine matters of child maintenance found that over half had experienced psychological and/or physical abuse from partners. Psychological abuse took the form of insults such as calling wives 'stupid', 'ugly', 'worthless', 'bad mothers' and so on, and actions such as leaving home and going out with other women. Physical violence, on the other hand, ranged from kicking, beating, slapping, pinching and biting (PANI, 1990:8). Interestingly, 48 per cent of married women had been the victims of physical violence as against 35 per cent of women in consensual unions, leading to the conclusion that in some ways marriage might act to endorse male abuse of women (see PANI, 1990:29–33; also CEFEMINA, 1994). Domestic violence is most likely to occur when men have been drinking, which, as in other parts of Central America, forms an integral part of 'machista' culture (Goldenberg, 1994:198). Given the mounting incidence of alcoholism in the country,[14] it is no surprise that the partners of nearly half the women who report domestic violence to the PANI in San José have problems related to alcohol or other forms of drug abuse (Amador, 1992:6).

Despite the problems attached to male household headship, the idea that women might choose to have a child out of wedlock, or set up their own homes, is far from condoned. As pointed out by PANI (1990:4–5), women in Costa Rica are expected to go from the house of their parents to the house of their husbands, because living alone indicates they are 'libertine'. This is echoed by Goldenburg (1994:221) who claims that because a woman who renounces marriage and family and becomes a lone mother does not have a master (*dueño*), this is tantamount to declaring she is sexually available. Having said this, in regions such as Limón where there is a significant Afro-Caribbean population (around one-third of the total in the province – see McIlwaine, 1993:7), and a long tradition of female household headship due to male overseas migration, female independence seems to be more accepted (*ibid.*: Chapter 6). In 1990, for example, 43 per cent of black women in Limón provice were heads of household, most being unmarried and having an average of two to four dependent children (CMF, 1994:141). In the city of Limón itself, as many as 36.9 per cent of Afro-Caribbean households in a survey of low-income communities were female-headed, compared with 19.4 per cent among the white/*mestizo* population (McIlwaine, 1993:163)

Yet despite the social pressures upon the bulk of Costa Rican women to marry and to hold their marriages together, the reality is that many may not have very much choice in the matter, with the National Centre for the Development of Women and the Family (*Centro Nacional del Desarrollo de la Mujer y la Familia*/CMF)[15] asserting that the vast majority of women-headed households in Costa Rica arise through abandonment or absence of men and/or paternal neglect (CMF, 1994:52). While the Costa Rican state is concerned to uphold the institution of two-parent families headed by a married couple[16] and perhaps for this reason not only fails to grant special welfare benefits or day-care facilities for women-headed households, but denies support to children whose fathers' names do not appear on their birth certificates,[17,18] in other respects its policies on gender could be regarded as lending some form of helping hand to women who find themselves in this position.

Gender legislation, family policy and social welfare

Compared with the other case study countries, Costa Rica boasts major achievements in respect of gender-aware legislation and policy that might contribute indirectly to its relatively high levels of female household headship. Since the Constitution of 1948, women have technically had the same legal rights as men (PANI, 1982:5), and the Costa Rican state has not only long professed a strong commitment to gender equality, but been active in backing and/or helping to finance women's organisations (Lara *et al.*, 1995: 105 *et seq.*; Méndez, 1988).

The Social Equality Law of 1990

One of the most solid manifestations of state support for gender issues has been the Law Promoting Social Equality for Women passed in 1990. Under the auspices of a general proclamation of gender equality in political, economic, social and cultural domains (IJSA, 1990:5), the law reinforces earlier legislation designed to improve women's position in Costa Rica, and more ambitiously, aims to *guarantee* equal rights by thorough monitoring and enforcement (Chant, 1991b:61). To this end, Article 21 of the law provided for the creation of a General Defence of Human Rights attached to the state judiciary, and within this, a special watchdog committee on women's rights (IJSA, 1990:10–12). Notwithstanding that the law took two years to reach the statute book and was watered down *en route* (see below), it contains a number of far-reaching prescriptions which have considerable relevance to the formation and survival of women-headed households. These include compulsory joint registration of property in marriage (or in non-formalised unions, registration in the woman's name), which potentially protects women's property rights in event of separation);[19] increased funding for day-care centres in rural areas and state institutions (which potentially helps mothers to work); prohibition of dismissal from jobs on the ground of pregnancy (which further entitles mothers to continue working), and in cases of domestic violence, greater rights for women in respect of ensuring that the perpetrator leaves the house immediately (which might conceivably make women less fearful about dissolving their partnerships) (*ibid.*). The law has also strengthened the property rights of women in *uniones libres* (consensual unions) of three or more years duration (Molina, 1993), and has succeeded in amending Article 138 of the Family Code which gave fathers the right to decide on the custody of children unless decreed otherwise by the courts (Facio, 1989a:74; Vincenzi, 1991:289). More recently (1994), ministerial offices for women (*Oficinas Ministeriales de la Mujer*/OMM) were created in all state ministeries which, in coordination with the CMF, are there to ensure that there is no discrimination against women and that their rights are protected (CMF, 1994:xiv).

Although many women in Costa Rica, especially low-income women, have not heard of the law, or if they have, have not benefited directly (see Latinamerica Press, 1995:6; McIlwaine, 1993: Chapter 3; also Chapter 6 this volume), various other elements of Costa Rican legislature do assist women. One is the welfare state which gives allowances for children, widow's pensions and some limited provision for childcare (see Notes 10 and 17), another is the Family Code, which provides back-up (in principle) to women concerned to extricate themselves from difficult relationships and to establish their own households.

The Costa Rican Family Code

Both divorce and legal separation in Costa Rica are permissible on fairly wide grounds. Divorce may be granted in the event of adultery on the part of either spouse, attack by one spouse on the other's life, an attempt to prostitute a spouse or to corrupt the children, or other actions which prejudice the welfare of household members (Article 48) (República de Costa Rica, 1986:192; see also Molina, 1994). As for legal separation, this may be decreed in cases where there has been wilful or malicious neglect of a spouse or children, failure to comply with basic household responsibilities, mental breakdown, dangerous conduct, imprisonment for a non-political crime, *de facto* separation for at least one year (two years from the date of marriage), or mutual consent (Article 58). The fact that only 'innocent parties' can apply for divorce also favours women since, in the context of limited sexual freedom, they are less likely than men to engage in adultery (see Chant, 1991b; Chaverría *et al.*, 1987). At the same time, procedures can be long-drawn-out and bureaucratic, commonly involving court appearances and a wait of at least three years after the date of the marriage. Difficult divorces can also be expensive, especially for poor women who have little recourse to legal aid (see Chapter 7).[20] Beyond this, and despite the fact that the number of divorces per year per 1000 women multiplied five-fold between 1973 and 1984 (Dierckxsens, 1992:25) (in 1975 there were 2 divorces for every 100 marriages, 12 in 1981 and 15.3 in 1991 – CMF, 1994:4), there is evidence to suggest that divorce is still not acceptable to the majority of Costa Ricans (Fernández, 1992:20).

As for other aspects of gender subordination which the Costa Rican state has so far failed to address, one is women's relatively limited political representation. The passage of the the Social Equality Law, for example, was delayed due to conflict over proposals for fixed quotas for female deputies and positive discrimination for women in public posts (see Facio, 1989a). Although by 1994 women were 15 per cent of the 432-member Legislative Assembly (CMF, 1994:xii) (see also Table 5.2), during the period 1953 to 1982, only 6 per cent of deputies were female (Escalante Herrera, 1990:27). At the other end of the spectrum, peasant women are routinely excluded from community-level political decision-making and union representation (Cartín Leiva, 1994:145). These patterns are usually attributed to women's limited knowledge of their political rights, compounded by an education system which does not encourage women to think for themselves nor to be more educated than their menfolk (Escalante Herrera, 1990:27; PANI, 1990:4–5). Although male–female differentials in years of schooling are now negligible, educational materials are often sexist, and there is considerable gender-typing at tertiary level (for example, few women undergraduates study technical subjects such as agronomy or architecture) (CMF, 1994:xvii).

Women's movements and organisations

Despite these restraints, it is important to recognise that the women's movement is fairly organised in Costa Rica, that there are numerous feminist groups, and around forty NGOs working with women in one form or another, half of whom specialise in women *per se* (CMF, 1994:xiv). These concentrate on fields such as training, finance, education, research, human rights, family planning, reproductive health and domestic violence (*ibid.*). The largest feminist NGO in the country, CEFEMINA, has been in existence for 20 years and is expanding programmes against violence, sensitising women to their rights, lobbying for legislative changes, providing refuges for women and so on (see CEFEMINA, 1995). The country has had a shelter for battered women since 1984 (Barry, 1991:68), and bottom-up initatives are frequently accompanied by efforts on the part of the state, with PANI now promoting therapeutic group sessions on violence against women (PANI, 1994),

FEMALE HOUSEHOLD HEADSHIP IN THE PHILIPPINES: CHARACTERISTICS AND CONTEXT

National profile of female-headed households

Compared with the other case study countries, the Philippines has the lowest level of female household headship (11.3 per cent). Moreover, referring to figures from the National Demographic Surveys conducted by the Population Institute of the University of the Philippines in 1968 and 1973 (when women-headed units were only 9.8 per cent of all households in both years – see Illo, 1992:196, Table 8.3), there seems to have been only a marginal increase in the last two-and-a-half decades.

Unlike in Mexico and Costa Rica, household headship in the Philippine census is defined on the basis of instrumental criteria, referring to the person 'responsible for the care and organisation of the household', and adding that this person (decribed as 'He') 'usually provides the chief source of income' (NSO, 1992:xv). This may well bias the designation of headship towards men and could be one reason why national figures are so much lower in relation to Mexico and Costa Rica, especially when community-level surveys in the case study centres reveal otherwise (see Chapter 6).

Census data also show that women-headed households in the Philippines are much more common among older women than in the other two countries, with 60 per cent being over 50 years of age (see Table 5.7).

Table 5.7 *The Philippines: percentage distribution of female and male household heads by age cohorts, 1990*

Age Group (years)	Female Heads %	Male Heads %
< 20	0.7	0.5
20–29	7.4	18.0
30–39	13.0	30.5
40–49	18.6	22.7
50–59	23.7	15.4
60–69	21.1	8.4
70+	15.5	4.5
TOTAL	100.0	100.0

Source: NSO (1992: Table 14 'Number of Households by Age Group and Sex of Household Head, Household Size and Region:1990').

Similar to the other countries, the average size of households headed by men in the Philippines is larger (5.5), than those headed by women (4.1) (NSO, 1992:97). A total of 12.5 per cent of female-headed households are single-person units compared with only 1.7 per cent of male-headed households, and 60 per cent of the former are in the 60-plus age group (*ibid.*). Although it is not possible to elicit data on the marital status of female heads from census data, it is probable that the vast majority are widows in the light of the fact that, excluding the 46.6 per cent of Filipino women aged ten years or more recorded as single in the 1990 census, 91.2 per cent are married, 7.4 per cent widowed, and only 1.3 per cent separated or divorced (*ibid.*:xxix). Low rates of marital breakdown seem to owe not so much to women's position in the economy, as to structures of gender and kinship in Philippine society, and particularly to family law, as discussed below.

Economic development, urbanisation and crisis

The Philippines is the poorest of the three case study countries with a per capita GNP of only $770 US in 1992 (see Table 5.3). Although the economy is increasingly reliant on 'modern' activities such as manufacturing and international tourism, both of which have drawn progressively greater numbers of people into towns and cities and/or contributed to the urbanisation of existing settlements, only 48.6 per cent of the country's 60.6 million inhabitants in 1990 were classified as urban (NSO, 1992:5, Table 3),[21] and only 16 per cent of the labour force was in industry in 1990–92, compared with 45 per cent in agriculture (UNDP, 1994:162–3, Table 17). The country's poverty is frequently deemed responsible for its huge numbers of overseas migrants, who, in 1994, generated $3 billion US in remittances through formal banking channels. This was equivalent to 22 per cent of total merchandise exports and 4.5 per cent of GNP (*ibid*.:29).

The slow progress of industrialisation in the Philippines is usually attributed to the grip maintained on the economy by the United States following Independence in 1946 (possession of the colony switched from Spanish to American hands in 1898). On one hand, Filipino producers could not compete with cheap US manufactured goods, and on another, fledgeling attempts at import substitution industrialisation made the country even more reliant on foreign technology and managerial expertise. Agriculture continued to be the main source of foreign revenue, notwithstanding that the modernisation programme set in train by President Ferdinand Marcos during the 1960s and 1970s allowed extensive penetration of foreign capital (Goodno, 1991; Putzel, 1992). It was also under Marcos that the country's foreign debt escalated to unprecedented proportions (swelling from less than 10 per cent of GDP throughout most of the 1950 and 1960s to an average of 28 per cent in the 1970s) (Cruz and Repetto, 1992:15). Much foreign borrowing (amounting to a total of $24 billion US by 1983) was diverted to the personal fortunes of the Marcos family and/or to secure political patronage (see Cammack *et al.*, 1993:69; Pineda-Ofreneo, 1991:7). This, together with the assassination of Marcos's main political rival, Benigno Aquino, in 1983, resulted in the downfall of Marcos in 1986 with the 'People Power' revolution, although successive governments (those of Cory Aquino, 1986–92, and the current administration of Fidel Ramos) have been able to do little to reduce the foreign debt, which presently stands at nearly $33 billion US (see Table 5.3). As in Mexico and Costa Rica, this has led to a series of stabilisation and structural adjustment programmes which have exacerbated hardship for low-income groups through reducing the quality and coverage of public services, raising costs of basic commodities such as fuel and foodstuffs, and increasing unemployment (Chant and McIlwaine, 1995a). Part and parcel of President Ramos's economic liberalisation project has been the 'Philippines 2000' plan which aims to turn the Philippines into a newly-industrialising country (NIC) by the turn of the century by means of stepping up manufacturing exports and increasing levels of foreign direct investment. Key industrial products targeted by the programme are garments, electrical components, furniture, and gifts and houseware (including fashion accessories and costume jewellery). Much of the manufacturing of these items takes place in factories in export-processing zones (EPZs) where again, multinational companies are the main profit-makers. None the less, after coconut oil, garments and electronics are the Philippines top two exports by value, and even amidst crisis have continued to generate vital foreign exchange (Chant and McIlwaine, 1995b). A bias towards the recruitment of women into export factories has contributed to raising female labour force participation in the country and to stimulating the movement of women to urban areas, although unlike in Mexico and Costa Rica, neither of these processes seems to have led to increases in female household headship.

Female labour force participation and rural–urban migration
Filipino women have a long history of economic activity; they have made up around one-third of the labour force since the 1970s, and in 1992 their share was nearly 38 per cent (Table 5.4). Indeed, in 1990 a total of 39.2 per cent of women aged 15 years or more were economically active (UN, 1991:107, Table 8). Yet despite the fact that female labour force participation is higher than in Mexico or Costa Rica, the incidence of women-headed households is lower. Beyond this, although women are 29 per cent of the rural labour force and 39 per cent of the urban labour force (NSO, 1992: Tables 16 and 18), and more specifically are strongly represented in urban-based sectors such as industry (where they are 46 per cent of workers), and services and commerce (44 per cent of workers), as opposed to farming, fishing and forestry (8 per cent) (Chant and McIlwaine, 1995a:23–4), the incidence of female household headship is by no means consistently higher in provinces with greater degrees of urbanisation (see Table 5.8).

Although the Philippine census does not give specific rural–urban breakdowns for household headship[22] which might yield a more precise idea of whether there was any systematic 'urban bias' in the distribution of female-headed households, it would certainly appear that rural–urban differentials are not as marked as in Costa Rica or Mexico. This, in some senses, is rather strange, since women have constituted a growing proportion of migrants to Philippine towns and cities since the 1960s (Eviota and Smith, 1984), and by 1990 the national urban sex ratio was only 97.7 men per 100 women (NSO, 1992:5, Table 3). Beyond this, data for some of the major cities indicate some relationship between urbanisation, women's share of employment, the feminisation of sex ratios and levels of household headship. In Cebu City, for example, the male : female ratio is only 94 : 100 and 14 per cent of households are headed by women (Chant and McIlwaine, 1995a:32;

see also Chapter 6), and the National Capital Region where Manila is located and where 100 per cent of the population is classified as urban, has a sex ratio of 94.2 men per 100 women, and 13.8 per cent of household heads are female. In these cities women also have above average shares of employment (42.8 per cent in Cebu City and 45.3 per cent in Manila).

Table 5.8 *Philippines: population, urbanisation, sex ratios, female employment and female household headship by region, 1990*

Region	Population	% of Population Urban	Sex Ratio (Men per 100 Women)	Female Share of Employed Population*	% of Households Headed by Women
Philippines	60,559,116	48.6	101.1	32.6	11.3
National Capital Region	7,907,386	100.0	94.2	45.2	13.8
Central Luzon	6,188,716	60.2	101.6	29.9	11.7
Southern Tagalog	8,247,120	51.0	102.1	29.1	11.1
Southern Mindanao	4,448,616	47.4	104.0	28.2	8.2
Northern Mindanao	3,502,674	43.4	103.6	31.6	8.9
Central Visayas	4,582,529	40.4	100.0	36.5	12.5
Ilocos	3,547,269	37.8	100.4	39.0	14.2
Western Visayas	5,385,222	35.8	101.2	29.7	12.6
Cordillera A.R.**	1,141,141	31.3	102.4	41.1	13.4
Bicol	3,904,793	31.2	103.4	25.9	10.7
Eastern Visayas	3,048,854	31.2	104.4	26.2	11.2
Western Mindanao	3,150,906	30.8	102.3	47.9	8.4
Central Mindanao	3,167,540	25.2	100.9	26.5	7.7
Cagayan Valley	2,446,350	23.5	104.1	27.9	9.2

Source: NSO (1992: Tables 3, 14 & 19).
NB Regions listed in order of levels of urbanisation.
* Excludes unemployed persons in labour force.
** A.R.= Administrative Region.

Family norms, gender and social identity

The lack of any clear correspondence between levels of female headship and economic and demographic factors may owe in part to emphasis on the male headed family throughout the Philippines. Notwithstanding that this might be most marked in the southern part of the country where most of the country's Muslim population are concentrated and where rates of female headship are lower than average (see Table 5.8 on the Mindanao provinces) family cohesiveness is also stressed in 'mainstream' ('lowland Christian' Filipino culture, with marriage and childbirth stressed from an early stag in women's lives. For example, data from the Asian Marriage Survey indicate that the average age of marriage for rural and low-income urban women in the Philippines is 21.4 years, and that of middle-class women, only slightly higher (22.7 years) (Domingo and King, 1992:97, Table 7.1). While the total fertility rate in the Philippines dropped to 4.1 in 1992 from a level of 6.4 in 1970 (Table 5.2), this is still high. More significant still perhaps, is that levels of marital breakdown are exceptionally low (as noted earlier, less than 2 per cent of non-single women are recorded as having separated from their spouses). Aside from the fact that divorce is illegal in the Philippines (see below), one factor which might play an important role in glueing marriages together is the persistence of an extremely strong attachment to kin, reflected in high levels of extended households, residential propinquity to relatives, and elaborate inter-household kinship networks (see for example Castillo, 1991; Chant and McIlwaine, 1995a; Medina, 1992; Peterson, 1993; Pineda-Deang, 1992; Shimuzu, 1991). While nuclear households may predominate, married couples are rarely isolated. This is important insofar as marital tensions may be attenuated by family support, and/or pressure on couples to stay together. The concept of 'smooth interpersonal relations' (SIR) (a widely-identified feature of Philippine culture), is pertinent here. SIR, as the term suggests, refers to harmonious human interactions, and to the avoidance of confrontation, aggression and dissent. Also important is the imperative of 'not losing face' or bringing shame upon one's family (expressed in the concept of '*hiya*') (see Enriquez, 1991:99; Shimuzu, 1991:118; Villariba, 1993:20). Marital disruption is likely to offend these norms and is therefore prone to be discouraged by the wider family, which is not to say that many marriages are not extremely conflictive (Chant and McIlwaine, 1995a). Another factor relating to family which may inhibit marital disruption is the widely-noted 'child-centredness' of Filipino culture. Love and duty towards children are uppermost in Filipino family life and this has been seen as important in keeping couples together (see Ramirez, 1984:30; also Chapter 6).

Resistance to splitting up is such that even where women have been subject to domestic violence and go as far as taking their cases to court, they frequently withdraw, especially if their husbands plead for a second (or subsequent) chance. As Banaynal-Fernandez (1994:41) points out: 'Many women just want the battering to stop. Many are not ready to leave the relationship, no matter how problematic.' Interestingly, of the 84 women who brought cases of domestic violence to the attention of the Support and Crisis Programme of the Lihok-Pilipina Foundation in Cebu between 1991 and 1993, a far greater proportion (67 per cent) suffered violence from husbands, than live-in partners (27 per cent) or boyfriends (6 per cent) (*ibid.*:43), although this could simply reflect the prevalence of formal marriage among the adult female population.

Related in part to the notion of family shame and to religious values, is the way in which female headship (and particularly lone motherhood) meets with stigmatisation on moral grounds: lone women, especially those with out-of-wedlock offspring, are often the butt of speculative gossip on the part of peers and neighbours. As such, they often continue to live with parents rather than form independent households, except in cases where they migrate away from home areas to work and have no kin in the destinations to which they move. 'Hidden' in the homes of parents or relatives, these 'embedded' female heads are not only less visible but are further likely to inure themselves from comment insofar as they have less freedom and privacy to engage in sexual liaisons. Some of these women may be the mistresses ('*keridas*') of married men, who due to sexual double standards are relatively free to indulge in extra-marital affairs (see Eviota, 1992;134).

In many respects, other aspects of gender roles and relations in the Philippines might be viewed as contributing to higher levels of female headship than there actually are. Among lowland Christian groups, for example, there is commonly argued to be greater fluidity between male and female roles than in several other cultures (see Illo, 1991), with men often being involved in various aspects of housework and childcare (see Aguilar, 1991:159; Illo and Polo, 1990:101; Pavia Ticzon, 1990:117; PROCESS, 1993:32; Sevilla, 1989:4). Women, on the other hand, while still shouldering the bulk of domestic duties, are no strangers to employment. In fact, among low-income groups in particular, those who take on remunerative work usually meet with 'approval and prestige' from their male and female peers (Hollnsteiner, 1991a:266; see also Bucoy, 1992; Sevilla, 1989).

Women's access to income in their own right seems to be associated with a strong role in the management of household finances and a prominent role in household decision-making (see Medina, 1991; Miralao, 1984; Ramirez, 1984), notwithstanding that responsibility is often assumed because of male disinterest in family matters, and a greater orientation on the part of men to extra-household activities (Chant and McIlwaine, 1995a: Chapter 3; Illo and Lee, 1991). Indeed, Dumont (1994:177) notes that men in the Visayan region spend very little time at home, and when they do, they often sleep in order to disengage themselves from any domestic responsibility. Whatever men's social class, 'the time spent at home was mostly subdued time that was constrained by having relinquished one's initiative and authority to the control of women. In short, from a male viewpoint, home was always a feminised space.' Yet gender relations in the Philippines are such that men's privileges in terms of access to resources and recreation are upheld even when they have no employment and/or contribute little to household welfare. Indeed, in many cases women finance men's personal expenditures out of their own earnings (Chant and McIlwaine, 1995a). Yet although these factors might arguably increase the likelihood of women breaking away and forming their own households, social emphasis on keeping their marriages together acts to dissuade them (see earlier). This may also be intensified by various legal-institutional elements of Philippine society, notwithstanding that the state seems to have taken a reasonably progressive stand on some gender issues.

Gender legislation, family policy and social welfare

As in Costa Rica, the Philippine government professes commitment to women's concerns. A Bureau of Women and Young Workers has existed within the the Department of Labour and Employment since 1969, and 1975 saw the creation by President Marcos of a National Commission on the Role of Filipino Women (NCRFW) (then the National Commission on Women/NCW), in direct response to International Women's Year (del Rosario, 1995:103; see also Chapter 3). In its early days, the organisation mainly concentrated on the education of rural women and livelihood projects for low-income groups, but after Aquino came to power and proclamations of gender equality were enshrined in the new Constitution, the NCRFW became responsible for drawing up the the first major development plan for women in the country, and advising the President and Cabinet on related policies, programmes and projects for women's advancement (Valdeavilla, 1995:94).

The Philippine Development Plan for Women (PDPW) of 1989 was instituted directly under the Office of the President and integrated into the Medium Term Development Plan of the Philippines (1989–92). One of the overriding aims of the plan was to 'alter the traditional concept of a woman's self-worth as being subordinate to a man' (NCRFW, 1989:8), with goals for equality and development in six major areas: individual, family, socio-cultural, economic, political and legal. Initiatives taken included strengthening laws against discrimination against women in employment, the extension of maternity leave payments to private sector workers, and the outlawing of the mail order bride business (the trafficking of Filipina brides to foreign countries) (see Reyes, 1992:45–6). Since the expiry of the PDPW, the NCRFW have been preparing a new 30-year Philippine Plan for Gender Responsive Development (PPGD) (Valdeavilla, 1995:94).

The Philippine Family Code
The other major achievement in respect of gender during Aquino's term was the revision of the Family Code. Although the Revised Code of 1988 still

aimed to strengthen marriage and the family (see below), a number of positive changes were made in respect of women's rights. One was that women no longer had to have their husband's permission to apply for credit (Illo, 1991:44), another that the family home became the common property of the husband and wife (Quisumbing, 1990:45), and another, the recasting of household management (including financial support) as the right and duty of both spouses (Sempio-Diy, 1988:100). On the other hand, various restrictive measures surrounding marriage and the family remain, one with particular relevance in restraining the emergence of female-headed households being the total prohibition of divorce (see Pineda, 1991:95–6). Although legal separation is now granted in limited cases (for example on grounds of incest or physical violence – see Sempio-Diy, 1988:73), neither party is entitled to remarry since the marital bonds themselves remain indissoluble (Medina, 1991:180; Villariba, 1993:33). Moreover, women's scope to obtain legal separated status on grounds of sexual infidelity is much less than men: a husband has to actually live with another woman for a wife to apply, whereas a husband may qualify even if his wife has only had intercourse with another man outside marriage (see Banaynal-Fernandez, 1994:52; Reyes, 1992:50). This legislative impediment to couples splitting up is important directly, and also indirectly insofar as it equates the dissolution of marriage with an extra-legal activity. The force of the latter is undoubtedly bolstered by high levels of Catholic religious observance.[23] Women in particular take their vows extremely seriously and often cite religion as a major reason for staying with husbands with whom they are unhappy (Chant and McIlwaine, 1995a). Catholicism is also important in putting pressure on young couples to marry, especially when women get pregnant, which clearly reduces potential numbers of never-married single mothers.[24]

Women's movements and organisations

Government resistance to extending women's rights across-the-board is to some extent compensated by the size and scope of the Philippine women's movement. Philippine women's organisations have been especially strong since the demise of Marcos, and a number are radical in their demands. The largest legal coalition in the women's movement is GABRIELA (General Assembly Binding Women for Reforms, Integrity, Liberty and Action) which was established in 1984, and amongst its various initiatives includes concerns such as female exploitation in bars and brothels, mail order brides, domestic violence, the cost of living, national debt, nuclear power and the environment. Along with several other groups, GABRIELA offers advice and assistance to women on their rights. A recent attempt at strengthening grounds for consensus and collective action among various strands of the women's movement has come about with DIWATA (Development Initatives for Women and Transformative Action) funded by the Women's Programme of the Canadian International Development Agency (CIDA). DIWATA has a total of 230 groups under its wing (St Hilaire, 1992:12). Aside from trying to streamline some of the concerns in the women's movement, DIWATA's main objectives are to support projects leading to gender equality and to promote and encourage the development of policies, programmes and services benefiting women (Israel-Sobritchea, 1994). Although this is in many respects a welcome initiative, it is important to recognise that there have long been major cleavages in the women's movement on grounds of differential allegiance to state and nationalist projects (*ibid.*; see also Valdeavilla, 1995:95). In addition, although many middle-class groups are concerned to work alongside low-income women and some have spawned organisations which specifically represent their interests, the latter are frequently excluded from mainstream feminist organisational structures. Beyond this, single mothers seem to have no special place in such initiatives.

CONCLUSIONS

This review of core economic, demographic, socio-cultural and legal-institutional features of Mexico, Costa Rica and the Philippines gives some indication of reasons behind variations in levels and types of female household headship among the countries. More than anything perhaps, it highlights the importance of considering different factors in conjunction with one another, especially since there are so many which favour *and* inhibit female headship in each context, the main ones being summarised for purposes of clarification and reference in Figure 5.1. Of all the countries, the Philippines arguably stands out as that in which forces pull most strongly in contradictory directions. Athough several factors might lead to the expectation of high numbers of female-headed units in the country (gender-selective migration, high female labour force participation, a strongly organised women's movement, some support on the part of the state for women's needs and rights, and major female responsibility for decision-making and financial management within households), these mean little in the face of constraints imposed on female independence by the institution of the family, high birth rates, and more particularly, the combined influences of religion and the state in terms of divorce prohibition.

Figure 5.1 *Factors influencing the formation of female-headed households in Mexico, Costa Rica and the Philippines*

Major Precipitating Factors		Major Inhibiting Factors
Feminised national sex ratio		Catholicism
Feminisation of urban sex ratios (due to female-selective urban migration)		Social ideals of marriage & motherhood
		Restricted gender roles for women
High levels of urban-industrial development		Increased household extension during economic crisis
Rising female labour force participation	**Mexico**	State support for 'traditional' family
Rising gap between male & female life expectancy		Limited popular organisation of women
Egalitarian Civil Code & access to divorce		Male–female earning differentials
Machismo and male sexual infidelity		
Feminisation of urban sex ratios (due to female-selective urban migration)		Low levels of urban-industrial development
Seasonal agriculture and male out-migration		Catholicism
		Social ideals of marriage & motherhood
State commitment to gender equality & major legislation in interests of women (including access to divorce and basic rights for women in consensual unions)	**Costa Rica**	Conservative Family Code (re. divisions of labour in household)
		Male–female earning differentials
Some state welfare provisions (e.g. family pensions, childcare services)		Restricted gender roles for women
Machismo and domestic violence		
Active/established women's movement		
Rising female labour force participation		
Feminisation of urban sex ratios (due to female-selective urban migration)		Low levels of urban-industrial development
High levels of female labour force participation		Masculinised national sex ratio
		High fertility
Broad gender roles for women (including household financial management and decision-making)	**The Philippines**	Catholicism
		Social ideals of marriage & motherhood
Sexual double standards (particularly re. husbands' entitlement to mistresses)		Conservative Family Code (particularly re. prohibition on divorce)
Pro-female government initiatives (e.g. NCRFW, PDPW)		
Active/established women's movement		

As for Mexico and Costa Rica where there are relatively marginal differences in levels of female headship, if not the routes by which women enter into the state, it is difficult to explain differences. The fact that greater proportions of female heads in Costa Rica are single, separated or divorced, however, and not as concentrated in older age groups, might reflect a better established women's movement, substantial pro-female legislation, and greater provision of social welfare. Having said this, generalised analysis on the basis of statistics and secondary source material can only produce speculative inferences. While national factors aid explanation to a greater extent than global ones, local factors are likely to be more illuminating still,[25] especially with reference to patterns and processes at the grassroots, as explored in the following chapters.

NOTES

1. More recent figures for Costa Rica indicate further increases. As of 1993, for example, an estimated 19.8 per cent of households were headed by women (DGEC, 1993a: Table 7).

2. All three countries, for example, were colonies of Spain between the sixteenth and nineteenth centuries, even if the forms of colonisation, and the indigenous cultures on which these were imposed, were highly variable.

3. This is especially the case with demographic characteristics and owes to variability between censuses. For example, for Costa Rica I am unable to give figures for household size according to headship or the proportion of households consisting of one woman alone. Neither am I able to show how many female-headed households contain kin or unrelated members, since although there are data on people's relationships to household heads, these are not tabulated in such a way as to enable calculation of the actual numbers of extended households, nor the sex of persons they are headed by (the latter also applies to the Philippines). In addition, even if the Mexican census indicates whether multi-person households consist of kin or non-kin, information on type of extension is unavailable.

4. According to Escobar Latapí and González de la Rocha (1995:62–4), the decade 1982–92 can be divided into three sub-periods. The first period ('crisis and adjustment', 1982–85), was marked, amongst other things by economic downturn, falling wages and several devaluations of the *peso*, but all within a context in which the basis of Mexican economic policy remained unaltered. The second period, 1985–87 was that of substantial restructuring, marked by large-scale privatisation, Mexico's signing of the GATT accord, and a rise in multinational investment. The third period, starting with President Salinas's administration in 1988, was characterised by renegotiation of the foreign debt under the Brady plan, restrictive pacts on wage rises and an increase in

precarious, casualised employment. In this last period, the sustained decline of state intervention in the economy became much more apparent.

5. Each state in Mexico has its own version of the Civil Code. The one referred to in the text is that which pertains to the Federal District as the blueprint for the rest of the country.

6. Interview with Lic Hector Padilla Ruiz, DIF, Puerto Vallarta, November 1994.

7. Interviews with Lic Miguel Angel Vásquez Nava and Lic Adriana Aviles Salas, Mujeres en Solidaridad, Querétaro, November 1994.

8. Women-headed households were 16 per cent of the total household population in Costa Rica in 1973 (DGEC, 1974: Table 24), 17.5 per cent in 1984 (DGEC 1987: Table 7), and 18 per cent in 1990 (DGEC, 1990: Table 4).

9. Urban areas in Costa Rica correspond with the administrative centres of the country's cantons (a canton is an intermediate entity between province and district and contiguous areas. These areas are demarcated by physical and functional criteria such as street plans, electric light, urban services and so on (see DGEC 1987:xxiv).

10. It should also be noted, however, that the Costa Rican state has made more attempts than many other governments in the region to shield the poor from the worst effects of cuts in real wages, jobs and private consumption. This includes the retention of fairly extensive social welfare programmes under the auspices of a state-sponsored health service and social security system which covers three out of four Costa Ricans and includes '*pensiones familiares*' (family pensions such as retirement, disability and widows' pensions, and child allowances (see Barry, 1991:59–61; Lara *et al.*, 1995:61–4; Sojo, 1989, 1994). In addition President José María Figueres of the National Liberation Party (PLN/*Partido Liberación Nacional*), whose four-year term began in 1994, seems to be more concerned (in principle) than his predecessor, President Rafael Angel Calderón of the more right-wing Social Christian Unity Party (PUSC/*Partido Unidad Social Cristiano*) to improve standards of social services and to assist the poor (EIU 1994a:11 *et seq.*). Having said this, the amount of the national budget devoted to health and education in Costa Rica declined from 31.2 per cent in 1975 to 27.9 per cent in 1980 and to 16.1 per cent in 1988 (Menjívar and Trejos 1992:47, Table 5).

11. As of 1993, 5.2 per cent of Costa Rican women were unemployed compared with 3.6 per cent of men (DGEC, 1993a: Table 3).

12. This figure relates to 1985, at which time 46.4 per cent of all Costa Rican women resided in urban areas, compared with only 42.6 per cent of men (Chant and Radcliffe, 1992:6). By 1988, 51.7 per cent of the female population was urban with men still lagging behind at 47.5 per cent (Facio, 1989b:67, Table 3.2.1)

13. More specific reasons offered to explain why women put up with violence from men include dependence on them for shelter, a lack of legal and social support the social pressures upon women (from the family, the church and so on) to keep their marriages going, and the belief that it is not right for women to live alone when wife- and motherhood are their primary sources of social legitimacy (PANI, 1990:10).

14. Alcoholism is currently regarded as Costa Rica's biggest single cause of ill health and is estimated to affect 15 per cent of the population aged 15 years and over (Amador, 1992:6).

15. The origins of the National Centre for the Development of Women and the Family (CMF/*Centro Nacional del Desarrollo de la Mujer y la Familia*) date back to 1974 with the creation of an Office of Women's Programmes attached to the Ministry of Sports and Culture. From 1986, the CMF became officially designated as a semi-autonomous body with its own legislative powers.

16. Although Evangelism is quite strong in some parts of the country, such as the Atlantic coast (see McIlwaine, 1993), and is by no means free of patriarchal ideology (Latinamerica Press, 1995:15; Lehmann, 1994a), Roman Catholicism is the dominant religion in the country and is reported as the religious affiliation of 85 per cent of the population (Lara *et al.*, 1995:98). Although the Catholic Church's influence over government decision-making may have waned since the 1980s, its influence is still felt in a number of areas (Barry, 1991:61–3). Although family planning services are now widely available, for example, it is largely as a result of religious pressure that the government has so far resisted demands by organisations such as the National Child Welfare Agency to recognise consensual unions (Interview with Lic Marta Espinosa, Director of Operations, PANI, San José, October 1994).

17. Recently (October 1995), however, the government has announced a scheme whereby single mothers may be paid a monthly child benefit of 10,000 *colones* ($51 US) for six months provided they attend a designated training course. This will be backed up by the strengthening of childcare facilities, principally '*hogares comunitarios*' (community homes) whereby women in the community are paid a small subvention by the state for looking after the children of other women in the neighbourhood (see *La República*, 4 October 1994, article by Zinna Varela Quiros entitled '135 mil hogares con una mujer a la cabeza'). Some day-care in Costa Rica has also been provided as part of the 'CEN-CENAI' programme which is oriented to children under seven years of age at high nutritional and psycho-social risk. Entry to the scheme is based on the calculation of points attributed to different risk factors such as mothers being out at work (10 points), mothers under the age of 18 (20 points), mothers with no more than primary education (10 points), presence of social pathology in the family (15 points), and items such as insecure employment, and informal housing being accorded 5 points apiece. Within this schema, single motherhood is attributed a high risk value of 15 points, although this by no means guarantees their children's eligibility (see Grosh, 1994:89–91).

18. I am grateful to Zeneida Ballesteros Zuñiga, CEFEMINA and Gina Valituti, CMF for their insights on this issue.

19. This also led to the introduction of a new clause in Article 572 of the Civil Code referring to legitimate heirs. The partner in a consensual union only has rights to property/goods acquired during the duration of the relationship (and when the union has been between a man and a woman legally able to enter marriage, and where their union has been monogamous and stable for at least three years) (see Vincenzi, 1991:86).

20. The only legal resources accessible to low-income women are via '*Consultorios Jurídicos*' (student lawyers who provide free legal help as part of their training), and trained lawyers working for feminist organisations such as CEFEMINA who charge women a small fee for their services. Beyond this, however, the Social Equality Law has increased the prospect of the police ejecting violent

husbands from their home by use of force (interview with Lic. Gina Valituti, International Relations Advisor, CMF, October 1994).

21. Urban areas are defined in the Philippine census as

(i) all cities and municipalities having a population density of at least 1000 persons per square kilometre;
(ii) towns or central districts of municipalities with a population density of at least 500 persons per square kilometre;
(iii) Towns or central municipal districts (not included in i or ii which have (a) a parallel or right-angled street pattern, (b) at least six commercial, manufacturing or similar establishments, (c) at least three of the following: 1. town hall church or chapel, 2. public plaza, park or cemetery, 3. market place or building where trading activities are carried out at least once a week, 4. a public building such as a school, hospital or library;
(iv) a *barangay* (administrative unit) having at least 1000 inhabitants where the occupations of the majority are not in farming and/or fishing (see NSO 1992:xii–xiii).

22. These are only possible to calculate where municipal boundaries correspond with city limits, or where data is available for major metropolitan areas.

23. The 1990 census reports 83 per cent of the Philippine population as Catholic (Chant and McIlwaine, 1995a:16).

24. This is also conceivably exacerbated by a lack of legal abortion, heavily influenced by the Catholic Church's anti-family planning lobby and endorsed by the Philippine state. The Constitution of 1987, for example, includes a specific clause protecting the rights of the unborn child (Reyes, 1992:47 although see Chant and McIlwaine, 1995a: Chapter 2 on recent attempts by Ramos's government to revitalise the country's birth control campaign, and Marcelo, 1991 on evidence for informal terminations).

25. See Duncan (1995) on the necessity for taking into account regional and local processes of gender differentiation in relation to theorising European gender systems.

6 Female Headship and the Urban Poor: Case Study Perspectives

INTRODUCTION

Having outlined some of the general context and features of female headship in Mexico, Costa Rica and the Philippines, this chapter moves on to look more specifically at key characteristics of women-headed households among the poor in selected urban and urbanising localities. Since the bulk of the discussion in this and the following two chapters draws on my own fieldwork, the introductory section to each country gives basic information on the case study areas and brief details of the surveys carried out there. This is followed by a resumé of the principal aspects of female headship among the poor, the routes by which women enter household headship (including their views on factors they personally identify as being critical in the process), and how predominant patterns relate to various social, economic and demographic features of the areas concerned. The organisation of each country section varies slightly according to differences in points I wish to emphasise. The final part of the chapter attempts to outline the major factors accounting for diversity in female household headship among (and within) the countries. It also indicates processes which seem to give rise to common features of female headship, and assists in explaining some of the similarities in experiences and outcomes of women heading households discussed in subsequent chapters.

MEXICO

Introduction to Mexican case study areas

My research in Mexico has concentrated in three cities in the country: Querétaro, León and Puerto Vallarta. My first project was carried out in relation to a doctorate on family structure and self-help housing in Querétaro for which fieldwork took place in 1982–83. This involved a questionnaire survey with adult women (heads or spouses) in 244 'owner-occupier' households in three low-income settlements, and in-depth semi-structured interviews with a sub-sample of 49 respondents.[1] In 1986 I returned to Mexico to do a second major project looking at women's work, household structure and local labour markets in all three cities. This entailed a questionnaire survey with an overall total of women in 189 households (including renters in Puerto Vallarta and León), and 51 semi-structured interviews. Subsequent fieldwork (in 1992 and 1994) consisted of one or more follow-up interviews with 25 respondents in the three areas to explore issues such as the impacts on households of economic restructuring, life-course changes, and meanings and images of female household headship. In this latter research I was also concerned to spend more time than previously talking with children and husbands, although some were absent on the occasions I conducted interviews. Women, therefore, remained my principal informants whose histories have continued to unfold in a manner which is not only direct, but personally meaningful, and about which it is important to say a few words.

In the course of my fieldwork in Mexico, beginning when I was 23 years old, and with return visits interspersed with correspondence, Christmas cards, photographs and so on, I have obviously not only come to know people extremely well, but they have got to know me, and enduring friendships have developed with several women. In some senses I started with an advantage in that being the first *'extranjera'* (foreigner) many had conversed with, let alone had in their homes, I was welcomed as a source of information about *'el otro lado'* (the 'other side' – this actually means the USA where many thought I came from in the initial stages; being from Britain, however, turned out to be just as advantageous in that the country made the news fairly regularly with royal weddings, scandals and *'la dama de hiero'* ('iron lady') (in which there was always lively interest). Being a foreigner was also positive in that women said they felt freer to talk with someone who was not part of their everyday lives and with whom they had felt there was greater confidentiality vis-à-vis the information they were kind enough to share with me. Right from the start, many of my interviews were two-way exchanges in which respondents wanted to know as much about my life as I did about theirs, and their reactions, comments, and advice on various of my own experiences I regard as highly illuminating in the context of the present discussions. Indeed, in general terms (and this also applies to interviewees in Costa Rica, whom I have known since 1989, and in the Philippines since 1993), considerable interest has always been registered in my marital status, my family background, and, above all, whether I would come on my next field trip with a baby in tow. Although I was married briefly, and some of my Mexican respondents came to meet my now ex-husband, this has never been of quite as much concern as the idea that I would have a son or daughter. For me, this is not only strikingly expressive of the importance attached to family by women in the three countries, but class, professional status and income as well, even in the Philippines where childbirth out of wedlock is normally seen as extremely 'amoral'. For someone like me, a man was not important, because, as a professional, I could provide a child with all it needed and pay for help in the home. Beyond this, as a foreigner, I was from a place where it was perceived that conventional rules of social conduct did not matter so much. Yet while alternatives to marriage and children as a source of legitimacy are extremely limited for women in the case study localities, a substantial minority devise strategies to free themselves from, or to avoid, oppressive conjugal relationships, as revealed in the course of the next three chapters.

Querétaro, the setting of my first year in Mexico, lies on the eastern edge of the Bajío about 200 kilometres north of Mexico City (Figure 6.1). During the 1960s and 1970s it began attracting manufacturing firms, partly as a response to incentives offered by government decentralisation schemes, and by 1980 had become one of the most dynamic industrial centres in the country. Many factories which settled in the city's new greenfield industrial sites were subsidiaries of major multinational companies. Leading products were (and continue to be) metal-mechanical goods, motors and car parts, chemicals and para-chemicals, and processed foods, much based on automated, capital intensive production methods. Although it was hard-hit by economic crisis in 1982–83, Querétaro had recovered its fortunes by the end of the decade, and population growth remained high (between 6 and 7 per cent per annum) (see Chant, 1994b:215). By 1994, the population was in the region of 600,000 and over one-third of the labour force was employed in industry.

León, which is just over 300 kilometres north of Mexico City (Figure 6.1), is also an industrial city, but of a very different type to Querétaro. Whereas Querétaro might be described as a 'modern' industrial centre, production in León is of a more artesanal, 'traditional' nature. Although León's major expansion occurred in the 1960s, this was almost exclusively based on the labour-intensive sector of shoe-making. The latter is now such an important part of the economy that out of the 50 per cent of the economically-active population in León engaged in secondary activities, around 70 per cent are employed either in footwear production itself, or in a related industry (Chant, 1994b:213). As of 1989, León had over 3000 shoe production outlets and occupied 38 per cent of the national workforce in shoe-making (Morris and Lowder, 1992). Many footwear enterprises are small-scale workshops under local ownership, and even in the larger factories, levels of overseas investment are relatively minimal. In fact, lower dependence on foreign capital and the flexibility of small-scale production seemed to make León slightly more resistant to crisis than Querétaro in the first part of the 1980s, although some firms were forced into closure. The latter could explain why in-migration to the city has fallen in recent years, and why the city's population only grew from 1.4 to 1.6 million between 1986 and 1992 (Chant, 1994b:213).

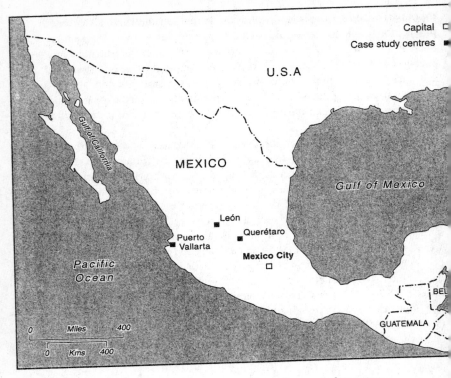

Figure 6.1: Mexico: Location of case study centres

Puerto Vallarta, the final Mexican case study locality (Figure 6.1), is distinguished from the other two centres by the fact that it is a tourist destination, where around three-quarters of the population are engaged in tertiary activities. It has traditionally represented for Jalisco, the state to which it belongs, and for Mexico as a whole, a major confluence for foreign investment and the generation of foreign exchange, with around half its visitors hailing from abroad, mainly from the USA (H. Ayuntamiento de Puerto Vallarta, 1992:11). During the 1970s and early 1980s, when the expansion of the resort was at its height, annual rates of population growth were in the region of 11–12 per cent, although these fell to just over 5 per cent by the 1990s. In 1992, its population stood at 250,000, and although it is still only around one-twentieth of the size of Guadalajara, the capital of Jalisco, it is actually the second biggest town in the state (*ibid.*:7).

Female household headship among the poor in Querétaro, León and Puerto Vallarta: key characteristics

On the basis of the major household interview surveys carried out in low-income settlements in each city (that is, Querétaro in 1982–83, and in León and Puerto Vallarta in 1986), women-headed households were 13.5 per cent of households in Querétaro, 10.4 per cent in León and 19.6 per cent in Puerto Vallarta, amounting to an overall average of 14.3 per cent.[2] With the exception of Puerto Vallarta, these figures are lower than the national census averages both for 1980 and 1990 (see Chapter 5), and may in part owe to the exclusion of certain types of household from the interview sampling frames (see Note 1).

Bearing in mind the fact that all households interviewed were family-based units, as with other studies of Mexican cities, the questionnaire surveys indicate a greater tendency for women-headed households to be extended (that is to consist of kin other than parents and children, generally daughters- or sons-in-law and their children) than male-headed units (55.9 per cent versus 28.3 per cent) (see also Chapter 1). Moreover, the number of relatives is greater in female- than male-headed extended households, being 3 to 4 as against 2. The mean number of co-resident children in households is just over 4, and does not differ radically between cities, nor according to male- or female-headship. The average size of female lone-parent units is 5.5 members, male-headed nuclear units 6.5, male-headed extended structures 8.2 and female-headed extended households 8.1 (see Chant, 1991a:204, Table 7.1). Female heads of household in all three cities are older than male heads, with a mean age of 45.3 years as against 40. In turn, female heads of extended households have an older average age than their counterparts in non-extended units (48.8 versus 41 years). Widows have the oldest average age across the three cities (52.9 years) and never-married female heads the lowest (37.8 years). In contrast to Costa Rica and the Philippines, the number of *de facto* female-headed households is minimal (only 2 out of a total of 34 women heads included in the interview survey across the three cities in 1986).

Except for León where 50 per cent of heads are widowed (which corresponds with national patterns – see Chapter 5), the other two cities reveal interesting differences in marital status. In Puerto Vallarta, for example, only 28 per cent of heads are widowed, whereas a further 28 per cent are divorced or separated, and the remainder are single (although around half had previously resided with a man). In Querétaro in 1982–83, even fewer female heads were widowed (20 per cent), whereas 15 per cent were unmarried, and as many as 65 per cent were separated.

Routes into female household headship in Querétaro, León and Puerto Vallarta

Non-marriage and 'marital breakdown' seem to be significant routes into female household headship in both Querétaro and Puerto Vallarta. Although elsewhere in Mexico, such as the town of Cuernavaca just south of the Federal District, LeVine (1993:95) reports that none of her older respondents or their mothers had elected to 'go it alone', some women in the case study cities do, albeit if their decisions are usually preceded by lengthy and/or soul-searching deliberation.

Separation: reasons and restraints
Exploration of the mechanisms of separation on the basis of in-depth interviews with a sub-sample of female lone parents in Querétaro in 1982–83 revealed that just over half (five out of nine) had been deserted by their husbands, in three cases because they had left to set up home with other women and in two cases had merely left the city 'to find work' and had never returned. The remaining four women, however, had taken the decision to leave their spouses on account of violence, infidelity and/or lack of financial commitment, notwithstanding that their religious beliefs had prevented them from so doing for some time, and those who had sought help from the church had usually been told: 'It's your cross and you have to bear it' (Chant, 1985b:646–7).

Religious counsel and/or pressure also dissuade women from leaving their spouses in the other cities. In Puerto Vallarta, for example, special sessions for women are held in the city's main Catholic church, where as one respondent, Fidelina, described: prayers are said *'por uno, por su familia de uno, y para que se cambie el esposo de uno'* ('prayers are said for oneself, one's family and in order that one's husband might change'). In Fidelina's case, attendance at the sessions coupled with the priest's assurance that she would get her rewards, if not in this life, in heaven, had been her only source of strength and comfort during six to seven years of trauma earlier on in her marriage when her husband David 'had things all his own way'. Despite giving her little money on which to subsist, David did not allow Fidelina to work, and when he discovered she had been doing some part-time cleaning, reacted by imposing a complete clampdown on her freedom. Aside from asking the neighbours to keep an eye on Fidelina's comings and goings, he even bribed their six-year-old son, David Junior, to report on his mother's activities when he was out at work (see also Chapter 8). Moreover, although David himself had mistresses, his routine rejoinder to Fidelina's questions about where he had been and who he had been with, was that she only interrogated him to deflect attention from the fact that she herself had been unfaithful! He even went as far as to blame Fidelina for a venereal disease he transmitted to her. It was only when Fidelina went against the advice of the church and threatened her husband with divorce on grounds of adultery that they finally reached a turning point in their relationship. The fear of losing his wife (and according to Fidelina, the even greater fear that she might meet someone else) has made him more responsible and less reluctant to let her go out to work.

Staying with one's husband 'for the sake of the children' is also stressed by many women as a reason for eschewing separation. One interviewee, Ana María, now a widow, but whose 46 years of married life she described as *'pura lágrima'* ('pure sorrow' [literally, tears]) on account of her husband Rogelio's wild moods and heavy drinking, declared that she had packed her bags and been on the point of leaving several times. However, when her children had 'tugged at her skirts' and 'pleaded with her to stay', she had always relented. Ana María claims that had it not been for the children, she would have walked out for good. At the same time, some women only find the strength to leave their husbands *because* of their children. For example, Lourdes was so worried about the example that her alcoholic husband was setting their five school-age children that she took them with her from their family home in Michoacán to a new life in Querétaro. Although relatives in the city gave Lourdes some assistance, holding down a full-time job as a kitchen assistant in a large hotel and putting all her children into new schools entailed considerable personal sacrifice. Yet every one of them has succeeded in getting a white-collar job, and Lourdes takes pride and pleasure in how things turned out: 'if I'd stayed with my husband, the children would have learned foul language, and the boys would probably have taken to drink'. Indeed even if things are hard to begin with, whether pragmatically or emotionally, women who do take the initiative to separate, are generally very glad they did so.

Lupe (Puerto Vallarta), for example, found the process of separation extremely difficult, especially from her second partner, Paco, with whom she lived in Guadalajara and with whom she was 'hopelessly in love'. According to Lupe, Paco was at one and the same time desirous and fearful of her good looks. Although Lupe would never have considered being unfaithful to him and repeatedly assured him of this, the only way Paco felt he could control his jealous passion was by seeing other women. As Lupe's distress at his infidelities mounted, she found herself becoming increasingly *'obsesiva'* (obsessive), and decided the only way to arrest the process was to terminate the relationship altogether. So, after their son was born, she moved out of their rented room and back to her mother's house with two other children from her first marriage. Lupe said that she cried every night for six months, and even two years later when she saw him again, her desire for him remained intense. None the less, finding the resolve to keep away from Paco and to protect herself from being hurt was aided by two factors. First, Lupe saw her primary responsibility as being towards her children, and while it was one thing if she suffered, she did not wish to impose her pain on them (when Paco upset her she became irritable, bad-tempered, and shouted at the children). Her second source of strength was that she saw herself as a young and reasonably attractive woman and imagined she might find a new love in the future, even if she was adamant that she would not go as far as to live with him.

Non-marriage: constraints and choices

Non-marriage as a route into female household headship seems to be most common in Puerto Vallarta. A major reason for women's unwillingness to commit themselves to wedlock (or sometimes even to reside with men) is local male notoriety for being 'spongers', 'ponces' or 'exploiters' ('padrotes', 'vividores de la mujer', 'convenencieros') who seek out women to live off. Distrust of men's motives for marriage means that women will often not accept proposals until they are in a position to make an informed judgement about whether or not they will be taken advantage of economically (see also Chapter 7). Respondents residing with men on an informal basis, for example, often talk about 'trying their partners out' before getting 'trapped' into marriage, whereas this is extremely rare in León or Querétaro where, in the case of first partners, at least, marriage is virtually always deemed preferable to cohabitation (see Chant, 1991a:173). Indeed, although women do remain single in these latter cities, the life histories of unmarried mothers reveal that it is usually because their partners or boyfriends already had wives and/or did not wish to marry. In Puerto Vallarta, however, it is preponderantly women who refuse wedlock, which, along with the fact that the resort draws in existing lone mothers and single women, contributes to high levels of female headship.

Inter-city differences in female household headship:
the influence of female labour force participation

One important factor giving rise to the above patterns in Puerto Vallarta is that women have traditionally had greater opportunities to generate their own income than in the other cities. As discussed earlier in the text, access to work is significant when female household heads, especially those with young children, may have few other means of support. Indeed, despite the fact that recession brought many married women into the labour force in Mexico during the 1980s (see Chapter 5), it is perhaps no surprise that female heads are still in a position where they are under greater obligation to find employment and have higher rates of labour force participation. Indeed, 65 per cent of female heads interviewed across the three cities in 1986 had an income-generating activity, compared with 53.5 per cent of female spouses, with most of the inactive heads being older and reliant on children's earnings.

Whereas women in the León and Querétaro settlements are mainly confined to low-paid, home-based, informal activities such as commerce, industrial piece-work, or taking in laundry, international tourism in Puerto Vallarta has created a wide and fairly lucrative variety of income-generating opportunities, with female residents in low-income settlements having access to formal occupations such as waitressing, restaurant kitchen work, and hotel chambermaiding (see Chant, 1991a: Chapter 4). Moreover, the spending power of foreign tourists together with the practice of tipping in tourism jobs means that women's average earnings in Puerto Vallarta are higher than in the other cities and closer to male wages (women in Puerto Vallarta in 1986 earned a little over 50 per cent of male earnings, as opposed to 30–40 per cent in León and Querétaro). In this light it is perhaps no surprise that among migrant female heads who had come to Puerto Vallarta as adults, 50 per cent moved to the city *as* lone mothers, whereas this applied to only 14 per cent of the female heads interviewed in the questionnaire survey in Querétaro, and none in León. Higher levels of female headship in Puerto Vallarta are thus partially explained by the fact that the resort attracts women in need of work to support children (see Chant, 1991a: Chapter 5).

As for women who grow up in the city or who arrive as young single women, women's actual (and perceived) access to employment seems to increase the likelihood of non-marriage and/or female headship in two main ways. One is that materially women are better able to fend for themselves. As one respondent, Dolores (now a widow) told me: 'Women can always find work here, so they don't really need a man to support them', adding, 'Like you Sylvia, what would they want a man for, unless they are really in love?' The other main set of considerations revolves around the fear of being saddled with an economic burden, whether because men abuse the situation where wives work by not working themselves or keeping more of their wages for their own use,[3] and/or by using marriage as a means of laying greater claim to women's earnings. For these kinds of reasons, Elba (38 years), who juggles numerous economic activities such as domestic service, pig-breeding and home-based food retail, withheld from legalising her relationship with her partner Teodosio for 13 years, even though they had had four children by this time. The only reason she finally gave in to Teodosio's demands was because in 1990 the *Registro Civil* (Civil Registry) arranged a free mass wedding in the community, and once one couple decided to take advantage of the opportunity, this had a domino effect. Whatever the case, whether women in Puerto Vallarta are single, married or cohabiting, paid work seems to be very much part of their lives and tends to translate into greater power within relationships, and greater ability to dissolve them if the need arises.

Added to the perception that cohabitation is seen to be a rather insecure arrangement for economic support, the fact that employment among women is less established in León and Querétaro possibly makes them more susceptible to accepting marriage proposals and/or resistant to leaving households in which men have traditionally been the main, if not only, providers. In Querétaro, for instance, although many wives had entered the labour force due to pressure on household incomes during the crisis of the early to mid-1980s, by 1992, some had withdrawn, either because husbands had gone back to work or sons and daughters had taken employment, and/or because they did not feel it was worth it to work for low wages (see Chant 1994b). Beyond this, a number of men still subscribe to the ideal that wives shoud not work (*ibid.*; see also Willis, 1993:71 on Oaxaca). Dependence on men of a practical and ideological nature is thus quite heavily inscribed in Querétaro. Even two mature 'long-term' female household heads had spent time out of the labour force between 1986 and 1992 due to transient involvement with men. Ana, for example, who was 50 in 1992, had given up a regular job as a municipal roadsweeper in the years 1989 through 1991 because the Canadian ('El Señor Alfredo Campbell') who had fathered her four children and abandoned her 15 years earlier, returned to Mexico from Montreal following the death of his wife. Because Campbell was by this time crippled with Parkinsons Disease, Ana gave up working to nurse him on a full-time basis. They survived during this period on his pension and a small reserve of savings. The other female head, Socorro, had given up her roadsweeping job in 1990 for one year when a new partner had moved in. This was in part so she could '*atenderle bién*' ('look after him properly'), with the other major consideration being that, as a fully-qualified welder, he earned a fairly substantial income (Chant, 1994b:221). Previously (in 1986), Socorro had considered the possibility of moving in with a widower 20 years her senior. Although she felt little physical attraction for him, she described him as a 'nice man' who was relatively well-off and had assets that could benefit her family. These factors could help to account for the limited feminisation of household headship in Querétaro between the 1980s and 1990s, with the only new additions to female-headed households during among this time being through widowhood or male migration to the USA.

Inter-city differerences in female household headship:
the influence of temporary male labour migration
Leading on from the above, it is not only female labour force participation which affects female headship in the Mexican study cities, but male

employment as well. Given fluctuations in employment in Puerto Valarta between the high and low season, and, more importantly, levels of tipping (which can more than double wages), men often migrate to rural areas to do agricultural work in the leaner months of May through September. Although seasonal male migration is much less marked than in northwest Costa Rica (see later), it could contribute to weakening ties between partners.

Inter-city differerences in female household headship:
the influence of neolocality and migrant status

Another factor potentially contributing to higher rates of female headship in Puerto Vallarta is neolocality and its association with greater informality in male–female relationships (see Chapter 4). Despite the fact that there are no differences in the migrant status of women in male- and female-headed households, 88 per cent of adult women were migrants in Puerto Vallarta in 1986, compared with 68 per cent in León and 58 per cent in Querétaro in 1982–83 (Chant, 1984a:165). The significance of these differences is heightened by the fact that the first major wave of in-migration to Puerto Vallarta did not commence until the 1970s (around 10–15 years later than in Querétaro and León). Since there has not been the same 're-grouping' among members of kin groups as in the other two cities, anonymity in Puerto Vallarta is more assured and may have permitted slightly greater relaxation of 'conventional' behaviour. As one respondent, Lupe, observed, when daughters are away from home and from the interference of parents and relatives, they feel freer to have relationships with the opposite sex, to move in with boyfriends on an informal basis, and/or even to have children out of wedlock. Indeed, the idea of moving to a city where nobody knew her had been very appealing to Lupe herself, who came to Puerto Vallarta as a lone mother. Aside from her confidence about getting a job in a tourist resort, Lupe felt that she would be more accepted than in the conservative city of Guadalajara where she previously resided, and, crucially, that her relatives would not be breathing down her neck and trying to persuade her to go back to her husband.

Inter-city differerences in female household headship:
the influence of international tourism

A final and related factor which seems to be connected with a greater incidence of female household headship in Puerto Vallarta is the relaxed and cosmopolitan atmosphere that accompanies its status as an international tourist destination. As a centre of leisure and 'holiday fun' (routinely associated with less restrained and/or less conservative behaviour), Puerto Vallarta is perceived to be a reaonably sympathetic environment for women on their own. Another important factor is that women come into contact in one form or another with foreign female tourists, whose relative economic and social freedom provokes interest, comment and seems in many cases to exert an influence on women's own behaviour and/or aspirations (Chant, 1991a:173). For example, women in the settlements frequently talk about how they would like to be able to travel and go out alone, not to mention how much they approve of *gringas'* casual modes of dress. Indeed, aside from the fact that Puerto Vallarta's tropical climate makes it difficult to wear the concealing blouses, cardigans, long skirts, pinafores and so on that women do in the central highlands, shorts and sleeveless tops are donned by older as well as younger age groups, and social mixing with foreigners of the opposite sex is increasingly occurring in discos, fast-food restaurants and beach bars. There is also greater awareness (if not tolerance) of alternatives to heterosexuality, even if some women claim that there are so many *'maricones'* (gay men) in Puerto Vallarta that they worry for their sons.

On balance, while rigorous comparative evaluation of reasons behind variations in the levels and nature of female household headship between these three Mexican cities is not possible on the basis of the small and uneven size of the original surveys, and the fact that they were undertaken in different years, it would seem that female labour force participation has an important role to play, with additional factors being distance from kin, exposure to or interaction with women from other cultures, informality of unions and male seasonal migration. These combine in different ways in the different areas with gender inequalities in male–female relations, including male control over women's freedom, the indulgence of men in activities such as drinking and infidelity, and the acquisition or abuse of women's earnings. All of these cast a destabilising influence on conjugal relationships, and while in Mexico men are preponderantly the ones to 'walk out', in situations where women have greater ability to take their own decisions (especially where they have access to jobs), they are more prone to leave husbands, or to take pre-emptive action by eschewing marriage altogether. Those who make such decisions are also prone to find the experience somewhat empowering.

The Mexican state and female household headship

What seems to have little effect on influencing women in any way in any of the case study localities is the state and legislation. Most women, whether heads or spouses, were unaware of any law or programme that helped women, and were sceptical about Mexican politics and government intervention in low-income neighbourhoods in general. Although many had heard of DIF and Solidaridad (see Chapter 5), very few had heard of *Mujeres en Solidaridad*, and those who had come into contact with a *Solidaridad* programme were highly dubious about objectives and effectiveness. Some women declared that there were no laws to help women, but there ought to be, with the need for some form of family allowance being particularly stressed by female heads. Women also felt that while it was more likely nowadays for men who beat their wives to be put in jail for a night or two, penalties for male violence should be stronger. There are one or two cases (such as that of Fidelina), where women have learned about their rights in the Mexican Civil Code, and have thought about petitioning for divorce. As for demanding maintenance from ex-partners, however, women seem either to be ignorant of their entitlements, reluctant to exercise them, and/or within a context where once-and-for-all desertion by men is commonplace, have few expectations of success. Having said this, an additional and important factor is pride. Socorro (Querétaro), for example, who discovered that her first partner had another 'wife' and three children, was so furious at the betrayal that she 'didn't want to touch his money'. As for her second partner (to whom Socorro was aware of her status as mistress from the outset), sexual relations became the basis of receiving cash for the children after the union broke up, and in the end Socorro did not deem the exchange worthwhile, even though he could sometimes be quite 'generous'. In some instances therefore, working outside the law can be a more effective strategy of resistance to attempts by absent fathers to perpetuate control over women through child support.

COSTA RICA

Introduction to Costa Rican case study areas

Guanacaste province, where the Costa Rican case study centres of Liberia, Cañas and Santa Cruz are situated (see Figure 6.2), is otherwise known (mainly for planning purposes) as the Chorotega Region, after its original indigenous inhabitants. Guanacaste has traditionally been one of the least urbanised areas of the country because most of its land is given over to cattle ranching, and rice and sugar production. These activities have been financially important for the province since large-scale government-backed promotion in the 1950s, but their low labour requirements (except seasonally in the case of sugar), mean that Guanacaste continues to be a net exporter of population to other parts of the country. Indeed, while Guanacaste covers around one-fifth of Costa Rica's land area, it has less than one-tenth of the national population (Chant, 1991c:240). The region also has levels of unemployment around twice the national average and scores poorly on indicators such as infant mortality (*ibid.*). In 1993, median monthly earnings in Guanacaste were only 73 per cent of those at a national level (DGEC, 1993a: Table 36). Although tourism is now expanding in the area, the inland towns which provided the context of research on gender, migration and employment in 1989 tend to be heavily dependent on agriculture in the surrounding hinterlands as a source of livelihood, especially for the male populace (see also Chapter 7). Fieldwork for this project entailed a random questionnaire survey with a total of 350 households in the three towns in April and May of 1989 and follow-up in-depth interviews with 70 households in July of that year (see Note 1). Subsequent fieldwork (in 1992 and 1994), as in Mexico, consisted of further in-depth interviews with an overall total of 20 of the original respondents oriented towards the impacts of economic crisis, household trajectories and perceptions of female headship.

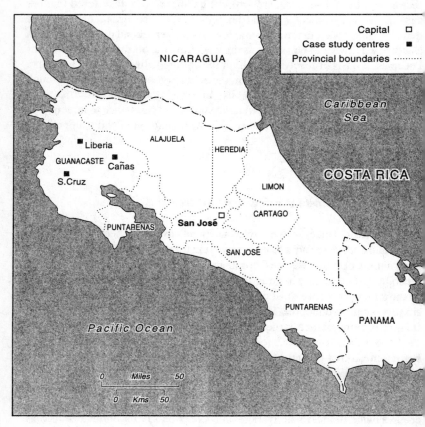

Figure 6.2: Costa Rica: Location of case study centres

The biggest of the three study centres and capital of the province is the town of Liberia, which in 1993 had a population of 30,191.[4] Here, less than one-third of the population work in the primary sector, partly because the main rural activities aside from cattle ranching in the immediate environs are rice and sorghum (both of which are highly mechanised), although there are also crops with higher labour requirements (albeit seasonal) such as sugar and cotton. Nearly half of Liberia's labour force are engaged in tertiary activities, mainly because the town has various provincial-level administrative functions and also houses Guanacaste's major health and educational facilities. This has drawn in professionals who, in turn, have created a demand for services lower down the hierarchy, such as domestic and personal service. What little industry there is, is confined to agro-processing. Despite the fact that 11.7 per cent of the town's labour force was recorded as out of work in the 1984 census, the town's annual population growth rate was actually greater than the national growth rate during the period 1973–84, being 2.7 per cent as against 2.3 per cent (INVU, 1985).

Cañas, lying 40 kilometres to the southeast of Liberia (Figure 6.2), also has higher than average growth rates, partly owing to its strategic location and route networks to other parts of the province. In 1993 it had a population of 22,144.[5] Commerce is an important employer of the local populace, with Cañas's municipal market, which specialises in the sale of fresh fruit, vegetables and flowers, being one of the largest in the region. More important still however, and employing over 40 per cent of the workforce, is agriculture, primarily sugar cane, and secondarily rice, sorghum and cotton. The town had an unemployment rate of 7.6 per cent in 1984, which was substantially lower than in Guanacaste as a whole (10.7 per cent), and population grew at a rate higher (2.8 per cent) than the national average during 1973–84.

Santa Cruz (Figure 6.2) is the smallest case study centre,[6] with a low growth rate and the highest incidence of poverty and unemployment. Over 50 per cent of the economically-active population work in agriculture, although the diversity of crops that have traditionally provided employment is being threatened by the continued expansion of stock raising and conversion of arable land to pasture (Chant, 1991c:242). As it is, in 1984, the town had a staggeringly high level of unemployment (14.4 per cent).

Female household headship among the poor in Liberia, Cañas and Santa Cruz: key characteristics

Compared with the case study localities in the other countries, the 1989 questionnaire survey reveals that the three towns in Guanacaste have the highest overall level of female household headship at 28.6 per cent, notwithstanding that 35 per cent of the women in this group in April/May 1989 were heading households on a *de facto* basis due to men working in other areas (see Chapter 1). Indeed, the figure for *de jure* female-headed households (18.6 per cent) is about the same as census figures for Guanacaste province as a whole (18.3 per cent) (the census excludes *de facto* household heads unless partners are habitually away from the household for more than six consecutive months of the year, in which case it does not disaggregate them from *de jure* female heads).

As for the community surveys in individual towns, Liberia has the lowest overall proportion of female heads (25 per cent, 41 per cent of whom are *de facto*), followed by Santa Cruz (30 per cent, 20.8 per cent of whom are *de facto*), and then Cañas (30.8 per cent, 29.6 per cent of whom are *de facto*). Although these are not particularly large variations, the lower total and *de jure* percentage in Liberia might be explained by the fact that more openings in secondary and tertiary sector employment (which offer more regular work than agriculture) place slightly less pressure on men to migrate elsewhere to find employment and, in this way, make for more enduring relationships between couples (see below). In terms of attitudes, experiences and routes into female headship on the part of respondents, however, there seemed to be very little difference between the towns, with the pattern of men engaging in seasonal labour migration being fairly generalised throughout the province (Ramírez Boza, 1987:22). For these reasons, it is apt to treat the towns collectively rather than individually. Indeed despite the fact that 14.9 per cent of respondents in the questionnaire survey were of Nicaraguan origin (most of whom were living in Liberia or Cañas), a similar proportion (30.8 per cent) of this group consisted of households headed by women, and processes, patterns and corollaries of female headship were virtually indistinguishable from those of the Costa Rican population (see Chant, 1991b).[7]

Compared with the three Mexican cities (as well as the Philippine study localities – see later), levels of female household headship in Guanacaste are high, which might in part owe to the fact that households of all tenures and composition were included in the questionnaire survey. However, although this brought in nuclear compound households, single women and grandmother-headed households, altogether these were less than 10 per cent of all households (see Chant, 1991b:64). Whatever, the number of *de facto* units in all three centres is substantial and undoubtedly owes in part to the fact that the major questionnaire survey took place in the months of April and May in 1989. This is the period immediately after the sugar harvest when men begin to move to other areas in search of employment. At the time of the survey, male heads were absent from 32 households and were spread over six of Costa Rica's seven provinces, generally in farm employment. Even if half the men were working in another part of Guanacaste, they were usually too far away to return on less than a fortnightly basis (which is when most get paid), and while the majority had only been away from home for two months or less, nearly one-fifth had been away for over a year (Chant, 1991b:67). Although not all men find work immediately, 82 per cent of *de facto* female heads reported receiving remittances. Notwithstanding that data on spouses' remittances were aggregated with remittances from others (for example non-resident children), the fact that between them these made up over three-quarters (77 per cent) of their average income (compared with only one-third in *de jure* female-headed households), indicates the importance of external income receipts for *de facto* female heads (see also Chapter 7).

As for their characteristics, female-headed households overall have slightly fewer co-resident children (2.5) than their male-headed counterparts (3.2), although the average size of female-headed households was 4.4, just over one less than male-headed units (5.8), which is similar to the Mexican (and Philippine) case study localities. As in Mexico, female-headed households have a greater tendency to be extended in composition (34 per cent) than male-headed units (25 per cent). Women are common in extended components, with 74 per cent of all extended households containing at least one female relative. The average size of extended components in female-headed units is 2.3, and in male-headed units 1.4.

Excluding grandmother heads, the average age of female heads is 42 years, about 7 years older than their counterparts in male-headed units, and 5 years older than the overall average (37.2 years) for male household heads themselves. As in Mexico, female heads of extended units have an older average age (48.7 years) than female heads of one-parent households (37 years). Single women (9 per cent of all female heads) have a mean age of 52 years, and grandmother heads of household (5.1 per cent of female heads) 67 years.

Grandmother-headed households

Grandmother-headed units in Guanacaste tend to emerge when daughters who have become separated from their partners (*compañeros*) or husbands have to migrate elsewhere in the country to find work (Chant, 1991b:66). For example, Justina, a Nicaraguan immigrant in Cañas, took responsibility for raising her grandson more or less from birth until the age of nine. In order to escape being beaten by the father of the child, Justina's youngest daughter Eugenia, then aged 16, left him when the boy was 8 months old. Since it was so difficult to find well-paid work in Cañas, Eugenia migrated to work as an apprentice in a tailor's shop in San José. Since she had to live on her employer's premises, she left her son with Justina and remitted money back for his upkeep as well as visiting him at least once a month. Two years ago, however, she linked up with another man in San José and took her son back to give him schooling in the capital. Now on her own, Justina feels sad since she had grown very accustomed to having her grandson around, declaring: *'uno los quiere como los propios hijos de uno'* ('one loves them like one's own children'). Indeed, loneliness can itself be a motive for the formation of grandmother-headed households. Elderly widows, for example, often appreciate having a grandchild to keep them company, as is the case with Juanita in Santz Cruz, whose daughter actually lives nearby but is happy for her son to be part of Juanita's household. This also alleviates the pressure on her own, overcrowded, accommodation. As it is, widows are a relatively small proportion of *de jure* female heads (24 per cent), whereas 9 per cent are single and the remainder (two-thirds), are separated.

Early consensual unions

The preponderance of separated women presents a different picture to the national pattern, where single women are the largest group and separated women the smallest (see Chapter 5). This could relate to the prevalence of early and informal unions among the population in Guanacaste, with 45.5 per cent of female heads and spouses in the questionnaire survey having entered a co-resident relationship with a man by the age of 16, and 88 per cent by the age of 20 (Chant, 1991b:74).[8] Courtships in Guanacaste are usually very brief (seldom more than one or two months), and once people start to have sexual relations, they are usually encouraged to move in with one another (if not to marry) by their parents. Although most respondents recognise this as premature in terms of assessing compatibility with partners, they explain it in terms of the fact that having sexual relations under one's parents' roof shows a *'falta de respeto'* (lack of respect). In the interests of 'decency', therefore, it is preferable for daughters to move out. Moving out also shifts the potential burden of child support from parents to partners. Only a fraction of these teenage relationships endure, however, let alone culminate in marriage. The impacts of this are undoubtedly reflected in the fact that whereas 73.3 per cent of women in conjugal unions at a national level are formally married, this applies to only 30.9 per cent of women in partnerships in the Guanacaste settlements (Chant, 1991b:74).

The prevalence of consensual unions in Guanacaste may also be influenced by historical antecedents. The original inhabitants of the area (the Chorotegas), did not practice formal marriage, and, given the peripheral location of the province, the imprint of Spanish customs was relatively weak (Chant, 1991b:74). However, another crucial element is male out-migration. Although male migration is clearly associated directly with *de facto* female headship, indirectly it seems to have some bearing both on the informality of unions and to conjugal discord which, in conjunction, often lead to *de jure* headship (see also below).

Male out-migration and de facto female headship

Regular, and often prolonged, periods of separation associated with male out-migration in Guanacaste place a variety of stresses on couples. The husband of Concepción, a 47-year-old Nicaraguan migrant living in Liberia, for example, spends only about six months in a year in the town, picking cotton between November and February, and cutting cane between February and late April/early May. Even though Concepción has five children and has had various relatives to stay for periods since their arrival in Cañas in 1978, she gets extremely lonely when Julio is away and dreads his annual departures. Although her eldest child is now 15 and, in 1994, Concepción's parents and brother were living with her, when the children were younger and Concepción was the sole adult in the household, she was constantly worried about '*ladrones*' (thieves). The feeling of being '*desprotegida*' ('unprotected') was exacerbated by the fact that their shack did not have a door. In order to waylay nocturnal intruders, they piled up furniture behind a curtain covering the entrance when darkness fell. Aside from this, Concepción's work became more arduous during Julio's absence because she had no-one to go collecting firewood with her. There was also the worry that he might not get a job and be able to send money home straight away. In addition, although she has a fairly happy marriage with Julio, she feels it is unhealthy for husbands and wives to spend time apart because this can sow the seeds of mistrust, and in the case of the women left behind means that there is a '*puerta libre*' (open door) through which other men might walk and take advantage of a potential sexual encounter. With the 'open door' motif also coming up as one of Concepción's primary fears during Julio's time away from home (especially at night), it seems that concerns not only about sexual infidelity, but the predatory sexuality of other men (and women's possible powerlessness to resist), might also be important in engendering anxiety about female headship.

Serial monogamy

Most women however, at least on the surface, claim that the hardest aspect of their partners' absences is lack of ready cash and/or guaranteed remittances. Indeed, whether couples adjust to a situation of repeated separation by keeping sentiments to a minimum, or whether some poor women rely so much upon male income that this overshadows the affective dimensions of relationships, men are more prone to be evaluated in economic rather than emotional terms, notwithstanding clear interconnections between the phenomena (for example, loving husbands are more likely to be reliable economically). In cases where migrant partners do not communicate for several months or rumours get back that they have had affairs or set up home with other women, women left behind usually attempt to find another man, and often get pregnant as a means of trying to retain them. Unfortunately this strategy is not always successful. Indeed, although women seldom reside with more than three male partners over the course of the lifecycle, they may have children by four or five different men, which probably helps to explain that women in the Guanacasteco settlements usually have five to six children (and more births but many die), which is well above the national average (see Chapters 5 and 8).

Routes into female headship in Liberia, Cañas and Santa Cruz

Informality of sexual unions and repeated male out-migration are undoubtedly important in helping to explain the fact that the most common route to *de jure* female household headship in Guanacaste is separation, but it may well exert an influence on non-marriage as well insofar as men are not accustomed to taking responsibility for their offspring.

Non-marriage and male desertion

In cases where women remain single, it is almost invariably men who play the determining role, usually through desertion (and often before the birth of the babies they have fathered). Although she is now '*ajuntada*' (living with a man), for example, Maiela (Liberia) was forced into having sexual relations at the age of 13 with a door-to-door pig seller. The man had been a regular caller at the house for six months and had been 'respectful', but after her mother died and Maiela was alone in the house during the day, he 'took advantage'. Two months after their first intercourse, Maiela worked out she was pregnant and on giving him the news he promptly extricated himself from the '*noviazgo*' (courtship/relationship). Maiela was nearly thrown out of her home by her remaining family, and one brother who was training to be a priest called her a 'harlot' and 'sinner' and has never spoken to her again. Maila describes it as fortunate that she met Victor, her present partner, a year later and that he suggested they move in together. A few years later they had their own child and they have been with each other since (23 years). Relationships of this length are uncommon however, with break ups usually owing, in the words of women, to 'irresponsibility' on the part of men.

Separation: constraints and choices

Stories of separation in Costa Rica pick up many of the threads in those recounted by respondents in Mexico, especially male economic neglect, domestic violence, and philandering. The latter, in the Costa Rican context, is often linked with men's periodic absences from home, but not always as a result of labour migration. For example, Maura, a 47-year-old resident of Liberia, had a 19-year relationship with a man called Carlos beginning at the age of 18. Although Maura had been keen to get married, Carlos saw marriage and living together as one and the same, and because, in Maura's words, 'a woman has no power to force a man', she had to conform with his decision. After they had been together four years and Maura had given birth to a couple of children, Carlos started coming home late and would sometimes disappear from the house for two to three weeks at a time. Maura suspected he was seeing other women ('like most men in Costa Rica'), but what affected her most was the lack of money to light a fire or to buy food. In order to get through these difficult intervals, Maura would have to take short-term jobs, usually as a domestic servant. Unfortunately, when Carlos returned and learned that Maura had been working, he would fly into a rage because she had been 'out on the streets' and undoubtedly in contact with other men. Arguments would lead to beatings, and on one occasion Carlos knocked two of Maura's teeth out. The downside of 'making up' in the aftermath of violence was usually a week or so of love-making that would lead to pregnancy and, in turn, make Maura even more dependent on his support. Despite these conflicts, Carlos did not want to leave Maura, and instead threatened her with all manner of consequences about what would happen to her if *she* left him. One of the few solutions Maura could think of to end the vicous cycle of conflict, reconciliation, pregnancy and vulnerability was to get herself sterilised. When she took this step, however, Carlos 'walked out of the door for the last time', accusing Maura of having had the operation as a means of allowing her to be sexually unfaithful.

Although men's '*mal comportamiento*' ('bad behaviour' – a catch-all for varying combinations of infidelity, alcoholism, financial irresponsibility and violence), is usually deemed a major factor in accounts of conjugal dissolution, it is crucial to note, as in Mexico, that it is not always men who leave women. Indeed, on the basis of the total number of separations (48) documented in semi-structured interviews with 70 households across the three Guanacasteco localities, 58.3 per cent had involved women making the move.[9] Layla (Cañas), for example, had taken the initative with both of her former co-resident partners, and had chosen not to move in with a third because she could not bear to undergo the experience of any further maltreatment at male hands.

Layla's first partner (with whom she had three children), worked on a banana plantation in the province of Limón but got caught up with the law for dealing *marijuana*. Once the police started pursuing him in earnest, Layla consented to marry him (after 10 years cohabitation) to give him greater 'respectability'. Shortly afterwards however, she discovered he had been seeing another woman. Layla challenged him with what she knew, and by the afternoon of the same day had installed herself and her children on the patio of her parents-in-law's house and began looking for work. Although his 'habit' of attacking her with a breadknife had made her consider leaving him in the past, infidelity was the last straw, so, despite the recency of their marriage she never considered reconciliation. Two years later, Layla met and moved in with a second man. Unfortunately he was also involved in drugs and ended up being jailed five months into their relationship. On finding out that he too had been unfaithful, Layla gave him 15 days to prove he could 'behave himself on coming out of prison. When he transgressed (as Layla anticipated he would), she left him. In desperation to get over the blow, she slept with another man who made her pregnant with a fourth child. Knowing him to be a womaniser, however, Layla never consented to live with him, although she does accept his occasional financial handouts for their now three-year old daughter. One possible reason why women in Layla's position are prepared to act so decisively in terms of ending relationships is because the generally transient presence of men in households in a region of high labour migration means that women are more accustomed to being alone and/or to asserting their authority than they would be if men were constant resident (Chant, 1991b:76–7).

While, at a personal level, reasons for separation and non-marriage given by women in Guanacaste are in many senses similar to those in Mexico, and owe largely to patterns of gender relations characterised by *machismo* and sexual double standards, in terms of related and intervening influences there are clearly differences. As already mentioned, seasonal out-migration of men and a high incidence of informal unions seem to be key to high levels of female headship in Costa Rica. Although similar processes may be discerned in Puerto Vallarta, women's own labour force participation seems to have less of an influence on female household headship in Guanacastec towns. Although, as in Mexico, female heads of household are more economically active than their counterparts in male-headed units (45 per cent compared with 34 per cent, with *de jure* heads having an economic activity rate of 50 per cent), it is significant that migrant women in Guanacaste (about two-thirds of the adult female population in the three towns) have not come so much for reasons of work (whether for their spouses or themselves) as for the better position of the centres in terms of transport and communication to other parts of the country, and for educational facilities, health care and other social services (see Chant, 1991c). Moreover, although women see themselves as having greater opportunities for employment than men, at least on a year-round basis, the openings available are far from profitable. The vast majority of women are engaged either in domestic service or home-based food production or trade, and their earnings are well below those of men (male weekly earnings across the three towns in 1989 averaged 2771 *colones* [$34.6 US], whereas those of women were only 1370 *colones* [$17.1 US] in full-time jobs, and only 1053 *colones* [$13.2 US] when part-time/occasional women workers are included).[10] Beyond this, pay for most jobs is lower than that for equivalent activities in other parts of the country. For example, wages for domestic service in Guanacaste are only one-third to one-half those that can be earned in the capital San José (Quiróz *et al.*, 1984:69).[11] The main reason that older women with children do not migrate to work in other areas (even if some of their daughters do), is because employers require them to reside on the premises, or because it is more costly to live in the capital (Chant, 1991b:71). Thus even if female heads seem to be a greater proportion of migrant households (32.4 per cent) than non-migrant households (22.7 per cent), with 73.5 per cent of all *de jure* female heads and *de facto* female heads respectively being migrants rather than natives of the towns, as against around 65 per cent for the adult female population in general (see Chant, 1991b:57–9), female heads had rarely come alone to the towns but instead had been accompanied by husbands or other relatives.

The state and female household headship in Guanacaste

Although around one-third of *de jure* female heads in Guanacaste receive government social welfare payments of some description, and in many respects the Costa Rican state could be argued to be more active in respect of women's rights than in Mexico (see Chapter 5), it can hardly be said that the government plays a major role in underpinning female headship in material terms. Less than 15 per cent of mothers as a whole in the communities receive child allowances or free milk, for example, and only 6 out of 16 widows report receipt of an old age or widow's pension. Moreover, according to Maiela (Liberia), applying for state support is not only a humiliating process, but the excessive red tape involved makes it exhausting as well. She herself has never pursued a claim for a '*pensión familiar*' because one has to turn up at the offices of the Social Welfare Ministry with old clothes on, queue for hours, and often go back the following day and still come away without seeing anyone.[12]

As for the possible impacts of progressive gender legislation on increasing women's prospects of assertiveness and/or independence in Guanacaste, effects

again seem to be fairly limited. For example, many women were not aware
of any law in favour of female rights (notably the Social Equality Law), and
Marta (Liberia) declared that if there was one: '*No se nota, yo sigo siendo
igual aquí*' ('You wouldn't really notice, life's still very much the same for
me'). By the same token, some women feel that the Equality Law has had
an important effect on both men and women, having made men more fearful
of acting violently with their wives in case of police intervention, and having
given women greater awareness of their rights. Ernestina (Cañas), for
example, thinks that violence is decreasing as a result of the law, and Marielos
(Liberia) believes that although educated women knew how to 'defend
themselves' already, the Equality Law has done a lot for poor women in terms
of sensitising them to problems of gender subordination and how they might
tackle them (although she did not specify precise ways).

Although divorce legislation is perhaps less relevant in an area where there
are low rates of formal marriage, it is significant that even though women
of limited means are technically entitled to legal aid in Costa Rica (see
Chapter 5), in outlying regions such as Guanacaste this is not apparent.
Even when divorces are relatively straightforward (that is, on the basis of
mutual consent), the costs are usually prohibitive. Although Layla (Cañas),
for example, would like to officially sever ties with her husband and he is
willing to go ahead with the process, he has also stipulated that Layla will
have to pay for it. Unfortunately, with legal fees in the region of $160 US
(equivalent to about six weeks of expenditure on food for Layla and her three
co-resident children), she cannot possibly entertain the prospect, unless, in
her own words, she wins the lottery!

As for the enforcement of child maintenance payments, this again seems
weak. Only a minority of women (under 20 per cent) in Guanacaste receive
maintenance from the fathers of their children. Those that do have ex
partners who wish to retain some kind of contact with their offspring and
according to various respondents, men see their donation of child support
as 'buying them the right'. In some cases, women eschew maintenance in
order to retain anonymity and/or independence. For example, for one female
head, Martilina, the desire to cut off contact with a husband who was having
an affair with a prostitute outweighed her desperation for cash. In fact, to
ensure complete severance of ties she left home with her five children and
as many belongings as they could carry in the dead of night. Her decision
to move to Liberia (rather than another part of Nicoya where they were living
at the time) was so he would stand less chance of ascertaining her whereabouts

THE PHILIPPINES

Introduction to the Philippine case study areas

The three case study areas in the Philippines (Cebu City, Lapu-Lapu City and Boracay) are located in the Visayas, which forms the middle group of islands in the country, wedged between Luzon to the north (where the capital, Manila, is situated) and Mindanao to the south (see Figure 6.3). For planning purposes the area is divided into three entities: the Eastern Visayas (NEDA Planning Region VIII); the Central Visayas (NEDA Planning Region VII), and the Western Visayas (NEDA Planning Region VI). Of these latter two regions, the Central Visayas (home to Cebu and Lapu-Lapu) is by far the more prosperous, having been designated by the national government as the Philippines' second major gateway for international trade and travel. As a predominantly industrial and commercial region, it has maintained high growth rates since the mid-to-late 1980s. The Western Visayas (where Boracay is situated), on the other hand, has a predominantly agricultural base, and as of the late 1980s was the second poorest region in the country after Bicol (Region V) (see Chant and McIlwaine, 1995a).

My research in the Visayas aimed to explore the interrelationships between female employment, migration and household organisation and involved a random questionnaire survey with women in 240 households and 30 in-depth semi-structured interviews in one low-income community in each case study locality in 1993. A total of 77 workers (male and female) from selected occupational groups (export-manufacturing, sex work and tourism in Cebu, export-manufacturing in Lapu-Lapu and formal and informal tourism workers in Boracay) were also interviewed with reference to their household arrangements (see also Note 1). Follow-up semi-structured interviews with particular reference to the images, meanings and practical and social implications of female headship were held with a sub-sample of ten of the original household survey respondents in Boracay in 1995.

Cebu City is the Philippines' second most important city, with a population of around 650,000. It is a port and major centre of trade, finance, and manufacturing (particularly rattan furniture, wood products and shellcraft). It is also home to one of the largest sex industries outside Manila, comprising a wide range of 'hospitality' establishments such as girlie bars, massage parlours, brothels and striptease venues (Chant and McIlwaine, 1995a). As of 1992, the Cebu City STD-AIDS Detection Centre estimated that there were 84 establishments servicing the sex industry (Law, forthcoming). Lapu-Lapu City, which forms part of the larger Cebu metropolis (Metro Cebu) (Figure 6.3), has a population of around 150,000 with its economic hub in

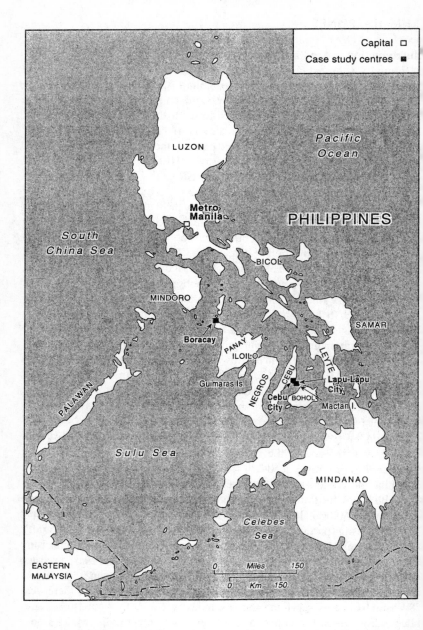

Figure 6.3: Philippines: Location of case study centres

the Mactan Island Export Processing Zone which employs over 15,000 people in a range of multinational export processing plants (mainly garments and electronics). Boracay Island, in the Western Visayas, has a population of around 8000 inhabitants and is the fastest-growing tourist resort in the Philippines. It is distinguished from other international tourism destinations in the country by its determined efforts to block the emergence of a formal sex industry.

Female household headship among the poor in Cebu, Lapu-Lapu and Boracay: key characteristics

The questionnaire survey of 240 households across the three localities showed that 14.6 per cent are headed by women (17 per cent in Cebu, 15 per cent in Boracay and 11.6 per cent in Lapu-Lapu).[13] In the cases of Cebu and Boracay, these figures are higher than locality-wide data from the 1990 census, which recorded the proportion of female-headed households as 14 per cent in Cebu, 13.9 per cent in Boracay,[14] and 11.6 per cent in Lapu-Lapu. The discrepancy owes largely to the fact that *de facto* female headship was recorded in the survey data, but remains under-recorded in the census, since unless men are away continuously for over a year, they are entered as household heads.

On the basis of the survey data, nearly two-thirds (65.7 per cent) of the overall total of 35 female-headed households in the localities are *de jure* female-headed units (that is, women who are widowed, permanently separated or have never lived with men), while the remainder are *de facto* women-headed households, with male partners working elsewhere (in four out of twelve cases overseas). Although *de jure* heads do receive remittances (mainly from children), the average sum amounts to only 10 per cent of household income, whereas in *de facto* units (which receive men's remittances as well), the proportion is 73 per cent. Although *de facto* heads are a smaller proportion of the total in Lapu-Lapu, greater overall levels of female headship in the Cebu and Boracay settlements owe primarily to the larger numbers of widows in the surveys (7 and 6.6 per cent respectively) as against 2.5 per cent. This may, in turn, relate to the fact that demand for labour in the Mactan Export Processing Zone is oriented to school leavers and/or inexperienced workers and has tended to lead to the settlement of younger families in the area (see Chant and McIlwaine, 1995b).

While 13 female-headed households across the three localities are independent lone-parent units consisting of mothers and children (6 of whom are *de facto*), 15 are extended households based upon lone-parent units where women have other co-resident relatives as well as their children (4 of which are *de facto*). On top of this, there are 3 lone-female households (one of which is *de facto*), 3 single-sex households (where female friends and/or kin live with one another – one of which is *de facto*), and one grandmother-headed household, where a woman lives with her grandchildren but without their mother (that is, her daughter).

While households headed by women have a greater tendency to be extended (48 per cent) compared with households headed by men (43 per cent), the differential is not nearly as marked as in the Mexican and Costa Rican communities (see earlier). Moreover, the average number of kin in male extended structures (2.3) is marginally higher than in female extended units (2.2), which differs from Mexico and Costa Rica. A total of 69 per cent of extended households contain at least one female relative (and 59 per cent one male), with the proportion of women among 130 people living in extended components being 57 per cent. As in the other two countries, extended households tend to be larger than their non-extended counterparts. For example, male-headed extended households have an average size of 7.1 and *de jure* female-headed extended units 5.3, compared with 5.2 among male-headed nuclear households and 4.9 among non-extended female-headed units. The overall average size of male-headed units is 6 and female-headed units, 4.3.

Female heads of *de jure* lone-parent units have an average age of 43.5 years and those of *de jure* extended households 52.5 years (both being considerably older than male heads, who have mean ages of 35 in nuclear households and 38.3 years in extended structures). This reflects the preponderance of widows among *de jure* female heads of lone-parent and extended households, whose mean ages are 50 years and 61.3 years respectively (separated women, on the other hand, have an average age of 37.3 years, and never-married women 32.1 years). The age profile of *de jure* female heads broadly corresponds with the national picture (see Chapter 5).

As for migrant status, while 62 per cent of female heads of household across the three localities are migrants, this applies to only 37 per cent of male heads. In some respects this could be due to the fact that independent female headship is more likely where people do not have relatives in the vicinity, with 'unwed mothers' often moving away from home areas in order to spare their kin embarrassment (see later). As for the marital status of the 23 *de jure* female heads, the biggest single group (13) are widows, followed by 7 who are single, and only 3 who are separated, indicating the strong social and legal constraints to marital break up (see below).

Routes into female household headship in Cebu, Lapu-Lapu and Boracay

Widowhood

That widowhood is the most common route into female headship in the Visayas (as well as in the Philippines more generally), owes in large part to the fact that for women married in church (the majority of the population – see Chant and McIlwaine, 1995a), matrimony is regarded as a 'contract for life'. Marriage is taken so seriously that it frequently influences female behaviour after their husbands' death as well. Engracia, now 77, in Cebu, not only never considered leaving her husband in the 36 years they were married, but has not entertained the thought of any male company in the 20 years since he died. Even though another widow, Elvira (40 years, Boracay), now has a new partner, she never thought of leaving her husband during the time he was alive, despite numerous bouts of violence and alcoholism, and long-running financial neglect.

Separation: restraints and reservations

Women in the Visayas tend to defend their resistance to separation on grounds of religious beliefs, but the legal prohibition on divorce in the Philippines is equally relevant (see Chapter 5). In fact this is frequently articulated by respondents in these terms. Evelyn (Boracay), for example, was one of many women who said: 'I never think of separating from my husband because there is not divorce in the Philippines.' Even if, technically speaking, divorce does not preclude separation, its illegality seems to make people feel it is a 'bad thing' (see Chant, 1995a). Indeed, fear of breaking a contract endorsed by both church and state appears to be so powerful that no matter what the circumstances, women claim never to have contemplated splitting up with spouses. The precedence of public over private concerns often costs dearly in terms of material well-being for women and other household members, not to mention personal emotional fulfilment.

For example, Minerva (Boracay), the 34-year-old wife of a fish-seller, Edwin, describes herself as 'not a successful married woman'. As a secretarial student in Iloilo City in the mid-1980s, Minerva became pregnant by her boyfriend, Octavio, with whom she was very much in love. At first Octavio seemed to take the news of the pregnancy quite well and there were plans to marry, but all of a sudden he left Iloilo and Minerva heard nothing of him until years after their daughter was born (she believes he escaped because he was 'ashamed' to be unemployed and was worried about providing for a child). Although Minerva's parents did not turn her out, as the years passed and her daughter started to grow, Minerva's unhappiness at putting her parents through the perpetual embarrassment of having an 'unwed mother' in the house, led her to leave her daughter with a married sister, and to move to Boracay to start a new life. She met Edwin shortly after arriving on the island, and was quite taken aback at his interest: 'He liked me even though I already have children!' They married in church and Minerva became pregnant almost immediately. In 1992, when the child was one year old and another baby was on the way, a letter from Octavio was passed on to her revealing that he had been working in Japan for a building firm and was keen to know whether she would now accept his hand in marriage. Although Minerva was thrown into emotional turmoil at this unexpected event, she declared that to leave Edwin was out of the question because 'we have made vows in church'. The decision, though irrevocable, however, has been hard to live with, not only due to Minerva's continued longing for Octavio, but because of the misery of her married life. Edwin never makes her feel appreciated, rarely helps around the home, and spends most of his free time gambling and/or going out to 'happy-go-lucky' (social gatherings).

Although some women may threaten to break their vows and leave, this is more usually a strategy to force change within the marriage than a genuine precedent for action. Moreover, since threats are seldom taken seriously by husbands, women's words are rendered a somewhat blunt tool in marital disputes. Rosamia, 42 years, in Lapu-Lapu, for example, suffered during ten years of her marriage because her husband, Godofredo, spent most of his time and money out of the home, drinking, gambling and smoking with his gang of male friends (*barkada*). When Rosamia scolded him for his '*bisyos*' (vices), he reacted by beating her, and even in the face of her repeated threats to leave, remained complacent because he knew she would not follow them through. Strangely enough, it was 'because of the children' that Godofredo eventually mended his ways and modified or eliminated most of his personal excesses. As his sons grew older, he wanted to set a 'good example', and is now relatively clean living, although Rosamia maintains that he still desires his cigarettes more than her: 'Better to lose a thousand women than a single stick of cigarette!'

While Rosamia managed to find the strength to stay in her marriage on account of the children, Dina, now 39 and one of the few separated women in the communities, could not. After contemplating doing so for five years, Dina left her husband, Bong, after a 17-year marriage at the age of 34. Dina and Bong had lived with his parents in Manila, and Dina helped out in their *sari-sari* store. Bong, on the other hand, was 'never responsible'. Instead of conceding to Dina's and his parents' pleas to work in the family business, Bong spent most of his days (and nights) drinking, gambling and frequenting the red light district of the capital. He would also take money from Dina for his recreation (as is the pattern in many households). Dina suspected Bong of having affairs, but had no proof until a prostitute who had become his mistress visited Dina to inform her she was having his child. Being pregnant herself for the sixth time at that stage, Dina demanded that Bong stop seeing his mistress. However, because the woman's brother was a policeman and Bong feared recriminations, he explained that he would have to keep the relationship going. The humiliation of knowing that her husband was not only sleeping with another woman but that she was going to have his child as well, was the last straw. So, leaving her eldest three children with her mother-in-law (who was paying their school fees), Dina returned to Boracay where her mother gave her a plot of land on which she built a nipa palm hut, and resumed the shellcraft work she had learned as a child. Bong is now living with his mistress and their current total of three children in Cagayan City.

Non-marriage and non-disclosure of male marital status

Some female heads in the Visayas have never married, and in virtually all cases because their present or former partners are/were already married. Married men's disclosure of their civil status often only takes place after sexual relations occur, and is sometimes delayed until after the birth of babies. Although now living with her daughter, Peachy, and the father of the child, Marylin (33 years, Cebu), did not learn that her lover already had a wife and three children until after Peachy was born. Peachy was three years old by the time the man took up residence with Marylin (the opportunity arose when his wife migrated to work as a domestic servant in Hong Kong and their children were fostered out to their maternal grandmother). In the intervening years, Marylin had lived as an embedded lone parent in her widowed mother's household, reflecting a common tendency for lone mothers to reside in the homes of others as opposed to establishing households of their own (see Chapter 5).

Embedded female-headed sub-families

Although it is not possible to tell from the household questionnaire survey precisely how many extended households contain 'embedded' female lone-parent units, on the basis of information collected in semi-structured interviews, the proportion would appear to be in the region of 30 per cent. Although this is about the same as Costa Rica (in Mexico, embedded female lone parents are found in only 21 per cent of extended households), it must also be set against the fact that a total of 43.7 per cent of households are extended in the Philippine case study localities, compared with only 27 per cent in Costa Rica and 33 per cent in Mexico. Indeed, as a rough estimate, a little under one in two Filipino lone mothers set up independent households with their children, whereas this applies to just over two out of three lone mothers in Mexico and Costa Rica.[15]

Although as in Costa Rica and Mexico, embedded female heads arise for economic or pragmatic reasons (lack of work and housing shortages, for example), in the Philippines (where labour force participation among low-income women is considerably higher – see below), living with kin also seems to play a strong symbolic role in respect of expressing moral restraint and/or 'reformed' intentions. Although single parents are often referred to rather pejoratively as 'unwed mothers', living with parents or other senior kin minimises the prospect of socially disreputable or embarrassing *'tsismis'* (gossip) (see Chapter 5). This tendency for kin to 'shelter' women who have had illegitimate births or indeed who are seen to have 'failed' in their marriages is conceivably exacerbated by the existence of an established sex industry in the Visayas (especially Cebu). Women who continue to live with kin rather than form their own households are less likely to be suspected to be involved in prostitution, let alone to actually be so. Two factors are important here: (a) women living with parents or other kin are under greater surveillance, and (b) the economic assistance provided by extended households means that women are less likely to need the comparatively high wages offered by the sexual service sector. Another benefit attached to living with kin in a context where the sexual commodification of women stands side by side with emphasis on female chastity and moral propriety, is the protection it offers from men keen to exploit the socially vulnerable position of lone mothers (Chant, 1995a). Those whose vulnerability is exacerbated by living alone are certainly prone to male advances. The widow Elvira referred to earlier, for example, declared that in the five years after her husband died she was approached by 'many no good people'. This was echoed by Dina, the separated woman, who said that several men 'dropped by' to see her under the illusion that she must want a boyfriend because she has no husband, although she has no hesitation in telling them that this is the very last thing on her agenda! Finally, being taken in by kin is sometimes the only hope for former sex workers whose legacy from the industry is incurable disease or addiction to life-threatening drugs. For example, one mother of three, Evangelin, living within her parents' household in Cebu, is addicted to *'shabu'* ('poor man's cocaine' – see Chant and McIlwaine, 1995a). According to her parents, unless they had controlled the money that used to be sent to Evangelin monthly by a long-term Italian 'boyfriend' as a retainer for her 'services' on his business trips to Cebu, she would probably have died by now.

The kinds of factors described above may help to explain why there is no obvious link between female labour force participation and household headship in the study localities. Although as in Mexico and Costa Rica, female heads have higher rates of labour force participation (74.2 per cent) than female spouses (66.8 per cent) (with as many as 82 per cent of *de jure* female heads being economically active), the fact that 83 per cent of all women work[16] in Boracay and, unlike in the other case study localities, earn more than men (with weekly average earnings of P741[$29.6 US] as against P642 [$25.7]),[17] is not reflected in record numbers of female heads on the island. Alternatively, although levels of female headship are highest in Cebu, the proportion of female respondents working (62 per cent) is the lowest of all three localities (Lapu-Lapu's figure for female labour force participation being 66 per cent), and gender differentials in earnings are greatest: women in Cebu earn a weekly average of P312 ($12.4 US) compared with P696 ($25.2 US) among men, whereas in Lapu-Lapu, women earn P426 ($17.4 US) per week as against a mean of P840 ($33.6 US) among their male counterparts.

Female household headship: links with specific occupations

Where there *would* appear to be a connection with female labour force participation and household headship is in the context of particular kinds of jobs. Although among the smaller surveys conducted among target occupational groups in the region (for example manufacturing workers, tourism workers and so on), levels of female headship are low, high proportions are found among sex workers in Cebu, and employees in formal tourism establishments (for example hotel, shop and restaurant workers) in Boracay.

The survey of sex workers in Cebu comprised 14 women working in some capacity or other (not always trading sexual intercourse) in the city's 'entertainment' establishments, with jobs ranging from dancers, hostesses, 'guest relations ladies', waitresses, to masseuses (Chant and McIlwaine, 1995a). In total, 79 per cent of these workers lived in female-headed households of one form or another, whether as independent single-person or lone-parent households, or with female kin or friends in female-dominant households (*ibid.*:267; see also Chapter 1, this volume).

Out of ten women with children in the sex worker sample, all but one were single parents, most having become pregnant out of wedlock and been abandoned by boyfriends.[18] Interestingly, it was only usually *after* this that they had entered the sex trade (in seven out of ten cases), indicating that while single parenthood is often an occupational hazard of sex work, it is also (and perhaps more commonly) a catalyst for women's entry into the industry. Indeed, many single mothers in the sample said prostitution was the only way they could earn enough money to support their children. Integral to the connections between sex work and lone parenthood is migration, with women often moving away from home areas in order to disguise the fact of being single mothers and of bringing shame upon their families. Once away from kin, and lacking the social and economic infrastructure provided by these networks, it is a relatively small step to starting work in a business which is almost universally condemned by 'decent society'. As Law (forthcoming) sums up on the basis of her research among sex workers in Cebu City: 'Once a woman loses her virginity or has a child out of wedlock, she is classified as a whore. Non-virgins and single mothers who have the opportunity to work in the sex industry often do because they are considered loose women and therefore unmarriageable.' While two of the five migrant single mothers had fostered their children to their own parents in home villages and were in fairly regular contact, the others had next to no communication as a means of concealing their activities.[19] For example, one woman, Arlene, with a two-year-old son had only seen her father who lived in Negros Oriental province once in three years and has never invited him to Cebu. Having told him that she is working as a cashier in a restaurant, she lives in fear that he will pay her an unexpected visit and discover the reality of her circumstances (see Chant and McIlwaine, 1995a:Chapter 6; also Law, forthcoming).

As for tourism workers in Boracay, the vast bulk of people working in hotels, shops and restaurants are young and single and live on the business premises in single-sex dormitories. These groups are referred to as 'live-ins', and a sum for their board and lodging is deducted from their wages at source (often providing employers with a smokescreen for underpaying their employees). Of the total of 13 female respondents working in formal tourism establishments in Boracay, 9 were 'live-ins', 8 of whom were migrants who had mostly arranged their jobs through relatives prior to coming to the island. In many respects, lodging in the form of 'apprentices' with their bosses restricts women's time and freedom and thereby allays parents' fears about what their daughters might 'get up to' when they leave home to work elsewhere. The female-dominated living arrangements of tourism workers in Boracay are therefore very different in origin and character from those of sex workers in Cebu, although, as I have argued elsewhere, they may be significant for women who might otherwise only have the experience of residing in households headed by fathers or husbands (see Chant, 1996b).[20]

The Philippine state and female household headship
Despite the seemingly progressive agenda of the Philippine state and the organised women's movement (see Chapter 5), none of the respondents either in the household or worker surveys had heard of the National Commission on the Role of Filipino Women, the Philippine Development Plan for Women, or any recent revisions to the Family Code. The only thing that was widely known, was that divorce was totally impossible, and that once tied to a spouse who was violent, or a drunkard, or who had other vices

such as gambling, there was a very slim chance indeed of getting out (see also Chapter 7).

CONCLUSIONS: PERSPECTIVES ON INTER- AND INTRA-COUNTRY VARIATIONS

In drawing conclusions and comparisons among the three countries, it is important to bear in mind that difference is inscribed into the analysis by virtue of the fact that the areas chosen in each country were originally selected for different reasons; although households and their survival strategies were central to my research in all three contexts, methodology in the initial surveys varied according to the specific aims and objectives of different projects. Morever, the questionnaire surveys from which many of the basic facts and figures are drawn were undertaken in different years. Recognising the significance of ongoing change not only in the countries themselves, and in the personal situations of the respondents, but also in my own life, marital status, experience, degree of familiarity with interviewees and so on (see earlier), comparisons clearly need to be treated with some caution. Having said this, much of the information gathered in semi-structured interviews over the years relates to marriage, children, household organisation, domestic labour, employment, gender and life histories, besides which return trips were made to all three countries during 1994–95 with the specific purpose of gleaning further insights on female headship in the different localities at one point in time. In this sense, I feel that the material I have (and my interpretations of it) is of comparable enough nature to offer tentative perspectives on key areas of correspondence and divergence in the formation and features of women-headed households.

Most of the similarities among the case study localities relate to the basic socio-economic and demographic characteristics of female-headed households. Female heads of household in low-income settlements in all three countries are generally older than their male counterparts, they have similar numbers of co-resident children, they are more economically active than women with male partners, and whether or not their households are extended in composition they tend to be smaller than male-headed units. Despite the fact that there is greater diversity in types of female-headed household in the Philippine Visayas, the vast bulk in all three contexts are headed by lone mothers. The Costa Rican and Mexican case study localities share greater similarities insofar as women-headed units are more often extended than male-headed units, and that heads tend to be unmarried and separated women rather than widows. In turn, female lone parents in Mexico and Costa Rica are more likely to head their own households than in the Philippines where they more frequently end up as embedded sub-families. Having said this, Costa Rica and the Philippines are more alike in respect of a greater prevalence of *de facto* female-headed households and heavier reliance on remittances.

While many characteristics of female-headed households in Mexico, Costa Rica and the Philippines are similar, however, levels of female headship and routes into this status are more variable, and not only between countries but within them as well. Whereas critical factors associated with variations in levels of female headship within Mexico include the relative labour force participation of women, patterns of migration of different groups of women to different places (for example, significant flows of lone mothers to Puerto Vallarta), and neolocality and distance from kin, in Guanacaste, Costa Rica, the prevalence of consensual unions together with the seasonal out-migration of adult males is extremely significant in giving rise to high levels of both *de facto* and *de jure* female headship, with state welfare possibly playing a contributory role. In the Philippine Visayas, by contrast, type of employment and its social significance distinguishes one group of independent female-headed households (those headed by unmarried mothers, preponderantly working in the sex industry), from the majority group of older female-headed units headed by widows.

Although gender roles, relations, ideologies and inequalities and the interplay between them in different domains – conjugal relationships, the household, the labour market and so on – impact in different ways in different places on the formation of female-headed households, a few features stand out as common to all localities. One is that conjugal unions are characterised by differences in the behaviour and range of activities socially-endorsed and/or expected of male and female partners. Generally speaking, while women are confined to a fairly small number of spheres (predominantly the household and the labour force – their presence in the latter largely justified by acting in the interests of the welfare of other household and/or family members) men's licence for personal freedom and movement is much greater. This allows them to disengage themselves with less practical difficulty, social penalty and/or psychological compunction from household needs, to be more mobile across space, and to be involved in a greater range of recreational activities (which may include sexual interaction with other women). This can lead directly to men's desertion of spouses or provoke conflict that precipitates separation. Despite variations in women's responses to the trauma generated by more extreme degrees of male orientation to personal/extra-domestic (as opposed to family/ home-centred) imperatives, there is little doubt that gender differences in the priority attached emotionally, normatively and pragmatically to household well-being are often catalytic in conjugal breakdown.

A second and related point of correspondence in the three localities, is that while routes into female headship vary widely, this is not prone to be a state which women enter of their own volition, and certainly not until after considerable thought on the matter. While it is incorrect to assume that women-headed households are 'victims' of forces beyond their control (as evidenced by those women in the Philippines who leave their husbands in the face of extreme social opprobrium and legal constraints), women do not generally choose to avoid marriage, to leave husbands, or to fuel the conflict which usually precedes marital breakdown (infidelity, heavy drinking and so on). This finds parallels with Schlyter's (1989:180) findings from Zimbabwe where she observes: 'Many of the interviewed women had become heads of household against their will, and they had elaborated their household strategies to adapt to their situation. The formation of a household of their own was for other women a strategy of resistance to a situation which they found unbearable.' Much of the scenario painted by Schlyter owes to the fact that marriage is highly emphasised in Zimbabwean women's lives: 'It was not the aim of any young girl to become a head of household. Love and children within a happy marriage is central to the dreams of young girls, and among the young women interviewed marriage remained the ultimate aim of their strategies' (*ibid.*). This latter observation, in turn, has considerable relevance in Mexico, Costa Rica and the Philippines, and reveals another gender issue common to all three contexts: while men do not have to 'prove' themselves as good husbands to qualify as 'male' (in fact, the contrary is arguably as, if not more, important), for women, the expectation that they will marry, have children and play a central role in maintaining the cohesiveness of the family unit places great pressure on women to legitimise themselves by being 'successful' wives and mothers.[21] On balance, therefore, the majority of women are unlikely to make a conscious decision to remain single or pursue a path to separation quite as readily as men,[22] notwithstanding that more systematic fieldwork with male respondents would be necessary to confirm this interpretation (see aso Chapter 9).

Piecing together the observations I have made, however, a very contradictory picture emerges, in which prevailing differences between masculine and feminine identities impose immense strain on the socially-sanctioned institutions of marriage and male household headship, which, in all three countries, are deemed to provide the most appropriate context for raising children (see Chapter 5). In past times, the male-headed household was possibly not quite so susceptible to dissolution, arguably because men's greater access to resources than women was more assured. Now, however, this is changing (see below), and the fundamental inequalities embedded in a pattern where women are expected to invest the bulk, if not all of their energy in upholding marriage and family life, whereas men (to be men), are not expected, nor encouraged, to demonstrate wholesale involvement in household activities, are hardly likely to be the best recipe for generating stability, enthusiasm and/or continued faith in couple-centred domesticity. This is especially so where men's ability to fulfil their main family function as economic providers is increasingly thwarted by lack of regular well-paid employment. Indeed, although male participation in the tasks of housework and childcare is far from unwelcome, breadwinning remains the key marker of being a 'good family man', and in view of labour market disadvantage, men may have little option but to resort to other signifiers of masculine identity – the more 'dangerous' extra-familial ones (summed up by respondents as 'bad behaviour') – as a means of achieving some kind of legitimacy, not to mention relief or solace from frustration, failure and their low-ranking socio-economic position (see Chant, 1991a; González de la Rocha, 1995b).[23,24]

As for women, a situation in which they are exposed not only to the problems of scant financial assistance from men, but to emotional turmoil, makes it difficult for them to achieve the goal of being good wives as well as good mothers, notwithstanding that in all three countries it seems that women have traditionally been expected to make greater personal sacrifices than men in the context of marriage and parenthood. Yet although the state, the church, and other social institutions such as kinship continue to bolster these patterns, whether by justifying women's suffering as 'fate' or glorifying it as martyrdom, and/or by penalising them for giving up the struggle, recent economic and demographic shifts such as recession, increased labour migration, rising opportunities for female employment and so on, seem to be bringing other factors into play that enable and/or enforce women to make choices. The 'choices' women make, however, lie not so much in making decisions between their personal happiness and that of their families, but in prioritising the interests of different members of their households. In short, where men's behaviour threatens children's well-being and where women feel they stand a better chance of ensuring this by going it alone, then their choice may fall on making a success of motherhood at the expense of keeping marriages intact. In some respects this could be seen as women using one aspect of their feminine identity (motherhood) to create space and power in another female arena (wifehood), the latter being a domain which, as an affinal relationship, is possibly more open to negotiation than a consanguineal one. This is not to say, of course, that depriving children of their fathers is an easy choice, regardless of the fact that men's behaviour is what really deprives them.[25]

Indeed, although women's decisions to dissolve conjugal unions arise in the context of harsh daily domestic realities which might well be understood and/or supported by intimate friends and family, they remain far from approved at wider societal levels. The idea that women might choose to live alone, and particularly, raise children as lone parents, is in all localities deemed anomalous, if not scandalous in the case of unmarried women. Although children are an important factor in this equation, a more important restraint still, perhaps, relates to the aspersions cast on the sexual proclivity of the women in question. This itself, however, may act to compound the 'problem', since if marriage or cohabitation is seen as the only acceptable framework for female sexual activity, the result may be hasty teenage unions with little chance of long-term survival. Notwithstanding these contradictory forces and the fact that respectability and reputation are important social imperatives, we have seen that some women pre-empt male abandonment and/or reject self-sacrificial resignation by creating alternative domestic environments for themselves and their children, the nature of which are more closely examined in the following chapters.

NOTES

1. 'Owner-occupiers' were classified as people who had legal title to their plots or who as squatters or illegal purchasers were likely to get their tenure regularised in due course and in the meantime were not paying rent. These were selected randomly from a sample universe that excluded non-owners and plots occupied by two or more households which did not share cooking and financial arrangements ('nuclear compound units'), the reason being that I was primarily concerned with the examination of house-building strategies among households and the latter group would have complicated the picture due to variable degrees of inter-household exchange (see Chant, 1984a: Appendix 1). Given the possibility that relative numbers of women-headed households might have been higher among renters or as sub-units of nuclear compound households (as 'sharers' – see Varley, 1995), some under-recording of female headship may be likely. Having said this, although renters were included in the 1986 survey of León and Puerto Vallarta, levels of rental tenure were about the same (one-fifth) in male- and female-headed units. The latter sampling universe did, however exclude a total of 133 out of 769 households on the basis of being nuclear compound units, or other (admittedly infrequently occurring) household types such as single person households, male-headed one-parent units and households where adolescent siblings reside without parents, so again there is a chance that female headship may be under-reported (see Chant, 1991a: Appendix 1). None the less, since the vast bulk of households in all settlements in all years were

'conventional' family-based units headed by men or women, I am reasonably confident that the Mexican questionnaire samples are typical for a large section of the urban poor. As for the questionnaire surveys in Costa Rica and the Philippines, these were totally random, including all household types and all tenures (see Chant, 1991b for details of the methodology in Costa Rica, and Chant and McIlwaine, 1995a: Appendix for details of the Philippine surveys).

2. Unless otherwise stated, data relate to the household questionnaire survey conducted in Querétaro in 1982–83, and in Puerto Vallarta and León in 1986. The reason for using 1982–83 data for Querétaro is because the first survey was based on a random sample of 244 respondents, whereas the 1986 questionnaire survey included only 20 of the original households.

3. This is even noted in the development plan produced by the Coordinating Commission of the Río Ameca Conurbation (to which Puerto Vallarta belongs) in 1980. The plan documents that men who are used to being breadwinners with dependent wives find it extremely difficult to adjust to a situation where women have an advantage in the labour market and may be the only members of the household with a secure wage, one reaction being to intensify '*macho*' behaviour (COCODERA, 1980:518–19; see also Chant, 1991a:168).

4. Data from Instituto de Fomento y Asesoría Municipal (IFAM), San José, October 1994.

5. Data from Instituto de Fomento y Asesoría Municipal (IFAM), San José, October 1994.

6. Figures for Santa Cruz in 1993 had yet to be calculated by IFAM in October 1994.

7. A minority of Nicaraguan immigrants in Guanacaste in 1989 had formal refugee status, but most were people who had crossed the border illegally as labour migrants.

8. In contrast, most women form partnerships a little later in the other countries: at 18–19 years in Mexico, and 21–22 years in the Philippines, possibly because formal marriage is more common.

9. That no cases were reported of a split which had been mutually agreed is possibly symptomatic of the frequently aggressive nature of male–female relationships in Guanacaste.

10. During 1989, there were roughly 80 *colones* to the US dollar.

11. In 1993, median monthly earnings in Guanacaste in general were only 68.7 per cent of those in the Región Central (where the capital, San José, is situated) (DGEC, 1993a:Table 36).

12. See also Eswara Prasad (1995) on the long and convoluted procedures attached to women's applications for widows' pensions in India.

13. Although use will be made of worker interviews in the Philippine case study localities later in this section, in the interests of greater comparability with the data from Mexico and Costa Rica, the bulk of the data is drawn from the household surveys.

14. The smallest scale at which published census data is available is at the level of municipalities. Although Cebu and Lapu-Lapu are municipalities in their own right, Boracay forms part of the municipality of Malay and data are given for the latter entity where information is not available for the island itself.

15. This is a classic case where census data are not revealing and where the inclusion of information on 'sub-families' might be helpful in cross-national comparisons of out-of-wedlock births, marital dissolution and so on (see also Chapter 9).

16. All these figures exclude women who are unemployed, but include part-timers/occasional workers, and women working on an unpaid basis in family businesses, along with full-time workers who actually constitute 94.5 per cent of total women workers.

17. The data pertain to 1993, since when the average rate of exchange has remained at around 25 Philippine pesos to $1 US.

18. This mirrors studies of sex workers in other developing countries. For example in their research on prostitutes in the city of Pune, India, Desai and Apte (1987) found that the majority were single parents.

19. In addition to suffering low levels of respect both from neighbours and relatives, 40 per cent of Desai and Apte's (1987:175) sample of sex workers had not maintained a relationship with their parents.

20. With reference to female garment workers in Bangladesh, Kabeer (1995) also observes that sharing lodgings with other women gives workers a novel residential opportunity.

21. See also Dallos (1995:184) on the advanced economies, who argues that women's sense of value may be seriously jeopardised by separation and divorce when a wife's role 'is contingent upon being in a relationship and being appreciated in that relationship'.

22. Schlyter (1989:181) also reveals that married women in Zimbabwe usually work hard to keep their unions intact whereas men more often file for divorce, and when women do take the initiative it is usually due to their husbands' taking a second wife, or because of domestic violence.

23. This has long been argued for Mexico in the context of the '*machismo*' complex (see for example, Arizmendi, 1980; Bridges, 1980; also Chapters 4 and 5).

24. With reference to the advanced economies, Collier (1995:192) also points out how economic restructuring, mass unemployment, and the shift of economies from an industrial to a service base, have thrown male familial commitment based on work into crisis, further noting that 'women's increased involvement in the workforce has rendered untenable the idea that the male/breadwinner, female/childrearer relation represents anything like the reality of family life for the majority'.

25. The extent to which this point may be relevant in other contexts is clearly questionable. For example, while making a case for differences between affinal and consanguineal kinship ties in the context of the Peruvian Andes, Harvey (1994:78) notes that women 'remain in violent partnerships for the sake of their children. For if a woman leaves her husband she deprives her children of the pivotal kinship relationship with the father, from whom the child receives a legitimate place in the hierarchy of local kin.' As for the present research, the point that men need to be interviewed is further reinforced (see Chapter 9).

7 Victims or Survivors?

INTRODUCTION

With further reference to case study material from Mexico, Costa Rica and the Philippines, this chapter explores whether and in which kinds of ways women-headed households suffer greater disadvantage than male-headed households. Picking up various threads from debates on female headship and poverty along with ideological and social marginality introduced in Chapter 2, particular attention is paid to how female heads view themselves and are viewed by others, what the nature of their experiences of heading households has been, and whether they deem their situations to be more difficult than they were (or might be) with men in their lives. These issues are examined not only in relation to practical and material aspects of female household headship (for example, incomes and domestic divisions of labour), but also to pyscho-social dimensions such as autonomy, stress, morality, status within the community and interactions with kin. The discussion also considers women's comparative satisfaction with existing household circumstances: to what extent do women in female- and male-headed units express desire to change their circumstances, and what are their views on marriage and remarriage? Responses to these questions shed additional light on whether women heads of household regard themselves primarily as 'victims' or 'survivors'.

In the interests of an integrated assessment of the above issues, I leave the bulk of my own reflections and interpretations until the conclusion of the chapter. An additional point is that since lone-parent units (whether extended or non-extended) predominate among women-headed households in the case study areas, the chapter concentrates mainly on this group. In fact, unless respondents have personal experience of other forms of female headship or are close to someone who has, female headship and lone motherhood are usually seen as one and the same, and preponderantly as a 'problem' of non-marriage.

IMAGES OF FEMALE HOUSEHOLD HEADSHIP

'Outsider' perspectives

As noted earlier in the book, women-headed households (particularly lone-parent units) are, in many countries, viewed rather negatively by the state and by wider society. Such attitudes also prevail among residents of the case study communities, although to different degrees and in different ways, with place, age, marital status and personal experience/relationships with lone mothers being some of the critical mediating factors. Using the term 'outsider' to describe residents of low-income settlements who are not female household heads themselves, the following section reviews predominant attitudes of male and female community members towards women who head their own households.

In Mexico, as in the other countries, the most hostile attitudes towards female heads of household (and particularly lone parents) are generally articulated by women in stable marriages. Rosa (Puerto Vallarta), for example, who has been married to Saul for 24 years, declared emphatically: *'madres solteras no me caen bién'* ('I don't like single mothers'), claiming that it would be better both for society and for their children if they got married. Rosa has no single parents in her own circle of relatives and friends, which possibly helps to explain that she could give no justification for her opinion other than the situation was 'not right'. Her statement also reveals an assumption that female lone parents have *not* been married in the past and that, in some senses, they have opted for the single state.

Where women have experienced troubles in their own marriages or those of their parents and/or have daughters who are lone mothers, there is generally greater sympathy towards female heads. For example, Idalia (Puerto Vallarta), whose father abandoned her mother and siblings when she was less than a year old, views single parenthood as a product of 'bad luck' for both mother and child, stating: 'This can happen to anyone ... it isn't always the woman's "fault"', notwithstanding that the addition of the proviso 'not always' suggests that women may have a role in the process. Alicia (Querétaro), whose daughter Rocío has been deserted by a succession of partners and been left with a total of five children, said that personally she has no problem with lone mothers, although the majority of the community – 'being Catholics' – think 'the worst' of them – that is, that they are 'immoral' or 'loose' women, which again confers a greater element of 'blame' on the part of mothers than on the men who father their children.

Similar attitudes come through in 'outsider' views of female headship in Costa Rica. Concepción (Liberia) acknowledges that not all single mothers are 'at fault', although she does maintain that a lot of women bring separation upon themselves, declaring: 'They go out, and sometimes they leave the children. Some of them drink with their friends as well. There's always conflict when this happens, and the men usually leave.' Aside from the fact that it is usually men who precipitate relationship problems through their own drinking and/or absences from home, Concepción's statement is interesting because it again implies that women are often the ones who are responsible (in this particular case, for marital breakdown), especially those who 'step out of line' with gendered norms. Concepción herself is very restrained in her activities. She rarely socialises outside the home, either with kin or friends, and fits very much into the normative model of obedient, dependent, full-time housewife and mother (see Chapter 5).

The idea that lone mothers have 'transgressed' in some way also comes through in parental reponses to teenage daughters who get pregnant through pre-marital sexual relations. Parental reactions to these events are often punitive, including scolding, withdrawal of support, making daughters leave home, and, in some instances, removing rights over their offspring, even if the latter is sometimes declared to be in young women's best interests. When Rosibel (Cañas) became a lone mother at the age of 18, for example, her parents, Jelba and José Alberto, were furious, although their dislike of Rosibel's partner was such that they decided not to turn Rosibel out. This has exacted its own price, however, in that it has extended their claims over Rosibel's child, Magda. Although a few years after Magda's birth, Jelba and José Alberto report that 'luck touched Rosibel' and she is now living with another man, they insisted on keeping Magda. They rationalised this action by declaring: 'We got used to having her around, and Rosibel's relationship will last longer if her new fellow doesn't have to support a step-child.'

An interesting slant on the above is provided by the fact that when young illegitimate children are absorbed into the homes of grandparents in Costa Rica, they often end up being referred to as 'sons' or 'daughters' as opposed to 'grandchildren'. The significance of this is multifaceted, including: (1) a sign or gesture to the outside world that the child is the *bona fide* offspring of an established conjugal union (although most neighbours would know that the grandmother is not the real mother), (2) an assertion of *de facto* custody rights on the part of grandparents (especially when children are often quite mature before they are informed of their true parentage), (3) the possibility of a better start in life for the child in question, whether materially, and/or in terms of social status (given the generally negative connotations of lone motherhood), and (4) a measure to dissuade the sisters of unmarried mothers from 'making the same mistake'.

In the Philippines, where pre-marital sex among women seems to be frowned upon to an even greater degree than the Latin American contexts, fostering occurs in the same way as in Costa Rica, or through the longer-term residence of lone mothers as embedded 'sub-families' in their parents' households (see Chapters 1 and 6). Attitudes towards female headship are also mixed. Although the idea was expressed by one or two women that if it mothers had good jobs and could afford to raise their children alone then lone parenting would be acceptable (especially as fathers were often not around much anyway), the emphasis among Visayan respondents was more on the matter of how lone motherhood offended 'tradition' and/or the 'sadness' attached to father absence for children. Again, there is a pervading assumption that lone parenthood is something women bring upon themselves, particularly through not having exercised sufficient restraint to withold from pre-marital relations. However, reactions to this are usually stated very euphemistically, mirroring a general tendency in the Philippines for considerable discretion in matters of sexuality and family affairs. Elvira (Boracay), for example, said she found it difficult to know what to think about female heads because they were not something she was 'accustomed to' and this was 'not tradition' in the Philippines. Her voice dropped to a virtual whisper while we discussed the subject, as if our very conversation was an unsavoury temptation of providence. Jocely (Boracay) declared she would want to 'keep her distance' if the female head in question had been a 'bad girl' (meaning she had had pre-marital sex or had left her husband), although she would be well-disposed if the man was 'at fault'. In brief, for Jocely, her reactions would 'depend on the girl, depend on the situation'. By the same token, the idea that women may be 'victims' of male abuse is also apparent, with Eden (Boracay), a relatively happily married woman with a large family declaring that she felt 'sorry' for 'solo mothers', and would like to take them and their offspring into her home in order to give them the experience of a 'normal family life'. With the exception of sex workers, however, very few women had lone parents (especially unmarried ones) in their family or social circle on which to base their opinion.

Men's attitudes towards lone mothers

The views of men towards lone mothers tend to mirror those of women in terms of suspecting lack of self-control, and find outward expression in predatory behaviour. The notion that female household heads are 'fair game' is present in all the localities, and, as noted in the context of the Philippines in the previous chapter, men frequently take the liberty of making propositions of a sexual nature. This also occurs in Mexico, where Emilia (Puerto Vallarta) claims that she has been asked out by several male neighbours, most of whom are married. Emilia believes that because of her status as an unmarried mother and the absence of a man in her home, men think she is 'desperate' for male company. In Emilia's particular case, this may be exacerbated by the fact that she has no use of her legs as a result of poliomyelitis in childhood. Whether or not this makes men think it will be easy to get into bed because 'minusválidos' ('disabled people') do not get many opportunities, or whether they desire an alternative type of sexual experience, she is often asked by the taxi drivers who ferry her between home and work whether they can pay her for sex. Emilia describes this as 'extremely degrading' but accepts it as part and parcel of being a lone mother in Mexico.

The existence of an abusive element in male advances to female heads also applies in Costa Rica. Lidia (Cañas) a Nicaraguan lone parent of 30 years who was abandoned by her husband seven years ago, has been asked for dates by at least five men during this time, even though she is always working or looking after her ten-year-old son, Elwin, and virtually never goes out except to see relatives. Lidia has refused every one of these '*pretendientes*' ('suitors'), not only because she knows they will try to take advantage of her sexually, but economically as well: 'Men know that single mothers have to work, so they not only come after you for sex, but also for your money!' Even if female heads manage to avoid and/or are able to resist direct approaches, they rarely escape comment or taunting. For example, Elsa, a lone mother of two in Cebu, routinely gets followed by young boys in her neighbourhood who call out 'you're a mother, but not an "*asawa*" (wife)'. In Costa Rica, too, jokes about illegitimate pregnancies abound, even among the young. For example, while I sat chatting one day amongst a crowd of school children in the settlement of Nazareth, Liberia, a group of 14-year-old boys recounted various refrains to do with male–female relations, one being: '*Las mujeres de Nazareth no saben tocar la marimba. A los quince años ya salen con garambimba*'. This effectively translates as: 'The women of Nazareth don't know how to play the marimba (a musical instrument), but at 15 years old their bellies are swollen (with child)'; in other words, women are not capable of doing much else but getting pregnant.

'Insider' perspectives on 'outsider' views

The general attitudes of others towards female heads of household are often deeply felt by those who are actually in this position (those we might term 'insiders'). Female heads realise not only that they are often regarded with caution, but with a combination of fear, disrespect and/or disdain. In Mexico, for example, women on their own are considered 'dangerous', particularly in respect of representing a sexual threat to married women. This is especially the case with younger single or separated women such as Lupe (39 years) in Puerto Vallarta, who summed up the prevailing view in her neighbourhood as: '*No tiene marido y tengo que cuidar el mío*' ('she doesn't have a husband so I have to look after mine'). On top of this, female heads feel not only that people often imagine them to be sexually promiscuous, but that they use their bodies to exact money from men '*como putas*' ('like whores'). Emilia (Puerto Vallarta), for example, says that her neighbours always gossip when male visitors call because they suspect she is having sex and getting paid for it. Even Dolores (Puerto Vallarta), who acknowledges that widows like herself are usually accorded more respect because they had no part to play in becoming female heads, claims that she has to be careful not to dress herself or her children too flamboyantly because people are likely to take this as evidence that she is 'going with men for money'.

Similar patterns are found in Costa Rica, where María Idalí in Santa Cruz declared that most of her neighbours are '*sapa*' (gossipy), and there is nothing they like doing better than commenting on what she and other lone mothers 'get up to'. As it is, María Idalí has become fairly thick-skinned about this now, and believes it has much to do with married women envying her freedom to come and go as she pleases. Indeed, many female heads in Mexico and Costa Rica have worked at hardening themselves over the years so that they worry less about what some of their neighbours might think of them, and in some cases have evolved quite positive self-images (see below).

In the Philippines, however, the situation seems less auspicious. Minerva, a former single mother, declared that for the four years she endured single parenthood as part of her parents' household in Iloilo City, she felt highly visible as an 'unwed mother' and utterly '*desgraciada*' (disgraced). Indeed, to spare her parents the embarrassment of having a daughter with 'loose morals' living under their roof, she eventually left her daughter with a married sister and moved to Boracay where no-one knew her. As discussed in Chapter 6, she sees herself as 'lucky' to have been able to marry Edwin, whom she met on the island, even though their wedded life is far from happy.

Dina, a separated mother in Boracay, has not felt quite as negative as Minerva about her lone-parent status, (a) because she has been married and did all she could to preserve the relationship, and (b) she has had no further contact with men. Moreover, because her husband, Bong, was '*so* bad', none of her relatives or friends has advised her to go back to him. At the same time, she recognises that people often seek out her company because 'they never tire of hearing about my husband's life in the whorehouses and discobars of Manila'. However, she takes this fairly philosophically, thinking: 'Never mind the *tsismis* (gossip), think of the children'; in other words, better to be a source of tales than with a man who could have ruined her family's life.

All in all, women in the case study communities in each of the three countries have strong identities as female heads. They see themselves as different from other women and know that their behaviour comes under close scrutiny from other people. In the Philippines in particular, this often encourages women to eschew any contact with men and to do the best they can to 'keep themselves to themselves' and to act as conservatively as possible. Having said this, lone parenthood also intermeshes with other identities, particularly those attached to being poor, and sometimes to being members of particular occupational groups, especially in more distinctive sectors such as the sex industry. At the end of the day, however, identity as female heads (and particularly lone mothers) seems to be prominent, although this may partly be due to the fact that the present research was oriented around this particular topic (see also Scott, 1994:200).[1]

PERSONAL EXPERIENCES AND EVALUATIONS OF FEMALE HOUSEHOLD HEADSHIP

When asked to evaluate their experiences as heads of household, past and present, women in all countries identified that it had been something of a struggle, especially at first. Yet as time passes and women become accustomed to being unpartnered and, more importantly, begin to make progress in coping on their own, pain, pessimism and vulnerability usually give way to feelings of a more optimistic nature. Hardey and Crow (1991:12) have noted similar processes in the advanced economies, where although the early stages of coming to terms with lone parenthood 'represent a lengthy period of adjustment during which the hardships can seem overwhelming', the progressive experience of 'coping alone and managing to deal with the various demands which the situation throws up allows a more positive identity to emerge'. This is echoed by Dallos and Sapsford (1995:129) who observe that:

> In describing the experience of becoming single parents, women frequently indicate that they go through initial periods of doubt, uncertainty and anxiety that they will not be able to manage. Following this, however, they tend to have feelings of increased self-confidence and a positive sense of freedom ... Emerging from such accounts by women is a sense of being in control of their lives, of a new-found feeling of autonomy.

In line with this notion of 'stages of adjustment', it is not surprising that appraisals of the long-term experience of female headship in the case study localities are mixed, although positive aspects are usually highlighted to a greater extent than negative ones, especially in Mexico and Costa Rica, and often fairly early on as well. In fact, one of the most striking things I came across in all three countries was women's very limited expressions of regret at losing partners, even where loss was relatively recent, and/or resulted from bereavement. In respect of the latter, my first encounter with the unexpected came in Querétaro in 1982, when one respondent informed me that she was a widow and had lost her husband a matter of weeks beforehand. When I

said how sorry I was to hear the news, she retorted 'I'm not. At last I'm free
to do what I want and go where I like … It was a dreadful marriage!'

Appraisals of female headship: the early stages

Reactions to bereavement

Although affirmations of the compensations of widowhood are fewer and
further between in the Philippines (see below), women in Mexico and Costa
Rica frequently talk about bereavement as a liberating and/or empowering
process, especially those who have extensive and ongoing contact with their
children. The latter, in turn, is frequently attributed to their having sacrificed
personal happiness for the well-being of offspring at earlier stages of the life
course. Ana María (Puerto Vallarta), for example, feels that now her husband,
Rogelio, is dead, she is reaping the rewards for having endured a long and
unhappy marriage. All her children 'look out for her', and 3 out of 11 adult
sons and daughters still live at home, including one son with his spouse. María
del Refugio, a 65-year-old widow in Querétaro, felt grief when her third partner,
Tito, died from liver failure in his fifties (*'le gustaba el trago'*/'he liked a
drink'), but within months felt considerably better off without him and had
no hesitation in declaring to friends and family: *'Bendito sea Diós que se
me llevó!'* ('Blessèd is God that he took him away!') While four years on
she still misses his company here and there, she claims she has had no
difficulty at all in getting over the absence of his laziness and financial irresponsibility. Currently surrounded by many of her grown-up children and
grandchildren, María feels that life is altogether easier and more peaceful,
declaring that she might as well be alone from now on, (a) because she is
going to die alone, and (b) would rather do so without worries about a man
on her plate. When news of her husband's death reached Lourdes (Querétaro)
in 1980 this came as a 'real relief' (as noted in Chapter 6, she had left him
because of his drink problem). Even Sabina (León) who had a relatively happy
marriage, reported grieving seriously for only four months, with her sons
having rallied round and made her feel loved and protected.

Reactions to desertion

As for women who undergo desertion during pregnancy, recollections of
breaking up with (or not being able to marry) their boyfriends often seem
to be less traumatic for them than the distress they caused people in their
lives at the time, particularly close relatives. For example, Ernestina (Cañas),
now 58, has been with her husband, Trini, for 35 years, but had her first child
at the age of 17 with a married man. This caused great consternation on the
part of her maternal grandmother with whom Ernestina had lived from an

early age, and who was '*muy recta*' ('very upright/moral'). Ernestina's misdeed made her grandmother feel that she had 'wasted her time' trying to educate Ernestina, and that Ernestina lacked 'respect'. Aside from scolding Ernestina severely for bringing a 'bad name' on their household, she took a very strong line on reminding her that the child was her own responsibility: while she herself had raised Ernestina (whose own mother had had a succession of partners), she was adamant about not bringing up a great-grandchild as well. When the baby was finally born, Ernestina was forced by her grandmother's detachment to take him with her to various cleaning jobs in houses and *sodas* (small restaurants) and to pay for the privilege by taking a cut in wages. Ernestina emphasised that: '*es duro ser madre soltera* responsable' ('it's hard to be a *responsible* single mother'). None the less, she takes pride in having worked around the clock in order to maintain her son, and to have done this single-handedly, when pressures on some single mothers can cause them to 'give their children away' ('*los regalan a otros*'), or even 'abandon them in the street' ('*los abandonan en la calle*').

Reactions to separation

As for women who are separated, and especially those who take the step to leave husbands or partners themselves, negative memories of their sufferings at the hands of men usually means that cynicism and anger take precedence over sadness or regret. For example, Layla, a mother of four in Cañas, has absolutely no misgivings about her decision to leave either of her two partners (one to whom she was married, the other whom she lived with). Aside from having extricated herself from violence and infidelity, she declares that financial neglect is not much fun either. According to Layla, neither of her ex-spouses (both of them drug-dealers) could support anyone if they tried, and '*no se puede enamorarse de hambre*' ('it's impossible to fall in love with hunger').

Appraisals of female headship: longer-term experiences

As already indicated, a sense of achievement in managing lone parenthood successfully (usually measured by children's educational progress and their own personal or conjugal happiness) is often a major compensation for women, and is frequently accompanied by other positive feelings. As such, while overviews of long-term experiences of female headship are mixed, for the most part the balance sheet is weighted favourably.

María Cruz in Querétaro, for example, worked hard to raise the three offspring arising from an 11-year relationship with a married man that terminated on account of his womanising. Although María Cruz claims that lone parenthood has been difficult economically, she is '*muy a gusto por la libertad*' ('very thankful for the freedom') it has given her. Indeed, even though she found a new boyfriend three years after the break-up and is still with him, she claims to be relieved that he wants to continue living with his mother rather than move in with her, because she does not want to have to do his washing and ironing (see later).

Even if she felt pain when she initially lost each of her three former partners, Socorro (Querétaro) also likes the feeling of being in charge of her own affairs and managing her time without having to answer to anyone. Although Socorro said that it had been hard economically as a mother of nine, having a man in the house rarely made much difference to her financial status. As such, although her first partner (with whom she lived for seven years) forbade her to take employment, she has worked more or less constantly since then, aside from a 12-month respite in the early stages of her third relationship. The major problem Socorro identified about being alone was the vulnerability attached to being their children's sole provider, and what might happen to them if she fell ill or met with an accident. On top of this, the pressure of having to perform the additional roles of nursemaid, cook and advisor and whether her energy would last out for all these tasks represented a constant source of worry. Now the children are older, however, Socorro is able to look back on her efforts with pride, declaring: '*Me siento a gusto*' ('I feel good').

Dolores (Puerto Vallarta), calls herself a 'heroine' for having raised her family virtually single-handedly. Although she was not a female head *sensu strictu*, in that she did have a husband until 1990, he was 30 years older than her and an extremely weak individual who soon after they got married allowed Dolores to support him more or less entirely. For this reason, Dolores had always described herself as the 'man *and* woman in this house' and took compensation in her early forties by having an extra-marital affair (with her husband's knowledge) which led to the birth of her two youngest children.

Layla (Cañas) feels in some way '*poderosa*' (powerful) to be a lone mother, especially in comparison with the fate of her ex-partners. This is partly because she has her children, which not only gives her emotional fulfilment and support, but forces her to plan sensibly for the future and to develop her capacities for independence and responsibility. Concerns for her children help her resist the temptations of encounters with other men, and as the children grow up she knows that the rewards for her investment in raising them will include financial security as well as psychological well-being. For men, on the other hand, Layla thinks there is often nothing left to show for a relationship but hurt, even if they have been the ones responsible for the breakdown. Because men cannot (or will not) accept that they were 'at fault' and/or deal easily with pain, they usually move on to other relationships quickly and

without thinking. This generally contributes to a cumulative trail of destruction
where they usually end up paying the price for 'harming women' in the
first place.

What emerges very strongly in this array of accounts from Mexico and
Costa Rica is pride among women for having managed single-handedly; the
way in which children have often compensated for the absence of male
partners; and a sense of greater personal power and freedom. What is equally
apparent is the way in which women have often suffered material and
emotional hardship as members of male-headed households, along with
limited control over their own lives (see also Vega, 1992:36). When living
with men means burdens and inequalities for women that can be lessened
by living alone, it is not surprising that some women not only opt out of existing
relationships, but do so on a long-term or permanent basis (see later). Indeed,
as Collins (1991:163) notes more generally, one important compensation of
lone parenthood is independence: 'not independence in the sense of freedom
to come and go at will, for no parent has that, but the control over decisions
that comes from needing to refer only to the well-being of family members,
not to someone else's opinions'. Even in the Philippines, where considerable
opprobrium is attached to lone parenthood, and/or because most are widows
who had no choice in the matter, it is interesting that many women still
emphasise advantages in being unpartnered. Virtually all the sex workers in
Cebu, for example, stressed that living without men gave them greater
freedom (it would certainly be very difficult for them to engage in their
professions with a partner, father or brother in the house) and less conflict,
violence and hard work. Moreover, while some sex workers recall their
experiences of male abandonment with anger or sadness, they often talk of
their households as a refuge from their degrading (and male-dominated) work
environments in a way that women with partners tend not to do (see Chant
and McIlwaine, 1995a: Chapter 7).[2] Where women live with female kin or
friends, they usually receive considerable practical help with childcare and
domestic labour, as well as steady emotional support (see Chant, 1996b),[3]
and sex workers who live independently can generally afford paid
childminders. This brings us to a more detailed analysis of domestic labour
and other practical aspects of female headship.

Domestic labour and household headship

Housework and childcare in Mexico are squarely identified with women, and,
despite quite significant increases in female labour force participation and
in women's roles in household decision-making, there has been no obvious
'masculinisation' of domestic labour in the last decade, especially in respect

of husbands' contributions (Chant, 1994b). None the less, female heads of household can usually expect some help from sons. In Querétaro in 1982–83, for example, 36 per cent of female lone parents had help with housework and childcare from male as well as female children, compared with virtually none of the female spouses in male-headed nuclear households (Chant, 1984a:242). Moreover, a greater prevalence of sharing domestic tasks in female-headed units in general meant that hours spent per person per week on tasks such as washing clothes and general cleaning were less in female-than male-headed households – ranging from 5.3 hours for these two activities in female-headed lone-parent households to 11.1 in male-headed nuclear units (*ibid.*:244, Table 5.2). This saving in time is critically important for female heads. Socorro (Querétaro), for example, who works a six-day week as an office cleaner and whose household presently consists of her elderly father and two sons (aged 14 and 22 years – both of whom are working students), could not manage unless everyone pitched in. Although boys of these ages are not commonly found helping their mothers, the pattern of each household member having a task was instilled in all of Socorro's nine children from an early age. Both sons do their chores with good grace and do not get embarrassed (as many do) to be *seen* doing housework. When I arrived to interview Socorro in 1994, for example, Juan Antonio, the elder son, was hanging up the washing and, following this, spent a good hour sweeping and tidying up the yard.

In Guanacaste, male help with housework (if not childcare) is a little more frequent, but mainly restricted to shopping rather than 'inside' chores such a washing dishes, washing clothes or ironing. Some women declared that men's willingness to shop stems not so much from a desire to collaborate or to show goodwill, but as a means both of controlling expenditure and keeping their wives indoors (Chant, 1991b:72). As such, the participation of husbands in reproductive labour is something of a double-edged sword. As for children, although as in Mexico, girls do more than boys around the house, the latter do help to collect firewood, and in female-headed households often take on a wider range of activities. The burden for female heads is further lessened in that when their partners are absent, whether temporarily or permanently, mealtimes are more flexible and women do not have the strain of washing and pressing men's clothes to order.[4]

Men seem to do slightly more around the home in the Philippines than in Costa Rica or Mexico, especially in respect of spending time with children (usually in the form of playing games and sharing affection). Cooking is also sometimes done by husbands, especially when they are unemployed, and it is customary for Filipino men to take charge of the household chores in the first month after a baby is born. In some households, however, many domestic tasks are done by a 'helper', who may or may not be a relative, but who lives as part of the family and does housework in return for free board and lodging (see Chant and McIlwaine, 1995a). Whatever the case, in male- and female-headed households alike, sons and daughters are expected to assist in some way, although depending on numbers, ages and sexes of children, there may be a gender division of tasks and girls often end up with more to do than boys. For example, when Elvira (Boracay) became a widow, her daughters tended to take on board the traditionally 'feminine' chores of cleaning and laundry, whereas the sons took over their father's former role in heavier tasks such as collecting firewood and water. Beyond this, however, the high proportion of extended households in the Philippines means that domestic labour is often shared by more than one adult as well as children, as is also the case among female-headed units in Mexico and Costa Rica, where extension is more prevalent than in households headed by men. In these latter two contexts, this is not only associated with the alleviation of chores for female heads, but greater prospects of labour force participation. Although household extension is also significant for women in the Philippines in this respect, external links with kin are often equally if not more important (see Peterson, 1993; also below).

Links with kin, friends and neighbours

As noted in Chapters 1 and 2, there is some debate as to whether the utilisation of kin and friendship networks is less or greater by female or male heads of household. At one level, networks may be very active because female heads need to look outside the household if there are insufficient resources (monetarily or in terms of labour) within it. Alternatively, it has also been suggested that female heads are either too busy to cultivate social networks, or an inability to meet requirements of symmetry in reciprocal obligations makes it preferable to remain relatively self-sufficient. On top of this, negative attitudes towards female heads within low-income communities may mean they have little choice in the matter due to social isolation from neighbours (see earlier).

The one group of female heads to which the scenario of self-sufficiency and social distancing particularly applies is lone-parent sex workers in the Philippines. These women are prone to keep themselves to themselves, and not only have limited contact with neighbours, but are often relatively isolated from their kin networks as well (Chant and McIlwaine, 1995a:302). This is often self-imposed in that distance fom kin preserves secrecy or discretion about what sex workers do and helps to avoid bringing shame on their families. Although many women call this 'sad', they see it as a necessity and often develop very strong relationships with colleagues as a means of compensating, often to the point of living with them. Ties with women in the same position can somewhat inevitably, however, be an immense source of strength for other lone parents as well. For example, one of Dina's best friends in Boracay is a woman who is separated like herself and who also experienced considerable distress at the hands of her husband before they split up. Dina says that she and her friend spend 'very good times together', talking through their problems and getting the anger they feel towards their spouses off their chests. Girlie (Boracay), while still in the preliminary stages of planning her escape from a long and unhappy marriage, finds great comfort talking with a friend whose husband sleeps every night at his girlfriend's house and only comes home to wash, change and eat. Girlie is always advising her friend to leave him and maintains that, in many ways, close contact with somebody else in a hopeless and difficult marriage has given her the strength to plan a new, independent future for herself.

Although negative attitudes towards lone parents are common within the case study communities (see earlier), it is also the case that as neighbours come to know each other, better relations can build up. Justina, a widow living alone in Cañas, for example, said that people are quite helpful because they know she is poor, and Layla, a twice-separated lone mother says that now people in the immediate vicinity have got to know her, she feels she actually gets more sympathy and assistance than if she were to have a man around.

For the most part however, links with kin are strongest. These are often felt to be critically important by lone mothers whose attempts to keep in close touch with blood relatives such as parents, siblings, grandparents, cousins and so on, usually derive from the imperative of giving their children a greater sense of having 'family' around. Generally speaking, ties are particularly close with female kin, such as mothers and sisters.[5] Links with kin not only comprise psychological and social dimensions, but economic ones as well, and are usually to the benefit of all parties. This is exemplified by Marrime's *de facto* female-headed household in Cebu.

Marrime (23 years) and her sister Velma (21 years) are both *de facto* female heads whose merchant seamen husbands remit to them a joint total of P1250 ($50 US) a week. Both women in 1993 were expecting their first babies, and worked together on an unpaid basis between 2 and 11 pm each day at their mother's *sari-sari* store in the port. Marrime herself used to work in the formal sector (as a sales assistant in one of Cebu's major department stores), but when her father died in 1988 and her mother moved to live at the *sari-sari* store, she felt bound to help her widowed parent. Although Marrime's and Velma's mother does not give them a wage, the sisters are allowed to take as much food as they like from the shop and usually eat there as well. The house they live in belongs to their mother and they do not pay rent. With so much assistance in kind, Marrime and Velma spend only P285 ($11.4 US) a week between them. This, coupled with remittances, means they have savings in the bank, which, as far as they are concerned, are available for any family member who runs into difficulty.

As for *de jure* female heads, although networks may be smaller due to lack of a spouse's kin (see Chapter 1, Note 8), in a significant minority of cases in the study localities, links with in-laws are retained after marital breakdown, and some in-laws even end up siding with the women if their sons are responsible for marital conflict or separation. For example, Girlie's in-laws in Boracay want her to stay with their alcoholic son, Dominico, and give her as much support as they can. Most of this is of an emotional nature, but money and practical assistance are forthcoming from time to time. Girlie finds this helpful, although she suspects that her in-laws' gestures might also be a means of trying to protect their son, to ensure that he does not become a burden on them, and/or to guarantee continued links with their grandson. The desire of grandparents to maintain contact with grandchildren is also important in the case of Dina (Boracay). Dina's mother-in-law, for example, currently provides bed, board and college fees for Dina's three eldest children who are studying at higher education institutions in Manila. Although Dina supports her youngest three children in Boracay, they too will go on to Manila when they graduate from high school. While Dina's mother-in-law is clearly very concerned for her grandchildren, however, she is also very fond of Dina in her own right. In fact she feels so wretched about the wrong her son has done his wife and children in taking up with a prostitute, that she even mooted the idea that Dina get a writ served upon him for adultery and negligence. Layla (Cañas) has also found solace with the parents of her first husband, who allowed her to camp on their patio with her three children when she first left him. Layla claims their desire to show support is partly motivated by their disapproval of their son's behaviour (drug-dealing, violence and womanising), although concern for their grandchildren is uppermost. All the above cases share similarities in this latter respect and indicate that sometimes greater importance may be attached to the wider family (that is, across three generations) than ties between parents and children *per se*.

Poverty and economic vulnerability

As for material aspects of life in female-headed households, there is little doubt that women have to struggle on several fronts, mainly because their earnings are usually less than half of men's (see Chapter 6), and because unlike male heads they have no 'wives' to perform non-market work on a full-time basis and/or who can supplement their incomes. Yet although this is one side of the picture, it is interesting that in none of the localities are women-headed households (as a whole) poorer than male-headed units measured in terms of average per capita incomes (that is, total household earnings and/or income receipts divided by household size) (see Chapter 2).

Clearly, however, women households heads are a heterogeneous group, one critical factor distinguishing them being whether they are *de facto* heads supported wholly or in part by the earnings of an absent partner, or *de jure* heads who in the vast majority of cases receive no financial help from ex-spouses (Chapter 6).

The only substantial numbers of *de facto* female heads are in the Philippines and Costa Rica, yet interestingly while *de facto* heads in the former are much better off in per capita income terms than their *de jure* counterparts (with weekly per capita incomes in 1993 of P363 [$14.5 US] against P244 [$9.8 US]), in Costa Rica this is the converse. Here (1989 data) *de jure* female heads have weekly per capita incomes of 660.5 *colones* ($8.3 US), but their *de facto* counterparts only 626.5 ($7.8 US) (Chant, 1991b:73). This difference owes to two reasons. First, men in Costa Rica seem to be less judicious about sending money home to their wives.[6] Second, one-third of migrant Filipino husbands are working overseas where earnings are far greater. For example, Carmencita in Cebu receives P10,000 a month ($400 US) by bank transfer from her husband who is on a two-year contract as a goldsmith in Japan. This is equivalent to nearly four times the legal minimum wage in the Philippines and is enough to support herself, their five children and a co-resident nephew, all of whom are studying. Analyn in Lapu-Lapu is sent P6000 a month ($240 US) by her husband who is working as a mechanic in Kuwait. Topped up with the weekly sum of $5–6 US she herself makes from selling 'banana-cue' (barbecued banana) to factory workers in the Mactan Export Processing Zone, this stretches to support their four children, Analyn's two co-resident student sisters and her mother.

As for *de jure* heads, it is possibly surprising that in both Costa Rica and Mexico, they have higher average per capita incomes than male heads. In Costa Rica, male-headed households had a mean per capita income of 636.5 *colones* ($17.9 US) per week, which is 96 per cent of that of their female-headed counterparts, and in Mexico in 1986, male-headed household per capita incomes were only 6549 *pesos* or 94 per cent of the average of 6949 *pesos* in women-headed units.[7] Even in the Philippines, where *de jure* female heads are less well off than male heads, the difference is not marked, with the former earning 94 per cent of the mean per capita income of P260 ($110.4 US) in male-headed households.

One explanation for the virtual parity in per capita incomes of male- and female-headed households is that there tend to be lower dependency ratios in female-headed units, partly due to their smaller size and partly because they make fuller use of their labour supply (which is often greater by virtue of their heading older households and/or being more likely to be extended) (see also Chapter 2). In the Philippines the mean number of 'dependants' per earner is 2.9 in male-headed households compared with 2.6 in female-headed units, and in Costa Rica, the figures are 3.6 and 3.2 respectively. The fact of sons working particularly helps to compensate for the low wages of female heads, and some older women come to regard them as something of a substitute for husbands. This is apparent in Girlie's case in Boracay, and Ana María (Puerto Vallarta) declared that once her sons started working and contributing to household income she felt much more secure than she had been with a husband who often returned from drinking sprees saying '*No hay para comer*' ('There's no money for food'). Fonseca's research in Porto Alegre, Brazil suggests this applies in low-income communities elsewhere: while a happy marriage is aspired to by many Porto Alegre women, experience 'slowly eats away at these aspirations. After the menopause, a single woman no longer represents a taunt to male virility; having gained a moment of respite in the battlefield of the sexes, she considers her options from a new vantage point – and, not uncommonly, her choice falls on sons rather than husbands' (Fonseca, 1991:157). Many of the single women interviewed by Fonseca claimed to live without partners 'not because they lacked opportunities, but by choice' (*ibid*.:156; see also Powell, 1986 on the Caribbean).

Although González de la Rocha's (1994a:210) work in Guadalajara, Mexico, reports that sons sometimes contribute to 'repeating established' patterns of gender relations' by determining whether mothers work or by retaining more of their wages for personal use than female household members, this was not the experience of the majority of women in the present case study areas. For example, although the sons of the widow Sabina (León) did not let her work (just as her husband had never done), they did look after her extremely well. Thus although such patterns conceivably perpetuate an ideology of the male provider, in no case in the Mexican, Costa Rican or Philippine study localities did I find sons abusing the situation by dominating their mothers or assuming the role of 'household head', usually because they had too much respect for them, as explored further in Chapter 8.

Another factor contributing to the economic health of *de jure* female-headed households (and part related to their more advanced stage in the life course) is that they are more likely than male heads to receive remittances from non-resident relatives, mainly children. For example, in the three Mexican cities in 1986, only 11 per cent of male-headed households were sent remittances by kin (representing an average of only 1.6 per cent of total income), whereas this applied to 31 per cent of *de jure* female-headed units, where the average contribution to household income was 12.5 per cent. Similar patterns are found in Costa Rica where some women also receive state transfer payments. In 1989, a total of 28 per cent of *de jure* female heads received remittances (mainly from children and other relatives), and an additional 27 per cent state transfers (one-third of these in conjunction with remittances). The average income from these sources as a proportion of total income receipts of *de jure* female heads was 27 per cent, compared with 10 per cent among male-headed households.

Perceived control and the distribution of household income

Over and above the fact that incomes in female-headed households may be bolstered by multiple-earning patterns within households and remittances from outside, gender differences in the allocation of earnings mean that money tends to be distributed more evenly to household members. While women devote most if not all of their wages to household use in Mexico, Costa Rica and the Philippines, this is much less the case with men. In Mexico, for example, the 1986 questionnaire survey showed that while women dedicated the equivalent of 106 per cent of their earnings to household income from their principal jobs (a number of women had more than one income-generating activity), the corresponding average for men was only 67.5 per cent (Chant, 1991a:203). Since female heads tend to be more economically active than their counterparts in male-headed units, this helps to make up the shortfall from their lower earning power (see also Chapters 6 and 8). Another factor is that female heads of household generally have greater control over the income that ends up in the pool for household use (whether from earnings, remittances or transfer payments), than women with male partners, and incomes tend to benefit other household members (as discussed in relation to children in Chapter 8). On top of this, it is not only the case that in male-headed households men may retain substantial amounts of their own earnings for personal use, but, in the Philippines in particular, are also accustomed to taking 'top-up' money from working wives (Chant and McIlwaine, 1995a:283).

For example, one married woman in Boracay, Sabing, who works as a caretaker for a small complex of holiday cottages, is frequently asked to hand over her entire pay-packet by her husband Leopoldo, who routinely loses it on cockfights and/or buying cockerels to train for fighting. The breeding of cockerels is an expensive process involving the purchase of special vitamins. Leopoldo has also put Sabing in serious difficulties by borrowing money from paying guests at the cottages and telling them that his wife will reimburse them. This has forced Sabing into pawning pieces of her jewellery and begging from her own friends and relatives. Although Leopoldo lost his job as a nightwatchman two years ago and has not worked since, he swears to Sabing that training fighting cocks will make him very rich one day. This has not transpired to date, however, and Sabing deplores Leopoldo's apparently greater concern for the birds than his wife and children. None the less, she sees herself as fortunate that her eldest son and daughter are now working and can afford to help her out (see also Dumont, 1994)

Girlie (Boracay) has similar problems with her husband, Dominico, whom she described in one breath as 'an alcoholic, a chainsmoker, a cardplayer, and unemployed'. Although Dominico has not worked for three years, he still gets through four packets of cigarettes a day, and, before getting out of bed in the morning, 'must drink at least one San Miguel' (beer). His only contribution to household survival is to do the cooking. Girlie, on the other hand, works seven days a week selling T-shirts and sarongs from a rented stall in the main tourist market on the island. Girlie gives Dominico P100 ($4 US) a day for his '*bisyos*' (vices), but when he runs out he gets his purchases on credit and to avoid public embarrassment, Girlie has to settle his bill at the *sari-sari* store at the end of each month, which sometimes comes to (P2000–3000) ($80–100 US). Although in 1995 Girlie was making about $150 US profit a week from her stall, her outgoings were also large since it costs $200 US per month to put her son, Denis, through a degree in marine transport studies in Manila. Although Girlie gives her husband money because 'I don't want to make trouble. I want to keep my husband quiet', and has long resisted the idea of splitting up, supporting a 'no-good man' has now become so intolerable that she plans to accept Denis's invitation for her to go and live with him in the capital when he finishes his studies, and is currently in the process of saving what she can to begin a new life there (see also Chapter 8). Indeed, whereas in the advanced economies, Dallos (1995:184) asserts that many women are 'shocked to realise the extent of their inequality and dependence' when their relationships disintegrate, this is often the converse in the case study localities, not to mention other developing countries.[8]

On balance, although the disadvantages of female household headship can include loneliness, pressure at having sole responsibility for children, a sense of economic vulnerability, and suspicion and isolation from others, not to mention social disgrace, women frequently articulate a range of advantages including less housework and/or a greater amount of shared labour within the home, less fear, less domestic conflict, more control over finances and decision-making, greater freedom, wider social and economic roles, and, among *de jure* heads at least, greater wealth and well-being within the household. Whether or not these benefits might be exaggerated by respondents in the interests of self-justification, there is little doubt that, at the bottom line, they expose a wide range of injustices to which women are often subjected in male-headed households, with the outcomes of female household headship often being better than anticipated. Accordingly, many women prefer to remain alone when they finally become accustomed to the state.

PERSPECTIVES ON SATISFACTION WITH FEMALE HOUSEHOLD HEADSHIP: VIEWS ON MARRIAGE AND REMARRIAGE

Despite the ambivalent position occupied by female heads of household within their communities, not to mention other social and economic pressures, going back to former partners was rarely considered by respondents in any of the three countries.[9] The vast array of popular Costa Rican refrains alluding to keeping away from problematic spouses indicates that this is often more than purely personal or idiosyncratic tendency, including: '*Agua que no debe beber, hay que dejarlo correr*' ('Water that isn't for drinking should be left to run away'), '*Basura que se bota, no se vuelve a recoger*' ('You don't go and pick up rubbish you've thrown away'), and '*Lo que hay que botar, no se vuelve a juntar*' ('what must be thrown away shouldn't be gathered up again').

Beyond this, the vast majority of female heads do not wish to meet or reside with another man, and in fact the only major group of women who *do* desire changes in their living arrangements belong to male-headed households. The latter either want their husbands to change their behaviour or to extricate themselves from their present circumstances – that is, leave home or get their husbands to leave. The only notable change desired by female heads, on the other hand, is to affirm their single status by getting a divorce. In fact, many respondents (even in the Philippines) expressed envy at the fact that I myself had been able to arrange a divorce within six months. Aside from high costs however (see Chapter 6), women are often unable to petition for one because the whereabouts of former spouses are unknown. Lupe (Puerto Vallarta), for instance, would now like to divorce, but cut off all contact with her husband when she split up with him. One of the reasons she gave for not arranging a divorce at the time was that subconsciously she did not want to remarry. Indeed, even the idea of meeting another man (let alone marrying them), is anathema to most female heads, and if considered at all, is an extremely low priority.

Older women are perhaps the most emphatic about remaining alone, with María del Refugio (Querétaro), a 65-year-old widow declaring '*Ya no más viejitos!*' ('No more blokes for me!'), although this also applies to younger women who had already been married or experienced a consensual union. For example, Dina (39 years) in Boracay, said that she never wanted another man in her life: 'I afraid already! My husband is bad, I might get worse!' and Lupe (39 years) (Puerto Vallarta) among many other Mexican and Costa Rican women, declared '*mejor sola que mal acompañada*' ('better alone than with bad company'). In sharing news of my personal circumstances of recent marital break up at the time, virtually all maintained that I should not take my husband back. Weighing up the evidence, most respondents concluded that my spouse did not 'deserve' to be taken back (because he had hurt me), besides which they could see no earthly reason why I was in need of him economically (since I had been the major breadwinner).

As for the notion that respondents might marry another man, this usually met with laughter, scorn and/or exaggerated shows of mock fear! Aside from protecting their independence, reasons given by women in the case study communities for remaining alone included reluctance to compromise, the desire to maintain a peaceful atmosphere in their homes, and unwillingness to subject themselves to male cruelty or irresponsibility. Such attitudes correspond with Safa's (1995:83) study of Puerto Rican manufacturing workers, where two-thirds of the women did not wish to remarry: 'They see men as restricting their freedom rather than assisting them with the responsibility of raising a family.' Similar patterns are reported in Shaw's (1991:149) research on the UK where attitudes towards remarriage are marked by 'wariness, reluctance or inability to trust, and fear of getting hurt again'. Resistance among women to subject themselves to male control is also noted by Collins (1991:163) who argues: 'For many lone mothers it is far from welcome – and a diminishing experience – to have coped so well for so long, and then to have a bossy man wading in, expecting to take over', further noting that 'Where a lone-parent household has come about through divorce, these new relationships created out of the wreckage of previous ones, embody a hard-won stability and sense of meaning and purpose of life, and all this is put in jeopardy by the remarriage' (*ibid*.:169).

Indeed, while one or two female heads in the case study communities do have boyfriends, they are reluctant to move in with them. Celia (León), whose husband left her for another woman at the end of a tormented nine-year relationship, is at present having an affair with a married man. This, for Celia is ideal, since it allows her to keep her distance and independence. In Celia's own words: 'I would never want to get married ever again or live with any man. It's better this way (alone). I protect myself.' In the event that co-residence is mooted, the general feeling among women in Mexico and Costa Rica is that a consensual union is preferable, primarily because it allows more freedom to split up and men cannot take women for granted in the same way

This is interesting because it reveals an expectation that marriage and living in a male-headed household implies an automatic transfer of rights to men. In other words, women do not have the confidence that ceding headship to men allows them to retain much in the way of power or freedom. Having said this, some women who had never married felt that formal matrimony might give them greater rights, even if this could simply indicate an element of the 'the grass being greener on the other side'. The only other reason for wanting to marry is religion: Astrid (Cañas) who has recently converted to Evangelism, would like to conform with religious edict by marrying Oscar, her third partner (of 12 years duration). Although Oscar is willing, however, she has no idea whether her first partner (to whom she was married) 'is dead or alive' and cannot for this reason get a divorce (see earlier). While women in Costa Rica often do end up living with a succession of partners, in Mexico and the Philippines, many women (even those currently with men), felt that if they knew what they knew now, they would not repeat the experience. This is possibly exemplified by the fact that in the three Mexican case study cities in 1986, only 6.8 per cent of women living with men were with a second or subsequent partner, and the rate is even lower in the Philippines. Indeed, whatever women's experiences of marriage, cohabitation, separation or widowhood, many remembered their happiest times as being single women. Eden (Boracay), for example, said that the highspots of her life were those spent 'larking around' with her female *barkada* (gang) in Manila, and Consuelo (Puerto Vallarta) declared rather miserably: '*Ya casada, no puede salir uno mucho – si no pides permiso a tu marido*' ('once married you can't go out much – unless you ask permission from your husband'). One important factor contributing to nostalgia for single status is that reality of marriage or marriage partners rarely matches up to ideals and expectations. Specifications of 'ideal' attributes of male and female spouses identified by respondents in semi-structured interviews in the case study areas are given in Tables 7.1–7.3. These are interesting not only because they are so removed from experience and/or reality (especially in the case of 'ideal husbands'), but also because of what they reveal about gender in the three countries.

In Mexico, for example, while women usually feel that men get what they are looking for in a wife (Table 7.1), this is not the case in terms of what women get with husbands. Most women are of the opinion that it is difficult to find an 'honourable' and 'honest' man. As Emilia (Puerto Vallarta) stated: '*Le hablan bonito a uno, luego le engañan a uno*' ('first they "sweet-talk" you, then they deceive you'). Dolores (Puerto Vallarta) said that trying to find a good man was like trying to find '*un aguja en las pajas*' ('a needle in a haystack'). Socorro (Querétaro) declared that there were no decent men: '*pues no hay ninguno – son unos cabrones bién hechos*' ('in fact, not one, they're right bastards'). María del Refugio (Querétaro) gave the comment that '*El mexicano – celoso de la honra pero desentido del gasto*' ('Mexican men are very concerned with honour but very dishonourable when it comes to financial support'). Even Saul, Rosa's husband (Puerto Vallarta), said that only 10 per cent of Mexican men would make good marriage partners, adding 'And believe me, I know the Mexican male!' Summing up responses from about 30 households, it seemed that women had less than a 10 per cent chance of finding an 'ideal' husband, but men had more than a 90 per cent chance of meeting the right kind of wife.[10]

Table 7.1 *Ideal characteristics of marriage partners according to interviewees in Mexican case study settlements*

Ideal characteristics of a husband	Ideal characteristics of a wife
Responsible	Good housekeeper/housewife*
Hardworking	Understanding
Non-abusive/ someone who does	Supportive
not take advantage	Sincere
Faithful /not unfaithful	Good conduct/behaviour
Understanding	Trustworthy
Not a drinker**	Hardworking (in home and labour market)
Not a wife-beater	Responsible
Honest	Unselfish
Honourable/someone who would	Respectful/respects husband
not abandon wife	Someone with assets
Supportive	Good looks
Respectful/respects wife	
Considerate of wife's needs	
Permissive of wife's employment	
Same age as wife	
Capable of feeling love	
Affectionate	
Not Mexican (!)	
Light skin colouring	

Source: Semi-structured interview surveys in Querétaro, León and Puero Vallarta, 1986, 1992 and 1994.

Notes:

*   This was defined variously as having the ability to cook beans well, of being happy to do men's washing and ironing, and a preference for being in the house (as opposed to outside it).

**   This, along with no wife-beating, was sometimes subsumed under the catch-all of 'no vices', which respondents were then asked to itemise.

NB. Phrasing in respondents' own words (literally translated from the Spanish), or as closely paraphrased as possible. Qualities specified for husbands are exclusively those identified by female respondents. Qualities specified for wives are based on a mixture of statements from male and female respondents. The lists for husbands and wives are arranged as far as possible to reflect the combined priority which respondents accorded to different attributes and the frequency with which the attributes were specified.

The ideal characteristics of male marriage partners in Costa Rica were similar to Mexico, yet more frequently articulated in an inverted manner – that is, in terms of men *not* being something or other (see Table 7.2).

Table 7.2 *Ideal characteristics of marriage partners according to interviewees in Costa Rican case study settlements*

Ideal characteristics of a husband	Ideal characteristics of a wife
Responsible	Good housekeeper/housewife*
Hardworking (preferably with a regular job)	Good conduct/behaviour
Not a drinker**	Faithful
Not a drug-user	Honest and trustworthy
Not a womaniser	Responsible
Not a thief	Hardworking
Not *machista*	Loving
Sincere	Obedient/defers to husband
Understanding	Physically attractive
Affectionate	Humble
Likes to do things *with* wife	No vices***
Not abusive of step-daughters	Good company
Physical appearance irrelevant	
Older, but not more than 10 years older than wife	
Humble (re. socio-economic status)	

Source: Semi-structured interviews in Liberia, Cañas and Santa Cruz, 1989, 1992 and 1994.
Notes:
*   This was defined variously as women being clean and tidy, having food on the table on time, being prepared to get up at any time of the night to make snacks, and being willing/happy to do men's washing and ironing, and to take their husbands' boots off! It also referred to women who were the 'stay-at-home sort'.
**   This, along with drug-use, womanising, thieving, *machismo*, was sometimes subsumed under the catch-all of 'no vices'.
*** For women, no vices meant not using make-up or spending time out of the home, as opposed, for example, to drinking or smoking.

Most women in Costa Rica deem the qualities of regular hard work and a responsible attitude to money as priorities in a spouse, although the reality is usually the converse (see also Chapter 6).

As for the chances of meeting someone that matched up to these ideals, Lidia (Cañas) said '*no hay buenos hombres – es un sueño*' ('there aren't any good men – it's a dream'). Athough Justina (Cañas) conceded that '*entre cién hay uno*' ('there is one in a hundred'), she was quick to qualify this by adding that '*Los hombres están tan corrumpidos*' ('men are hopelessly corrupt'), and 'they will always be the same, whether old or young'. Ernestina

(Cañas) claimed that 'If you find a good man, you'd better make the most of it, because there won't be another one!' As in Mexico, the odds on finding an ideal husband were less than 10 per cent, but on finding an ideal wife, around 90 per cent.

Sexual promiscuity on the part of men figures largely as a fear and reality among women in Costa Rica and is often identified as casting a fatal blow to conjugal bonds. Marta (Liberia) talked about the '*hombre machista*' (macho man), being the only one allowed to have any say in the household, and being womanisers who '*riegan la semilla en todos lados*' ('scatter their seed everywhere'). Braulia (Liberia) declared that whether men are married or not they cannot help '*buscando la carne*' (literally 'hunting for flesh'). Astrid (Cañas) felt that men are capable of much greater cruelty and deception than women, with their favourite pastime being '*brincando de mujer a mujer como conejitos*' ('jumping from woman to woman like rabbits'). Men's 'addiction' to sexual activity is highlighted by the importance of a wife's physical attributes for men, yet is also recognised as a major reason for unsuccessful partnerships. Juana (Liberia), for example, claims that men often move in with or marry women '*sólo porque son bonitas y ya!*' ('only because they're pretty'). The trouble here, according to Juana, is that this is very superficial: 'Once the looks wear off, men start behaving very badly, usually by taking another woman.' In turn, however, according to Concha (Cañas), this fulfils a further function for men. Concha claims that 'men like to have two women on the go' because they then achieve their aim of feeling powerful by making women suffer: 'There's nothing men like better than to see women crying over them.'

In the Philippine study communities, a rather different set of qualities were itemised for ideal male and female spouses, with good fatherhood and a sense of family being emphasised among the ideal characteristics for men, and for women, kindness, a 'good family background' (that is, a 'reputable' home without history of 'scandal'), and femininity – the latter usually taken to mean calm, quiet and peaceful with a 'soft' heart (that is tender/emotional) (see Table 7.3). This undoubtedly owes to the extreme importance attached to family cohesion in Filipino culture, and to notions of 'smooth interpersonal relations' effected through non-confrontational behaviour, concession and female propriety (see Chapter 5).

Although respondents felt that the prospects of finding a 'decent' husband were better than in Mexico or Costa Rica, with one or two people in about 30 households suggesting that there may be a 30 per cent chance, most women were less optimistic, with Dina (Boracay) declaring that if she could live her life again, she would want a man who was a 'responsible father – not like my husband!' As for women living up to 'ideal' specifications, the vast bulk of respondents said 'Most women are like this' (kind, understanding, responsible and so on), and estimated percentages of women living up to the ideal attributes of a wife were invariably above 90 per cent. None the less, however limited the expectation of finding an ideal husband in the Philippines, marriage is generally seen as preferable to a free union, not only because of the benefits attached to conformity with moral codes for the people concerned, but, more importantly, for children. As Jocely (Boracay) said: 'Marriage is not for sex. It is about living together, harmoniously, as a family ... with children.' Related to this, various respondents noted that it was difficult for children to get a birth certificate unless parents were married, which, in turn, meant problems proving age for important events such as school enrolment. Another concern was that if children ever tried to get an overseas work permit, they might be discriminated against if they had been born illegitimately. Eden (Boracay) recounted that someone that she knew with a Bachelor of Education (B.Ed) degree had been unable to get a passport because her parents were unmarried. Beyond this, women are very much of the opinion that there should be one man for life, and if married in church, one stays with the man forever, no matter how unhappy the relationship (see also Chapter 6).

Table 7.3 *Ideal characteristics of marriage partners according to interviewees in Philippine case study settlements*

Ideal characteristics of a husband	Ideal characteristics of a wife
Responsible	Good housekeeper
Not a drinker	Responsible
Not interested in cockfighting*	Kind
Good father/family man	Understanding
Not a smoker	Hardworking
Not an adulterer	Loyal
Hardworking	No vices
Not very handsome	Physically attractive
Helpful	Reputable family background
Good advisor	'Feminine'
	Good company

Source: Semi-structured interviews in Cebu, Lapu-Lapu and Boracay, 1993 and 1995.

Notes:

* Cockfighting is the main form of male gambling in the Philippines. Mahjong also involves betting, but is a pastime which attracts both sexes and usually entails smaller financial stakes.

The open articulation of the limited prospects of finding an 'ideal husband' reveals a strong awareness of women's disadvantage in the marriage market and of gender inequality in general. Women in all the case study communities, for example, seem to be very conscious of the fact that different sets of rules apply to men. Married men can have mistresses, but if anyone challenges them about this, they laugh, or according to Mary Lovely, a single woman in Cebu, retort 'So what? I'm a man.' As for women's sexuality, this is seen as 'shameful' and something which should be restrained, especially before marriage. Although this is particularly marked in the Philippines, the mother of Ana, a lone parent in Querétaro, had always impressed upon her '*Una sola vez vale la mujer*' ('women only have value one time') that is, as virgins.

Beyond this, gender differences seem to be very much embroiled in people's attitudes towards 'ideal partners'. Very rarely, for example, are the same qualities itemised for husbands as for wives. Indeed the 'male breadwinner/female housekeeper' model is evident in all places. It is also interesting, however, that in none of the countries was it specified that women should be 'good mothers'. This possibly indicates that men are more interested in how their wives will 'serve' them than their children (especially in Mexico and Costa Rica), or that it is assumed that 'good motherhood' comes 'naturally' to women. Moreover, it may also be because men are less concerned about the long term (and children), although children usually come along quite early on in married life.

Women's resistance to remarriage or cohabitation is not only based on negative experiences and the difficulties attached to finding the 'right man' but to some degree may also stem from reluctance to resume duties associated with heterosexual partnerships. For example, it was noted earlier that María Cruz (Querétaro) was unwilling to live with her boyfriend because she did not want to do his laundry. María's fear is probably justified if we recall the case of Socorro (Querétaro), who gave up her job when a new boyfriend moved in (see Chapter 6). Although Socorro had been on her own since our first meeting in 1982, I remember Socorro in the 'honeymoon period' of her third partnership in 1992 proudly unlocking a wardrobe full of beautifully laundered shirts and trousers and claiming how happy she was to be looking after a man again. A year later (by which time he had left), however, she felt betrayed, disillusioned, and above all angry that she had 'given so much' of herself. The persistence of gendered responsibilities indicates difficulties in throwing off the influence of socialisation and wider social norms, and is by no means unknown in other contexts (see for example, Shaw, 1991:148).

A final consideration (and usually a very powerful restraint) in respect of remarriage or living with someone else, is children. Braulia, a 53-year-old woman in Liberia whose husband left her for another woman nearly 20 years ago, has had no boyfriend since. Aside from the fact that Braulia does not want to put herself through any pain again, exclaiming '*ya no!*' ('not anymore') at the prospect of a further partnership, the children get very jealous, although like many other lone parents in the case study localities: '*no faltan hombres*' ('there's no lack of men') who have propositioned her (see earlier). Layla (Cañas) has already put her three eldest children through the experience of having a stepfather and when Juliana, her 10-year-old daughter was asked about whether she would mind if her mother lived with another man, the response was '*mejor no*' ('better not'). Jealousy on the part of children seems to be especially strong among elder sons in their teenage or early adult years, possibly because they come to see themselves as occupying the role of their mothers' male support. For example, the eldest son of Socorro, a lone parent in Querétaro, used to resent Socorro making herself up and putting on her best clothes to meet her boyfriend, and did not like it if she brought him back to the house. This also applies to María Cruz's (Querétaro) eldest son whose jealousy took the form of uncharacteristically argumentative and uncooperative behaviour when her boyfriend stayed overnight. Out of respect for her children, Lupe (Puerto Vallarta) never has a boyfriend back to the house when the children are there.

Mothers are also fearful about possible sexual interference with their daughters if men move in with them. One of the reasons Emilia (Puerto Vallarta) gives for never marrying is her concern for the 'welfare' of her now 14-year-old daughter Brenda. María Idalí (Santa Cruz) actually fostered her first two children when she moved in with a new boyfriend, since one was a girl and she was worried about what might happen to her if he was alone with them. The same applies to a Nicaraguan, Carmen (Cañas): the two children by her first partner were female and her mother kept them out of concern about possible abuse on the part of a stepfather, even before Carmen teamed up with someone else.

There is also the more general fear that stepfathers might maltreat the children to a greater extent than their own fathers, as discussed in the context of Cuernavaca, Mexico, by LeVine (1993:95), and which is echoed by Collins (1991:171) with reference to the UK, who notes that: 'Welcome as the prospect of a break from single-handed responsibilities is to many lone parents, the relief may be dearly bought' (see also Chapter 8).

CONCLUSION

In summing up the profile of female household headship in the case study localities, it is possible to discern a range of practical and ideological benefits linked with independence from a male partner. In all areas, for example, most women heads (and their children) feel more secure economically than their counterparts in male-headed units, in respect of their ability to mobilise household labour supply and to control earnings. In terms of daily reproductive labour, female heads are also more likely to be able to activate the help of sons and daughters and to reduce their overall share of domestic work and childcare. In psychological and ideological terms, the very process of coping with the difficulties of restricted female employment opportunities, sole responsibility for dependants when children are young, and some marginalisation from kin and neighbours, seems to give women a sense of achievement and empowerment. These findings share several similarities with Hardey and Crow's (1991:3) observation for advanced economies that despite 'unrelieved responsibilities and frustrations in the face of adverse economic and social processes of marginalisation', lone parenthood is also associated with considerable 'resilience and inventiveness'.

Clearly, however, we have to bear in mind that female household heads might overemphasise the positive aspects of their situations as a means of denying less auspicious elements, both to themselves and to the outside world, especially given the tendency towards negative images of female headship at community and wider societal levels. Among sex workers in the Philippines, for example, the shame attached to their employment is such that an emphasis on happy home lives and investment in children perhaps represents some way of justifying their livelihoods and lifestyles, and showing what their earnings can achieve. At the same time, there is no reason to suppose that women in male-headed households do not try to paint a 'rosy picture' either, whether to 'save face' or to convince themselves that they have satisfactory marriages.

In fact, it is patently obvious from many of the case studies in this and the preceding chapter, that the realities of life in male-headed households may be far from appealing, and that despite women's fantasies and aspirations, they are often very disillusioned by marriage and/or cohabitation. Disappointment, in my view, is very clearly registered by the fact that most women who end up alone, for whatever reason, are not only adamant about not taking their husbands back, but also about living with any man again. Most female heads are satisfied with their home lives and seem to enjoy greater peace, stability and security than they did as wives in male-headed households. If they do have further relationships with the opposite sex, these are usually on a non-cohabiting basis, except in Costa Rica where women seem to find it particularly hard to make a living on their own and may have to rely on men's financial support. Yet even the difficulties of getting work in

Guanacasteco towns are not so great as to dissuade some female residents from making a conscious choice to stay alone.

Having said this, the power to resist (re)marriage and male household headship is much greater among separated women than those who have never married, especially those who have remained single out of personal choice. While separated women may be viewed with suspicion for having failed to keep their unions together, they are at least able to demonstrate some conformity with social norms in the past, particularly in respect of sexuality: having done the 'decent thing' at one point in their lives gives women the chance to contest criticisms that they are 'loose' women by nature. Another relevant factor is that separated women's personal experiences of conjugal life are often horrific enough to elicit sympathy from those around them and to excuse their reluctance to repeat the dose with another man. Beyond, this, if women took the decision to leave their spouses for the sake of the children, then this lends respectability to their cause, and, in turn, may be backed up by the idea that children need to be protected against possible abuse from stepfathers. In some ways, too, staying on their own and adopting conservative patterns of behaviour not only signifies martyrdom on account of children, but can also show that these women have controllable sexual appetites and are not, as the majority might assume, living alone to fulfil promiscuous fantasies.

As for women who remain single by choice or as a result of male desertion following pre-marital sexual relations, approval and respect are harder to win, and, as suggested previously, owe to prevailing patterns of sexual double standards where women's licence for 'physical indulgence' is minimal. It is only in contexts where women do not have kin in the immediate vicinity and/or are protected by an atmosphere of greater sexual tolerance (as in the tourist resort of Puerto Vallarta, or among sex workers in Cebu), and/or where female household headship is more common, that there is some margin for acceptance (albeit among people in the same place or position). As it is, although there is considerable awareness that prospective husbands are more than likely to let women down, if matrimony (or in Costa Rica, cohabitation) is the only effective passport to sexual activity then it is hardly surprising that many single women succumb to social pressures to get married and/or set up homes with men. In addition to the influence exerted by kin and kinship ideologies, an elaborate religious, civil, commercial and state infrastructure peddling images of conjugal bliss, rewards in heaven, moral virtue, responsible parenthood and so on, exists to remind women that their proper place is with a man, and to support him whatever his failings.

In juxtaposition with the positive endorsement of married life for women, social and civic disapproval of lone motherhood acts as a powerful and persistent reminder to women of the dangers of female sexuality outside the confines of marriage or cohabitation, and is undoubtedly a major reason for continued adherence to normative ideals. While not denying that some women exercise agency and empower themselves through negotiating alternative domestic environments for themselves and their children, their continued minority presence means that their private battles (and successes) are waged (and won) against considerable public odds. Moreover, despite the fact that female household heads may feel satisfied with their situations in personal terms, the ways in which outsiders treat their children (especially those of unmarried mothers) may be such cause for concern among some, that the notion of encouraging sons as well as daughters to conform with mainstream social practices and to marry themselves proves irrepressibly attractive, as explored further in the next chapter.

NOTES

1. Scott's (1994) work on class and gender consciousness in Peru shows that people overwhelmingly identify themselves in class terms, although she noted that: 'To be fair, gender interests and gender consciousness were not specifically investigated in the research, a different set of questions might have produced different answers' (*ibid.*:200). (Open-ended questions in Scott's research revolved around family and class rather than men and women.)

2. This finds parallels with work among courtesans in Lucknow, India, who 'unanimously agreed that living amongst a host of nurturing and supportive women without the fear of men, and freedom from the pressure of the "marriage market" ... gave them the inner courage to develop their skills and treat men as equals, or even inferiors' (Oldenburg, 1992:39). Having said this, the experience of living with and/or interacting with female kin is not always viewed positively. For example, research on a Sri Lankan slum found that families with many women were regarded 'as a problem rather than an advantage or strength' (Thorbek, 1994:117), and that while the 'emotional and moral support married women and their mothers got from one another was important in everyday life, judging by the frequent visits and long chats ... this was not highly valued by the women themselves being seen merely as "natural" or "self-evident"' (*ibid.*:120).

3. Emotional and practical support from female friends is also noted among prostitutes in Pune, India (Desai and Apte, 1987).

4. These findings about the impacts of male absence on housework are not dissimilar to those in advanced economies. For example, Fassinger's (1993:208) work in the USA shows that women place less emphasis on housework when they end up on their own, partly because they work longer hours and have additional burdens, but also because they feel fewer social pressures from friends and neighbours, with their self-esteem 'less intimately linked with

household work'. This is echoed by Folbre and Abel's (1989) research on growth of boarding and lodging arrangements for single women in the USA in the nineteenth century, where 'increases in residential independence had particularly important implications for women, freeing them of the traditional obligation of performing domestic labour for male kin and allowing them far more control over their leisure time' (*ibid*.: 559).

5. The pattern of sisters maintaining strong bonds echoes the findings of Cicirelli's (1994:11) comparative research on sibling relationships, where he finds that sister–sister relationships in both industrialised and non-industrialised societies are usually particularly close, whereas cross-sex sibling relationships are of intermediate closeness, and brother–brother relationships least close.

6. See also Brydon and Legge (1996: Chapter 3) for similar patterns in Ghana.

7. It is difficult to convert these general figures to dollars because the exchange rate fluctuated so much during 1986. None the less, there were approximately 490 *pesos* to the US dollar in 1986 (when the fieldwork was conducted in Puerto Vallarta), 720 between July and August (when the fieldwork was done in León), and 850 by September (when I conducted my fieldwork in Querétaro).

8. Men's financial exploitation of women occurs in other Southeast Asian countries such as Thailand where Blanc-Szanton (1990b:93) observes that it is culturally acceptable for husbands to gamble and go drinking with friends after work and to demand money from their wives. For this reason, female market vendors earning good incomes were 'aware that such marriage traps awaited them. Many therefore, openly preferred to remain single.'

9. This is also found in other developing contexts such as India, where a study of deserted women in the slums of Madras showed that although 17 per cent of women wanted their spouses back for the sake of the children and for their own protection (mainly in respect of harrassment from other men) (Srinivasan, 1987:291; see also Vera Sanso, 1994) over four-fifths rejected the prospect for fear of financial dependency (especially where the husband in question was an alcoholic), or because they feared the conflict and violence routinely linked with heavy drinking (Srinivasan, 1987:291; also Bradshaw, 1996a on Honduras).

10. Thirty is an approximate figure since not all respondents in all households gave answers to particular questions. For example a few older women said they were so fed up with men or so 'past it' that they saw no reason in specifying the ideal characteristics a husband should have! Alternatively, in some households, men, sons, daughters and other relatives chipped in with answers to certain questions.

8 Growing Up in Women Headed Households

INTRODUCTION

This chapter is concerned with people's experiences of growing up in male- and female-headed households, and the manner in which material and psychosocial well-being might be affected by different types of home environment. The discussion draws mainly on qualitative information gathered in semi-structured interviews in the case study localities on sons and daughters in existing households, and on the backgrounds and histories mainly of women who are the heads (or spouses) in these households now. Despite the relatively small number of cases, the in-depth nature of the material adds dimensions to issues which have emerged largely on the basis of inference from cross-sectional statistics (see Chapter 2), and provides insights which might usefully be explored in further research. For example, children's comments and interpretations of 'father absence' (or presence) provide grassroots perspectives on the impacts of female headship on children. Moreover, considering the circumstances not only of current children but the life histories of their parents, throws light on household trajectories and generational continuity and change, particularly in respect of whether there are signs that female household headship might 'repeat itself' intergenerationally. The analysis of this and a number of other issues in the chapter are confined mainly to Mexico and Costa Rica where my contact with households extends over a longer period, thereby allowing direct tracking of children's evolution into adulthood. In the Philippines, by contrast, my first household interviews did not take place until 1993 and many households are still at a stage in the life course when their children are young. This means that discussion of the effects of female headship on offspring's education, marital circumstances and so on in the Visayas is mainly based on the retrospective life histories of adult women rather than current children.

IMPACTS OF FEMALE HEADSHIP ON YOUNGER GENERATIONS: PERSPECTIVES ON MATERIAL WELL-BEING

Incomes and expenditure

As noted in Chapter 2, one factor often cited as characterising female-headed households is the negative effects of lower incomes on child welfare.

However, the poverty gap between male- and female-headed units in terms of gross earnings, remittances and transfer payments per capita is by no means wide in the case study localities, besides which there is considerable evidence to suggest that in terms of the average income which ends up being allocated to household needs, members of women-headed units fare better since money ear-marked for basic consumption tends to benefit children.

On the basis of data from the household questionnaire survey in the Philippines in 1993, for example, mean per capita expenditure on household necessities (mainly food, rent, clothing, school and transport costs) is P169.5 ($6.8 US) per week in female-headed units (representing 58.8 per cent of per capita income [earnings plus remittances and transfer payments]), yet only P142.3 ($5.7 US) per week in male-headed households (equivalent to 54.7 per cent of per capita income), and even *de jure* women heads with the lowest per capita income still manage to devote P149.8 ($6 US) a week to each member of the household (61.4 per cent of their per capita income).

In Mexico too, the money available for collective household expenditure among households in the questionnaire survey in Puerto Vallarta, León and Querétaro in 1986 worked out as 3989 *pesos* per capita in households headed by women and 3677 in those headed by men. More specifically, female lone-parent households allocated the equivalent of 4526 *pesos* per head per week to household needs compared with 3156 *pesos* in male-headed nuclear households, and while spending on food averages 3524 *pesos* per capita per week in the former households, this is only 2155 in male-headed nuclear units (Chant, 1991a:204–5).

Beyond the fact that female heads of household appear to devote more in the way of income to children's needs, it follows that children in women-headed units fare just as well, if not better than their counterparts in male-headed households in respect of other 'material' factors such as physical aspects of their home environments, their health and well-being, education, and the utilisation of child labour in household survival strategies.

Housing

As the nexus of daily life and reproduction, housing is extremely important for children's welfare and well-being. Although it was noted in Chapter 2 that not all low-income women in developing countries have access to owner-occupied housing, where female household heads occupy their own land plots in self-help settlements, they often make dwelling construction and improvement a high priority and thereby attempt to ensure reasonable living conditions for their children. Bearing in mind that house consolidation may be more expensive for female heads whose lack of time or specialised

building skills may make them particularly reliant on hired labour (see
Chant, 1996a), a detailed survey of the dwellings of owner-occupier female
household heads in Querétaro showed that many were only able to begin
investing in their homes following desertion or the death of their husbands
(Chant, 1984a,1987). Moreover, although a larger proportion of female
heads reside in shacks (45 per cent) than male heads (21 per cent) (as
opposed to brick-and-board or concrete dwellings), relative to their household
incomes, greater sacrifices seem to be made in order to improve residential
infrastructure. In short, the modest housing conditions of some female heads
owe not so much to the fact that they are not prepared to spend money on
house-building, but because of residential assets inherited from their previous
relationships. That former husbands might not have invested much money
in house consolidation is possibly not surprising given that marriages are often
conflictive prior to separation. They may be conflictive *because* men commit
little money to household well-being, in which case housing is unlikely to
be a recipient of investment anyway, or, when conflict is associated with men
spending time away from home, men's interests in consolidating their
dwellings as environments to share with wives and children are less. Indeed,
the best consolidated houses among male-headed nuclear households are
generally those in which husbands dedicate the bulk of their 'free time' to
their homes and families, rather than spending it in bars or socialising with
male companions (*ibid.*). Although detailed surveys were not conducted of
housing investment and quality in Costa Rica or the Philippines, there is no
indication that owner-occupier female household heads live in dwellings of
markedly inferior quality. As such, children's physical environments may
not be so much affected by household headship *per se* in the case study
localities, as by women's control over income and the quality of husband–wife
relationships within male-headed units.

Infant and child mortality

In respect of infant and child mortality,[1] there is again no strong evidence
to suggest that this is influenced by household headship in any substantial
or systematic way, even if the data on this subject from the questionnaire
surveys of Costa Rica and the Philippines suggest that risks may be slightly
higher in female-headed units. For example, while women in male-headed
households in Costa Rica have an average of 5.2 births and there is a 1 in 6
to 7 chance that the child will die within five years of being born, female
heads of household have an average of 6.4 births and one child out of every
4 or 5 dies. In the Philippine Visayas, the differences are greater: while female
heads have an average of 4 pregnancies, the mean chance of miscarriage is

1 in 7, and the average number of child mortalities 1 in 10. In male-headed households, alternatively, where women have an average of 4.3 pregnancies, there is only a 1 in 11 chance of miscarriage, and 1 in 22 chance of experiencing the death of a child under five years of age. Yet, what the questionnaire data do *not* show is what the headship (or structure) of households was at the precise time the children died, nor the illnesses that caused the deaths. This information was only gathered systematically in the smaller samples of in-depth semi-structured interviews, and my investigation of this material yielded interesting insights. First, although reasons for infant and child mortalities vary in all three countries, most seem to be due to so-called 'diseases of poverty' (that is, diseases which owe to malnutrition, insanitary living conditions and so on). Second, and related to this, women who have experienced the death of children were either partnered at the time their children died, and/or, in the small minority of cases where they were not, lone parenthood *per se* was not something women deemed to be relevant in contributing to the poverty associated with morbidity. Indeed, although it is undeniable that, all things being equal, households with male earnings are *potentially* better placed to ward off the tragedy of young deaths and/or to deal with the consequences (in the form of post-mortems and burial arrangements), the reality is often different insofar as earnings do not necessarily translate into benefits for other household members.

Astrid (Cañas), for example, was living with men during the five occasions she lost babies. Astrid had four children with her first husband, with one dying at the age of two months from an asthma attack. With her second spouse (with whom she lived for 11 years), she had a further eight children, and lost four of them early on in their lives — one of a 'fever', one of gastroenteritis, one of a brain haemorrhage, and one due to misdiagnosis of a premature birth. In this latter case, the baby was thought to be stillborn and was wrapped in paper and put in the rubbish. By the time they heard the baby's cry, it was too late to get it to hospital and it died *en route*. Like most of her neighbours, Astrid had all her babies at home with no medical supervision. Neither of her spouses offered to pay anything towards medical treatment, injections and so on, and in the case of the second partner, Astrid maintained that financial neglect was a major factor in the deaths. Although Astrid herself had worked selling foodstuffs, the monetary resources available to the family were depleted by their diversion to her spouse's drinking and extra-domestic activities, which, as Astrid later learned from a friend, included regular visits to another woman over a number of years.

Concha, a Nicaraguan migrant in Cañas, also lost a total of four out of nine children when she was partnered: one of the two children that died was with her first spouse, and three out of seven with her second. In all cases, the mortalities were sparked by routine ailments such as worms, gastric infections and fevers associated with poor living conditions, inadequate preventive health care and insufficient funds to obtain emergency medical intervention. Again, the presence of a man did not seem to make any difference.

Education

As with infant mortalities, the impacts of household headship on children's educational achievements cannot be meaningfully assessed on the basis of the questionnaire survey data since (a) there is no way of knowing whether fathers were present or absent in households when children were at school, and (b) because I only have data on the schooling of eldest co-resident sons and daughters. For this reason, I am reliant on the semi-structured interviews conducted in 1994 and 1995 in Mexico, Costa Rica and the Philippines which documented the schooling of all children.

In the sub-sample of Mexican interviews in 1994, there was a total of 15 households with at least one child who had finished their education. Although wide disparities of educational achievement among offspring within the same household are common, it is interesting that in all the long-term female-headed households (of which there were five with at least one son or daughter who had finished their education in 1994), no child had less than a completed primary education (six grades). Moreover, in three of these five female-headed households, there was at least one child who was in the process of doing a university degree. As for nine households headed by the natural fathers and mothers of the children, only two in this group had children who were or had been to university, and another two of the households actually contained children who had failed to complete their primary education. Although these figures are far from representative, they suggest at least that the basic education of children (which is usually financed wholly by parents) is no more compromised in female-headed than in male-headed households. This is important since thereafter (that is in relation to secondary school and further and higher education), most children, regardless of household type, take a part-time job to help fund their studies.[3]

Ana, a 52-year-old long-term single parent in Querétaro, for example, managed to see her two sons and two daughters through primary school, and her younger daughter, Alejandra, nearly completed her *preparatoria* education (equivalent to 'A'-level college) (that is pre-university). Having said this, her younger son, Alfredo, who got no further than completing secondary school, blames the absence of paternal support for failing to give him 'a good start in life'. He presently works as a driver for a cleaning products firm and feels that he could have done better had his father helped out, especially given the fact that as a Canadian engineer employed by a multinational company he potentially had the resources to do so. To some extent, a similar sense of deprivation is felt by the eldest son of Socorro, a 49-year-old single parent in Querétaro, even though she has managed to put all seven of her older children through primary school and her two youngest, Jorge Luís, 13 and Silvia, 11, are presently interned in religious schools (these are single-sex charitable foundations where she gives voluntary contributions to the governing body; she has sent her youngest here because she does not have time to look after them properly now that her older sons and daughters have left home and/or are working, besides which she feels they will probably get a better education as boarders with no distractions). As the oldest of three children who self-financed both secondary and *preparatoria* education, and who is currently studying for a language degree while doing a day job as a factory worker, Jaime (26 years), has been the only child of Socorro's to ask (in moments of frustration) why she did not stay with his father who now has two or three businesses and is relatively wealthy. Although Jaime appreciates that his mother could not tolerate his sexual duplicity, he has also mentioned that it would have been easier if he had been able to benefit from a father's support. Such cases as Jaime and Alfredo might indicate that even if the reality is that children in female-headed households are able to do as well, if not better, educationally, than children in male-headed units, they may *perceive* disadvantage and/or attribute what they see as a lack of achievement to father absence, although this can also act as an impetus for children to push ahead under their own steam to succeed, especially among women.

In fact, a very interesting point to emerge from the Mexican material, is that while most children are now achieving higher levels of education than their parents did (undoubtedly as a result of expansion in public provision in recent decades), this is especially marked in the case of those from one-parent households. In other words, the children of current lone mothers seem to be doing considerably better in educational terms than women who were themselves raised by single parents. Indeed, although many older women in the case study localities had little or no education, the lowest levels of attainment are mainly among women brought up in step-families and/or who had spent the bulk of their formative years in female-headed households. For example, four out of five women (now in their late thirties and upwards) raised by lone mothers had not completed primary school. The only woman with an upbringing combining lone motherhood and step-parenthood who had gone on to complete a secondary education (Lupe, a 39-year-old lone parent in Puerto Vallarta), did so as a mature student and is now extremely proud to have a 25-year-old daughter who is doing a degree in business administration at the University of Guadalajara. The desire to pursue education as mature students in both Lupe's and Giovana's case seems to be motivated by a strong desire to avoid the disadvantages faced by their own mothers, and to be able to fend for themselves if necessary, which is also found among women from lone-parent backgrounds in Costa Rica.

Education levels of the children of adult female respondents in Guanacaste tend to be lower than in the Mexican case study localities, which, given high levels of schooling and literacy at a national scale, testifies to the marginalisation of the region (see Lara *et al.*, 1995:67–9; also Chapter 5). For example, only one out of nine households with at least one child who had completed their schooling by 1994 had offspring who had gone beyond secondary school. The household in question was that of Juana, currently in a third conjugal union. Her eldest daughter (the product of a former relationship with a schoolteacher who provided maintenance for the three children he had with Juana) had completed a nursing degree in San José, and her eldest son (also fathered by the schoolteacher) had pursued a post-secondary school training in mechanics. Other than this, there were few households in which all children had finished their primary education, let alone in which children had entered secondary school, and no consistent relationship between the conjugal circumstances of parents and educational achievement among offspring was apparent.

The same applies to the older generation (that is, current female heads and spouses) in Costa Rica, with household background seeming to have made less difference to their educational attainment than their Mexican counterparts where lone parenthood appears to have put daughters at a particular disadvantage. Of six women heads/spouses with no education, for example, two had been raised by both their natural parents, two in step-families, one had been fostered out to a grandmother and only one had been raised by a lone mother. However, while one woman who had spent most of her childhood being raised by a lone mother had not been to school, two others with single-parent backgrounds (like Lupe in Puerto Vallarta – see above), had put themselves through secondary education evening classes.

For example, Marielos (Liberia), now 26 years, married and with a five-year-old daughter, recalls her childhood with sadness and attributes her drive for self-improvement to the immense poverty and vulnerability she suffered in her youth. Marielos was the youngest of seven girls and her father left her mother before she was born. Two years later, her mother entered a union with another man with whom she had a son. Yet this man was also very poor, so in the short time they were together (he deserted a few months after the boy was born), his presence did not substantially improve household finances. According to Marielos, life was very difficult for women on their own in Guanacaste 20 years ago, especially those with several children. Since her mother was unable to scratch more than a meagre income from sowing beans, Marielos always felt it was a personal responsibility to 'drag herself up'. Fortunately her mother encouraged all the children to go to church and the school (Catholic) attached to it, and from this basis Marielos was able to make progress. She used to beg the teachers to let her borrow books, and prayed regularly to God for help and strength. Typically, Marielos attributes her success in pursuing knowledge not to her own efforts but to religion: '*El único fue Diós*' ('It was all down to God'). At the age of seven Marielos started selling '*churros*' (sugared doughnut sticks) to make money and help put her half-brother through school, which she did, as well as completing her own primary education, and managing one year of secondary school. After her daughter Evelyn was born, Marielos started part-time classes in secondary education as a mature student, and hopes eventually to do a course in computer-based secretarial skills. This, in turn, will allow her to generate the resources necessary to give Evelyn all the education she needs to '*defenderse*' (defend herself).

Women's keenness to equip their daughters with the means of 'defending themselves' is also strongly felt by women who have been abandoned, such as Braulia (Liberia). For example, although only one of Braulia's three daughters managed to complete their primary education (the others making it solely to the fifth grade), Braulia herself had none and she feels that being able to read and write and do arithmetic gives them a greater chance to '*manejarse solas*' ('manage their own lives') if, like her, they end up being unable to rely on men (see also McIlwaine, 1993 on mothers' encouragement of their daughters' education among the Afro-Caribbean population of Limón).

As for the Philippines, there are insufficient numbers of households with children who have completed their schooling to come to any kind of conclusion about the effects of family background on educational attainment among today's youth. Moreover, as for the experiences of their mothers, given that only 8 out of 30 respondents interviewed on an in-depth semi-structured basis in Cebu, Lapu-Lapu and Boracay had *not* been raised in nuclear units headed by natural parents, the basis for inter-group comparisons among the parents' generation is limited. None the less, of the 8 women who had been brought up either by a lone mother (3), by their mother and grandparents or just grandparents or other relatives (4), or in a step-family (1), only 2 managed to graduate from high school, whereas 14 out of the 22 women from 'stable' homes did so, and 3 of these proceeded to college courses in commerce or teaching as well. In short, in the Philippines, it seems as if a 'conventional' two-parent household might have been a more conducive basis for educational attainment in the past.

Although in Mexico and the Philippines it appears that current female heads and spouses may have been disadvantaged by growing up in one-parent households, the data on the younger generation in both countries suggest important changes. Moreover, notwithstanding that children in all localities (that is including Costa Rica) seem to be benefiting from expanded educational provision, those in female-headed households are often given even more encouragement to take advantage of educational opportunities than their counterparts in male-headed units. None the less, despite a particularly strong desire on the part of lone mothers to ensure that their daughters are able to stand on their own two feet, boys' educational achievements often remain higher because they are able to get better-paid part-time jobs to help fund their secondary and further studies.

Child labour and household survival
Schooling and educational attainment are not just affected by the money available to support studies, but by the relative onus on children to contribute time and labour to household survival. The labour required of children may be economic, of an unpaid domestic nature, or may straddle the two in respect of helping parent(s) on an unremunerated basis in family businesses.

As for the implications for education of child labour, a range of studies have suggested that young women (especially eldest daughters) have to assume larger burdens of childcare and domestic work when mothers are employed outside the home, and this may be more pronounced among female heads who generally have higher rates of labour force participation (see Chapters 2 and 4). As Ennew (1982:560) notes of working heads of single-parent households in Jamaica: 'When the mother has to be the father, it is inevitable that in many cases the children have to be the housewives.' Such pressure, in turn, is argued to prejudice daughters' educational prospects by forcing absenteeism, by leading to poor grades through lack of time for homework, and/or provoking premature withdrawal from school. The consequences may include inferior employment and, ultimately, further 'feminisation of poverty' (see Chalita Ortiz, 1992; Dierckxsens, 1992; Ennew and Young, 1981; Moser, 1989; Rodríguez, 1993). However, the evidence from the case study localities does not support a picture of limited educational achievement among daughters in female-headed households, one reason being that housework and the care of siblings is more likely to be shared with their brothers (see Chapter 7). For example, in the household of Lupe, a lone mother in Puerto Vallarta, Giovana was not only the eldest child but also the only girl. Yet because the two brothers she grew up with were expected to participate in the daily running of the household and learned how to look after themselves early on, she was never overburdened to the extent that she was unable to attend school regularly. Indeed, in addition to housework Giovana also managed to have a part-time job as a photographic assistant to help get her through secondary school and *preparatoria*. The fact that she is now doing a Business Studies degree at the University of Guadalajara (see earlier) actually makes her the most educated member of the family.

In the household of another single parent in Puerto Vallarta (Emilia), housework is again shared by all members, in this case comprising an 8-year-old son, a 14-year-old daughter and a 14-year-old niece of Emilia's. Although on top of housework, the daughter, Brenda, helps her mother out on her fruit stall during her vacations from secondary school, Emilia is extremely keen for her to finish her studies and prepare herself for a life in which she can be self-sufficient if necessary. Over and above mothers' concerns for their daughters to be able to fend for themselves and greater fluidity in gender divisions of labour within female-headed households, another reason why girls in these units may do as well, if not better educationally than their counterparts in other households, is because lone parents are potentially freer to make decisions and/or allocate resources on their daughters' behalves. In male-headed households, by contrast, wives may be in the position of having to fight their husbands to ensure that their daughters get equality of treatment with sons. In Querétaro, for example, María Asunción's desire for her daughter, Rosalba, to be educated has never met with enthusiasm from her husband, Antonio. Ever since Rosalba finished primary school, Antonio has constantly complained that it is a waste of time for women to study because they will only get married. Moreover, he bemoans the fact that it is costing him money he claims he can ill afford, despite the fact that he is willing to commit resources to the education of his three sons, and has actually enrolled the two youngest boys (eight-year-old twins) in a private junior school. Although Rosalba works hard in the family grocery store after school and at weekends, Antonio never ceases to maintain how much better off they would be if Rosalba were to work in the shop full-time. María Asunción feels that an additional factor might be that Antonio himself has no more than primary education and it offends his sense of masculinity and authority if his daughter is more educated than he is. While María Asunción so far seems to have won the battle over educating Rosalba, Antonio has demonstrated his annoyance by being unsupportive, by passing remarks about how much it is costing him to keep her in school (she is presently 17 and studying *preparatoria*), and by threatening to take her out of education if she so much as entertains the thought of having a boyfriend. In short, Rosalba's education is being acquired under considerable duress. Yet Rosalba hopes eventually to go to university and although she is gifted in the arts and humanities, María Asunción is encouraging her to think of a chemistry degree since this will be more vocational. If she ends up making money, María Asunción hopes that Antonio may come round to conceding that it was right to educate their daughter after all, and that Rosalba will reap the benefits for having spent a youth bereft of social contact with her peers and laced with hostility and resentment from her father.

As for the use of children in economic aspects of household survival, various studies have emphasised that this is likely to be greater in female-headed households (especially non-extended units) for reasons of having to supplement the low earnings of mothers (see Ennew and Young, 1981 on Jamaica; Moghadam, 1995c on Egypt). In turn, this may act to the detriment of children's life chances, with González de la Rocha (1995a:392) arguing for the Mexican cities of Guadalajara and Monterrey that:

> Going to work at an early age undoubtedly has consequences for young people's levels of schooling, medium and long-range remuneration levels, and type of insertion into the labour market, throughout their working lives. What at one point is a survival mechanism later becomes part of the reproduction of poverty.

Yet differences according to headship are by no means marked in any of the study localities (see also Note 3). People from all kinds of family background, past and present, claim that they had to work as children because their families were/are poor, whether running errands, selling goods, or doing small-scale production jobs such as sorting beads, stringing necklaces, or fabricating simple industrial components such as shoe straps.

Whether or not early entry into remunerated work has major effects on their labour market position in later life cannot be answered by the present data. What *does* seem apparent, however, is that children in non-extended female-headed units feel a greater sense of responsibility because their mothers are on their own. As Layla (Cañas) put it, her children's experience of fatherlessness and knowing their mother had no other help means that they 'han tenido que madurarse a muy temprana edad' ('had to mature at a very early age'). As soon as they were able, they started running errands to help out with household expenditure and so on (see also the case of María Cruz later in this chapter). Whether or not this is a 'bad thing' is not an easy question to answer, when enforced responsibility and the need to assist mothers, whether in the home or in the labour market, often means that children take little for granted and continue to be very hard-working when they have their own families. Indeed, the contacts they make in the labour market as youngsters sometimes assist them with part-time jobs as teenagers and can help their entry into full-time work in later life a well. Similar patterns are noted in other areas. For example, in their study of child labour in Jamaica, Ennew and Young (1981:59) report that the self-reliance and independence that children develop through their early participation in household responsibilities may deprive them of their childhood, but as 'proto-adults', they are also eminently 'adept at surviving in the midst of poverty and unemployment' (see also Valladares, 1989 on Brazil). It is also the case that children's practical responsibilities seem to be accompanied by an intellectual and emotional maturity, and a respect for women among boys, that distinguishes them from many of their counterparts in male-headed households. This leads us to explore some of the psychological dimensions of growing up in female-headed households.

IMPACTS OF FEMALE HEADSHIP ON YOUNGER GENERATIONS: PERSPECTIVES ON EMOTIONAL AND PSYCHOLOGICAL WELL-BEING

How children interpret the experience of growing up in female-headed households is conditioned by many things. As noted in Chapter 2, the psychological effects of 'father absence' on children are often viewed as damaging, and type of loss (whether through death, desertion or divorce) is deemed important in affecting how children respond to not having a father around. Factors which seem to be particularly significant in the case study areas include the age at which children lost their fathers and the amount of time which has elapsed since, and, in the case of older children, recollections of life when their fathers were at home. The amount and nature of contact retained with fathers over time is also important, although in most cases this seems to be minimal or non-existent. As one 70-year-old Nicaraguan respondent in Cañas, Justina, put it: 'When men are with you they say they love the children, but once they're gone, they don't look back, because they know the mother will look after them.'[4] In her particular case she has no idea where her husband is since he has not communicated since he walked out. Although her children gradually learned to accept his departure and began not to refer to it, family get-togethers on Christmas Day and during *Semana Santa* (Holy Week) were always rather sad because the children could not resist speculating about what he might be doing and whether or not they might see him again. Lidia, another Nicaraguan in Cañas, also felt that it was easy for men to forget their children – her own father did not want his name to go on her birth certificate which, in Lidia's view, was tantamount to denying that she existed.

Yet, as Collins (1991:168) has stressed in relation to Western societies, children may be wont to preserve distorted and/or idealised memories of absent or deceased parents, with the pain of the loss they undergo often being so immense as to block out the reality of their experiences. Hewitt and Leach (1993:15) identify that this is particularly the case where death has been the cause of loss, claiming that, although 'Bereavement is socially recognised, and good memories of a father are usually allowed and supported by a widowed mother', this is much rarer when parents divorce (see also Chandler, 1991). However, as with widows (see Chapter 6), children in the case study localities reveal little pain or sorrow when they talk about the death of fathers, possibly because so many men have been poor parents. For example, the children of a 40-year-old widow in Boracay, Elvira, were so traumatised when her husband was alive – he used to beat Elvira and the children, and once tried to drown one of his sons – that when he died of heart failure at the age of 35, the children rarely spoke about it afterwards, and the younger ones did not even ask where he had gone.

As for cases where husbands have deserted mothers or provoked separation, resentment seems to be as strong as sadness. María Asunción (Querétaro), for example, recalls how embarrassed she felt at having to use her mother's surname twice (routine practice both in Mexico and Costa Rica when children are born illegitimately), and María del Refugio (Querétaro) reports being an angry child because she did not know her father's surname. She always felt she needed to know who her father was, although at the age of 20 when she met him for the first time, she described finding him *'chaparro y feo'* ('small and ugly'), and stressed what a disillusion this was for her. Idalia (Puerto Vallarta) also felt resentful about the fact that her father left her mother with four children when Idalia herself was only eight months old to marry another woman. The first time she saw him was when she was eight years old, but it was only as an adult that they began to develop a relationship. By this time he was in his nineties and in many respects Idalia felt betrayed by the fact that she was there for him when he needed her, but he had never given her the chance of depending on him.

Feelings of estrangement, if not betrayal, are also common in Costa Rica and undoubtedly relate to the fact that children never knew their fathers or were abandoned at a young age and have had little or no contact since. For example, Lidia in Cañas was the third child of her mother, Concha's, second union, and her father abandoned them when Lidia was only 40 days old. The first time she saw him she was aged seven (he bought her shoes for her first communion), and the second and last time was at her wedding 13 years ago, when he gave her away. Lidia declared: 'I feel strange with him ... *no me nace "papá" así* ['it doesn't come easily to me to call him "Dad"'] ... *No me hace ni falta'* ('I don't miss him at all'). In Liberia, Lisa (20 years), the youngest child of her mother Juana's first union (she is presently in her third), declared that the loss of her father (her mother left him once he started to beat her) *'no me afectó porque estaba muy pequeña'* ('didn't affect me because I was very young'). ·

This latter point highlights the importance of time, and suggest that children gradually adjust as the immediacy of their fathers' departures fades. As Layla's ten-year-old daughter, Juliana (Cañas) said *'Ya me acostumbré – no me hace falta'* ('I've got used to it now, I don't miss him'). Although time can also help to heal past wounds, however, where major conflict has occurred, these are difficult to close completely, even where there is some form of ongoing relationship. For example, six out of seven of Braulia's children (Liberia) see their father once or twice a year (the youngest, Enrique, was only three when they split up so he never really knew him). Although the children have borne him less malice and resentment as time has gone on, they still cannot really come to terms with the pain he caused Braulia and the way this affected the happiness and security of their home lives. In some respects, however, there have been positive spin-offs in that they attribute their own fairly stable and *'cumplido'* ('responsible') relationships to the fact that they knew at first hand the suffering that comes from growing up in a 'broken home' (see later). Yet, as mentioned earlier in relation to bereavement, children may be much more traumatised by having a father who is difficult to live with, especially if he is aggressive or violent, and in such circumstances, loss may well be compensated by the benefits of 'father absence'. In fact, in some cases, this leads to children actively splitting the family home.

Seventeen-year-old Denis's distress at his father, Dominico's, behaviour, for example, is such that he plans to take his mother, Girlie, away from Boracay to live with him in Manila as soon as he has completed his university degree. Although Denis says he does not feel like an 'odd-one-out' in that many men in Boracay, like his father, have taken to drink and to living off their wives' earnings, he declared in a characteristically understated way that he is 'sometimes sad, sometimes angry' about Dominico's cavalier treatment of Girlie. With the exception of cooking, Denis's fragile mother has to do all the household chores as well as working seven days a week on a market stall to earn enough income to run the household and to put Denis through college. Denis was particularly upset when his father did not turn up at Girlie's bedside in Caticlan on the mainland when she collapsed with a blood disorder and was rushed to hospital for a transfusion. In many ways he hoped that this might jolt his father into mending his ways and help to pull them together as a family unit. Unfortunately this was not to be. Recognising that his ability to study and further himself is entirely due to his mother's efforts, one way of repaying Girlie's kindness and to free her from further exploitation, is to give her a legitimate (that is family-linked) excuse to move elsewhere, and let herself be looked after for a change.

Sometimes children not only witness their mothers' suffering, but experience violence themselves, and/or rather than make a bid to change things may be drawn into their fathers' cruelty. In Puerto Vallarta, for example, David Junior, the eldest son of a married couple, Fidelina and David, was made an accomplice in a programme of intra-family espionage. Following the discovery that Fidelina had been working as a cleaner behind his back, David placed an outright ban on Fidelina doing the same again and asked neighbours to tell him if they found out this was otherwise. As part of his strategy, David bribed David Junior (only six years old at the time) with money and sweets (backed up by threats of physical violence) to report on his mother's comings and goings, with whom she talked, who visited the house and so on. David impressed upon his son that his mother was 'bad' and that as a male he had to help him keep her 'under control'. The situation was unbearable for Fidelina, who had to put up with a six-year-old behaving assertively, rudely and uncooperatively as a result of paternal pressure, and who made her feel 'like a prisoner in her own home' for an entire year.

In light of the above kinds of circumstances, it is no surprise that some female heads do not feel that father absence wreaks undue damage upon their children. Emilia (Puerto Vallarta), for example, feels that if there is enough love from the mother, the presence of a father is not important. This is her own experience and is one reason why she feels perfectly content not to have married any of the men with whom she has had children. Lupe (Puerto Vallarta) also does not feel that she has deprived her children to any great extent and feels that her inner peace has probably made her a better mother than she would have been had she stayed with the men concerned and undergone the torment of sexual jealousy. By the same token, she had difficulty communicating with one of her sons, Luís, when he reached adolescence and became somewhat unruly. He works presently in Guadalajara and is not in nearly as much contact with Lupe as her daughter. Lupe feels that this situation may in part be explained by the fact that '*le falta la mano del papá*' ('he lacks the hand of his father'). When Lupe split up with her partner, however, Luís was very young and in such circumstances, the notion of father possibly replaces the actual individual. In Gordon's (1994:173) study of single women in Finland, the USA and the UK, for example, she found that some children of single mothers 'did not necessarily miss a particular person (they may not have known their fathers well or at all), but they missed a father figure: a completion of the familial unit'. In other words, social ideals can be extremely pervasive and may act to neutralise the pain some children undergo as a result of living with problematic fathers and/or in situations where parents have conflictive relations.

Indeed, while Lupe experienced problems with her elder son, her daughter and younger son have been extremely easy to live with, mirroring a more general pattern for the children of long-term female-headed households to be strikingly well-behaved and responsible, to keep in close touch with their mothers once they have left home, and to continue giving financial assistance. Part of this may have to do with the fact that from an early age a sense of vulnerability encourages household members to pull together and survive through difficulty. Another is that lone mothers tend to impress upon sons and daughters the need for responsibility, if not to demand it. Certainly, the fact that sons tend to help out with domestic labour in female-headed units and are subject as children to the authority of adult women, seems to result in their being more helpful and respectful to their own wives in later life, as well as retaining close ties with their mothers. Although this could conceivably be a source of conflict between mothers and daughters-in-law, there was little evidence of this in the case study localities.

María Cruz (Querétaro), for example, has three children: two sons, Ramiro and Rodolfo aged 22 and 20 respectively, and a daughter, Ana Erica, of 17. Ramiro was only 8 years old and Rodolfo 6 in 1980 when Cruz and her partner split up, but by 1983 (when I first interviewed the family), both Ramiro and Rodolfo were not only skilled in household tasks, but had a well-established series of strategies for topping up Cruz's own earnings from her part-time breakfast business (they gave her half their money), and to help fund their schooling. These included running errands for neighbours, helping people clear stones from their land plots, and making charges for trips to the water standpipe in the settlement. Ramiro completed secondary school and is now a taxi driver with a part-share in a cab. Rodolfo works part-time in a pizza bar and is in his second year of an accountancy degree. Although Rodolfo is single and still lives at home, Ramiro is living a few doors down with his partner and 3-year-old child on his parents-in-law's plot. He and his family are constant visitors to María's home and relationships are so good that his partner sees María as a '*segunda mamá*' ('second mother'). Ramiro feels that support and understanding are vital ingredients of a happy union, and he is proving to be such a good spouse and father (as well as a son), that María declares she can see 'no earthly resemblance to his "black sheep" of a father'. Part of this is due to the fact that the sons of lone parents are usually tutored in the skills and attitudes that their mothers would ideally like to have had their own husbands to have, and partly because sons themselves do not want their children to remember them with the same angst, disdain or disappointment that colours the images they have of their own fathers.

Socorro (Querétaro), another long-term single parent, claims that she has not only taught her sons to respect women, but also has trained them in household tasks which makes them better able to help their own wives. This has certainly proved to be the case with her eldest son Jaime who assists his partner Mariana with household chores and the care of their two children, and has had a happy, stable relationship with his partner for seven years. Mariana thinks that Jaime is far better than most Mexican men who do not know even how to boil a pan of water. She is also delighted about his strong sense of sexual fidelity, which in Jaime's view is a product of wanting to spare his own family the pain that resulted from his father's philandering when he was young. In fact, Jaime is so family-oriented that he has no desire to move from the piece of Socorro's plot that they presently occupy, even though they could afford to do so.

Tereso (Querétaro), another son of a single parent, is 46 and is described by his wife Paula as an 'exceptional husband'. Tereso had grown up in a household where his father regularly beat his mother and was '*muy desobligado*' ('very irresponsible'). When his father eventually left home, Tereso took it upon himself to help his mother out as much as he could and resolved never to cause the same suffering to his own wife. Throughout his 26-year marriage to Paula, Tereso has been devoted to the family and if anything has taken a greater share of the housework because Paula's job as a school cleaner-cum-dinner lady means she is out most of the day. Tereso hopes he has set a good example to his four sons who are thus far unmarried, preferring to follow their father's advice to save money and become economically secure before taking on the commitment of looking after a family.

Although Tereso decares that he hopes in some way to rectify the mistakes his father made, both as a son and as a father, and has made a determined effort to do so, he maintains that he might well have followed in his father's footsteps given that this was the '*imágen masculino*' ('masculine image') with which he was most closely acquainted. In fact, Ana María (Puerto Vallarta), now a widow, attributes the heavy drinking habits of three of her sons to the fact that her husband was an alcoholic. None the less, Ana María also feels that a male household head is good for keeping discipline in the home, and there is certainly more respect from other people. In fact, picking up an earlier point about idealised images attached to the notion of a 'complete' family, many of the problems of female-headed households owe not so much to what goes on within their homes, as to how they are treated by 'outsiders' (see Chapter 7). For example, Lupe (Puerto Vallarta) feels that there is often lack of respect for daughters of *madres solteras* because it is imagined that such mothers have 'loose morals'. In other words, the perceptions about what other people think can be immensely preoccupying for lone mothers, again highlighting the disjuncture between normative prescriptions and realities. While not denying that being part of a lone-parent household may make children feel they are marked as 'different', there seem to be few who welcome the prospect of their mothers marrying another man in the interests of social confomity.

Experiences of step-parenthood

Although many children seem to become accustomed to living without fathers in their day-to-day lives, and in many instances find this an improvement on previous circumstances, this is less the case when mothers take new partners. Indeed, while we saw how concern about children figures prominently in women's attitudes to remarriage or cohabitation with a new partner in Chapter 7, it is worth exploring briefly the experiences of step-parenthood for children in the case study localities.

Resentment of and resistance to stepfathers arises for a number of reasons. One is that children may not be able to come to terms with 'replacing' their fathers with someone else. This seems especially marked where natural fathers have retained contact. Although Marta's (Liberia) former partner left her with two young girls to marry another woman (whom he has since divorced), he continued giving money to Marta for the children and to see them every other weekend. Although the elder daughter accepted this relatively limited contact and gets on well with her mother's new husband, Franklin, the younger daughter, Angélica, is described by her mother as 'maladjusted' as a result of the split. Years later she would still announce in front of her stepfather and half-siblings that she wanted her father back, and when her father used to come for her on alternate Saturdays, she would make him come right to the door to collect her, thereby emphasising his presence and her continued attachment.

Another issue is that children who get used to having power and playing a greater part in decision-making in lone-parent households may be threatened when a parent establishes a new relationship (see also Collins, 1991:170). This seems particularly relevant to sons in Mexico and Costa Rica, as noted in the previous chapter, where jealousy of their mothers' boyfriends can take the form of antagonistic or uncooperative behaviour. Another point made by Collins (1991:168–9) is that in the process of a lone-parent household evolving into a step-family, 'the theme and experience of loss are often resurrected'. In other words, children may not want to be reminded of the past or to enter a situation where the past might 'repeat itself'. When Maura

(Liberia) found a second partner, Bernardo, for example, most of her older children refused to share the same home as them and insisted that Maura go to his house while they stayed behind in the family residence. Maura believes this is partly because they had witnessed terrible scenes of rage and violence between Maura and their own father.

The single greatest factor affecting children's reluctance to welcome stepfathers, however, is the anticipation that step-children are not particularly well treated. Sadly this often turns out to the case, with Lidia (Cañas) recalling her mother's third partner (with whom she had no children), becoming increasingly aggressive during their seven years of cohabitation. He began resenting the presence of the children and would turn the television off when they were watching it, eventually hurling it across the floor and breaking it. In Lidia's view, having a stepfather was worse than having no father. Lupe (Puerto Vallarta), also had a very unhappy home life from the age of six onwards. Her stepfather, whom she describes as a '*déspoto*' ('despot'), treated her and her mother extremely badly. Lupe remembers him eating first and ordering them about, and withdrawing her from school at the age of 11 because he was envious of her mental agility. The domestic slavery into which Lupe was forced thereafter was the major reason she eloped with an older man at the age of 14, an event she refers to now as '*salida número uno*' ('escape route number one'), the second and third 'exits' being from her marriage, and from her union with a man she claimed to love too much for her own good (see Chapter 6).

Some step-families seem to 'work' however. Doña Lupe (Querétaro) loved her stepfather, possibly because she was so young when her mother married him that she always saw him as her real father.

Maiela's daughter, María Lorena (Liberia), was also taken to live with her stepfather as a baby. Although she used to ask Maiela what her father was like from time to time, since she had a kindly stepfather in Victor, '*no me hacía falta mi papá*' ('I didn't miss my father'). Having said this, Victor has a somewhat restrained relationship with María Lorena, and generally transmits his grievances about her through Maiela. This is not surprising given Collins' (1991:171) point that: 'a biological parent who attempts to discipline and control children starts with the advantage of a generally sanctioned right to do it, and a general expectation that he or she will'.

GENERATIONAL TRAJECTORIES: CONTINUITY OR CHANGE?

Having considered various dimensions of growing up in female- and male-headed households (and step-families), it is important to consider how the experience of living in different types of household may affect the types of household which people go on to create themselves. Do people tend to repeat patterns of their own childhood when they grow up, and, if so, what kinds of factors are at play? As noted in Chapter 2, 'culture of poverty' and 'underclass' debates tend to assume that inadequate discipline, poverty, lack of a male role model and so on in female-headed households give rise to a tendency for weak family structures in younger generations. Yet, it could also be argued, that if children grow up in situations where their fathers are present but have conflictive relations with their wives, this is even more likely to generate fears about making marital commitments. Another important issue is whether children 'imitate' the behaviour of their parents or whether, in the process of living through traumatic times in their natal families, they determine to 'do better'. We have seen, for example, that the sons of lone mothers who are responsible from an early age seem to learn something of value from their hardship, as well as being actively taught by mothers to be respectful. As for daughters, it seems as if lone mothers are particularly concerned to arm them with the means for independence. Although, again, data is drawn from small numbers of semi-structured interviews, they provide some indication of the ways in which people make sense of their experiences and use them in shaping their own lives. The first part of the discussion concentrates on the household backgrounds of existing female heads and spouses, and the second part on the household arrangements of the sons and daughters of these women.

Household backgrounds of current female heads and spouses

Only one in five long-term lone mothers among a total of 18 respondents interviewed in Mexico in 1994 had been raised by a lone parent. The woman in question was Emilia, a 39-year-old unmarried mother in Puerto Vallarta. Emilia's mother was abandoned by her partner (with whom she was in an informal union that had already given rise to the births of two boys) when Emilia was only eight months old. They lived at this time on a smallholding in the village of La Cruz, Tomatlán, Jalisco state, where her mother bred pigs and took in washing to make a living. Although her mother went on to have a further two children with a second partner, she never set up home with him. This second man, like Emilia's father, was of a mean disposition and because he rarely gave Emilia's mother money towards the children's upkeep, Emilia remembers whole weeks where the family would have nothing to eat but *tortillas* and salt. In fact when Emilia and one of her younger brothers were both crippled by polio (Emilia was seven years old when she woke one morning to find that she could not straighten either leg, and has been on crutches ever since), the desperate nature of her family situation forced her to see the positive side of her predicament, namely that she would be able to get more money from begging on Sundays in the village plaza. Talking of her childhood, Emilia claims that '*Estaba duro, pero vivía*' ('it was hard, but we lived'). Her mother managed to send all the children to school for three years, although they had to leave to help out financially. In Emilia's case, farm work was not felt to be appropriate because of her disability and because her mother thought she would be taken advantage of by male labourers, so until the family moved to Puerto Vallarta in 1970, Emilia's main activities were begging, making *tortillas* and doing the housework.

The move to Puerto Vallarta in 1970 was prompted by the completion of the international airport and the promise of a massive expansion of employment in the resort. Emilia was by this time 16 and had been repeatedly warned by her mother to stay away from men because '*te hacen daño*' ('they do you harm'). In fact Emilia's mother was so worried about her daughter's safety that she did not allow her to take a job until she was 18. As soon as Emilia was outside the home and began selling *artesanía* (handicrafts) from a stall in the municipal market, men started asking her out. The fact that she was inundated with offers she attributes to her height – being only three feet tall with her crutches, Emilia was referred to by everyone as '*la chaparrita*' ('the tiny one'). She claims that men felt very 'protective' towards her. Given her mother's words and experiences, however, she was wary, and consistently refused invitations. As it was Emilia was raped at the age of 25 by a fellow market worker who had propositioned her repeatedly for three years (he stole a locket she was accustomed to wearing and tricked her into visiting his lodgings to get it back). When he learned she was pregnant, he proposed marriage but Emilia was so offended by the rape that she opted to stay single. In addition to the fact that she enjoyed living with her mother and younger brother, she was also worried at the thought of a stranger witnessing her physical disabilities at close quarters and seeing her on her 'bad days'. While she was pregnant with her first child, Brenda, however, she met another man who was very keen on her and with whom she later had voluntary relations. This gave rise to the birth of a son, Edgar, in 1980. Although Emilia entertained the prospect of marriage as a means by which she might be better able to support her children, her mother dissuaded her by insisting that she keep Brenda, to whom she had grown very attached. Since Emilia also felt guilty about abandoning her mother, her choice fell again on continuing to live as a lone parent with her mother and younger brother. This worked fairly well because they were able to share work and childcare until, in 1984, Emilia's mother died suddenly. Soon after this, Emilia was visited by a childhood friend with whom she ended up sleeping for comfort, and subsequently became pregnant with her third child, Jorge. While she could also have married Jorge's father and was in some respects torn when he offered help around the time of her second child Edgar's death at the age of three-and-a-half years, she chose not to, although she later accepted money to help support his own son for the first two years of his life. Although she has absolutely no regrets about remaining single, and manages to earn a reasonable income, she sees herself as poor and declares somewhat wistfully '*A mí me tocó la suerte que le tocó a mi mamá*' ('I got the same luck my mother had'). It is poverty, however, rather than the absence of a man about which Emilia feels regretful. She made a conscious choice to opt for control over her own life and is happy with this decision.

Just as much as history does not necessarily seem to repeat itself in terms of women who are currently heads of household, it is also interesting to note that of four other women in Mexico who had been raised by a lone mother, only one, Ana María, now widowed, had had an unhappy marriage (mainly because of her husband's drinking), whereas three of them have stable, happy married lives. In other words, no pattern of generational continuity is discernible. Having said this, mothers in difficult relationships had forewarned their daughters about the problems of marriage. María del Refugio's mother, for example, had always impressed upon her the importance of working since '*El hombre no va a estar estable en la vida*' ('a man isn't going to be stable in life'). This turned out to be very relevant in María del Refugio's case, where two of her total of three relationships with men ended in separation and she had to work throughout because she could never rely on them for financial support.

As for Costa Rica, only 2 out of 12 female heads and spouses interviewed in 1994 had come from homes with happily married parents, and both of them now have stable marriages themselves. Yet although instability of women's household backgrounds was much more pronounced than in Mexico, and seems to display more of a tendency to be repeated in their own lives, I sense this is because family disruption is relatively generalised in northwest Costa Rica and has much less to do with individual circumstances. This is not to say, however, that people do not rationalise their actions by referring to personal household histories.

Lidia, a Nicaraguan lone parent in Cañas, is very philosophical about being the child of a single parent, and now one herself. Lidia's mother Concha had been raised by an aunt in Rivas, Nicaragua and at the age of 15 had run off to Managua to 'get to know more of the world'. She found a job as a domestic servant and a year later met her first partner. He was nearly ten years older than Concha and treated her very badly. She had two children with him in the two years they were together, although one died. Shortly after the death, the man began to beat Concha severely to provoke her into leaving and make space for him to install another woman. Once out on the streets again, it was a lot harder for Concha to get work as a lone parent and for this reason she accepted an invitation to live with another man (Lidia's father), although he insisted that she foster out her existing son. This second union lasted seven years and was happier, although the man eventually abandoned Concha and their three children when Lidia was only 40 days old. Lidia takes this philosophically, however, declaring: '*son cosas que ya tenían que pasar*' ('these things were meant to happen'). Indeed, living with her mother's third partner (see the earlier section on step-families) was a much harder thing to bear. This third man walked out on Concha a matter of weeks after their arrival in Costa Rica in 1987 when he met and moved in with a '*tica*' (Costa Rican woman). The family feels that he probably did this to stand a better chance of staying in the country, and, although Concha was traumatised, Lidia was relieved and feels her mother suffers much less than when she has a man in her life.

As for Lidia herself, she says her mother's experience made her opt for marriage under the illusion that this might give her more protection and security. Unfortunately, this did not turn out to be the case: Lidia's husband was very irresponsible with money, resented Lidia pursuing her education at night school, and picked constant fights with her. On top of this, his desertion from the *Frente Sandinista* (Sandinista army) meant that Lidia and her baby son, Elwin, were harrassed and once put in prison for three days, where they were made to sleep sitting up and only given water to drink. This event was crucial in prompting the family's flight to Costa Rica where they managed to secure refugee status. Soon after the move, however, Lidia's husband met another woman and left his wife and son (then three years of age). In order to sever contact and to dodge maintenance payments he moved with his lover to Limón, on the other side of the country. Ignorant of his exact whereabouts Lidia cannot even get the divorce which she would very much like in order to cut herself off from the past. After all she (and her mother) have been through, she is not after reconciliation and is quite happy to remain alone. In fact, having witnessed at first hand the calming influence that being alone eventually had on her mother, she takes this as a lesson that, young as she is, she should cease her involvement with men before she makes matters any worse.

In the Philippines, as noted earlier, as many as 22 out of 30 female heads and spouses in Cebu, Lapu-Lapu and Boracay came from homes where parents stayed together and/or were not so poor that they had to foster their children out. In other words, their home lives were more stable and dovetailed more closely with the normative ideal than those of women in Mexico or

Costa Rica. Of the eight remaining respondents, two came from foster households (one being due to the natural parents having too many children to feed, and the other where the aunt of the child did not have children of her own), three came from homes where a parent had died (one had moved in with her mother to her grandmother's house, one had a stepmother, and one was raised by her mother), and three came from homes where women were separated. Interestingly, two out of the three women who had been raised by lone mothers were unmarried when they had their first child, and the other one is presently a lone parent. The reasons given for one of the pre-marital pregnancies was that it was an accident, and the other, that the woman's mother was never around to discipline her, although it is clearly not possible to draw any pattern.

Household circumstances of children

As for household headship among the younger generations (that is, the sons and daughters of adult female respondents), it is again extremely difficult to discern any generalised trajectories. Out of five separated daughters (all heading lone-parent households) in the Mexican case study localities, only one had been raised by a single mother, two came from step-families, and two from households headed by their natural parents. One of the latter two, however, had been the product of a very conflictive marriage. Moreover, among three children aged 25 years or more who are still single by choice, two came from unhappy marriages and one from a single-parent household. A further individual (female) who elected not to get married until she was 32 did so partly because she was training as a deputy bank manager, and partly because she came from an unhappy family and did not want to suffer as her mother had done. In other words, people in Mexico nowadays may be slightly more circumspect about marriage when their own home lives have been traumatic or 'broken'.

Marriage

As for the incidence of marriage among the younger generation in Mexico, 31 out of a total of 38 children in unions in 1994 were formally married (84 per cent), and the bulk had a church ceremony as well as a civil wedding. Out of six children in informal unions, four come from two households where parents are not formally married, one from a single-parent household and one from a household where parents did not marry until very recently (Elba – see Chapter 6). By the same token, only 61 per cent of formally married sons and daughters came from households where parents were or are married.

Most of the rest come from long-term lone-mother households or households with stepfathers. In short, marriage seems to be equally, if not more, likely when children come from homes from which their natural fathers were absent.

In Costa Rica, informality of unions is more widespread among both younger and older generations. Of all sons and daughters currently in a union, only 43 per cent are formally married and half of these come from two households where, although their mothers are with second partners, they are married to them. Looked at another way, 88 per cent of the children from homes where their mothers are married are also married themselves. Alternatively only 2 out of a total of 13 children from four households in which men and women are in an informal union are formally married (15.3 per cent). Interestingly 7 out of 15 children (46.6 per cent) who come from the three relatively long-term lone-mother units are formally married, and in two cases mothers themselves were before separation. The three separated sons and daughters (two of whom are lone mothers) are all from step-families where their mothers are currently in their third union. Unfortunately there are insufficient numbers of households in the Philippine case study localities with children who are in unions to draw any patterns, although it is instructive that, as in the other countries, marriage remains a pervasive ideal.

ATTITUDES TO GENDER AND CHILDREN'S FUTURES

Returning to adult respondents, despite being rather jaundiced about marriage themselves (see Chapter 7), many unmarried or separated lone mothers want their own daughters to marry, as much, if not more, than women who are currently with men.

Although in Mexico some relaxation of attitudes to non-marriage and illegitimate pregnancy seems to be discernible over the last decade (see Chant, 1994b), Lupe (Puerto Vallarta), believes there still continues to be more respect for married mothers. Although she herself would never marry again, she hopes her daughter will do so since '*la mujer se ve más mal si tenga hijos sin casarse*' ('women look worse if they have children without being married'). By the same token, she wants Giovana to complete her university degree before she gives serious consideration to matrimony.

Doña Lupe (Querétaro) felt '*engañada*' ('deceived') when her daughter Flor became pregnant at the age of 19. She has never met the father, but would like to put '*un balazo en donde es hombre*' (literally: 'a bullet in his masculine parts'). Doña Lupe felt particularly sad because she and Don Teno had set a good example by being married. Yet Alicia and her daughter Rocío

(Querétaro) feel that marriage and living together are one and the same since nothing stops men from going off with other women. In fact Alicia has given her full support to her youngest daughter, Araseli, to leave a husband who is much older than her and with whom she is unhappy. Although they got married in church, which Alicia confesses to having been very proud of at the time, she sees no point in her daughter leading a miserable life and has given her blessing to the new relationship in which Araseli is currently involved. This may partly be because Alicia herself is in a very humdrum relationship and has heard rumours that her common-law husband, Daniel, is in love with a young girl on his home ranch. He will not leave Alicia, however, because the papers for their house plot are in her name, and he would lose an asset that has appreciated in value. At the same time, people also think it's getting easier for women to live independently now. As María Cruz (Querétaro) suggested, nowadays women *'no tienen miedo de enfrentar la vida'* ('aren't afraid of facing up to life'). As far as she is concerned she would rather see her daughter, Ana Erica, in a good job than living with a man who was a wastrel or made her life unhappy. In other words, there may be some shift towards the idea that women may not need marriage quite as much as they did in the past, although this is not to say that sex outside marriage is by any means condoned (see Chapter 6 and 7).

This also applies in Costa Rica, where although marriage is relatively uncommon in Guanacaste and there are large numbers of female heads, early motherhood and out-of-wedlock births are disapproved of in principle, with matrimony regarded as preferable to cohabitation on religious and economic grounds. Concepción (Liberia), for example, feels that marriage is *'para siempre'* ('forever'), and couples are not as likely to part *'por el temor de Diós'* ('for the fear of God'). Although this is undoubtedly influenced by the fact that her own marriage, thus far, has 'worked', she would not want anything less for her daughters. María Levi (Santa Cruz) feels that with marriage, one is *'más seguro con Diós y más seguro con la tierra'* (literally: 'more secure in heaven and on earth'), although it is bad luck if a man does not ask because the move had to be made by him. As far as Braulia (Liberia), an abandoned mother, is concerned, her main reason for favouring marriage for her daughters is that women have greater recourse to the law to make a claim on men's cash if they desert, although she also added that marriage was better in the eyes of *'él de arriba'* ('him up there' that is, God). Braulia's sentiments were echoed by an evangelical, Elda (Liberia), who feels that by getting married, women are accorded rights under the law that ensure greater security for their children. Marielos (Liberia) also felt that marriage was good from the point of view of earning social respect, and certainly hoped that God would give her the strength to survive her own, increasingly loveless, union. Although as discussed in Chapter 6, cohabitation is regarded as the next best thing to marriage for daughters who are having sexual relations, and for this reason they are encouraged to leave home and set up home with their boyfriends, parents will sometimes adopt additional measures to protect daughters. This applies to Maiela in Liberia, whose 17-year-old daughter, Yorlenes, fell pregnant in 1994 with a young man of 25 who Maiela describes as a 'layabout'. In order to keep an eye on things and to spare them the indignity of '*andar rodando*' ('going around renting one room to the next'),[5] Maiela has offered Yorlenes and her partner a room in their house, which allows Maiela to look after Yorlenes' health, to bully her boyfriend into going to look for work (Yorlenes would be less likely to do this), and also to ensure that he does not sleep with other women. Apart from the fact that Maiela does not see much point in marriage when '*Ya cuando uno fracasó*' ('when the dirty deed is done'),[6] she is not keen for Yorlenes to tie herself to someone who in her opinion is 'second best'. Maiela, like many mothers, expresses the hope that her daughters will find a 'good man' (usually defined as one with a regular job) (see also Chapter 7). Since such men are perceived as rare in Guanacaste, however, then it is sometimes better to fall back on one's own resources. For example, Ernestina's daughter Margot (23 years, Cañas) has quite a profitable business selling gold jewellery, and neither mother nor daughter believe it is worth her getting married because she has a trade and a good income.

In the Philippines, where female labour force participation is much more widespread, women certainly do not like the idea of 'live-in'. Sexual relations before marriage are still relatively uncommon, and Minerva (Boracay) said: 'The Maria Clara image ... you know ... women being virginal, is what most people want. The body is sacred, and women should keep it for only one man ... not like me.'[7] Winnie (Boracay), further emphasised that marriage was the only means of having children, who, in turn, would be a vital source of security in later years. Following this line of reasoning, Eden (Boracay) stressed that she was particularly keen her sons would marry since, as household heads, they would have more say over what happened to household income and thus be in a better position to give her money. Daughters, on the other hand, can usually only provide substantial economic support to parents when they have their own jobs, which is why, in Eden's opinion, so many nowadays are taking active advantage of education and training opportunities. Related to this, most women are concerned that daughters (and sons) complete their education before embroiling themselves in family commitments (Chant and McIlwaine, 1995a:127). However, although many women expressed the idea that as long as children had finished their studies it would '*depende sa aron*' ('depend on them') when and whom they married, some, like Dina, a separated woman in Boracay, added that she would only be interested in her daughters marrying if they found 'good guys'. Marilyn (Cebu), also noted that it could be problematic if her daughter, Peachy, married before she became really established in a career, because most employers 'don't like married; they prefer singles'.

Forward household projections

Aside from the marital arrangements of sons and daughters, it is interesting that lone parents (or women who are planning to leave their spouses) are often a projected part of the future households of their offspring. For example, Emilia's daughter Brenda (Puerto Vallarta) will not marry unless her husband accepts that Emilia lives with them. Denis, too, wants his mother Girlie (Boracay) to live with him when he gets married, which also means that she will be able to look after the children. In many cases, the children of older female heads such as María del Refugio, Socorro and María Cruz (Querétaro) continue to live very near their mothers and to see them regularly, further testifying to the frequently close bonds between children and unpartnered mothers.

CONCLUSIONS

Although, as stated at the beginning of the chapter, the discussion of the effects of female headship on children is impressionistic given the small number of case studies, there are interesting indications in a range of areas. One is that while, in the past, the children of lone mothers (particularly in Mexico and the Philippines) often started life with a distinct disadvantage, this seems to be less the case nowadays. For example, many children of long-term single parents go on to attain comparable levels of schooling as their counterparts in male-headed households, if not more. This seems to be especially marked among daughters, owing to a combination of their mothers' concerns about them being able to survive alone, and the fact that they are able to put their goals into practice more easily than women who are answerable to husbands and have less power over household decisions and finances. An additional factor is that domestic duties have a greater tendency to be shared between the sexes as well as the generations in female-headed units meaning that individual girls do not end up with exclusive or even major responsibility for housework and the care of siblings. Whatever the case, it is very clear that lone mothers are particularly keen to equip their daughters with both the means of being independent, and of bettering themselves. The fact that a greater proportion are achieving this testifies to the fact that there may be more opportunity nowadays for women to obtain education, training and/or experience, and to enjoy alternatives to early marriage and motherhood. In short, many aspects of the context of female roles and women's relations with men seem to be changing (in terms of widening educational opportunities, greater access by women to the labour force and so on), and daughters in lone-parent households seem to be in a privileged position to take advantage of them.

On top of this, lone mothers seem to be particularly concerned to impress 'responsible' attitudes upon their sons, which appear in many cases to lead to happier marriages. If these valuable lessons are passed on to their own sons and bolstered by a less authoritarian masculine role model, there are seeds here for positive change. Indeed, sons from lone-mother households seem to be much more engaged in the daily lives of their natal households and the ones they create, and to be more family-oriented than those from male-headed households. This tends to break with a pattern (especially in Mexico and Costa Rica) where mothers have been the thread of continuity in family life against a backcloth where men tend to come and go, even when they are nominally resident in the household. Although this pattern is in some respects (particularly at the domestic, if not the community level) taken as 'normal', and children are rarely unduly distressed by 'father absence', they might be considerably happier if their fathers were to devote more time, effort and emotional investment in contributing to household security and well-being.

In this light, the desire among lone mothers (and their children) that both sons and daughters will marry (albeit following the conclusion of their education), is not as conservative or contradictory as it might first appear. While not denying that this is a bid for 'respectability', in many respects it is also a sign of hope that marriage itself can be reworked, or at least renegotiated, so that both women and men benefit from an institution that formalises their togetherness and mutual commitment to children.

NOTES

1. Infant mortality refers to deaths among children within the first year of life, and child mortalities to deaths occurring within the first five years.
2. This also applies in the Costa Rican and Philippine case study localities and is counter to the findings of other studies, such as that of Merrick and Schmink's (1993:265) on low-income groups in Belo Horizonte, Brazil, where they found

that lack of money meant that women-headed households were less likely to have their children registered in school than male-headed households.

3. Although data from the questionnaire survey in Mexico in 1986 show that the incidence of school children or students working is higher among female-headed households (where 1 in 6 children have part-time jobs), compared with male-headed households (where the rate is 1 in 12), this could in part owe to the higher average age of female heads (see Chapter 6). This to some extent is borne out by the fact that the mean age of lone mothers with offspring contributing income to their studies is 42.9 years, compared with 39.4 years among those whose children do not have jobs. Household composition is also a mediating factor. Whereas there is at least one school child/student working in 42.9 per cent of lone-mother households, this applies only to 6.6 per cent of female-headed extended households. It is also interesting that the Costa Rican questionnaire data reveal a higher rate of school children working in male-headed households (1 in 8 children) than in female-headed households (1 in 15).

4. This also applies in the UK, where surveys have shown that nearly 50 per cent of fathers lose contact with their children (see Bradshaw and Millar, 1991), and an estimated three-quarters of a million children have no communication with their fathers (Collier, 1995:228). Collier further points or that research prior to the 1989 Children's Act (which dispensed with the term 'custody' but retained the idea of 'welfare' uppermost in determining arrangements concerning children), that it was mainly mothers who both demanded and obtained custody of children, whatever their position in divorce, and that custody cases were seldom contested (*ibid.* 178).

5. Other common ways to describe this in Costa Rica are '*ser como un gitano*' ('to be like a gipsy'), and '*no tener un lugar fijo*' ('to have no fixed abode').

6. '*Hacer una torta*' is another common Costa Rican expression for 'making a mess of things'/'screwing-up'.

7. The 'Maria Clara' image sums up the concept of women being yielding, loyal, enduring, anxious to please, maternal, permissive with their husbands, chaste and so on (see Church, 1986:6).

9 Whither Women-Headed Households? Directions for Theory, Research and Policy

INTRODUCTION

This chapter attempts to draw together the different threads of the book with a view to considering their theoretical and policy implications, and to suggest directions for future research on female household headship. These interlinked issues are important because in most parts of the world it looks not only as if women-headed households are here to stay, but are set for further increases. One of the crucial elements in the discussion is assessing the utility of comparative research in aiding our understanding of women-headed households and how we might enhance its feasibility. In a related vein, to what extent is it worthwhile to strengthen communication across the North–South divide for conceptual and pragmatic ends? The first section of the chapter summarises the major findings of the present analysis and their theoretical relevance. The discussion then proceeds to offer suggestions for future research and action.

MAJOR FINDINGS AND THEIR RELEVANCE FOR THEORISING FEMALE HOUSEHOLD HEADSHIP

In sifting out the key conclusions, it is important to bear in mind that the analysis has probably raised more questions than answers, and that I see this resumé mainly as a means of pointing us down particular pathways in studying female household headship. I also recognise that there are a number of positions from which summarisation might start: not only has the analysis moved through different scales of resolution – global, regional, national and local, but it has drawn on a variety of sources – micro-level, primary data such as interviews and life histories in relation to the case study discussions, and macro-level and/or secondary sources for the national accounts of Mexico, Costa Rica and the Philippines, and for the regional and global overviews. While I do not necessarily privilege the findings of my field research over arguments developed in the wider literature, it has been through my personal contact with individual women that I feel I have best come to learn (and care) about the formation, survival and implications of women-headed

256

households. As such, and in light of the fairly lengthy summaries given at the end of each chapter, I will confine myself to picking out the most salient points from the case study discussions and to indicate how these relate (or not) to the broader picture. In the interests of clarity and in line with the treatment of topics in the case study chapters, it is helpful to divide the discussion into two main parts: first, conclusions concerning the formation of female-headed households, and second, their survival and implications.

The formation of female-headed households

Aside from the rather obvious fact that women-headed household differ in frequency within as well as among Mexico, Costa Rica and the Philippines, and that routes into female household headship also vary, the case studies suggest that some factors are more consistently associated with the emergence of female-headed households than others. Notwithstanding that 'factors' do not arise or operate in isolation and need always to be contextualised with reference to place and the persons involved, the three which seem to stand out as most important in affecting levels (and types) of female headship in the case study countries are: (i) that women have the means of surviving economically without male partners and/or can support children partly or wholly through their earnings; (ii) that women are able to some degree or in some way to cope with the social pressures to which they are frequently subjected for not residing with spouses (whether through long-distance migration, independence from kin, situating themselves in environments [places or occupational sectors, for example] where they are freer to act autonomously and/or have contact with women in like circumstances, and so on); (iii) that the financial and/or psychological gains of living with men do not outweigh those attached to living alone, with other women, and/or with their children.

Lest this summing-up comes over as instrumentalist and/or implies undue degrees of voluntarism on the part of women in processes of household formation, it should be stressed that the majority of women in the case study localities (as in many other parts of the world), tend not to choose to head households and/or to raise children alone with great willingness (or facility) unless they have actually lived with men previously. Only separated or widowed women (usually with negative experiences of male household headship), stand to more easily resist resuming such an arrangement (whether through returning to former spouses or taking up with a new one). Beyond this, the process of women establishing independent households before or from within marriage or cohabitation is often a response to, or result of, men's actions. Aside from the 'involuntary' event of death (which may in some instances be hastened by personal behaviour or lifestyle), the biggest direct cause of women's non-marriage or separation is male desertion, and indirectly, the conflict induced by their partners' disengagement from household commitments and/or pursuit of 'outside' activities (for example, socialising with male peers, drinking, gambling, extra-marital affairs).

This generalised summary of what we might term 'proximate' influences on female household headship (that is factors which in a very direct and personal sense impinge upon the formation and viability of these units in respect of material and social considerations, inter-spousal conflict and/or inequality and so on),[1] arise from aspects of gender which, in turn, seem to be common to all the case study localities. First and foremost these include the social legitimacy which women derive from marriage and motherhood, constraints upon female extra-marital sexuality, women's secondary economic status (within male-headed households and in the labour market), and the greater orientation of men to extra-domestic activities (especially in situations where inadequate or inferior employment offers little chance of fulfilling expectations to be primary or major breadwinners). Yet while gender roles, relations, identities and ideologies share much in common in terms of what they prioritise and how their normative prescriptions impact upon individuals at the grassroots, the frameworks within which these are constructed, mediated and negotiated in the case study areas vary considerably and provide important clues as to differentiated patterns of household organisation *between* localities. More particularly, the influence exerted on gender and familial norms by kinship, culture, religion, law, economic development, demographic trends and so on differ in nature, degree and impact from place to place and time to time, and examination of these in combination with one another helps to explain spatial and temporal variations in frequencies and types of female household headship.

For example, although there are many processes involved in the configuration of gender identities in the Philippine Visayas which might arguably lead to high levels of female household headship and/or greater action on the part of women in determining household arrangements (high rates of female economic activity, the acceptance of employment as part of married women's roles, male detachment from family and home life, the appropriation of women's earnings by husbands and so on), the combined forces of religion, ideologies of family coherence, and legal prohibition of divorce are significant deterrents. This is one major reason why the bulk of women heads in the Visayas are widowed and/or disproportionately represented among particular occupational groups such as sex workers, who are marginalised from mainstream society (Chapters 5 and 6). In Guanacaste, Costa Rica, alternatively, where most female heads are separated, the barriers to female headship presented by religion, law and kinship seem to be less resistant to the destabilising influences exerted on marriage and male household headship by economic, demographic and interlinked social factors such as seasonal labour migration and informal conjugal arrangements. In Mexico, comparisons between the case study centres further suggest that economic and employment factors may be more powerful in affecting inter-urban differences in household headship than other variables, notwithstanding their interplay with related demographic and social processes in particular places at particular times (see Chapter 6).

Such variegated scenarios raise extremely interesting issues and questions for the analysis of gender and household organisation. Aside from emphasising the multiplicity of interacting influences on the formation of female-headed households, it seems that certain factors operating at a personal or proximate level are reasonably systematic in respect of inhibiting their emergence (particularly the construction of feminine identities and female legitimacy around the family), and those which tend to precipitate them (for example, gender divisions of labour, power and resources within male-headed units, and women's access to earnings). The findings also show, however, that in order to see where these influences come from and to evaluate their relative importance at a wider spatial scale (in this instance, the locality level), we have to look beyond meanings and interpretations to what, for want of a better term, we might call structures and mechanisms of gender inequality (Duncan, 1995; see also later), and to analyse them not only in their own right but in the context of their interrelations.

For example, if we accept that in all three countries male household headship remains the dominant normative ideal (and there is considerable evidence to support this at every level of analysis – see Chapters 5–8), it is interesting to note that where the power of social and ideological institutions such as kinship, culture, religion and the law is strong and there is some consensus in respect of preserving male household headship, then economic shifts, however dramatic, are unlikely to have major effects to the contrary. In turn, this begs questions not only about the nature of these institutions in themselves and their roles in shaping certain outcomes, but how these intermesh with contingencies of place, time and their interplay with one another. It is tempting, for example, to ask whether greater secularisation in Costa Rica and Mexico has played a prime role in making marriage a less powerful and rigid institution than where religion has greater influence in government and political life, as in the Philippines (see Chapter 5).[2] Moreover, to what extent has the success of the Church lobby against birth control in the Philippines meant greater emphasis on the ideal of family coherence (for pragmatic as well as ideological reasons) than in Mexico and Costa Rica where birth rates have dropped considerably as a result of family planning programmes? While these particular lines of enquiry would necessitate greater in-depth historical research in the context of the countries concerned, their formulation owes in large part to the fact that comparative analysis helps to single out factors affecting household diversity and dynamics likely to be worthy of further consideration. In turn, it is undoubtedly important to think about how particular social, institutional and economic constellations in space and time interrelate with broader global processes. This is especially relevant in light of the fact that macro-economic forces such as globalisation, the increasing integration of markets, and new international division of labour have imposed a range of pressures on familial relations, the allocation of resources within households, and childcare arrangements (Moore, 1994b:i).

For example, could the fact that Mexico and Costa Rica are often argued to be more 'developed' than the Philippines help to explain the relatively greater influence of global economic change in these countries on undermining male household headship? If so, what particular kinds of economic development are likely to be most associated with rises in women-headed households, and why? For example, is the fact that tourism in Puerto Vallarta is driven both by multinational capital and clients (and in this sense is more exposed to global economic and social influences) an important exogenous element explaining its greater levels of female headship than other cities? In fact similar patterns are discernible in the Philippines, albeit among particular groups of workers directly associated with the international tourist trade in Cebu and Boracay (see Chapter 6). While global processes cannot necessarily be tied to national or local ones, and certainly not in any functionalist or instrumental manner, exploring links between factors operating at a variety of spatial scales as well as between places could be valuable for enriching research at different levels of geographic resolution, as I return to later.

The survival and implications of female-headed households

Parallel arguments apply when considering the survival and outcomes of female headship. Notwithstanding that the character of women-headed households is likely to be affected by factors leading to their formation in particular cases, the case study discussions of Mexico, Costa Rica and the Philippines indicate a number of similarities in respect of women's perceptions of their circumstances. For instance, heading a household is often deemed by women to be preferable to their previous experiences as spouses in male-headed households. Beyond this, several material and psycho-social aspects of life in female-headed units compare favourably with those of women and children in existing male-headed households; in other words, it is not just the most conflictive male-headed households which split up and thereby make female household headship look positive by contrast.

More specifically, the data from all areas showed that women-headed households are by no means always the 'poorest of the poor', and that there is considerable support for deconstructing the notion of poverty and analysing it with reference to intra-household factors. The case study findings also tend to echo those of a small but growing body of research in both developing and advanced economies that children may be less traumatised by growing up with their mothers alone than in homes where parents have conflictive relationships. The field research further suggests that children's achievements (in respect of education, jobs and so on) may be comparable, if not better, in long-term female-headed units and this is especially marked among daughters. It would certainly appear that women growing up in female-headed households in contemporary Mexico and Costa Rica are less vulnerable and/or disadvantaged than their counterparts in the past (Chapter 8). Moreover, there are few signs that household histories tend to 'repeat themselves' among successive generations and that female household headship leads to a weakness in the conjugal unions of their offspring. Indeed, for a range of reasons, both sons and daughters of lone mothers seem to be better placed to have more enduring adult relationships. Daughters, for example, are possibly more aware of the pitfalls of marriage, more careful in selecting partners, and/or are in a stronger position to negotiate their lives with men by virtue of being better educated. Sons, on the other hand, may have healthier unions because they are more familiar with domestic chores, accustomed to taking responsibility for contributing to household well-being and/or are concerned not to transpose the suffering they might have experienced from paternal neglect onto their own children.

Female household headship may thus bring benefits for women themselves, their children, and their grandchildren, even if these are usually personal in nature. Indeed, gains in narrowing male–female gaps and inequalities within the household are often held in check by gender inequalities in society at large. Female household headship does not have a framework in which it is accorded the same respect as male headship, and this can act as a powerful deterrent to validating and popularising the notion that 'alternative' households (and/or alternative patterns of gender) are viable and/or desirable. This in turn feeds back into factors which depress the formation of these units.

Theoretical insights from the analysis and building blocks for future theory

As for the theoretical importance of the above findings (and the analysis in general), I noted in the introductory chapters to the book that it was unlikely that one theory could explain how and why female household headship was growing at a world level, or which might systematically account for differential emergence. I also argued, however, that weaving together observations from a range of contexts might be a helpful basis for a form of theorisation that, in line with post-modern feminist objectives, would not be concerned with making universal claims but with helping us better explain (and represent) difference. I also pointed-up (and in many respects this has been borne out by the findings, not just from the case studies, but from the wider literature) that while properly contextualised meanings of female household headship should be a central component of theorisation, this should not preclude the importance of factors which, while culturally-embedded themselves, might be more amenable to cross-cultural and/or quantitative analysis, and in turn aid the investigation of diversity. These factors included women's access to land and resources, female labour force participation, and state policies on gender and the family (see Chapters 2 and 4), and would certainly seem to be important, if not in respect of explanation at any general level, in provoking questions that help us better explore reasons for specificities in particular times and places.

The value of comparative research and analysis as a basis for theorisation
Leading on from the above, I remain convinced about the relevance of comparative work for enhancing theorisation. The exercise of evaluating the case study findings from Mexico, against those of Costa Rica and the Philippines, has been immensely important in directing me to what I believe are critical influences on female household headship and which I hope future research will further clarify. I have also found it extremely helpful to look at the literature on other developing countries and the advanced economies, not only in terms of rejecting notions I may previously have held about the general importance of factors observed in specific field locations, but in respect of detecting similarities.

'Similarities', of course, are far from conceptually unproblematic: the legacy of modernist social science makes generalisation one of our greatest weaknesses, and while difference is possibly more frequently the rule than the exception, it is much more difficult to deal with, not least because it distances us from an ability to codify, to categorise, and, in our limited ways, to explain. While theorising from the 'bottom-up' may well help us to check the views we bring with us to the analysis of a situation, how we interpret and present what we 'find' is usually irresistibly straitjacketed by our prior conceptions. Indeed, as soon as we begin to talk across households, let alone regions, the chances are that multiple realities are drowned under the tide of larger arguments. At the same time, although aggregation tends to iron out the variegated details of individual cases, one obvious theme in common between North and South is that men tend to appropriate a disproportionate share of household resources, leading many women (especially when resources are short), to *feel* they are better off when they head their own households, even among the very poor.

If similarities such as these are genuine and relevant (and it would seem that I am not the only one who sees them), where does that leave us in terms of explanation? Far from advocating that we return to modernist concepts of 'patriarchy', the idea of 'structural concepts of gender inequality' which embrace the notion that patriarchal relations take different forms and have different impacts in different times and places and which gets us thinking about *how* structures and their outcomes vary, seems appealing (see Duncan, 1995:264). Here comparative research is important because it arguably helps us construct explanations not only for difference but for sameness, in that similiar outcomes may owe to particular constellations of factors and processes in given locations. At the same time, there are so many features that would seem to be similar about the situations faced by women-headed households (particularly in respect of social marginalisation), not just in developing countries but in the industrialised economies as well, that it is important to think not just about local processes but national, regional and global ones (see Perrons, 1995a). These can perhaps best be reached by comparative research not only at different levels of resolution, but of different types (see below).

Drawing the global picture is important because, aside from being a means of exposure and allowing us to see common threads, it is also likely to indicate differences which not only press us to explore reasons for diversity and dynamics but may give important clues as to what to look for. If differences display systematic associations with different regions of the world, then regionally-comparative research is likely to be a useful step in this process. The national picture is particularly important regarding legal-institutional frameworks for gender equality and family law, whereas the local level indicates the scope and/or limitations of rights-based equity frameworks against local economic and social variations, how ideologies work out at the grassroots and how men and women interact and organise their households as individuals (Perrons, 1995b).

As suggested above, theorisation might also benefit from drawing on research which is comparative in other ways. While research comparing households among different ethnic groups is reasonably established in advanced economies, for example, there is still room to expand this in developing nations in order to explore interconnecting influences of colonial and post-colonial, as well as gender and ethnic constructs on household headship (see for example, McIlwaine, 1993; Trotz, 1996). Cross-class research which has begun to make an appearance in the literature on female-headed households in developing societies could also be developed, particularly as a means of examining the influence of economic and social factors affecting the formation of women-headed units at intra-national levels (see González de la Rocha, 1994b; Willis, 1994). Comparative research on female-headed households in rural and urban areas might also be an interesting means of evaluating different types of influence. For example, Bradshaw's (1996a) work on Honduras not only underlines the importance of assets and access to the means of production as affecting different frequencies and types of female household headship between rural and urban settings, but social and political factors as well. When considering the longer-term viability of women-headed households it is not only important to compare them with their male-headed counterparts, but to compare similar types, for example, lone-male and lone-female households, and households headed by lone mothers and lone fathers. The need for more research on this latter group is perhaps especially pertinent to developing societies, and to low-income groups in advanced economies, given that most work on single fathers to date has focused almost exclusively on employed middle- and upper-middle-income men (Grief *et al.*,1993:177).

Methods to strengthen the empirical bases for theorisation
While modes of strengthening comparative research are discussed in more detail later in the chapter, it is important here to stress that this would be an empty exercise if we did not manage to incorporate insights fom the grassroots (see Chapter 2). This makes it important to present other major theoretical implications of the analysis here, most of which have to do with methodological approaches and/or ethical/political considerations.

Grassroots perspectives
Perhaps one of the strongest messages that emerges from the present research is that we cannot afford to neglect what female heads and the members of their households think about how they evolve and the circumstances they find themselves in. Incorporating the opinions of women at the grassroots breathes life and meaning into the analysis of female household headship, and acts to challenge ideas that are often given in studies of a more generalised and/or abstract nature. For example, the case study discussions indicate that in many instances the lives of a number of low-income women in Mexico, Costa Rica and the Philippines sit at odds with portrayals of disadvantage or formation by default.[3] While this is not to suggest that women heads in poverty do not face huge difficulties (and in some places these are likely to

be greater than others – see Chapters 3 and 4), it is clear that households are not merely passive entities buffeted by larger economic, social, political and demographic forces, but represent sites in which active decision-making goes on and power and ideology are contested. Taking on board Netting *et al.*'s (1984:xxii) point that households have an 'emergent character that makes them more than the sum of their parts', and constitute arenas where the 'very stuff of culture is mediated and transformed into action', theorisation needs to take on board the role of agency, and the circumstances which affect its differential operation and outcomes in different contexts.

Representation and responsibility

Finding ways to more accurately depict and express women's personal rationalisations and realities are an essential part of such a process. This is difficult, however, when views about female household headship are usually not expressed directly by women themselves, but edited, translated, and/or paraphrased by others (the present text being no exception). The best I myself have been able to do in this situation is to conduct open-ended (and usually two-way) interviews, to spend as much time with people over a number of occasions, and to discuss my ideas and interpretations with respondents as they evolve. At the very least, it would appear that participatory feedback is one mechanism by which theorisation might become not only more accurate and comprehensive, but responsible and accountable. Here, feminist researchers are taking a pioneering line, with Chen and Drèze (1995) holding workshops and conferences with their respondents as a means of developing interaction and feedback in their work on widows in rural India, and Townsend *et al.* (1994) using similar methods of participatory research in relation to women in the Mexican and Colombian rainforest (see also Chapter 1). At the same time, it is important to acknowledge that feedback procedures and processes are unlikely to be straightforward, given power relations between researcher and researched, and the ways in which group feedback may be compromised by intra-group relations.[4]

Positionality and objectives

Theorisation will also require much more consistent and comprehensive clarification of the position of the author, the reasons why he or she is writing about the subject, the perspectives and context in which they are writing from, how this shapes their analysis, and what omissions they have made. With regard to the latter, for example, it is disturbing to see how writers from the North who write about the North often fail even to specify what country they are referring to in the titles of their books or articles, thereby perpetuating an idea that 'family trends' in the UK or the USA, for example, are somehow representative of worldwide patterns.[5] Moreover, in several texts with purported relevance for the study of households at a world scale, developing countries get scant mention. It is also important to recognise that the policy context in which Northern authors write means that what they argue is likely to have much more immediate implications for interventions than in the South. Here audiences are either likely to be smaller and less receptive to policy ideas because there is simply not the money for states to intervene in any direct way in 'family life', and/or audiences may be more diffuse because even if progressive policy prescriptions are adopted by multilateral agencies, First World development organisations and NGOs at a conceptual level, they may take time to 'filter down' to the grassroots. For these kinds of reasons, target readership should be specified, and an honest appraisal given as to how this may have influenced the analysis. At the bottom line, all writers should give details about themselves, about the fieldwork and methodology, and about the aims of the research in question. The main objective of the present book, for example (as discussed in Chapter 1), was to dispel stereotypes and to make the case for tolerance of a multiplicity of household forms. This was not just an academic exercise, but a personal and political one. From my very first visit to Mexico I have been aware that pathological discourses of female headship are both misleading and unjust, and in some way I hope to make some kind of contribution to creating a context in which women's efforts as female heads are acknowledged (and celebrated), and where the social, legal and economic environments in which they operate become less hostile than at present. Hence, my hope that the text would have a readership beyond academia. In setting out aims and position, analyses can at the very least be better evaluated for selectivity and bias, and theorisation should thereby become more transparent. This is not to say, of course, that theory should be reduced to a vehicle for political motives at the expense of balance and open-mindedness.

Men and masculinities: a place in the home

In fact, in the process of rectifying what I detected as a bias in much of the literature on female household headship, by paying greater attention to women's agency and interrogating portrayals of disadvantage, I recognise that my methodological approach may at some level run the risk of stereotyping in other directions. While in several respects, for example, I felt it was important to excavate the determinants and corollaries of female household headship from women's perspectives, I am well aware that this may have given a very one-sided view. Awareness of this is not only important analytically, but in respect of policy, since blanket ideas about and prescriptions for 'categories' of people have in many ways led us to where we are now. As Lehmann (1994b:6) has argued:

> female-headed single parent households need to be treated in a coherent analytical context, and this means in particular 'bringing men back in', for the image currently presented includes them only by pathologising them: poor urban men in particular tend to be dismissed *en bloc* as violent and drunken, so that the analysis of household dynamics is too often side-tracked into the denunciation of the consequences of male misbehaviour.

'Bringing men back in', as Lehmann suggests, will be a critical part of future, and more comprehensive, theorisation. Already there is a welcome appearance of new research which has begun to question and problematise masculinities, even if reference to men in feminist analyses of gender is still somewhat token and very few studies are based on large-scale fieldwork with male respondents. In the context of my own research I recognise that apart from considering sons, I have not included much on men except what women say about them (partly due to the legacy of my previous fieldwork, partly due to unavailability of men for interview, and partly because a feminist stance has possibly prevented me from coming round to the idea that we need to expose what men think when their views have dominated for centuries!). However, the explanatory weakness of field-based gendered research without full inclusion of men is now so obvious that I cannot countenance excluding them to any degree in future fieldwork.

Beyond this, I also sense that the time is long overdue to think much more fundamentally about changing constructions of masculinities and femininities not only in relation to men's and women's responsibilities within households but in terms of how they interrelate with other domains of activity and identification. This is clearly felt by others. Aside from decrying the long-standing and unproblematised equation of men's family role with economic provider, Collier (1995:229) points out that there seems to be no understanding of the ways in which:

> *cultures of masculinity* which are inimical to men's involvement with childcare have themselves been reproduced through the law and how they continue to inform understandings of the morality, economics and the politics of single parenthood. It is this failure to engage with cultures of masculinity which has been particularly evident in the historical construction of the errant father discourse ... The idea of the 'errant' and irresponsible father, which has surfaced so clearly in recent debates taps into and and reproduces deep-seated ideas about respectable familial masculinity. (Collier's emphasis)

Aside from thinking about masculinities and femininities against a broader canvas, we also need to think about male household headship alongside female household headship, to question the institutions involved in partnerships and parenting, and to recognise that biological parenthood is but one element in family lives and structures (Millar, 1992a:159). Referring to the UK, for example, Collier (1995:204) argues that cohabitation is increasingly an important context for parenthood, and that formal marriage is by no means a guarantee of paternal responsibility. Notwithstanding that the 'ideal-traditional' family unit centred around a married couple may be more an invention than a reality (see Chapter 2), we need to embrace the fact that other arrangements exist and function admirably despite the constraints imposed upon them (see Hewitt and Leach, 1993:42; Shaw, 1991:146).

Women-headed households: a place in the 'malestream'
A final major issue concerns the place we give to women-headed households within theory more generally. I believe the discussions in the book have indicated the merits of theorising female household headship in its own right, but this should not preclude the incorporation of women-headed households within wider theories of household and family change. Indeed this could be a very important basis for acknowledging (and tolerating) diversity in household forms, and is especially important in the light of current trends, not only in the 'feminisation' of household headship, but in terms of differentiation among women-headed households themselves.

Trends in female household headship

Despite the fact that the timeframe of most retrospective data on female household headship has been so limited that any talk of 'trends' must remain speculative, there seems to be some consensus that in most parts of the world, female household headship will continue to grow. Although in proportional terms women-headed households have not risen as much in the case study countries as in other areas in developing regions over the last two to three decades, in absolute terms they have, and this is especially true of lone mothers. Similar tendencies are noted in advanced economies with Cashmore (1985:3) suggesting that:

> The signs are that one parenthood is going to become even more prevalent. A mixture of choice and circumstances will guarantee that. The choices are those of those women and men whose deliberate intention it is to steer clear of the cultural scripts and write their own. The circumstances are those surrounding marriage: greater accessibility to divorce, easier

arrangements over the custody of children, and generally, a slight erosion of the values people place on marriage and a tendency towards the establishment of common law or *de facto* partnerships.

Notwithstanding the above, Winchester (1990:83) points out with reference to Britain, Australia and other advanced economies, that although it is probable that lone-parent households will increase in absolute terms, the rate of increase may diminish. Moreover, while lone-parent households in general are on the increase, the proportion headed by women may *decrease*. For example, US Bureau of the Census figures suggest that the percentage of lone-parent households headed by men grew from 10 per cent to 14 per cent between 1970 and 1990 (see Greif *et al*, 1993:176). The relative frequency of male and female lone parenthood is clearly fundamentally grounded in interactions between gender roles and relations, customary practices, legal aspects of family organisation and parenting, economic change and demographic factors in different places. At present, however, lone fatherhood seems to be minimal in developing countries, and virtually non-existent in the case study localities, although our bases for explanation are limited (see earlier).

Another group of female heads likely to witness some increase are women who live alone. In the UK, for example, this tendency is already in place, and many of the individuals it will concern in future are elderly women. Indeed, Sykes (1994:77) talks about the 'major growth area' over the coming decade being in single-person households, the vast majority of whom will be widows. This is also likely to occur in the USA, where presently half of all women aged over 75 live alone, compared with only 22 per cent of men in this age group (Keigher, 1993:379). If kinship obligations continue to weaken, and labour migration increases among the young, the frequency of elderly lone-female households could also grow in the developing world (see Chapters 3 and 4).

Another group of female heads which may increase in number are single-sex households of young childless women. These are most associated with formal sector workers engaged in multinational operations and may increase if the so-called 'feminisation of labour' continues and draws women into jobs which make it difficult to combine employment and family life. By the same token, there are more general signs that gender-selectivity in rural–urban migration in developing countries is diminishing over time, which may play a part in counteracting this process.

Whatever the case, maintenance or growth in current levels of female headship give rise to a number of possible outcomes. Looking at the global picture, world birth rates may drop still further as women postpone or avoid marriage, or as lone mothers decide to limit their fertility. On a more ideological note, an increase in female household headship could mean that women in this position come to gain greater acceptance and legitimacy over time, especially if growth persists at a world scale.

Back in the 1970s, for example, Chester (1977) argued for Britain, that lone parents looked like becoming more accepted in society, and, as such, to be regarded more as a 'variant' rather than 'deviant' family form. Yet while growth may be accompanied by greater acceptance, as in Canada, where Rose (1993:194) argues that the growth in mother-led families means that they 'are no longer regarded as unusual', there is little evidence of this in Britain. In the USA, too, female heads still face considerable prejudice and downgrading/hostility, especially if they 'choose' to be single parents (Gelles, 1995:6). To a large extent this applies in the case study countries, particularly the Philippines, although this could in part owe to their smaller numbers (Chapters 5 and 6). Whatever the case, accepting Winchester's (1990:83–4) point in relation to Britain and Australia that 'The implications of this changing family structure are at least as dramatic and far-reaching as the well-publicised decline in fertility and the ageing of western populations', there is little doubt that we need to make our research responsive to changing household realities.

DIRECTIONS AND PRIORITIES FOR RESEARCH

Many points raised under the heading of theoretical implications are also crucial questions for future research, particularly the need to 'bring men back in', and to more accurately assess the roles people themselves play in negotiating household arrangements. Aside from improving the quality of our context-specific research, creating a basis for work of a more comparative nature is also likely to be helpful, particularly in light of the inadequacies of existing statistics. Two possible ways of doing this are first, to work at developing some form of common terminology and definitional criteria for female-headed households, and second, to continue a process to which I hope I have contributed, namely to extend interdisciplinary dialogue (see below).

Data and definitions

One critical basis both for improving our conceptualisation and understanding of female household headship and to strengthen comparative research, is that of bettering the quality and quantity of data. A useful starting point might be the standardisation of definitions of female headship, which is not to say (as noted back in the Chapter 1), that standardisation is not beset with problems, particularly in respect of selecting criteria that are in some way intelligible or meaningful to all parties in all situations and in all places. One possible solution might be for international bodies such as the United Nations to set a standard according to the majority view (ideally based on the findings of in-depth case study work), and for member countries to submit returns along these lines. Even if we were to stick with the conventional definition (that is, female-headed households are those in which the main adult woman in the unit has no male partner), we could at least aim for less asymmetrical definitions for other households: for example, male-headed units could be defined as households headed by men with no adult woman, and households comprising an 'intact' couple could be termed 'couple-headed households'. This would help to dispense with the way in which the terminology of 'headship' obscures the fact that women in all sorts of household often take a large share of responsibility for survival and/or reinforces ideas of male authority. It would not, of course, preclude individual nations from gathering and tabulating data in a way that is more useful for their own purposes.

Over and above asking nation states to produce returns along internationally-agreed guidelines, and resources permitting (some of which might come from a central fund for poorer countries), additional data ought to be collected on whether women who are living alone are still linked to a male partner through an extant relationship or remittances (which would provide information about whether households are *de facto* or *de jure* female-headed). Indeed, even if headship definitions remain unstandardised, comparisons could also be assisted by giving the marital status of female heads since as Folbre (1991:93) argues: 'The percentage of households with female heads, excluding those legally or consensually married (not separated) represents a measure of households which lack a formal claim on male income, an approximate lower boundary for the percentage of families primarily maintained by women alone.'

Although the size of households is often given in headship breakdowns, ideally it would also be useful to have more information on the gender and age composition of households, the existence of embedded 'sub-families', and flows of income within and between households (Folbre, 1991:93–4). This would help not only to get away from looking at heads *per se* (*ibid.*:99), but to evaluate headship and implications for its members in more meaningful ways. As Baden and Milward (1995:45) argue, the need for more attention to gender-disaggregated data collection in large-scale household surveys is paramount with respect to the control and allocation of labour, and other productive resources such as assets and incomes (see also INSTRAW, 1992:239). Maintaining the breadth of surveys, of course, remains important for 'representativeness'. Yet while Netting *et al.* (1984:xxiii) point out that 'Resolution of the sampling problem requires collection of a large number of cases at several points in time, a solution not often available to historians or anthropologists', it is critical to acknowledge that small surveys and case study material can greatly enhance the meaning of large-scale statistics, and could be a vital basis for improving macro and census measures (see also Perrons, 1996). Indeed, I hope the present book has shown just how important micro-level surveys are in terms of capturing the diversity and dynamics of female household headship, the reasons behind their formation and their access to resources. To build on this in the future, micro-studies by individual researchers and teams of researchers should be very precise about their methodology (sampling procedures, numbers and dates, 'typicality' and so on), and deposited alongside sources of large-scale quantitative data for ready consultation by interested parties. As mentioned earlier, we also need to hear voices of women themselves in micro-level material, and use this to help bridge the gaps between analysis, policy and action.

Interdisciplinary interchange

The question of strengthening research on female headship for geographically comparative work is clearly not just a matter of data, but considering that data with a view to tackling the multiplicity of factors influencing household diversity and dynamics. A helpful strategy for so doing would be to make more sustained moves to open up dialogue and interchange between disciplines whose different languages and approaches have frequently proved inimical to integrated enquiry. As Folbre (1991:113) points out, different disciplines are likely to bring different insights to the questions surrounding different elements of female headship:

Changing family structures invite interdisciplinary research because they are the outcome of complex political, cultural and economic processes. Historical demography offers new methodologies that could be applied to the construction of comparable data sets. Social historians could address the highly contested cultural meaning of female economic and residential independence. Political history is also relevant: forms of collective action aimed to defend or challenge patriarchal authority must be analysed in terms which are sensitive to differences in nation, race and class. Anthropological research could contribute to our understanding of traditional law and implicit contracts governing informal kin networks. Legal historians have only just begun to trace the evolution of family laws that determine women's and children's formal claims on male income. With the patriarchal aspects of the welfare state already receiving notable attention in the United States and Europe, similar attention should be focused on state policies in the developing world.

The synthesis of factors associated with the emergence of women-headed households in different parts of the world in Chapter 3 and particularly in the context of developing countries in Chapter 4, might prove to be helpful guidelines for issues that could usefully be explored in a range of areas by a variety of researchers and help to strengthen interdisciplinary methodologies and cross-cultural knowledge. Beyond this, Folbre's point about welfare states is critical not only from an analytical perspective, but insofar as it beckons closer involvement between academics and policy-makers. This could create a healthier basis for interventions, especially if interaction takes place not only within nation states but at a world scale.

DIRECTIONS AND PRIORITIES FOR POLICY

Considering the issue of comparative analysis not only as a basis for policy, but in respect of policy itself, it is clearly vital to assess whether it is possible for countries to learn from one another about policy approaches and interventions that might be appropriate to strengthen the position of women-headed households within a framework of support to all citizens. Kamerman and Kahn (1988:71) argue for industrialised countries, for example, that:

> even if there are legitimate doubts about the ability of one country to 'borrow' directly from the experiences of another, given the importance of total societal context, culture, and history in these matters, insights can be obtained from the experiences of other countries and from an analysis of how they have addressed the problems they have identified, with what consequences.

Whether or not such possibilities are relevant in respect of transferability to developing country contexts, however, is another question. As pointed out in Chapter 2, while advanced economies have higher overall incomes, a wider tax base and fairly well-established (albeit eroding) systems of social security and family support, these are only weakly evolved in most developing nations. Moreover, projects to assist target groups such as the poor in general and/or women-headed households in particular, are frequently dependent on external aid (whether in grant or loan form) and for this reason, coverage is rarely comprehensive or long term. Moreover, as indicated in the case study discussions, very few women in Mexico, Costa Rica or the Philippines are aware of existing government programmes for women or low-income groups, and have little trust in government motives for intervention (Chapter 6). None the less, at some level, the underlying bases and general outcomes of policy between North and South may be worthy of examination, particularly if grant aid for women in developing countries could be stepped up as a result of international pressure and/or in the process of learning about common characteristics and problems of female-headed households in different parts of the world, factors come to light that are responsible for core difficulties and about which something might be done through global action.

The relevance of targeting and differentiation

One of the first questions we must ask ourselves (and more importantly, female heads perhaps!) is whether the latter desire specific policy interventions, or whether they would prefer more general programmes for women and/or parents that they could tap into as required. As discussed in Chapter 2, one of the problems of targeting female heads is that there is a danger of missing other women. Another problem is that of perpetuating the assumption that women-headed households are disadvantaged. As should be obvious from the bulk of the discussion in the present book, women-headed households are highly heterogeneous. As Lewis (1993:24) sums up: 'lack of male' should not necessarily indicate 'poor' or 'weak', and 'Both the construction of sound analytical categories and the questioning of common preconceptions about female-headed households are necessary for the provision of poverty-focused development assistance.'

If we are going to target women-headed households, therefore, we need to be aware of who this broad group consist of in different contexts and who is likely to be most 'in need'. With reference to developing countries in general, INSTRAW (1992:237) propose that three types of household headed by women are of special relevance in respect of social policy:

(1) one-person households of lone women (where it will also be helpful to know more about their age and marital status);

(2) households where there are women and children but no adult males (and here, data on the receipt of remittances would be useful); and

(3) households which have adult males, but where women are the principal or sole economic providers ('women-maintained' households – see Chapter 1, this volume).

INSTRAW's schema would mean not only different types of female head might be reached, but women in other households as well. This is important since the analysis not only of the case study areas, but of other developing (and advanced) economies, show very clearly that gender inequalities affect all women. Yet while female-headed households seem to find strategies to resist these at a domestic level, the bulk of the problems they face in their communities, in the labour market, and in society may be greater than among other women for the very reason that they lack a 'male buffer' in their households. Beyond this, it is important to acknowledge that disadvantage is likely to be affected by intersecting differences in female headship in accordance with 'race', class, and the life course (Varley, 1996).

What sorts of intervention?

As for the types of policy intervention that might be welcomed and/or would benefit women, the case study discussions and analyses of female household headship in other developing countries suggest that these might be of two main types – short-term needs revolving around material and practical concerns, and longer-term initiatives of a more ideological nature geared to such questions as women's rights and empowerment (see Lewis, 1993:36–8).[6] In many respects, this mirrors the distinction made by Molyneux between practical and strategic gender interests, and which was first translated in the gender planning context as practical and strategic gender 'needs' by Moser (1987, 1993a).[7] Having drawn this distinction, however, it is critical to bear in mind that needs/interests are often overlapping and can evolve out of one another in multiple and interacting ways (see Moser, 1987; also Kabeer, 1994). As Wieringa (1994:836) reminds us, the matter of defining interests is never a 'one-off activity' but a 'constant process'.

'Immediate' needs and interests of female-headed households

Notwithstanding that needs are likely to vary in different parts of the world and according to the particular group concerned (see above), the case study findings and the literature on other developing countries, suggest that basic material factors such as housing, access to employment and earnings, and provision for childcare may be vital in strengthening the position of women in general, and women-headed households in particular (Chant, 1996a; Shanthi, 1994). For example, women's rights to land are often emphasised as a critical prerequisite for gender equality, even if, as Tinker (1993:23) argues: 'nowhere is the move toward equity more difficult than in policies to change women's rights to land and housing'. Yet a simple step such as registering land and property in the names of wives as well as husbands (see Larsson, 1993:114) would not only allow women greater security and stability in the event of conjugal breakdown, but could also enhance their possibilities for determining household arrangements. In other words, women might find it more feasible and/or easier to ask men to leave home if they know that separation will not entail leaving home themselves and forfeiting their assets (Chant, 1996a). Given that owner-occupied dwellings are also frequently the locus of income-generating activities among women, enforcement or rights over domestic property could also help to prevent the situation where women may resort to taking another partner for financial reasons (*ibid.*). Protection of land rights is also stressed for widows in rural India, alongside the provision of pensions and increased access to gainful employment (see Chen and Drèze, 1992:38).

In respect of earnings, it is clear from the case study discussions that although women-headed households develop several imaginative strategies for earning, conserving and stretching income, that their financial position would be better still if female earnings were closer to men's.[8] This, in turn, could also strengthen their ability to opt for separate residence (see Chapters 6 and 7). The matter of earnings disadvantage is by no means a developing world phenomenon. For example, Kamerman and Kahn (1988:100) point out for industrialised economies that:

> The relative economic deprivation experienced by mother-only families can be alleviated – but not eliminated – when women's wages are closer to male wages and when earned income is supplemented if low. The income of one-parent families will not equal that of the two-parent, two-earner family because transfers do not substitute fully for earnings, but the difference can be partially reduced.

This is also stressed by Folbre (1994a:258–9) who proposes specific recommendations to compensate women for the greater share of unpaid family labour they do and affirmative action to promote equal opportunity. Yet the extent to which this scenario is likely anywhere in the world is limited. As Cleves Mosse (1993:47) argues with reference to developing economies: '... the myth that the male breadwinner and the female housewife is the normal and best arrangement for human beings clings tenaciously, despite overwhelming evidence to the contrary'.

In light of the above, and accepting that it is likely to be extremely difficult to 'de-gender' labour markets overnight, complementary initiatives to make up the shortfall from women's labour market returns could include stepping up men's responsibilities for child support (see Bruce and Lloyd, 1992; Folbre, 1994a,b; also Chapter 2).[9] Athough we saw that women in the case study countries often reject maintenance from former partners because it ties them into ongoing contact they do not desire, the maintenance process might be changed to allow women to retain their independence while receiving economic help.

Over and above enforcing child maintenance payments (which would also reduce men's economic incentives to desert), another option is to keep men within households with redefined roles as partners and parents. This could take the form of what Folbre (1994a:257) calls 'a social contract modeled on an egalitarian family'. Another option suggested by Folbre is to encourage men and women to combine family work and market work by making changes in the workplace (*ibid.*:258–9). Certainly, men's abilities to parent may be aided by more supportive work environments where fathers are entitled to flexible shifts, time off for medical reasons, access to childcare facilities and so on. As Grief *et al.* (1993:192) point out: 'to recognise that men as well as women are parents and that, as working parents, they must make adjustments in their work to respond to family needs. If work organisations do not begin to take men's parenting needs more seriously ... both fathers and children will continue to suffer the consequences.' Hewitt and Leach (1993:16) add that some provision for statutory paid paternity leave could help fathers to believe their parenting counts.

Yet arguments for paternity leave are scarcely relevant in developing nations, where even maternity leave is a 'privilege' confined to a very small (and possibly shrinking) section of the (formal) labour force. Moreover, arguments about workplace changes assume that men will continue to be main breadwinners in households, when macro-economic circumstances seem to be making it increasingly difficult for men everywhere to fulfil this function (see Collier, 1995:192 on advanced economies). Another contradictory pressure is that employers are facing an increasingly competitive world market and as such are unlikely to want to make greater accommodations and concessions to the needs of workers, let alone be interested in struggles for gender inequality.

On the more general question of income, regardless of the way in which women might get hold of it and how much they might receive, it is important to acknowledge that this is by no means a guarantee of improved status. Indeed, although in the advanced economies, many female-headed households, particularly lone mothers, are already linked into welfare programmes, state assistance has hardly done a great deal for compensating economic inequality, and the associated ideological fall-out has often been worse. As noted in Chapter 2, the links between lone mothers and welfare have often led to greater negativity in images of female household headship, with the possible exception of places like Sweden where state assistance is based on the idea of people as parents, workers and citizens (see Hobson, 1994). My overwhelming impression, North and South, however, is that improving women's material position in relation to men via anti-poverty strategies is insufficient to make female households headship a legitimate option. Accordingly, needs and interests of a more ideological and strategic nature must also be addressed.

Longer-term ideological and strategic interests

Reiterating the point made earlier about the interweaving of practical and strategic interests and how these should ideally evolve from the 'bottom-up', my perception is that the really critical item on the agenda for women-headed households lies in creating ideological, political and economic environments in which they and other 'alternative' households can enjoy the same legitimacy as others. From my perspective, this would revolve around two main interlinked imperatives. The first (and this is particularly relevant to lone mothers) is recognising that children are not necessarily disadvantaged by the number and sex of their carers, but by the quality of care they receive, the love they are given, and the basic means of material survival. As Hewitt and Leach (1993:11) so forcefully summarise: 'It is a travesty of the facts – and desperately damaging to many children – to make lone parents scapegoats, as many politicians do, for the problems which many children face and some of them cause', when 'Individual children thrive in any kind of family where they are well cared for by loving parents and parent figures, and in no kind of family where they are not' (*ibid.*:14). Advocating tolerance of female-headed households, however, does not mean advocating an ideal family state and is not about justifying male neglect of dependants, especially when the process of 'going solo' can tie women even more to gendered duties in the context of state regimes that see women's mothering work as 'natural' and leave it largely unsupported (see Folbre, 1994a,b; Moore, 1994b). Rather, my argument is that depressing and/or denigrating female headship represents a fundamental infringement of women's human rights, and that it will not be only women who suffer from this injustice, but society in general. This is again illustrated by Hewitt and Leach's path-breaking analysis of the situation in Britain:

> The inequities and deprivations suffered by children in the UK are not our misfortune, but our shame. We cannot continue to scapegoat lone mothers and irresponsible fathers for them or to distance ourselves from them with talk of 'cycles of deprivation' or an 'underclass' that sounds as if these misfortunes had a will and an existence beyond our understanding or control. Child poverty, the abuse of children's human rights and the undervaluation, in different ways, of both mothers and fathers are profoundly

damaging not only to children and their immediate families, but to the whole of our society. (Hewitt and Leach, 1993:43)

Leading on from this, the second imperative ought to involve equalising the status of and relations between men and women in society at large, both ideologically and pragmatically. This would not only mean that women who are currently alone and/or who head their own households can take full advantage of their situations, but so that others who may want to live independently have greater freedom to do so. As Hobson (1994:176) sums up with reference to female lone parents: 'Solo motherhood is the reflector or rearview mirror for the dynamics of power and dependency – the more difficult and stigmatised solo motherhood is in a society, the greater the barriers against opting out of a bad marriage.' While women's freedom and happiness are often limited by male household headship, their bid to escape this situation seems to meet with so many hurdles at community and societal levels that it is no surprise that some do not attempt to do so in the first place. For those who do, their marginalised position may have grave repercussions for younger generations considering that children need 'positive role models and can find them best in mothers who are not peripheral or excluded but are part of mainstream society' (Kamerman, 1984:268–9). Part and parcel of this process is to promote the idea that female household headship of any description is not a 'bad thing', and to get backing for the struggle from as many quarters as possible.

Cooperation for change

Having emphasised the role of policy, I realise that I have privileged the role of the state, and it is crucial to recognise that widespread change will require the active involvement of a much larger range of actors: individual persons, popular organisations, NGOs, multilateral institutions and so on.

In the UK, for example, the National Council for One Parent Families, which is supported largely by charitable trusts and private donations, is now such an important presence on the political scene that it is rarely excluded from public debates on the subject. Having garnered information about one-parent families, campaigned for 'a life in the mainstream' for several years, and influenced public and political opinion in a range of ways, this may well have helped to divert arguments on the subject 'away from moral panic to rational debate' (NCOPF, 1994b:2). At the same time, the strategic political work of the Council has been accompanied by practical efforts such as 'return to work' programmes which appear to have enjoyed substantial success rates (Monk, 1993:27–30).

The existence of local lone-parent support groups is also likely to be important. For example, in her study of 25 separated and divorced lone parents in the United Kingdom, Shaw (1991:145) found that the majority were attending groups which provided a social outlet for parents and children alike, as well as practical and emotional support. In Costa Rica, NGOs such as CEFEMINA have also been concerned to provide advice and legal aid concerning divorce, separation and child maintenance to women at the grassroots, and to provide refuge for battered wives. While these operations have undoubtedly benefited women in the capital, San José, however, women in marginal regions such as Guanacaste remain excluded (Chapter 7).

Exclusion, in turn, is not only a spatial but a profoundly symbolic and personal matter, and breaking down the isolation of female household heads in all respects is long overdue. There are several steps we might take towards this. In providing a resource that attempts to synthesise information and analysis of female headship from a range of places and perspectives, and to expose correspondencies and continuities as well as diversity and dynamics, I hope the present text represents one of them.

NOTES

1. 'Proximate' is not a term I particularly like, but it seems to sum up what I mean with fewer problems than other alternatives. Possible substitutes could have included 'immediate', although the aspect of time implied in this is not appropriate when the process of changing household arrangements is often long drawn-out. While 'self-assessed' is helpful insofar as I am referring to factors that are perceived and acknowledged by people, I do not feel that this is sufficient to cover the fact that most of those I refer to (for example, labour and income opportunities, social opprobrium towards lone motherhood) have an independent existence as well. I am grateful to Simon Duncan for talking through these terminological problems with me.
2. One of the reasons that it would be easier to examine this question in relation to the case study countries is because Catholicism is the dominant religion in all three of them.
3. Women-headed households are clearly not always presented as forming by default, but when they are discussed as evolving out of 'design', particularly in policy and media circles in the North, the tendency has been to portray this in negative terms, emphasising the irresponsibility of illegitimate childbirth or women using single parenthood as a means of eliciting money, housing or other welfare benefits from the state (see Chapter 2).
4. I am grateful to Penny Vera-Sanso for drawing attention to this point.

5. While writers on developing countries more commonly discuss 'households', those writing on households in advanced economies often work with the term 'family'. This is an interesting difference considering that a greater proportion of households in developing economies are family-based units than in the advanced regions. One possible reason why 'household' has been the preferred term in developing societies is because the members of individual residential units are often embedded within strong networks of wider family and kin and it accordingly makes little sense to confine 'family' to small domestic groups. Alternatively, people in Northern countries often have less contact with relatives beyond the immediate household or their natal families and so the concept of family becomes prioritised in a household setting. Another possibility is that the 'family' becomes more relevant in contexts where there are more established social policy frameworks.

6. It is important to bear in mind Wieringa's (1994:836) argument here that people's definition of needs is 'culturally specific, historically contingent and subject to symbolic processes of identification'.

7. Molyneux (1984, 1986) used the term 'interests' in her ground-breaking work on the distinction between practical and strategic gender interests in the context of the Sandinista government's policies towards women in Nicaragua in the 1980s. Moser (1987, 1993a), who drew on Molyneux's work in formulating her 'Triple Roles' framework for gender policy and planning, substitutes the term 'interests' with 'needs'. The theoretical distinction between 'interests' and 'needs' is important, and a helpful discussion on the subject is provided by Kabeer (1994) who, in her own 'Social Relations' framework for gender planning, refers to 'practical gender-based needs', but retains Molyneux's original terminology for 'strategic gender interests'. Kabeer's reasons for so doing revolve around the fact that although Molyneux herself did not specify exactly what she meant by 'interests', her work was grounded within a Marxian theoretical tradition where interests arise out of power relations and are defined differently according to people's places in society. In respect of disadvantaged groups, for example, interests are likely to differ from those in positions of power and the true identification of those interests emerges 'from below'. The term 'needs', however, belongs to planning discourse, and in this light is 'generally a perspective from above' (Kabeer, 1994:297). Kabeer further notes that 'the distinction between needs and interests would be a purely semantic one if all planning processes were transparent, participatory, democratic and accountable' (*ibid.*). This is rarely the case, however. Institutions are sites of contested power relations between different groups, where men's strategic gender interests (which might include protecting their position or extending their privileges) may clearly pose obstacles to the pursuit and/or attainment of women's strategic gender interests (see also Goetz, 1995; White, 1994). Beall (1995) also adheres to the practical needs/strategic interests schema, further clarifying the importance of terminological differences by identifying that interests are held by political or organisational categories of people – that is, interest groups who advance their *demands*, whereas needs are identified *for* beneficiaries or *by* users within the planning process, whether in a 'top-down' or 'bottom-up' way. Unlike Moser, therefore, Beall does not regard political/organisational and political/planning processes as interchangeable. See also Wieringa's (1994) critique of the distinction between practical and strategic gender interests.

8. Although the strategies women heads evolve to maximise income may not necessarily have negative repercussions on other members of their households (Chapter 8), in certain contexts the use of child labour may be problematic insofar as affecting their education, and as Lewis (1993:33) argues in relation to Bangladesh, raises additional dimensions to policy questions.

9. Another key element would perhaps be to make child custody less biased in favour of women. In the UK at present, for example, the rights of fathers are much less than those of mothers. Unmarried fathers do not automatically have rights over their children and must either apply to the courts for a Parental Responsibility Order or be given express responsibility by the mother via a Parental Responsibilty Agreement (NCOPF, 1991:5; see also Collier, 1995:178).

Bibliography

Abu, Katherine (1983) 'The Separateness of Spouses: Conjugal Resources in an Ashanti Town', in Christine Oppong (ed.), *Female and Male in West Africa* (London: George Allen and Unwin) 156–68.

Achío, Mayra and Krauskopf, Dina (1994) *Programa: Población y Desarrollo* (San José: Instituto de Investigaciones Sociales, Universidad de Costa Rica, Avances de Investigación No.89).

Achío, Mayra and Mora, Patricia (1988) 'La Obrera Florista y la Subordinación de la Mujer', *Revista de Ciencias Sociales*, 39, 47–56.

Acosta-Belén, Edna and Bose, Christine (1995) 'Colonialism, Structural Subordination and Empowerment: Women in the Development Process in Latin America and the Caribbean', in Christine Bose and Edna Acosta-Belén (eds), *Women in the Latin American Development Process* (Philadelphia: Temple University Press) 1–36.

Acosta Diaz, Felix (1992) 'Hogares Más Pobres con Jefaturas Femeninas', *Demos*, 2, 30–1.

Afshar, Haleh (1987) 'Women, Marriage and the State in Iran', in Haleh Afshar (ed.), *Women, State and Ideology: Studies from Africa and Asia* (Basingstoke: Macmillan) 70–86.

Aguilar, Delia (1991) *Filipino Housewives Speak* (Manila: Rainfree Trading and Publishing).

Ahmad, Asmah (1993) 'Gender and the Quality of Life of Households in Raft Houses, Temerloh, Pahang, Peninsular Malaysia', in Janet Momsen and Vivian Kinnaird (eds), *Different Places, Different Voices: Gender and Development in Africa, Asia and Latin America* (London: Routledge) 183–96.

Albee, Alana (1995) 'Living in Transition: Women in Rural Vietnam'. Paper presented at the 15th annual conference of the Association of Southeast Asian Studies in the United Kingdom, 'Gender and the Sexes in Southeast Asia', University of Durham, 29–31 March.

Albert, Michèlle (1982) *Sex Selectivity in Internal Migration: A Exploratory Study of Costa Rica* (Ottawa: International Development Studies Group, Institute for International Development and Cooperation, University of Ottawa, Working Paper No.827).

al-Khayyat, Sana (1990) *Honour and Shame: Women in Modern Iraq* (London: Saqi Books).

Amador, Giselle (1992) 'El Alcoholismo en Costa Rica. ¿Causa de Divorcio Familiar?', in CEFEMINA, *Mujer, Violencia y Mitos* (San José: CEFEMINA) 8.

Anderson, Patricia (1986) 'Conclusion:WICP', *Social and Economic Studies* (Institute of Social and Economic Research, University of the West Indies), 35:2, 291–324.

Appleton, Simon (1991) 'Gender Dimensions of Structural Adjustment: The Role of Economic Theory and Quantitative Analysis', *IDS Bulletin* (Sussex), 22:1, 17–22.

Arizmendi, Fernando (1980) 'Familia. Organización Transicional. Estructura Social. Relación Objetal. In Carlos Corona (ed.), *Antropocultura* (Guadalajara: Universidad de Guadalajara) 68–87.

Arizpe, Lourdes (1982) *Etnicismo, Migración y Cambio Económico* (México DF: El Colegio de México).

Armstrong, Warwick and McGee, T.G. (1985) *Theatres of Accumulation: Studies in Asian and Latin American Urbanisation* (London: Methuen).

Baden, Sally (1992) *Social, Economic and Health Implications of Adjustment for Women in Developing Countries* (Sussex: Institute of Development Studies, Bridge Report No.2).

Baden, Sally (1993) *'The Impact of Recession and Structural Adjustment on Women's Work in Selected Developing Countries'* (Sussex: Institute of Development Studies, Bridge Report No.15).

Baden, Sally with Milward, Kirsty (1995) *Gender and Poverty* (Sussex: Institute of Development Studies, Bridge Report No.30).

Baden, Sally and Goetz, Anne-Marie (1996) ' Discourses on Gender at Beijing: The Depoliticisation of Feminism'. Seminar, Development Studies Institute, London School of Economics, 16 February.

Baerga, Maria del Carmen (1992) 'Puerto Rico: From Colony to Colony', in Joan Smith and Immanuel Wallerstein (eds), *Creating and Transforming Households: The Constraints of the World Economy* (Cambridge: Cambridge University Press/Paris: Editions de la Maison des Sciences des Hommes) 121–42.

Banaynal-Fernandez, Tessie (1994) 'Fighting Violence Against Women: The Experience of the Lihok-Pilipina Foundation in Cebu', *Environment and Urbanisation*, 6:2, 31–56.

Bane, Mary Jo (1986) 'Household Composition and Poverty', in Sheldon Danziger and Daniel Weinberger (eds), *Fighting Poverty* (Cambridge, Massachusetts: Harvard University Press) 209–31.

de Barbieri, Teresita (1982) 'Familia y Trabajo Doméstico'. Paper presented at the seminar 'Domestic Groups, Family and Society', El Colegio de México, México DF, 7–9 July.

de Barbieri, Teresita and de Oliveira, Brígida (1989) 'Reproducción de la Fuerza de Trabajo en América Latina: Algunas Hipótesis', in Marta Schteingart (ed.), *Las Ciudades Latinamericanas en la Crisis* (México DF: Editorial Trillas) 19–29.

Barrett, Michèle (1986) *Women's Oppression Today: Problems in Marxist Feminist Analysis*, 5th impression (London: Verso).

Barry, Tom (1991) *Costa Rica: A Country Guide*, 3rd edn (Albuquerque: Inter-Hemispheric Education Resource Center).

Barry, Tom (1992) *Mexico: A Country Guide* (Albuquerque: Inter-Hemispheric Education Resource Center).

Barrow, Christine (1986) 'Finding the Support: A Study of Strategies for Survival', *Social and Economic Studies*, 35:2, 131–76.

Beall, Jo (1995) MSc Course Outline: 'Gender, Development and Social Planning' (SA412), Department of Social Policy and Administration, London School of Economics.

Beittel, Mark (1992) 'The Witwatersrand: Black Households, White Households', in Joan Smith and Immanuel Wallerstein (eds), *Creating and Transforming Households: The Constraints of the World Economy* (Cambridge: Cambridge University Press/Paris: Editions de la Maison des Sciences des Hommes) 197–230.

Bell, Peter F. (1995) 'Thailand's Economic Miracle: Built on the Backs of Women'. Paper presented at the 15th annual conference of the Association of Southeast Asian Studies in the United Kingdom, 'Gender and the Sexes in Southeast Asia', University of Durham, 29–31 March.

Benería, Lourdes (1991) 'Structural Adjustment, the Labour Market and the Household: The Case of Mexico', in Guy Standing and Victor Tokman (eds), *Towards Social Adjustment: Labour Market Issues in Structural Adjustment* (Geneva: International Labour Office) 161–83.

Benería, Lourdes (1992) 'The Mexican Debt Crisis: Restructuring the Economy and the Household', in Lourdes Benería and Shelley Feldman (eds), *Unequal Burden: Economic Crises, Persistent Poverty and Women's Work* (Boulder, Colorado: Westview Press) 83–104.

Benería, Lourdes and Roldan, Martha (1987) *The Crossroads of Class and Gender: Industrial Homework, Subcontracting and Household Dynamics in Mexico City* (Chicago: University of Chicago Press).

Bernard, Jessie (1972) *The Future of Marriage* (New York: Souvenir Press).

Berquó, Elza and Xenos, Peter (1992) 'Editors' Introduction', in Elza Berquó and Peter Xenos (eds), *Family Systems and Cultural Change* (Oxford: Clarendon Press) 8–12.

Blanc-Szanton, Cristina (1990a) 'Collision of Cultures: Historical Reformulations of Gender in the Lowland Visayas', in Jane Atkinson and Sherry Errinston (eds), *Power and Difference* (Stanford, California: Stanford University Press) 345–83.

Blanc-Szanton, Cristina (1990b) 'Gender and Inter-generational Resource Allocation among Thai and Sino-Thai Households', in Leela Dube and Rajni Palriwala (eds), *Structures and Strategies: Women, Work and Family* (New Delhi: Sage) 79–102.

Bledsoe, Caroline (1980) *Women and Marriage in Kpelle Society* (Stanford: Stanford University Press).

Blumberg, Rae Lesser (1978) 'The Political Economy of the Mother-Child Family Revisited', in André Marks and René Römer (eds), *Family and Kinship in Middle America and the Caribbean* (Leiden: University of the Netherlands Antilles and Department of Caribbean Studies, Royal Institute of Linguistics and Anthropology) 526–75.

Blumberg, Rae Lesser (1991) 'Income Under Female Versus Male Control: Hypotheses from a Theory of Gender Stratification and Data from the Third World', in Rae Lesser Blumberg (ed.), *Gender, Family and the Economy: The Triple Overlap* (Newbury Park: Sage) 97–127.

Blumberg, Rae Lesser (1995) 'Introduction: Engendering Wealth and Well-Being in an Era of Economic Transformation', in Rae Lesser Blumberg, Cathy Rakowski, Irene Tinker and Michael Monteón (eds), *Engendering Wealth and Well-Being: Empowerment for Global Change* (Boulder: Westview) 1–16.

Blumberg, Rae Lesser with García, María Pilar (1977) 'The Political Economy of the Mother–Child Family: A Cross-Societal View', in Luís Leñero-Otero (ed.), *Beyond the Nuclear Family Model* (London: Sage) 99–163.

Bolaños, Bernardo and Rodríguez, Hannia (1988) 'La Incorporación de la Mujer en el Proceso Productive de Flores en Costa Rica', *Revista de Ciencias Sociales*, 39, 57–68.

Bolles, A. Lynn (1986) 'Economic Crisis and Female-headed Households in Urban Jamaica', in June Nash and Helen Safa (eds), *Women and Change in Latin America* (Massachusetts: Bergin and Garvey) 65–83.

van den Bosch, Lourens (1995) 'The Ultimate Journey: Sati and Widowhood in India', in Jan Bremmer and Lourens van den Bosch (eds), *Between Poverty and the Pyre: Moments in the History of Widowhood* (London: Routledge) 171–203.

Boyden, Jo with Holden, Pat (1991) *Children of the Cities* (London: Zed).

Bradley, Christine (1994) 'Why Male Violence Against Women is a Development Issue: Reflections from Papua New Guinea', in Miranda Davies (ed.), *Women and Violence: Realities and Responses Worldwide* (London: Zed) 10–27.

Bradshaw, Jonathan and Millar, Jane (1991) *Lone-parent Families in the UK* (London: HMSO).

Bradshaw, Sarah (1995a) 'Women's Access to Employment and the Formation of Women-headed Households in Rural and Urban Honduras', *Bulletin of Latin American Research*, 14:2, 143–58.

Bradshaw, Sarah (1995b) 'Female-headed Households in Honduras: Perspectives on Rural–Urban Differences', *Third World Planning Review* (Special issue on 'Gender and Development'), 17:2, 117–31.

Bradshaw, Sarah (1996a) 'Female-headed Households in Honduras: A Study of their Formation and Survival in Low-income Communities'. Unpublished PhD thesis (Department of Geography, London School of Economics).

Bradshaw, Sarah (1996b) 'Inequality Within Households: The Case of Honduras'. Paper presented at the Symposium 'Vulnerable Groups in Latin American Cities', Annual Conference of the Society of Latin American Studies, University of Leeds, 29–31 March.

Bridges, Julian (1980) 'The Mexican Family', in Man Singh Das and Clinton Jesser (eds), *The Family in Latin America* (New Delhi: Vikas) 295–334.

Brink, Satya (1995) 'Steering Between Policies of Difference and Policies of Indifference: Assuring Gender Neutral Outcomes in the Residential Environment'. Paper presented at the XIII meeting of CIB Commission 69 'Housing Sociology: New Challenges and New Directions in Housing Sociology', Warsaw, 15–18 September.

Brodie, Janine (1994) 'Shifting the Boundaries: Gender and the Politics of Restructuring', in Isabella Bakker (ed.), *The Strategic Silence: Gender and Economic Policy* (London: Zed in association with The North-South Institute) 46–67.

Browne, Harry (1994) *For Richer For Poorer: Shaping US-Mexican Integration* (Albuquerque/London: Resource Center Press/Latin America Bureau).

Browner, C.H. (1989) 'Women, Household and Health in Latin America', *Social Science and Medicine*, 28:5, 461–73.

Brownlee, Helen (1989) 'Female Sole-parent Households', in Duncan Ironmonger (ed.), *Households Work* (Sydney: Allen and Unwin) 97–112.

Bruce, Judith and Dwyer, Daisy (1988) 'Introduction', in Daisy Dwyer and Judith Bruce (eds), *A Home Divided: Women and Income in the Third World* (Stanford: Stanford University Press) 1–19.

Bruce, Judith and Lloyd, Cynthia (1992) *Finding the Ties that Bind: Beyond Headship and the Household* (New York: Population Council/Washington DC: International Center for Research on Women).

Bruner, Edward (1982) 'Models of Urban Kinship', in Helen Safa (ed.), *Towards a Political Economy of Urbanisation* (New Delhi: Oxford University Press) 105–18.

Brydon, Lynne (1979) 'Women at Work: Some Changes in Family Structure in Amedzofe-Avatime, Ghana', *Africa*, 49:2, 97–111.

Brydon, Lynne (1987a) 'Women in the Family: Cultural Change in Avatime, Ghana', *Development and Change*, 18, 251–69.

Brydon, Lynne (1987b) 'Who Moves? Women and Migration in West Africa in the 1980s', in Jeremy Eades (ed.), *Migrant Workers and the Social Order* (London: Tavistock, Association of Social Anthropologists Monograph No.26) 165–80.

Brydon, Lynne and Chant, Sylvia (1989) *Women in the Third World: Gender Issues in Rural and Urban Areas* (Aldershot: Edward Elgar).

Brydon, Lynne and Legge, Karen (1996) *Adjusting Society: The IMF, the World Bank and Ghana* (London: I.B. Tauris).

Bucoy, Rhodora (1992) 'Some Notes on the Status of Women in Cebu', *Review of Women's Studies* (University of the Philippines, Quezon City) 3:1, 33–50.

Buitelaar, Marjo (1995) 'Widows' Worlds: Representations and Realities', in Jan Bremmer and Lourens van den Bosch (eds), *Between Poverty and the Pyre: Moments in the History of Widowhood* (London: Routledge) 1–18.

Bullock, Susan (1994) *Women and Work* (London: Zed).

Burghes, Louie (1994) *Lone Parenthood and Family Disruption: The Outcomes for Children* (London: Family Policy Studies Centre, Occasional Paper 18).

Burns, Elaine (1992) 'Women and Feminism', in Tom Barry, *Mexico: A Country Guide* (Albuquerque: Inter-Hemispheric Education Resource Center) 213–21.

Butterworth, Douglas (1975) *Tilantongo: Comunidad Mixteca en Transición* (México DF: Instituto Nacional Indigenista y Secretaría de Educación Pública).

Buvinic, Marya (1990) 'The Vulnerability of Women-headed Households: Policy Questions and Options for Latin America and the Caribbean'. Paper presented at the Economic Commission for Latin America and the Caribbean Meeting on 'Vulnerable Women', Vienna, 26–30 November.

Buvinic, Mayra (1993) 'The Feminisation of Poverty? Research and Policy Needs'. Paper presented at the Symposium: 'Poverty: New Approaches to Analysis and Poverty', International Institute for Labour Studies, Geneva, 22–24 November.

Buvinic, Mayra and Gupta, Geeta Rao (1993) 'Responding to Insecurity in the 1990s: Targeting Woman-headed Households and Woman-maintained Families in Developing Countries'. Paper presented at the International Workshop 'Insecurity in the 1990s: Gender and Social Policy in an International Perspective', London School of Economics and European Association of Development Institutes, London, 5–6 April.

Buvinic, Mayra; Valenzuela, Juan Pablo; Molina, Temistocles and González, Electra (1992) 'The Fortunes of Adolescent Mothers and Their Children: The Transmission of Poverty in Santiago, Chile', *Population and Development Review*, 18:2, 169–97.

Buvinic, Mayra and Youssef, Nadia, with Von Elm, Barbara (1978) 'Women-headed Households: The Ignored Factor in Development Planning'. Report submitted to the Office of Women in Development, USAID (Washington DC: ICRW).

Cain, Mead; Khanam, Syeda Rokeya and Nahar, Shamsun (1979) 'Class, Patriarchy and Women's Work in Bangladesh', *Population and Development Review*, 5:3, 405–38.

Caldwell, John C. (1976) 'Towards a Restatement of Demographic Transition Theory', *Population and Development Review*, 2:3/4, 321–65.

Caldwell, John C. (1977) *Population Growth and Family Change in Africa* (London: C. Hurst and Company).

Caldwell, John C. and Caldwell, Pat (1992) 'Family Systems: Their Viability and Vulnerability', in Elza Berquó and Peter Xenos (eds), *Family Systems and Cultural Change* (Oxford: Clarendon Press) 46–66.

Cammack, Paul; Pool, David and Tordoff, William (1993) *Third World Politics: A Comparative Introduction*, 2nd edn (Basingstoke: Macmillan).

Caplan, Patricia (1985) *Class and Gender in India: Women and their Organisations in a South Indian City* (London: Tavistock).

Carter, William and True, William (1978) 'Family and Kinship among the San José Working Class', in André Marks and René Römer (eds), *Family and Kinship in Middle America and the Caribbean* (Leiden: University of the Netherlands Antilles and Department of Caribbean Studies, Royal Institute of Linguistics and Anthropology) 227–50.

Cartín Leiva, Nancy (1994) 'Patriarcado, Prácticas Cotidianas de la Mujer Campesina y Construcción de su Identidad', *Revista de Ciencias Sociales*, 63, 141–59.

Carvajal, Manuel and Geithman, David (1985) 'Income, Human Capital and Sex Discrimination: Some Evidence from Costa Rica, 1963 and 1973', *Journal of Economic Development*, 10:1, 89–115.

Cashmore, E.E. (1985) *The World of One Parent Families: Having To* (London: Unwin Paperbacks).

Casinader, Rex; Fernando, Sepalika and Gamage, Karuna (1987) 'Women's Issues and Men's Roles: Sri Lankan Village Experience', in Janet Momsen and Janet Townsend (eds), *Geography of Gender in the Third World* (London: Hutchinson) 309–22.

Castillo, Gelia (1991) 'Family and Household: The Microworld of the Filipino', in Department of Sociology-Anthropology (ed.), *SA 21: Selected Readings* (Quezon City: Ateneo de Manila University, Office of Research and Publications) 244–50.

Centro Feminista de Información y Acción (CEFEMINA) (1986) *Mujer 4: Sexualidad* (San José: CEFEMINA).

Centro Feminista de Información y Acción (CEFEMINA) (1994) *Mujeres Hacía el 2000: Deteniendo la Violencia* (San José: CEFEMINA).

Centro Feminista de Información y Acción (CEFEMINA) (1995) *CEFEMINA: Su Historia, Su Gente, Sus Sueños* (San José: CEFEMINA).

Centro Nacional para el Desarrollo de la Mujer y la Familia (CMF) (1994) *Informe Nacional Sobre la Situación de las Mujeres en Costa Rica,1985–1994* (San José: CMF).

Chalita Ortiz, Patricia (1992) 'Sobrevivencia en la Ciudad: Una Conceptualización de las Unidades Domésticas Encabezadas por Mujeres en América Latina', in Alejandra Massolo (ed.), *Mujeres y Ciudades: Participación Social, Vivienda y Vida Cotidiana* (México DF: El Colegio de México) 271–97.

Chambers, Robert (1995) 'Poverty and Livelihoods: Whose Reality Counts?', *Environment and Urbanisation*, 7:1, 173–204.

Chandler, Joan (1991) *Women Without Husbands: An Exploration of the Margins of Marriage* (Basingstoke: Macmillan).

Chant, Sylvia (1984a) '"*Las Olvidadas*": A Study of Women, Housing and Family Structure in Querétaro, Mexico'. Unpublished PhD dissertation, Department of Geography, University College London.

Chant, Sylvia (1984b) 'Household Labour and Self-Help Housing in Querétaro, Mexico', *Boletín de Estudios Latinoamericanos y del Caribe*, 37, 45–68.

Chant, Sylvia (1985a) 'Family Formation and Female Roles in Querétaro, Mexico', *Bulletin of Latin American Research*, 4:1, 17–32.

Chant, Sylvia (1985b) 'Single-parent Families: Choice or Constraint? The Formation of Female-headed Households in Mexican Shanty Towns', *Development and Change*, 16:4, 635–56.

Chant, Sylvia (1987) 'Domestic Labour, Decision-Making and Dwelling Construction: The Experience of Women in Querétaro, Mexico', in Caroline Moser and Linda Peake (eds), *Women, Human Settlements and Housing* (London: Tavistock) 33–54.

Chant, Sylvia (1991a) *Women and Survival in Mexican Cities: Perspectives on Gender, Labour Markets and Low-income Households* (Manchester: Manchester University Press).

Chant, Sylvia (1991b) 'Gender, Households and Seasonal Migration in Guanacaste, Costa Rica', *European Review of Latin American and Caribbean Studies*, 50, 51–85.

Chant, Sylvia (1991c) 'Gender, Migration and Urban Development in Costa Rica: The Case of Guanacaste', *Geoforum*, 22:3, 237–53.

Chant, Sylvia (1992) 'Migration at the Margins: Gender, Poverty and Population Movement on the Costa Rican Periphery', in Sylvia Chant (ed.), *Gender and Migration in Developing Countries* (London: Belhaven) 49–72.

Chant, Sylvia (1993) 'Women's Work and Household Change in the 1980s', in Neil Harvey (ed.), *Mexico: Dilemmas of Transition* (London: Institute of Latin American Studies/British Academic Press) 318–54.

Chant, Sylvia (1994a) 'Women and Poverty in Urban Latin America: Mexican and Costa Rican Experiences', in Fatima Meer (ed.), *Poverty in the 1990s: The Responses of Urban Women* (Paris: UNESCO/International Social Science Council), 87–115.

Chant, Sylvia (1994b) 'Women, Work and Household Survival Strategies in Mexico, 1982–1992', *Bulletin of Latin American Research*, 13:2, 203–33.

Chant, Sylvia (1994c) 'Female-Headed Households and Development: A Research Agenda for the 1990s'. Paper given at the panel 'Population, Health and Social Policy', Conference 'Gender Research and Development: Looking Forward to Beijing', University of East Anglia, Norwich, 9–10 September,

Chant, Sylvia (1995a) 'Women-headed Households in the Philippines: Social and Economic Dimensions'. Paper presented at the 15th annual conference of the Association of Southeast Asian Studies in the United Kingdom, 'Gender and the Sexes in Southeast Asia', University of Durham, 29–31 March.

Chant, Sylvia (1995b) 'Editorial Introduction: Gender and Development in the 1990s', *Third World Planning Review* (Special issue on 'Gender and Development'), 17:2, 111–16.

Chant, Sylvia (1996a) *Gender, Urban Development and Housing* (New York: United Nations Development Programme, Publication Series for Habitat II, Vol. 2).

Chant, Sylvia (1996b) 'Gender and Tourism Employment in Mexico and the Philippines', in M. Thea Sinclair (ed.), *Gender, Work and Tourism* (London:Routledge) 120–79.

Chant, Sylvia and McIlwaine, Cathy (1995a) *Women of a Lesser Cost: Female Labour, Foreign Exchange and Philippine Development* (London: Pluto Press).

Chant, Sylvia and McIlwaine, Cathy (1995b) 'Gender and Export Manufacturing in the Philippines: Continuity or Change in Female Employment? The Case of the Mactan Export Processing Zone', *Gender, Place and Culture*, 2:2, 149–78.

Chant, Sylvia and Radcliffe, Sarah (1992) 'Migration and Development: The Importance of Gender', in Sylvia Chant (ed.), *Gender and Migration in Developing Countries* (London: Belhaven) 1–29.

Chant, Sylvia and Ward, Peter (1987) 'Family Structure and Low-income Housing Policy', *Third World Planning Review*, 9:4, 5–19.

Chaverría, Carmen; Elizondo, María Elena; García, Carmen and Martínez, María del Refugio (1987) 'Algunas Consideraciones Sobre Familias Guanacastecas Organizadas: Análisis de Tres Grupos Femeninos Productivos'. Unpublished thesis for Licenciado en Trabajo Social (Liberia: Universidad de Costa Rica, Centro Universitario de Guanacaste).

Chen, Marty and Drèze, Jean (1992) 'Widows and Health in Rural North India'. Paper presented at Workshop on 'Health and Development in India, National Council of Applied Economic Research and the Harvard Center for Population and Development Studies, India International Centre, New Delhi, 2–4 January.

Chen, Marty and Drèze, Jean (1995) 'Recent Research on Widows in India: Workshop and Conference Report', *Economic and Political Weekly* (Bombay), 30 September, 2435–50.

Chester, Robert (1977) 'The One-Parent Family: Deviant or Variant?' in Robert Chester and John Peel (eds), *Equalities and Inequalities in Family Life* (London: Academic Press) 149–61.

Chinchilla, Luisa (1992) 'Cambios en la Agricultura Costarricense en los Ultimos Años', in Juan Manuel Villasuso (ed.), *El Nuevo Rostro de Costa Rica* (Heredia: Centro de Estudios Democráticos de América Latina) 457–70.

Church, Timothy (1986) *Filipino Personality: A Review of Research and Writing* (Manila: De la Salle University Press, Monograph Series No.6).

Cicirelli, Victor (1994) 'Sibling Relationships in Cross-Cultural Perspective', *Journal of Marriage and the Family*, 56, 7–20.

Clarke, Edith (1957) *My Mother who Fathered Me: A Study of Family in Three Selected Communities in Jamaica* (London: George Allen and Unwin).

Clarke, Noel (1981) 'A Study on Perceived Mobility: Life Experiences of Selected Families in a Cebu Squatter Community'. Thesis presented to the Faculty of the Graduate School, University of San Carlos, Cebu City.

Cleves Mosse, Julia (1993) *Half the World, Half a Chance* (Oxford: Oxfam).

Colimoro, Claudia (1994) 'A Prostitute's Election Campaign', in Gaby Küppers (ed.), *Compañeras: Voices from the Latin American Women's Movement* (London: Latin America Bureau) 92–6.

Collier, Richard (1995) *Masculinity, Law and the Family* (London: Routledge).

Collins, Patricia Hill (1994) 'Shifting the Center: Race, Class and Feminist Theorising About Motherhood', in Evelyn Nakano Glenn, Grace Chang and Linda Rennie Forcey (eds), *Mothering: Ideology, Experience and Agency* (New York: Routledge) 45–65.

Collins, Stephen (1991) 'The Transition from Lone-Parent Family to Step-family', in Michael Hardey and Graham Crow (eds), *Lone Parenthood: Coping with Constraints and Making Opportunities* (Hemel Hempstead: Harvester Wheatsheaf) 156–75.

Comisión Coordinadora de Desarrollo de la Desembocadura del Río Ameca (COCODERA) (1980) *Programa de Ordenación de la Zona Conurbada del Río Ameca* (Puerto Vallarta: COCODERA).

Comisión Económica para América Latina y el Caribe (CEPAL) (1994) 'El Sector Informal Urbano desde la Perspectiva de Género: El Caso de México'. Paper presented at workshop on 'El Sector Informal Urbano desde la Perspectiva de Género: El Caso de México', México DF, 28–29 November.

Connell, John (1984) 'Status or Subjugation? Women, Migration and Development in the South Pacific', *International Migration Review*, xviii:4, 964–83.

Coote, Anna (1992) 'Families in the Future: New Policy Directions'. Seminar, Gender Institute, London School of Economics, 29 October.

Cordera Campos, Rolando and González Tiburcio, Enrique (1991) 'Crisis and Transition in the Mexican Economy', in Mercedes González de la Rocha and Agustín Escobar Latapí (eds), *Social Responses to Mexico's Economic Crisis of the 1980s* (San Diego: Center for US-Mexican Studies, UCLA, Contemporary Perspectives Series 1) 19–56.

Cornia, Giovanni Andrea; Jolly, Richard and Stewart, Frances (eds) (1988) *Adjustment with a Human Face: Vol. II: Country Case Studies* (Oxford: Clarendon).

Craske, Nikki (1993) 'Women's Political Participation in Colonias Populares in Guadalajara, Mexico', in Sarah Radcliffe and Sallie Westwood (eds), *'Viva': Women and Popular Protest in Latin America* (London: Routledge) 112–35.

Craske, Nikki (forthcoming) 'Mexican Women's Inclusion into Political Life: A Latin American Perspective', in Victoria Rodríguez (ed.), *Women in Contemporary Mexican Politics* (Phoenix: University of Arizona Press).

Croll, Elisabeth (1983) *Chinese Women Since Mao* (London: Zed).

Croll, Elisabeth (1994) *From Heaven to Earth: Images and Experiences of Development in China* (London: Routledge).

Cruz, Wilfrido and Repetto, Robert (1992) *The Environmental Impacts of Stabilisation and Structural Adjustment Programmes: The Philippine Case* (Washington DC: World Resources Institute).

Cutrufelli, Maria Rosa (1983) *Women of Africa: Roots of Oppression* (London: Zed).

Dabir, Neela (1993) 'Shelter Homes: A Need to Develop a New Approach for Women in Familial Distress', in Hemalata Dandekar (ed.), *Women, Shelter and Development: First and Third World Perspectives* (Ann Arbor, Michigan: George Wahr Publishing Co.) 23–32.

Dallos, Rudi (1995) 'Constructing Family Life: Family Belief Systems', in John Muncie, Margaret Wetherell, Rudi Dallos and Allan Cochrane (eds), *Understanding the Family* (London: Sage) 173–211.

Dallos, Rudi and Sapsford, Roger (1995) 'Patterns of Diversity and Lived Reality', in John Muncie, Margaret Wetherell, Rudi Dallos and Allan Cochrane (eds), *Understanding the Family* (London: Sage) 125–70.

Dandvate, Pramila (1989) 'Social Legislation and Women', in Pramila Dandvate, Ranjana Kumari and Jamila Verghese (eds), *Widows, Abandoned and Destitute Women in India* (London: Sangam Books) 84–9.

Davies, Miranda (ed.) (1994) *Women and Violence: Realities and Responses Worldwide* (London: Zed).

Davis, Carol (1995) 'Hierarchy or Complementarity? Gendered Expressions of Minangkabau Adat'. Paper presented at the 15th annual conference of the Association of Southeast Asian Studies in the United Kingdom, 'Gender and the Sexes in Southeast Asia', University of Durham, 29–31 March.

Deere, Carmen Diana (1990) *Household and Class Relations: Peasants and Landlords in Northern Peru* (Berkeley: University of California Press).

Dennis, Norman (1993) *Rising Crime and the Dismembered Family: How Conformist Intellectuals Have Campaigned Against Common Sense* (London: Institute of Economic Affairs, IEA Health and Welfare Unit).

Dennis, Norman and Erdos, George (1992) *Families Without Fatherhood* (London: Institute of Economic Affairs, Health and Welfare Unit).

Desai, Murli and Apte, Meenakshi (1987) 'Status of Prostitutes and Deprivation of Family Care Among their Children', *The Indian Journal of Social Work*, XLVIII:2, 171–80.

Desarrollo Integral de la Familia (DIF) (1994) *3er Informe de Actividades* (DIF: Querétaro).

Dey, Jennie (1981) 'Gambian Women: Unequal Partners in Rice Development Projects', in Nici Nelson (ed.), *African Women in the Development Process* (London: Frank Cass) 109–22.

Dhillon-Kashyap, Perminder (1994) 'Black Women and Housing', in Rose Gilroy and Roberta Woods (eds), *Housing Women* (London: Routledge) 101–26.

Diagne, Sény (1993) 'Defending Women's Rights – Facts and Challenges in Francophone Africa', in Joanna Kerr (ed.) *Ours By Right: Women's Rights as Human Rights* (London: Zed in association with The North South Institute) 43–51.

Dierckxsens, Wim (1992) 'Impacto del Ajuste Estructural Sobre la Mujer Trabajadora en Costa Rica', in Marvin Acuña Ortega (ed.), *Cuadernos de Política Económica* (Heredia: Universidad Nacional de Costa Rica) 2–59.

Dirección General de Estadística y Censos (DGEC) (1974) *Censo de Población 1973, Tomo 1* (San José: DGEC).

Dirección General de Estadística y Censos (DGEC) (1987) *Censo de Población 1984, Tomo 1* (San José: DGEC).

Dirección General de Estadística y Censos (DGEC) (1990) *Encuesta de Hogares por Zona 1990* (San José: DGEC).

Dirección General de Estadística y Censos (DGEC) (1993a) *Encuesta de Hogares por Región 1993* (San José: DGEC).

Dirección General de Estadística y Censos (DGEC) (1993b) *Encuesta de Hogares por Zona 1993* (San José: DGEC).

Domingo, Lita and King, Elizabeth (1992) 'The Role of the Family in the Process of Entry to Marriage in Asia', in Elza Berquó and Peter Xenos (eds), *Family Systems and Cultural Change* (Oxford: Clarendon Press) 87–108.

Dore, Elizabeth (1995) 'Public Patriarchy in Rural Nicaragua, 1830–1875'. Paper given at 'Gender Issues' Symposium, Annual Conference of the Society of Latin American Studies, University of Swansea, 24–26 March.

Douglas, Anne and Gilroy, Rose (1994) 'Young Women and Homelessness', in Rose Gilroy and Roberta Woods (eds), *Housing Women* (London: Routledge) 127–51.

Dresser, Denise (1991) *Neopopulist Solutions to Neoliberal Problems: Mexico's National Solidarity Program* (San Diego: UCLA, Center for US-Mexican Studies, Current Issues Brief No.3).

Drèze, Jean (1990) *Widows in Rural India* (London: Suntory Toyota International Centre for Economics and Related Disciplines, LSE, Development Economics Research Programme No.26).

Dube, Leela (1992) 'Preface', in K. Saradamoni (ed.), *Finding the Household: Methodological and Empirical Issues* (New Delhi: Sage) 9–14.

Dumont, Jean-Paul (1994) 'Matrons, Maids and Mistresses: Philippine Domestic Encounters', *Philippine Quarterly of Culture and Society*, 22, 174–91.

Duncan, Simon (1991a) 'Gender Divisions of Labour', in Keith Hoggart and David Green (eds), *London: A New Metropolitan Geography* (London: Edward Arnold) 95–122.

Duncan, Simon (1991b) 'The Geography of Gender Divisions of Labour in Britain', *Transactions of the Institute of British Geographers NS*, 16, 420–39.

Duncan, Simon (1994) 'Theorising Differences in Patriarchy', *Environment and Planning A*, 26, 1177–94.

Duncan, Simon (1995) 'Theorising European Gender Systems', *Journal of European Social Policy*, 5:4, 263–84.

Duncan, Simon and Edwards, Rosalind (1994) 'Lone Mothers and Paid Work: State Policies, Social Discourses and Neighbourhood Processes'. Mimeo, Gender Institute, London School of Economics.

Duncan, Simon and Edwards, Rosalind (1996) 'Lone Mothers and Paid Work:Neighbourhoods, Local Labour Markets and Welfare State Regimes', *Social Politics: International Studies in Gender, State and Society*, 3:4.

Dunn, Leith (1994) 'A Sociological Analysis of Methods of Organising Used by Women in Caribbean Free Trade Zones: Implications for Development'. Unpublished PhD thesis (Department of Sociology, London School of Economics).

Dwyer, Daisy and Bruce, Judith (eds) (1988), *A Home Divided: Women and Income in the Third World* (Stanford: Stanford University Press).

Economist Intelligence Unit (EIU) (1994a) *Costa Rica, Panama: Country Report 3rd Quarter 1994* (London: EIU).

Economist Intelligence Unit (EIU) (1994b) *Mexico: Country Report 1st Quarter 1994* (London: EIU).

Economist Intelligence Unit (EIU) (1994c) *Mexico: Country Report 3rd Quarter 1994* (London: EIU).

Economist Intelligence Unit (EIU) (1995a) *Mexico: Country Report 2nd Quarter 1995* (London: EIU).

Economist Intelligence Unit (EIU) (1995b) *Costa Rica, Panama: Country Report 2nd Quarter 1995* (London: EIU).

Economist Intelligence Unit (EIU) (1995c) *Philippines: Country Report 3rd Quarter 1995* (London: EIU).

Editorial Porrua (1992) *Código Civil para el Distrito Federal*, 60a edición (México DF: Editorial Porrua).

Edley, Nigel and Wetherell, Margaret (1995) *Men in Perspective: Practice, Power and Identity* (London: Prentice Hall/Harvester Wheatsheaf).

Edwards, John; Fuller, Theodore; Vorakitphokatorn, Sairudee and Sermsri, Santhat (1992) 'Female Employment and Marital Instability: Evidence from Thailand', *Journal of Marriage and the Family*, 54:1, 59–68.

Edwards, Rosalind and Duncan, Simon (1996a) 'Lone Mothers and Economic Activity', in Fiona Williams (ed.), *Social Policy: A Reader* (Cambridge: Polity Press).

Edwards, Rosalind and Duncan, Simon (1996b) 'Rational Economic Man or Lone Mothers in Context? The Uptake of Paid Work', in Elizabeth Bortolaia-Silva (ed.), *Good Enough Mothering? Feminist Perspectives on Lone Motherhood* (London: Routledge).

Ellis, Pat (1986) 'Introduction – An Overview of Women in Caribbean Society', in Pat Ellis (ed.), *Women of the Caribbean* (London: Zed) 1–24.

Elmendorf, Mary (1977) 'Mexico: The Many Worlds of Women', in Janet Zollinger Giele and Audrey Chapman Smock (eds), *Women: Roles and Status in Eight Countries* (New York: John Wiley) 127–72.

Elson, Diane (1989) 'The Impact of Structural Adjustment on Women: Concepts and Issues', in Bade Onimode (ed.), *The IMF, the World Bank and the African Debt Vol.2: The Social and Political Impact* (Zed: London).

Elson, Diane (1992) 'From Survival Strategies to Transformation Strategies: Women's Needs and Structural Adjustment', in Lourdes Benería and Shelley Feldman (eds), *Unequal Burden: Economic Crises, Persistent Poverty and Women's Work* (Boulder: Westview) 26–48.

Elson, Diane and Pearson, Ruth (1981) '"Nimble Fingers Make Cheap Workers": An Analysis of Women's Employment in Third World Export Manufacturing', *Feminist Review*, 7, 87–107.

Engle, Patrice (1995) 'Father's Money, Mother's Money, and Parental Commitment: Guatemala and Nicaragua', in Rae Lesser Blumberg, Cathy Rakowski, Irene Tinker and Michael Monteón (eds), *Engendering Wealth and Well-Being: Empowerment for Global Change* (Boulder: Westview) 155–79.

Ennew, Judith (1982) 'Family Structure, Unemployment and Child Labour in Jamaica', *Development and Change*, 13, 551–63.

Ennew, Judith and Young, Patsy (1981) *Child Employment in Jamaica* (London: Anti-Slavery Society, Child Labour Series No.6).

Enriquez, Virgilio (1991) 'Kapwa: A Core Concept in Filipino Social Psychology', in Department of Sociology-Anthropology (ed.), *SA 21: Selected Readings* (Quezon City: Ateneo de Manila University, Office of Research and Publications) 98–105.

Escalante Herrera, Ana (1990) *El Subdesarrollo, la Paz y la Mujer en Costa Rica* (San José: Instituto de Investigaciones Sociales, Universidad de Costa Rica, Contribuciones).

Escobar Latapí, Agustín and González de la Rocha, Mercedes (1995) 'Crisis, Restructuring and Urban Poverty in Mexico', *Environment and Urbanisation*, 7:1, 50–75.

Espinosa Damián, Gisela (1987) 'Feminism and Social Struggle in Mexico', in Miranda Davies (ed.), *Third World, Second Sex 2* (London: Zed) 31–41.

Eswara Prasad, K.V. (1995) 'Social Security for Destitute Widows in Tamil Nadu', *Economic and Political Weekly* (Bombay), April 15, 794–6.

Etienne, Mona (1983) 'Gender Relations and Conjugality among the Baule', in Christine Oppong (ed.), *Female and Male in West Africa* (London: George Allen and Unwin) 32–53.

Etienne, Mona (1993) 'The Case for Social Maternity: Adoption of Children by Urban Baule Women', in Caroline Brettell and Carolyn Sargent (eds.) *Gender in Cross-Cultural Perspective* (Englewood Cliffs, New Jersey: Prentice Hall) 25–37.

Etienne, Mona and Leacock, Eleanor (eds) (1980) *Women and Colonization* (New York: Praeger).

Evans, Alison (1992) 'Statistics', in Lise Østergaard (ed.) *Gender and Development: A Practical Guide* (London: Routledge) 11–40.

Eviota, Elizabeth (1986) 'The Articulation of Gender and Class in the Philippines', in Eleanor Leacock and Helen Safa (eds), *Women's Work* (Massachusetts: Bergin and Garvey) 194–206.

Eviota, Elizabeth (1992) *The Political Economy of Gender: Women and the Sexual Division of Labour in the Philippines* (London: Zed).

Facio, Alda (1989a) 'La Igualdad Entre Hombres y Mujeres y las Relaciones Familiares en la Legislación Centroamericana', *Estudios Sociales Centroamericanos*, 50, 55–75.

Facio, Alda (1989b) 'Costa Rica', in Ana Isabel García and Enrique Gomáriz (eds), *Mujeres Centroamericanas Ante la Crisis, la Guerra y el Proceso de Paz Vol.1* (San José: FLACSO) 41–103.

Falú, Ana and Curutchet, Mirina (1991) 'Rehousing the Urban Poor: Looking at Women First', *Environment and Urbanisation*, 3:2, 23–38.

Fassinger, Polly (1993) 'Meanings of Housework for Single Fathers and Mothers: Insights into Gender Inequality', in Jane Hood (ed.), *Men, Work and Family* (Newbury Park: Sage) 195–216.

Feldman, Shelley (1992) 'Crises, Poverty and Gender Inequalities: Current Themes and Issues', in Lourdes Benería and Shelley Feldman (eds), *Unequal Burden: Economic Crises, Persistent Poverty and Women's Work* (Boulder, Colorado: Westview Press) 1–25.

Fernández, Oscar (1992) '¿Qué Valores Valen Hoy en Costa Rica?', in Juan Manuel Villasuso (ed.), *El Nuevo Rostro de Costa Rica* (Heredia: Centro de Estudios Democráticos de América Latina).

Fernández-Kelly, María Patricia (1983) 'Mexican Border Industrialisation, Female Labour Force Participation and Migration', in June Nash and María Patricia Fernández-Kelly (eds), *Women, Men and the International Division of Labour* (Albany: State University of New York Press) 205–23.

Flandrin, Jean-Louis (1979) *Families in Former Times: Kinship, Household and Sexuality* (Cambridge: Cambridge University Press).

Folbre, Nancy (1988) 'The Black Four of Hearts', in Daisy Dwyer and Judith Bruce (eds), *A Home Divided: Women and Income in the Third World* (Stanford: Stanford University Press) 248–62.

Folbre, Nancy (1991) 'Women on their Own: Global Patterns of Female Headship', in Rita S. Gallin and Ann Ferguson (eds), *The Women and International Development Annual, Vol. 2* (Boulder: Westview) 69–126.

Folbre, Nancy (1994a) *Who Pays for the Kids? Gender and the Structures of Constraint* (New York: Routledge).

Folbre, Nancy (1994b) 'Children as Public Goods', *American Economic Review*, 84:2, 86–90.

Folbre, Nancy and Abel, Marjorie (1989) 'Women's Work and Women's Households: Gender Bias in the US Census', *Social Research*, 56:3, 545–69.

Fonseca, Claudia (1991) 'Spouses, Siblings and Sex-linked Bonding: A Look at Kinship Organisation in a Brazilian Slum', in Elizabeth Jelin (ed.), *Family, Household and Gender Relations in Latin America* (London: Kegan Paul International /Paris: UNESCO) 133–60.

Fraser, Nancy and Nicholson, Linda (eds) (1990) *Feminism/Postmodernism* (London: Routledge).

Freeman, Marsha (1993) 'Women, Development and Justice: Using the International Convention on Women's Rights', in Joanna Kerr (ed.) *Ours By Right: Women's Rights as Human Rights* (London: Zed in association with The North South Institute) 93–105.

Froebel, Folker; Heinrichs, Jurgen and Kreye, Otto (1980) *The New International Division of Labour* (Cambridge: Cambridge University Press).

García, Brígida (1992) 'La Femenización en la Actividad Económica', *Demos*, 2, 23–4.

García, Brígida; Muñoz, Humberto and de Oliveira, Orlandina (1982) *Hogares y Trabajadores en la Ciudad de México* (México DF: El Colegio de México/UNAM).

García, Brígida; Muñoz, Humberto and de Oliveira, Orlandina (1983a) *Familia y Mercado de Trabajo: Un Estudio de Dos Ciudades Brasileñas* (México DF: El Colegio de México/UNAM).

García, Brígida; Muñoz, Humberto and de Oliveira, Orlandina (1983b) 'Familia y Trabajo en México y Brasil', *Estudios Sociológicos*, 1:3, 487–507.

García, Brígida and de Oliveira, Orlandina (1994) *Trabajo Femenino y Vida Familiar en México* (México DF: El Colegio de México).

Gardner, Katy (1995) *Global Migrants, Local Lives: Travel and Transformation in Rural Bangladesh* (Oxford: Clarendon Press).

Gelles, Richard (1995) *Contemporary Families: A Sociological View* (Thousand Oaks, California: Sage).

Gerber, Stanford and Rasmussen, Knud (1978) 'Further Reflections on the Concept of Matrifocality and its Consequences for Social Science Research', in André Marks and René Römer (eds), *Family and Kinship in Middle America and the Caribbean* (Leiden: University of the Netherlands Antilles and Department of Caribbean Studies, Royal Institute of Linguistics and Anthropology) 576–87.

Gilbert, Alan (1994) 'Third World Cities: Poverty, Unemployment, Gender Roles and the Environment during a Time of Restructuring', *Urban Studies*, 31:4/5, 605–33.

Gilbert, Alan and Gugler, Josef (1992) *Cities, Poverty and Development: Urbanisation in the Third World*, 2nd edn (Oxford: Oxford University Press).

Gindling, T.H. (1993) 'Women's Wages and Economic Crisis in Costa Rica', *Economic Development and Cultural Change*, 41;2, 277–97.

Gledhill, John (1995) *Neoliberalism, Transnationalisation and Rural Poverty: A Case Study of Michoacán, Mexico* (Boulder: Westview).

Glenn, Evelyn Nakano (1994) 'Social Constructions of Mothering: A Thematic Overview', in Evelyn Nakano Glenn, Grace Chang and Linda Rennie Forcey (eds), *Mothering: Ideology, Experience and Agency* (New York: Routledge) 1–29.

Goetz, Anne Marie (1995) 'Institutionalising Women's Concerns and Accountability to Women in Development', *IDS Bulletin* (Sussex) 26:3, 1–10.

Goldenberg, Olga (1994) 'En Clave de Género', in Olga Goldenberg and Victor Hugo Acuña, *Género y la Informalidad* (San José:FLACSO) 185–233.

González de la Rocha, Mercedes (1986) *Los Recursos de la Pobreza* (Guadalajara: El Colegio de Jalisco).

González de la Rocha, Mercedes (1988a) 'Economic Crisis, Domestic Reorganisation and Women's Work in Guadalajara, Mexico', *Bulletin of Latin American Research*, 7:2, 207–23.

González de la Rocha, Mercedes (1988b) 'De Por Qué las Mujeres Aguantan Golpes y Cuernos: Un Análisis de Hogares Sin Varón en Guadalajara', in Luisa Gabayet, Patricia García, Mercedes González de la Rocha, Silvia Lailson and Agustín Escobar (eds), *Mujeres y Sociedad: Salario, Hogar y Acción Social en el Occidente de México* (Guadalajara: El Colegio de Jalisco/CIESAS del Occidente) 205–27.

González de la Rocha, Mercedes (1991) 'Family Well-being, Food Consumption and Survival Strategies during Mexico's Economic Crisis', in Mercedes González de la Rocha and Agustín Escobar (eds), *Social Responses to Mexico's Economic Crisis of the 1980s* (San Diego: Center for US-Mexican Studies, UCLA) 115–27.

González de la Rocha, Mercedes (1993) 'Household Headship and Occupational Position: Notes Towards a Better Understanding of Gender and Class Differences in a Mexican Urban Context'. Paper prepared for the Conference 'Engendering Wealth and Well-being', Center for Iberian and Latin American Studies, University of California, San Diego, 17–20 February.

González de la Rocha, Mercedes (1994a) *The Resources of Poverty: Women and Survival in a Mexican City* (Oxford: Blackwell).

González de la Rocha, Mercedes (1994b) 'Household Headship and Occupational Position in Mexico', in Eileen Kennedy and Mercedes González de la Rocha, *Poverty and Well-being in the Household: Case Studies of the Developing World* (San Diego: Center for Iberian and Latin American Studies, University of California, Working Paper No.5) 1–24.

González de la Rocha, Mercedes (1995a) 'Social Restructuring in Two Mexican Cities: An Analysis of Domestic Groups in Guadalajara and Monterrey', *European Journal of Development Research*, 7:2, 389–406.

González de la Rocha, Mercedes (1995b) 'El Nuevo Perfil de los Grupos Domésticos Urbanos en la Era del Trabajo Precario en México'. Paper presented at the session 'Globalisation and the New Latin American Household', XIX International Congress of the Latin American Studies Association, Washington DC, 28–30 September.

Goode, William (1963) *World Revolution and Family Patterns* (New York: Free Press of Glencoe).

Goode, William (1964) *The Family* (Englewood Cliffs, New Jersey: Prentice Hall).

Goodno, James (1991) *The Philippines: Land of Broken Promises* (London: Zed).

Goody, Esther (1975) 'Delegation of Parental Roles in West Africa and the West Indies', in Jack Goody (ed.), *Changing Social Structures in Ghana* (London: International African Institute) 137–66.

Gordon, Elizabeth (1981) 'An Analysis of the Impact of Labour Migration on the Lives of Women in Lesotho', in Nici Nelson (ed.), *African Women in the Development Process* (London: Frank Cass) 60–76.

Gordon, Lorna (1986) 'Women in Caribbean Agriculture', in Pat Ellis (ed.), *Women of the Caribbean* (London: Zed) 35–40.

Gordon, Tuula (1994) *Single Women* (Basingstoke: Macmillan).

Graham, Hilary (1987) 'Being Poor: Perceptions and Coping Strategies of Lone Mothers', in Julia Brannen and Gail Wilson (eds), *Give and Take in Families: Studies in Resource Distribution* (London: Allen and Unwin) 56–74.

Graham, Hilary (1993) *Hardship and Health in Women's Lives* (Hemel Hempstead: Harvester Wheatsheaf).

Green, Duncan (1995) *Silent Revolution: The Rise of Market Economics in Latin America* (London: Cassell/Latin America Bureau).

Greif, Geoffrey; DeMaris, Alfred and Hood, Jane (1993) 'Balancing Work and Single Fatherhood', in Jane Hood (ed.), *Men,Work and Family* (Newbury Park: Sage) 176–94.

Grosh, Margaret (1994) *Administering Targeted Social Programs in Latin America: From Platitudes to Practice* (Washington DC: World Bank).

Gudmundson, Lowell (1986) *Costa Rica Before Coffee: Society and Economy on the Eve of the Export Boom* (Baton Rouge: Louisiana State University Press).

Gugler, Josef and Flanagan, William (1978) *Urbanisation and Social Change in West Africa* (Cambridge: Cambridge University Press).

Gulati, I.S. and Gulati, Leela (1995) 'Social Security for Widows', *Economic and Political Weekly* (Bombay), 30 September, 2451–3.

Guyer, Jane and Peters, Pauline (1987) 'Introduction' to Special Issue 'Conceptualising the Household: Issues of Theory and Policy in Africa', *Development and Change*, 18, 197–214.

Hackenberg, Robert; Murphy, Arthur and Selby, Henry (1981) 'The Household in the Secondary Cities of the Third World'. Paper prepared in advance for participants in the Wenner-Gren Foundation Symposium 'Households: Changing Form and Function', New York, 8–15 October.

Haddad, Lawrence (1991) 'Gender and Poverty in Ghana: A Descriptive Analysis of Selected Outcomes and Processes', *IDS Bulletin* (Sussex), 22:1, 5–16.

Hagan, George Panyin (1983) 'Marriage, Divorce and Polygyny in Winneba', in Christine Oppong (ed.), *Female and Male in West Africa* (London: George Allen and Unwin) 192–203.

Hall, Carolyn (1985) *Costa Rica: A Geographical Interpretation in Historical Perspective* (Boulder, Colorado: Westview, Dellplain Latin American Studies No.17).

Hardey, Michael and Crow, Graham (1991) 'Introduction', in Michael Hardey and Graham Crow (eds), *Lone Parenthood: Coping with Constraints and Making Opportunities* (Hemel Hempstead: Harvester Wheatsheaf) 1–18.

Hardey, Michael and Glover, Judith (1991) 'Income, Employment, Daycare and Lone Parenthood', in Michael Hardey and Graham Crow (eds), *Lone Parenthood: Coping with Constraints and Making Opportunities* (Hemel Hempstead: Harvester Wheatsheaf) 88–109.

Harris, Ian (1995) *Messages Men Hear: Constructing Masculinities* (London: Taylor and Francis).

Harris, Kathleen Mullan (1993) 'Work and Welfare Among Single Mothers in Poverty', *American Journal of Sociology*, 99:2, 317–52.

Harris, Olivia (1981) 'Households as Natural Units', in Kate Young, Carol Wolkowitz and Roslyn McCullagh (eds), *Of Marriage and the Market* (London: CSE Books) 48–67.

Harris, Olivia (1982) 'Latin American Women: An Overview', in Olivia Harris (ed.), *Latin American Women* (London: Minority Rights Group) 4–8.

Harriss, Barbara and Watson, Elizabeth (1987) 'The Sex Ratio in South Asia', in Janet Momsen and Janet Townsend (eds), *Geography of Gender in the Third World* (London: Hutchinson) 85–115.

Harvey, Penelope (1994) 'Domestic Violence in the Peruvian Andes', in Penelope Harvey and Peter Gow (eds), *Sex and Violence: Issues in Representation and Experience* (London: Routledge) 66–89.

Harvey, Penelope and Gow, Peter (1994) 'Introduction', in Penelope Harvey and Peter Gow (eds), *Sex and Violence: Issues in Representation and Experience* (London: Routledge) 1–17.

Haskey, John (1991) 'Lone Parenthood and Demographic Change', in Michael Hardey and Graham Crow (eds), *Lone Parenthood: Coping with Constraints and Making Opportunities* (Hemel Hempstead: Harvester Wheatsheaf) 19–46.

H. Ayuntamiento de Puerto Vallarta (1992) *Plan de Desarrollo Urbano de Puerto Vallarta 1992–5* (Puerto Vallarta: H. Ayuntamiento/Gobierno del Estado de Jalisco/SEDEUR).

Hetler, Carol (1990) 'Survival Strategies and Household Headship (Java)', in Leela Dube and Rajni Palriwala (eds) *Structures and Strategies: Women, Work and Family* (New Delhi: Sage) 175–99.

Hewitt, Patricia and Leach, Penelope (1993) *Social Justice, Children and Families* (London: Institute for Public Policy Research).

Heyzer, Noeleen (1986) *Working Women in Southeast Asia: Development, Subordination and Emancipation* (Milton Keynes: Open University Press).

Hill, Polly (1969) 'Hidden Trade in Hausaland', *Man*, 4:3, 392–409.

Hobson, Barbara (1994) 'Solo Mothers, Social Policy Regimes and the Logics of Gender', in Diane Sainsbury (ed.), *Gendering Welfare States* (London: Sage) 170–88.

Hoddinott, John and Haddad, Lawrence (1991) *Household Expenditures, Child Anthropomorphic Status and the Intra-Household Division of Income: Evidence from the Côte d'Ivoire* (Oxford: Unit for the Study of African Economics, University of Oxford).

Hoffman, Kristi; Demo, David and Edwards, John (1994) 'Physical Wife Abuse in a Non-Western Society: An Integrated Theoretical Approach', *Journal of Marriage and the Family*, 56, 131–46.

Hollnsteiner, Mary (1991a) 'The Wife', in Department of Sociology-Anthropology (ed.), *SA 21: Selected Readings* (Quezon City: Ateneo de Manila University, Office of Research and Publications) 251–75.

Hollnsteiner, Mary (1991b) 'The Husband', in Department of Sociology-Anthropology (ed.), *SA 21: Selected Readings* (Quezon City: Ateneo de Manila University, Office of Research and Publications) 276–84.

Hood, Jane (ed.) (1993) *Men, Work and Family* (Newbury Park: Sage).

Hugo, Graeme (1992) 'Women on the Move: Changing Patterns of Population Movement of Women in Indonesia', in Sylvia Chant (ed.), *Gender and Migration in Developing Countries* (London: Belhaven) 174–96.

Hulme, David and Turner, Mark (1990) *Sociology and Development: Theories, Policies and Practices* (New York: Harvester Wheatsheaf).

Illo, Jeanne (1991) 'Putting Gender Up Front: Data, Issues and Prospects', in Jeanne Illo (ed.), *Gender Analysis and Planning* (Quezon City: Ateneo de Manila University) 39–58.

Illo, Jeanne (1992) 'Who Heads the Household? Women in Households in the Philippines', in K. Saradamoni (ed.), *Finding the Household: Methodological and Empirical Issues* (New Delhi: Sage) 185–201.

Illo, Jeanne and Lee, Rona (1991) 'Women and Men in a Rainfed Farming Systems Project: The Cahabaan Case', in Jeanne Illo (ed.), *Gender Analysis and Planning* (Quezon City: Ateneo de Manila University Press) 65–74.

Illo, Jeanne and Polo, Jaime (1990) *Fishers, Farmers, Traders, Wives* (Quezon City: Ateneo de Manila University, Institute of Philippine Culture).

Instituto Nacional de Estadística, Geografía e Informática (INEGI) (1993) *La Mujer en México, Edición 1993* (Aguascalientes: INEGI).

Instituto Nacional de Vivienda y Urbanismo (INVU) (1985) *Tasas de Crecimiento Anual de Todos los Distritos del País Según Censos 1973–1984* (San José: INVU).

INSTRAW (1992) 'Women and the Household', in K. Saradamoni (ed.), *Finding the Household: Methodological and Empirical Issues* (New Delhi: Sage) 233–40.

Investigaciones Jurídicas, S.A. (IJSA) (1990) *Ley de Promoción de la Igualdad Social de la Mujer* (San José: IJSA).

Israel-Sobritchea, Carolyn (1994) '"Getting the Right Mix of Feminism and Nationalism": Some Reflections on Recent Developments in the Women's Movement in the Philippines'. Paper given at the panel 'Negotiating Gender in the Philippines', European Conference on Philippine Studies, School of Oriental and African Studies University of London, 13–15 April.

Itzin, Catherine (1980) *Splitting-Up: Single Parent Liberation* (London: Virago).

Jacobsen, Joyce (1994) *The Economics of Gender* (Cambridge, Massachusetts: Blackwell).

Jayawardena, C. (1960) 'Marital Stability in Two Guianese Sugar Estate Communities', *Social and Economic Studies*, 9, 76–100.

Jeffery, Roger and Jeffery, Patricia (1993) 'Traditional Birth Attendants in Rural North India', in Shirley Lindenbaum and Margaret Lock (eds), *Knowledge, Power and Practice in Medicine and Everyday Life* (Berkeley: University of California Press) 7–31.

Jeffery, Roger and Jeffery, Patricia (1996) *Don't Marry Me to a Plowman! Women's Everday Lives in Rural North India* (Boulder/San Francisco/Oxford: Westview/HarperCollins).

Jelin, Elizabeth (ed.) (1991) *Family, Household and Gender Relations in Latin America* (London: Kegan Paul International/Paris: UNESCO).

Jelin, Elizabeth (1992) 'Celibacy, Solitude, and Personal Autonomy: Individual Choice and Social Constraints', in Elza Berquó and Peter Xenos (eds), *Family Systems and Cultural Change* (Oxford: Clarendon Press) 109–24.

Joekes, Susan (1985) 'Working for Lipstick? Male and Female Labour in the Clothing Industry in Morocco', in Haleh Afshar (ed.), *Women, Work and Ideology in the Third World* (London: Tavistock) 183–213.

Joekes, Susan (1987) *Women in the World Economy: An INSTRAW Study* (Albany: State University of New York Press).

Johnson, Chris (1992) *Women on the Frontline: Voices from Southern Africa* (Basingstoke: Macmillan).

Joseph Rowntree Foundation (1994) *Children Living in Re-ordered Families* (York: Joseph Rowntree Foundation, Social Policy Research Findings No.45).

Jules-Rosette, Benetta (1985) 'The Women Potters of Lusaka: Urban Migration and Socio-economic Adjustment', in Beverly Lindsay (ed.), *African Migration and National Development* (Pennsylvania: Pennsylvania State University) 82–112.

Kabeer, Naila (1991) 'Gender Dimensions of Rural Poverty: Analysis from Bangladesh', *Journal of Peasant Studies*, 18:2, 241–62.

Kabeer, Naila (1994) *Reversed Realities: Gender Hierarchies in Development Thought* (London: Verso).

Kabeer, Naila (1995) 'Necessary, Sufficient or Relevant? Women's Wages and Intra-household Power Relations in Urban Bangladesh'. Seminar, Gender Institute, London School of Economics, 6 December.

Kabeer, Naila and Joekes, Susan (1991) 'Editorial', *IDS Bulletin* (Sussex), 22:1 (Special Issue 'Researching the Household: Methodological and Empirical Issues') 1–4.

Kalpagam, U. (1992) 'Women and the Household: What the Indian Data Sources Have to Offer', in K. Saradamoni (ed.), *Finding the Household: Methodological and Empirical Issues* (New Delhi: Sage) 75–131.

Kamerman, Sheila (1984) 'Women, Children and Poverty: Public Policies and Female-headed Households in Industrialised Countries', *Signs*, 10:2, 249–71.

Kamerman, Sheila and Kahn, Alfred (1988) *Mothers Alone: Strategies for a Time of Change* (Dover, Massachusetts: Auburn House Publishing Company).

Kandiyoti, Deniz (1991) 'Bargaining with Patriarchy', in Judith Lorber and Susan Farrell (eds), *The Social Construction of Gender* (Newbury Park: Sage) 104–18.

Kanji, Nazneen (1991) 'Structural Adjustment Policies: Shifting the Costs of Social Reproduction to Women', *Critical Health*, 34, 61–7.

Kanji, Nazneen (1994) Gender and Structural Adjustment: A Case Study of Harare, Zimbabwe. Unpublished PhD dissertation, Department of Geography, London School of Economics.

Kawar, Mary (1996) Gender, Employment and the Life-Course: Working Daughters in Amman, Jordan. PhD thesis in preparation, Department of Geography, London School of Economics.

Keigher, Sharon (1993) 'In Search of the "Golden Girls": Why is Affordable, Adaptable and Assisted Housing for Older Women so Hard to Find?', in Hemalata Dandekar (ed.), *Women, Shelter and Development: First and Third World Perspectives* (Ann Arbor, Michigan: George Wahr Publishing Co) 377–95.

Kennedy, Eileen (1994) 'Development Policy, Gender of Head of Household, and Nutrition', in Eileen Kennedy and Mercedes González de la Rocha, *Poverty and Well-being in the Household: Case Studies of the Developing World* (San Diego: Center for Iberian and Latin American Studies, University of California, Working Paper No.5) 25–42.

Kertzer, David (1991) 'Household and Gender in a Life-course Perspective', in Eleanora Masini and Susan Stratigos (eds), *Women, Households and Change* (Tokyo: United Nations University Press) 18–29.

Khasiani, Shanyisa (1993) 'Reproductive Rights Among Women in Kenya', in Wanjiku Kabira, Jacqueline Oduol and Maria Nzomo (eds), *Democratic Change in Africa: Women's Perspective* (Nairobi: Association of African Women for Research and Development and Acts Press, African Centre for Technology Studies) 55–72.

Kodras, Janet and Jones, John Paul (1991) 'A Contextual Examination of the Feminisation of Poverty', *Geoforum*, 22:2, 159–71.

Koopman, Jeanne (1991) 'Neoclassical Household Models and Modes of Household Production: Problems in the Analysis of African Agricultural Households', *Review of Radical Political Economy*, 23:3–4, 148–73.

Koussoudji, Sherrie and Mueller, Eva (1983) 'The Economic and Demographic Status of Female-headed Households in Rural Botswana', *Economic Development and Cultural Change*, 21, 831–59.

Kumari, Ranjana (1989) *Women-headed Households in Rural India* (New Delhi: Radiant Publishers).

Kuznesof, Elizabeth Anne (1980) 'Household Composition and Headship as Related to Changes in Modes of Production: São Paulo 1765–1836', *Comparative Studies in Society and History*, 22:1, 78–108.

Land, Hilary (1977) 'Inequalities in Large Families', in Robert Chester and John Peel (eds), *Equalities and Inequalities in Family Life* (London: Academic Press) 163–76.

Land, Hilary (1995) 'Families and the Law', in John Muncie, Margaret Wetherell, Rudi Dallos and Allan Cochrane (eds), *Understanding the Family* (London: Sage) 81–123.

Land, Hilary and Rose, Hilary (1985) 'Compulsory Altruism for All or an Altruistic Society for Some?', in Philip Bean, John Ferris, and David Whynes (eds), *In Defence of Welfare* (London: Tavistock) 74–96.

Lara, Silvia with Barry, Tom and Simonson, Peter (1995) *Inside Costa Rica* (Albuquerque: Interhemispheric Resource Center).

Lardinois, Roland (1992) 'Family and Household as Practical Groups: Preliminary Reflections on the Hindu Joint Family', in K. Saradamoni (ed.), *Finding the Household: Methodological and Empirical Issues* (New Delhi: Sage) 31–74.

Larsson, Anita (1989) *Women Householders and Housing Strategies: The Case of Gaborone, Botswana* (Gävle: The National Swedish Institute for Building Research)

Larsson, Anita (1993) 'The Importance of Housing in the Lives of Women: The Case of Botswana', in Hemalata Dandekar (ed.), *Women, Shelter and Development: First and Third World Perspectives* (Ann Arbor, Michigan: George Wahr Publishing Co.) 106–15.

Laslett, Peter (1972) 'Introduction: The History of the Family', in Peter Laslett and Richard Wall (eds), *Household and Family in Past Time* (Cambridge: Cambridge University Press) 1–89.

Laslett, Peter (1984) 'The Family as a Knot of Individual Interests', in Robert McC Netting, Richard R Wilk and Eric J Arnould (eds), *Households: Comparative and Historical Studies of the Domestic Group* (Berkeley: University of California Press) 353–79.

Latinamerica Press (1995) 'Women on the Move', *Latinamerica Press*, 27:3 (Lima).

Law, Lisa (forthcoming) 'A Matter of "Choice": Discourses on Prostitution in the Philippines', in L. Manderson and M. Jolly (eds), *Sites of Desire/Economies of Pleasure: Sexualities in Asia and the Pacific* (Chicago: University of Chicago Press).

Leacock, Eleanor (1972) 'Introduction', in Frederick Engels *The Origin of the Family, Private Property and the State* (London: Lawrence and Wishart) 7–67.

Lehmann, David (1994a) 'Pentecostal Women'. Paper delivered at the Symposium 'Gender in Latin America', Annual Conference on the Society of Latin American Studies, University of Liverpool, 25–27 March.

Lehmann, David (1994b) 'Bringing Society Back In: Latin America in a Post-Development World'. Draft appplication for British Academy Research Fellowship, Centre of Latin American Studies, University of Cambridge.

Leonardo, Micaela di (1993) 'The Female World of Cards and Holidays: Women, Family and the Work of Kinship', in Caroline Brettell and Carolyn Sargent (eds), *Gender in Cross-Cultural Perspective* (Englewood Cliffs, New Jersey: Prentice Hall) 322–3.

Lerner, Gerda (1986) *The Creation of Patriarchy* (New York: Oxford University Press).

Lessinger, Joanna (1990) 'Work and Modesty: The Dilemma of Women Market Traders in Madras', in Leela Dube and Rajni Palriwala (eds), *Structures and Strategies: Women, Work and Family* (New Dlehi: Sage) 15–55.

LeVine, Sarah (in collaboration with Clara Sunderland Correa) *Dolor y Alegría: Women and Social Change in Urban Mexico* (Madison, Wisconsin: University of Wisconsin).

Levinson, David (1989) *Family Violence in Cross-Cultural Perspective* (Newbury Park: Sage).

Levy, Caren (1992) 'Transport', in Lise Østergaard (ed.) *Gender and Development: A Practical Guide* (London: Routledge) 94–109.

Lewin, Ellen (1994) 'Negotiating Lesbian Motherhood: The Dialectics of Resistance and Accommodation', in Evelyn Nakano Glenn, Grace Chang and Linda Rennie Forcey (eds), *Mothering: Ideology, Experience and Agency* (New York: Routledge) 333–53.

Lewis, David (1993) 'Going It Alone: Female-Headed Households, Rights and Resources in Rural Bangladesh', *European Journal of Development Research*, 5:2, 23–42.

Lewis, Jane (1989) 'Lone Parent Families: Politics and Economics', *Journal of Social Policy* 18:4, 595–600.

Lewis, Jane (1995) *The Problem of Lone Mother Families in Twentieth Century Britain* (London: London School of Economics, Suntory-Toyota International Centre for Economics and Related Disciplines, Welfare State Programme Discussion Paper 114).

Lewis, Oscar (1966) 'The Culture of Poverty', *Scientific American* (October), 19–25.

Lily, Fazila Banu (1987) 'The Role of Rural Bangladeshi Women in Livestock Rearing', in Andréa Menefee Singh and Anita Kelles-Viitanen (eds), *Invisible Hands: Women in Home-based Production* (New Delhi: Sage) 93–108.

Lloyd, Cynthia and Gage-Brandon, Anastasia (1993) 'Women's Role in Maintaining Households: Family Welfare and Sexual Inequality in Ghana', *Population Studies*, 47, 115–31.

Lomnitz, Larissa (1977) *Networks and Marginality - Life in a Mexican Shanty Town* (México DF: Siglo Veintiuno).

Lomnitz, Larissa and Pérez-Lizaur, Marisol (1991) 'Dynastic Growth and Survival Strategies: The Solidarity of Mexican Grand-Families', in Elizabeth Jelin (ed.), *Family, Household and Gender Relations in Latin America* (London/Paris: Kegan Paul International/UNESCO) 123–32.

Lustig, Nora (1992) *Mexico: The Reshaping of an Economy* (Philadelphia: Brookings Institute).

Macaskill, Hilary (1993) *From the Workhouse to the Workplace: 75 Years of One-parent Family Life 1918–1993* (London: National Council for One Parent Families).

MacDonald, J.S. and MacDonald, L. (1979) 'The Black Family in the Americas: A Review of the Literature', *Sage Race Relations Abstracts* 3:1, 1–42.

Machado, Leda (1987) 'The Problems for Women-headed Households in a Low-income Housing Programme in Brazil', in Caroline Moser and Linda Peake (eds), *Women, Human Settlements and Housing* (London: Tavistock) 55–69.

Mackintosh, Maureen (1979) 'Domestic Labour and the Household', in Sandra Burman (ed.), *Fit Work for Women* (London: Croom Helm) 173–91.

Mädje, E. and Neusüss, C. (1994) 'Lone Mothers on Welfare in West Berlin: Disadvantaged Citizens or Women Avoiding Patriarchy?', *Environment and Planning A*, 26, 1419–33.

Maier, Elizabeth (1994) 'Sex and Class as a Single Entity', in Gaby Küppers (ed.), *Compañeras: Voices from the Latin American Women's Movement* (London: Latin America Bureau) 40–5.

Mangahas, Fe and Pasalo, Virginia (1994) 'Devising an Empowerment Paradigm for Women in the Philippines: The Importance of the Family in Micro-Urban Enterprises', in Fatima Meer (ed.), *Poverty in the 1990s: The Responses of Urban Women* (Paris: UNESCO/International Social Science Council) 243–68.

Mann, Michael (1994) 'Persons, Households, Families, Lineages, Genders, Classes and Nations', in *The Polity Reader in Gender Studies* (Cambridge: Polity Press) 177–94.

Marcelo, Alexandrina (1991) *State Policies and Women's Health and Reproductive Rights* (Manila: Institute for Social Studies and Action).

Masini, Eleanora Barbieri (1991) 'The Household, Gender and Age Project', in Eleanora Masini and Susan Stratigos (eds), *Women, Households and Change* (Tokyo: United Nations University Press) 3–17.

Massiah, Joycelin (1986) 'Work in the Lives of Caribbean Women', *Social and Economic Studies* (Institute of Social and Economic Research, University of West Indies), 35:2, 177–239.

Mather, Celia (1985) '"Rather Than Make Trouble, It's Better Just to Leave": Behind the Lack of Industrial Strife in the Tangerang Region of West Java', in Haleh Afshar (ed.), *Women, Work and Ideology in the Third World* (London: Tavistock) 153–82.

Mather, Celia (1988) 'Subordination of Women and Lack of Industrial Strife in West Java', in John Taylor and Andrew Turton (eds), *Sociology of 'Developing Societies': Southeast Asia* (Basingstoke: Macmillan) 147–57.

Maynard, Mary (1994) 'Methods, Practice and Epistemology: The Debate about Feminism and Research', in Mary Maynard and Jane Purvis (eds), *Researching Women's Lives From a Feminist Perspective* (London: Taylor and Francis) 10–26.

Maynard, Mary and Purvis Jane (1994) 'Doing Feminist Research', in Mary Maynard and Jane Purvis (eds), *Researching Women's Lives From a Feminist Perspective* (London: Taylor and Francis) 1–9.

McAdoo, Hariette Pipes (1986) 'Strategies Used by Black Single Mothers Against Stress', in Margaret C. Simms and Julianne Malvaux (eds), *Slipping Through the Cracks: The Status of Black Women* (New Brunswick, New Jersey: Transaction Books) 153–66.

McCreery, John (1993) 'Women's Property Rights and Dowry in China and South Asia', in Caroline Brettell and Carolyn Sargent (eds) *Gender in Cross-Cultural Perspective* (Englewood Cliffs, New Jersey: Prentice Hall) 269–78.

McDonald, Peter (1992) 'Convergence or Compromise in Historical Family Change?', in Elza Berquó and Peter Xenos (eds), *Family Systems and Cultural Change* (Oxford: Clarendon Press) 15–30.

McIlwaine, Cathy (1993) 'Gender, Ethnicity and the Local Labour Market in Limón, Costa Rica'. Unpublished PhD thesis (Department of Geography, London School of Economics).

McIlwaine, Cathy (1994) 'People in Glass Boxes: Gender and Ethnic Constraints on Labour Mobility in Limón, Costa Rica'. Paper delivered at Symposium 'Gender in Latin America', Annual Conference on the Society of Latin American Studies, University of Liverpool, 25–27 March.

McIlwaine, Cathy (1995) 'Gender, Race and Ethnicity: Concepts, Realities and Policy Implications', *Third World Planning Review* (Special issue on Gender and Development) 17:2, 237–43.

Medina, Belen (1991) *The Filipino Family: A Text With Selected Readings* (Quezon City: University of the Philippines Press).

Mencher, Joan (1989) 'Women Agricultural Labourers and Land Owners in Kerala and Tamil Nadu: Some Questions about Gender and Autonomy in the Household', in Maithreyi Krishnaraj and Karuna Chanana (eds), *Gender and the Household Domain: Social and Cultural Dimensions* (New Delhi: Sage) 117–41.

Méndez, Zinnia (1988) 'Socialización y Estereotipos Sociales en Costa Rica', *Revista de Ciencias Sociales* 39, 29–45.

Menjívar, Rafael and Trejos, Juan Diego (1992) *La Pobreza en América Central*, 2nd edn (San José: FLACSO).

Mernissi, Fatima (1985) *Beyond the Veil: Male-Female Dynamics in Modern Muslim Society* (London: Al Saqi Books).

Merrick, Thomas and Schmink, Marianne (1983) 'Households Headed by Women and Urban Poverty in Brazil', in Mayra Buvinic, Margaret Lycette and William McGreevey (eds), *Women and Poverty in the Third World* (Baltimore: John Hopkins) 244–71.

Millar, Jane (1992a) 'Lone Mothers and Poverty', in Caroline Glendinning and Jane Millar (eds), *Women and Poverty in Britain in the 1990s* (Hemel Hempstead: Harvester Wheatsheaf) 149–61.

Millar, Jane (1992b) 'Individual, Family and State Responsibilities: Lone Mothers and the 1992 Child Support Act'. Seminar, Suntory-Toyota Institute for Economics and Related Disciplines, London School of Economics, 10 June.

Millar, Jane and Glendinning, Caroline (1989) 'Gender and Poverty', *Journal of Social Policy* 18:3, 363–81.

Millar, Jane; Leeper, Sandra and Davies, Celia (1992) *Lone Parents: Poverty and Public Policy in Ireland* (Dublin: Combat Poverty Agency).

Miralao, Virginia (1984) 'The Impact of Female Employment on Household Management', in Gavin Jones (ed.), *Women in the Urban and Industrial Workforce: Southeast and East Asia* (Canberra: Australian National University) 369–86.

Mir-Hosseini, Ziba (1996) 'Women and Politics in Post-Khomeini Iran: Divorce, Veiling and Emerging Feminist Voices', in Haleh Afshar (ed.), *Women and Politics in the Third World* (London: Routledge) 142–70.

Mishra, Kiran (1992) 'Nishing Longhouse as a Household', in K. Saradamoni (ed.), *Finding the Household: Methodological and Empirical Issues* (New Delhi: Sage) 135–42.

Mitterauer, Michael and Sieder, Reinhard (1982) *The European Family* (Oxford: Blackwell).

Moghadam, Valentine (1994) 'Women in Societies', *International Social Science Journal*, 139, 95–115.

Moghadam, Valentine (1995a) 'Gender Aspects of Employment and Unemployment in a Global Perspective', in Mihály Simai with Valentine Moghadam and Arvo Kuddo (eds), *Global Employment: An International Investigation into the Future of Work Vol.1* (London: Zed) 111–34.

Moghadam, Valentine (1995b) 'Gender Dynamics of Restructuring in the Semiperiphery', in Rae Lesser Blumberg, Cathy Rakowski, Irene Tinker and Michael Monteón (eds), *Engendering Wealth and Well-Being: Empowerment for Global Change* (Boulder: Westview) 17–37.

Moghadam, Valentine (1995c) *Economic Reform and Women's Employment in Egypt: Constraints and Opportunities* (Helsinki: United Nations University, World Institute for Development Economics Research).

Moghadam, Valentine (1995d) 'Gender and Revolutionary Transformation: Iran 1979 and East Central Europe 1989', *Gender and Society*, 9:3, 328–58.

Moghadam, Valentine (1995e) 'The Fourth World Conference on Women: Dissension and Consensus'. Mimeo, World Institute of Development Economics Research, United Nations University, Helsinki.

Moghadam, Valentine (1995f) 'Introduction and Overview: Economic Reforms, Women's Employment and Social Policies', in Valentine Moghadam (ed.) *Economic Reforms, Women's Employment and Social Policies* (Helsinki: United

Nations University, World Institute of Development Economics Research, World Development Studies 4) 1–9.

Mohanty, Chandra Talpade (1991) 'Under Western Eyes: Feminist Scholarship and Colonial Discourses', in Chandra Mohanty, Ann Russo and Lourdes Torres (eds), *Third World Women and the Politics of Feminism* (Bloomington: Indiana Univerity Press) 51–80.

Molapo, Lesego (1987) 'Women and Agriculture in Botswana', in Christine Qunta (ed.), *Women in Southern Africa* (London: Allison and Busby) 204–6.

Molina, Giselle (1989) 'La Administración de Justicia en la Violencia Conyugal', *Mujer*, 5, 32–40.

Molina, Giselle (1993) *¿Cómo Obtener Protección Legal?* (San José: CEFEMINA).

Molina, Giselle (1994) *Matrimonio, Separación, Divorcio (Derechos y Deberes)* (San José: CEFEMINA).

Molyneux, Maxine (1984) 'Mobilisation Without Emancipation? Women's Interests, State and Revolution in Nicaragua', *Critical Social Policy*, 10:4:7, 280–302.

Molyneux, Maxine (1986) 'Mobilisation Without Emancipation? Women's Interests, State and Revolution', in Richard Fagan, Carmen Diana Deere and José Luis Coraggio (eds), *Transition and Development: Problems of Third World Socialism* (New York: Monthly Review Press) 280–302.

Momsen, Janet (1987) 'The Feminisation of Agriculture in the Caribbean', in Janet Momsen and Janet Townsend (eds), *Geography of Gender in the Third World* (London: Hutchinson) 344–7.

Momsen, Janet (1991) *Women and Development in the Third World* (London: Routledge).

Momsen, Janet (1992) 'Gender Selectivity in Caribbean Migration', in Sylvia Chant (ed.), *Gender and Migration in Developing Countries* (London: Belhaven) 73–90.

Momsen, Janet and Kinnaird, Vivian (eds) (1993) *Different Places, Different Voices: Gender and Development in Africa, Asia and Latin America* (London: Routledge).

Monk, Sue (ed.) (1993) *From the Margins to the Mainstream: An Employment Strategy for Lone Parents* (National Council for One Parent Families: London).

Monteón, Michael (1995) 'Gender and Economic Crises in Latin America: Reflections on the Great Depression and the Debt Crisis', in Rae Lesser Blumberg, Cathy Rakowski, Irene Tinker and Michael Monteón (eds), *Engendering Wealth and Well-Being: Empowerment for Global Change* (Boulder: Westview) 39–64.

Morgan, Patricia (1995) *Farewell to the Family: Public Policy and Family Breakdown in Britain and the USA* (London: Institute for Economic Affairs, Health and Welfare Unit)

Moore, Henrietta (1988) *Feminism and Anthropology* (Cambridge: Polity).

Moore, Henrietta (1994a) *A Passion for Difference: Essays in Anthropology and Gender* (Cambridge: Polity).

Moore, Henrietta (1994b) *Is There a Crisis in the Family?* (Geneva: World Summit for Social Development, Occasional Paper 3).

Moore, Henrietta and Vaughan, Megan (1994) *Cutting Down Trees: Gender, Nutrition and Agricultural Change in the Northern Province of Zambia, 1890–1990* (Portsmouth, New Jersey: Heinemann).

Morris, Arthur and Lowder, Stella (1992) 'Flexible Specialisation: The Application of Theory in a Poor Country Context: León, Mexico', *International Journal of Urban and Regional Research*, 16, 190–201.

Morrison, Jean (1995) '"The Circulation of Men": Marriage Practices and Gender Relations among the Bajou of Sabah, East Malaysia'. Paper presented at the 15th annual conference of the Association of Southeast Asian Studies in the United Kingdom, 'Gender and the Sexes in Southeast Asia', University of Durham, 29–31 March.

Moser, Caroline (1987) 'Women, Human Settlements and Housing: A Conceptual Framework for Analysis and Policy-Making', in Caroline Moser and Linda Peake (eds), *Women, Human Settlements and Housing* (London: Tavistock) 12–32.

Moser, Caroline (1989) 'The Impact of Structural Adjustment at the Micro-level: Low-income Women and their Households in Guayaquil, Ecuador', in UNICEF (ed.), *Invisible Adjustment Vol.2* (New York, UNICEF Americas and Caribbean Office), 137–62.

Moser, Caroline (1992) 'Adjustment from Below: Low-income Women, Time and the Triple Role in Guayaquil, Ecuador', in Haleh Afshar and Carolyne Dennis (eds), *Women and Adjustment Policies in the Third World* (Basingstoke: Macmillan), 87–116.

Moser, Caroline (1993a) *Gender Planning and Development: Theory, Practice and Training* (London: Routledge).

Moser, Caroline (1993b) 'Women, Gender and Urban Development: Challenges for the 1990s'. Paper prepared for the Final Workshop of Ford Foundation Research Project on Urban Research in the Developing World: Toward an Agenda for the 1990s, Cairo, 14–18 February.

Moser, Caroline (1995) 'Women, Gender and Urban Development Policy: Challenges for Current and Future Research', *Third World Planning Review* (Special issue on 'Gender and Development'), 17:2, 223–35.

Moser, Caroline and Levy, Caren (1986) *A Theory and Methodology of Gender Planning: Meeting Women's Practical and Strategic Needs* (London: Development Planning Unit, University College London, Gender and Planning Working Paper No.11).

Moses, Yolanda (1977) 'Female Status, the Family and Male Dominance in a West Indian Community', in Wellesley Editorial Committee (ed.), *Women and National Development: The Complexities of Change* (Chicago: University of Chicago Press), 42–53.

Mulder, Nils (1994) 'Filipino Culture and Social Analysis'. Paper delivered at the panel 'Religion, Ritual and Identity', European Conference on Philippine Studies, School of Oriental and African Studies, University of London, 13–15 April.

Muncie, John and Sapsford, Roger (1995) 'Issues in the Study of "The Family"', in John Muncie, Margaret Wetherell, Rudi Dallos and Allan Cochrane (eds), *Understanding the Family* (London: Sage) 7–37.

Muncie, John; Wetherell, Margaret; Dallow, Rudi and Cochrane, Allan (eds) (1995) *Understanding the Family* (London: Sage).

Muñoz, Hugo Alfonso (1992) 'El Papel de la Defensoría de la Mujer', in CEFEMINA *Mujer, Violencia y Mitos* (San José: CEFEMINA) 11–13.

Murray, Charles (1994) *Underclass: The Crisis Deepens* (London: Institute of Economic Affairs, Health and Welfare Unit in association with the *The Sunday Times*, Choice in Welfare Series No.20).

Murray, Colin (1981) *Families Divided: The Impact of Migrant Labour in Lesotho* (Cambridge: Cambridge University Press).

Murray, Colin (1987) 'Class, Gender and the Household: The Developmental Cycle in Southern Africa', *Development and Change*, 18, 235–49.

Muthwa, Sibongile (1993) 'Household Survival, Urban Poverty and Female Household Headship in Soweto: Some Key Issues for Further Policy Research'. Paper given in seminar series 'The Societies of Southern Africa in the 19th and 20th Centuries: Women, Colonialism and Commonwealth', Institute of Commonwealth Studies, University of London, 19 November.

Nagot, Ma Cristina D. (1991) 'Preliminary Investigation on Domestic Violence Against Women', in Sister Mary John Mananzan (ed.), *Essays on Women*, revised ed. (Manila: St Scholastica's College, Institute of Women's Studies) 113–28.

Nash, June (1980) 'A Critique of Social Science Roles in Latin America', in June Nash and Helen Safa (eds), *Sex and Class in Latin America* (New York: Bergin) 1–21.

National Commission on the Role of Filipino Women (NCRFW) (1989) *Philippine Development Plan for Women, 1989–1992* (Manila:NCRFW).

National Council for One Parent Families (NCOPF) (1991) *Legal Rights of Single Mothers* (London: NCOPF).

National Council for One Parent Families (NCOPF) (1993) *Annual Report 1992–3* (London: NCOPF).

National Council for One Parent Families (NCOPF) (1994a) *Maintenance and the Child Support Agency* (London: NCOPF).

National Council for One Parent Families (NCOPF) (1994b) *Annual Report 1993–4: A Watershed Year for Lone Parents* (London: NCOPF).

National Statistics Office (NSO) (1992a) *1990 Census of Population and Housing, Report No.3: Socio-Economic and Demographic Characteristics, Philippines* (Manila: NSO).

Nelson, Nici (1979) 'How Women and Men Get By: The Sexual Division of Labour in the Informal Sector of a Nairobi Squatter Settlement', in Ray Bromley and Chris Gerry (eds), *Casual Work and Poverty in Third World Cities* (Chichester: John Wiley), 283–302.

Nelson, Nici (1987) 'Rural–Urban Child Fostering in Kenya: Migration, Kinship Ideology and Class', in Jeremy Eades (ed.), *Migrants, Workers and the Social Order* (London: Tavistock, Association of Social Anthropologists Monograph No.26) 181–98.

Nelson, Nici (1992) 'The Women who have Left and Those who have Stayed Behind: Rural–Urban Migration in Central and Western Kenya', in Sylvia Chant (ed.), *Gender and Migration in Developing Countries* (London: Belhaven) 109–38.

Netting, Robert McC; Wilk, Richard R. and Arnould, Eric J. (1984) 'Introduction', in Robert McC Netting, Richard R Wilk and Eric J Arnould (eds), *Households: Comparative and Historical Studies of the Domestic Group* (Berkeley: University of California Press) xiii–xxxviii.

Nimpuno-Parente, Paula (1987) 'The Struggle for Shelter: Women in a Site and Service Project in Nairobi, Kenya', in Caroline Moser and Linda Peake (eds), *Women, Human Setlements and Housing* (London: Tavistock) 70–87.

O'Connell, Helen (1994) *Women and the Family* (London: Zed).

Oldenburg, Veena Talwar (1992) 'Lifestyle as Resistance: The Case of the Courtesans of Lucknow', in Douglas Haynes and Gyan Prakesh (eds), *Contesting Power: Resistance and Everyday Social Relations in South Asia* (Berkeley: University of California) 23–61.

Oliveira, María Coleta F.A. de (1992) 'Family Change and Family Process: Implications for Research in Developing Countries', in Elza Berquó and Peter Xenos (eds), *Family Systems and Cultural Change* (Oxford: Clarendon Press) 201–14.

Oliveira, Orlandina de (1991) 'Migration of Women, Family Organisation and Labour Markets in Mexico', in Elizabeth Jelin (ed.), *Family, Household and Gender Relations in Latin America* (London/Paris: Kegan Paul International/ UNESCO) 101–18.

Pahl, Jan (1995) 'Money, Power and Access to Resources within Marriage', Seminar, Gender Institute, London School of Economics, 22 November.

Pahl, Ray (1984) *Divisions of Labour* (Oxford: Blackwell).

Palriwala, Rajni (1990) 'Introduction', in Leela Dube and Rajni Palriwala (eds), *Structures and Strategies: Women, Work and Family* (New Delhi: Sage) 15–55.

Parashar, Archana (1992) *Women and Family Law Reform in India: Uniform Civil Code and Gender Equality* (New Delhi: Sage).

Parker, Hermione (1995) *Taxes, Benefits and Family Life: The Seven Deadly Traps* (London: Institute of Economic Affairs).

Parnwell, Mike (1993) *Population Movements and the Third World* (London: Routledge).

Parpart, Jane (1995) 'Deconstructing the Development "Expert": Gender, Development and the "Vulnerable Groups"', in Marianne Marchand and Jane Parpart (eds), *Feminism/Postmodernism/Development* (London: Routledge) 221–43.

Parpart, Jane and Marchand, Marianne (1995) 'Exploding the Canon: An Introduction/Conclusion', in Marianne Marchand and Jane Parpart (eds), *Feminism/Postmodernism/Development* (London: Routledge) 1–22.

Patronato Nacional de la Infancia (PANI) (1982) *La Mujer: Un Estudio Sobre la Madre Sola, Jefe de Familia que Hubiere Tenido Intervención por parte de as Unidades de Servicios Integrales del Area Central (USIS)* (San José: PANI, Oficina de Planificación).

Patronato Nacional de la Infancia (PANI) (1990) *Características de la Mujer Agredida Atendida en el PANI* (San José: PANI).

Patronato Nacional de la Infancia (PANI) (1994) *Estrategia de Intervención con Grupos de Mujeres Agredidas* (San José: PANI).

Patterson, Sybil (1994) 'Women's Survival Strategies in Urban Areas: CARICOM and Guyana', in Fatima Meer (ed.), *Poverty in the 1990s: The Responses of Urban Women* (Paris: UNESCO/International Social Science Council) 117–33.

Pavia Ticzon, Lucia (1990) 'A Feminist Reflection on Organisation Development', in Marjorie Evasco, Aurora Javate de Dios and Flor Caagusan (eds), *Women's Springbook: Readings on Women and Society* (Quezon City: Fresam Press) 115–20.

Peach, Ceri and Byron, Margaret (1993) 'Caribbean Tenants in Council Housing: "Race", Class and Gender, *New Community*,19:3, 407–23.

Pearson, Maggie (1987) 'Old Wives or Young Midwives? Women as Caretakers of Health: The Case of Nepal', in Janet Momsen and Janet Townsend (eds), *Geography of Gender in the Third World* (London: Hutchinson) 116–30.

Peña Saint Martin, Florencia (1992a) '¿A Quienes Considerar Mujeres Jefas de Familia en la Investigación Antropológica?', *Nueva Antropología*, XII:41, 159–72.

Peña Saint Martin, Florencia (1992b) 'Los Grupos Domésticos Encabezados por Mujeres: El Caso de las Maquiladoras Domiciliarias Emeritenses', *INAJ: Revista de Divulgación del Patrimonio Cultural de Yucatán*, 7, 1–21.

Peña Saint Martin, Florencia (1994) 'Women, Work and Family: The Case of the Garment Workers in Mérida, Yucatán'. Unpublished dissertation submitted to the Graduate School of the University of Florida in partial fulfilment of the requirements for the degree of Doctor of Philosophy.

Peña Saint Martin, Florencia and Gamboa Cetina, Marcial (1991) 'Entre Telas e Hilos de Colores: Mujeres y la Confección de Ropa en Yucatán', in Vania Sales and Elsie McPhail (eds), *Textos y Pre-textos: Once Estudios Sobre la Mujer* (México DF: El Colegio de México, Programa Interdisiplinario de Estudios Sobre la Mujer) 309–80.

Perlman, Janice (1976) *The Myth of Marginality: Urban Poverty and Politics in Rio de Janeiro* (Berkeley: University of California Press).

Perrons, Diane (1995a) 'Gender Inequality in Regional Development', *Regional Studies*, 29:5, 465–76.

Perrons, Diane (1995b) 'Welfare Regimes, Regulatory Frameworks and Gender Inequality in the Regions of Europe', *European Urban and Regional Studies*, 2:2, 99–120.

Perrons, Diane (1996) 'Gender as a Form of Social Exclusion: Gender Inequality in the Regions of Europe', in Paul Lawless (ed.), *Unemployment and Social Exclusion: Landscapes of Labour and Inequality* (London : Jessica Kingsley Publishers).

Pescatello, Ann (1976) *Power and Pawn: The Female in Iberian Families, Societies and Cultures* (Westport, Connecticut: Greenwood).

Peters, Pauline (1983) 'Gender, Development Cycles and Historical Process: A Critique of Recent Research on Women in Botswana, *Journal of Southern African Studies*, 10, 100–22.

Peterson, Jean Treloggan (1993) 'Generalised Extended Family Exchange: A Case from the Philippines', *Journal of Marriage and the Family*, 55,570–84.

Phoenix, Ann (1994) 'Practising Feminist Research: The Intersection of Gender and 'Race' in the Research Process', in Mary Maynard and Jane Purvis (eds), *Researching Women's Lives From a Feminist Perspective* (London: Taylor and Francis) 49–71.

Pietilä, Hilkka and Vickers, Jeanne (1994) *Making Women Matter: The Role of the United Nations*, revised and expanded ed. (Zed: London).

Pine, Frances (1982) 'Family Structure and the Division of Labour: Female Roles in Urban Ghana', in Hamsa Alavi and Teodor Shanin (eds), *Sociology of Developing Societies* (Basingstoke:Macmillan) 387–405.

Pineda Deang, Lionel (1992) 'Living Arrangements of Mothers Following Childbirth: Do They Affect Subsequent Fertility'. Unpublished PhD dissertation, Department of Sociology, University of North Carolina at Chapel Hill.

Pineda-Ofreneo, Rosalinda (1991) *The Philippines: Debt and Poverty* (Oxford:Oxfam).

Pittin, Renée (1989) 'The Control of Reproduction: Principle and Practice in Nigeria', in Ayesha Imam, Renée Pittin and H. Omole (eds), *Women and the Family in Africa* (Dakar: CODESRIA) 93–115.

Pollack, Molly (1989) 'Poverty and the Labour Market in Costa Rica', in Gerry Rodgers (ed.), *Urban Poverty and the Labour Market: Access to Jobs and Incomes in Asian and Latin American Cities* (Geneva: International Labour Office) 65–80.

Pothukuchi, Kameshwari (1993) 'Non-traditional Living Arrangements: Beyond the Nuclear Family', in Hemalata Dandekar (ed.), *Shelter, Women and Development: First and Third World Perspectives* (Ann Arbor, Michigan: George Wahr Publishing Co.) 286–94.

Powell, Dorian (1986) 'Caribbean Women and their Response to Familial Experiences', *Social and Economic Studies* (Institute of Social and Economic Research, University of the West Indies), 35:2, 83–130.

Prakash Singh, Indu and Singh, Renuka (1989) 'Sati: Its Patri-Politics', in Pramila Dandvate, Ranjana Kumari and Jamila Verghese (eds), *Widows, Abandoned and Destitute Women in India* (London: Sangam Books) 54–62.

Prior, Marsha (1993) 'Matrifocality, Power and Gender Relations in Jamaica', in Caroline Brettell and Carolyn Sargent (eds) *Gender in Cross-Cultural Perspective* (Englewood Cliffs, New Jersey: Prentice Hall) 310–18.

PROCESS (1993) *Gender Needs Assessment in PROCESS-supported Areas in Panay, Bohol and Northern Luzon* (Iloilo City: PROCESS).

Programa Nacional de Solidaridad (PNS) (1991) *Mujeres en Solidaridad* (México DF: PNS).

Pryer, Jane (1992) 'Purdah, Patriarchy and Population Movement: Perspectives from Bangladesh', in Sylvia Chant (ed.), *Gender and Migration in Developing Countries* (London: Belhaven) 139–53.

Pulsipher, Lydia (1993) '"He Won't Let She Stretch She Foot": Gender Relations in Traditional West Indian Houseyards', in Cindi Katz and Janice Monk (eds), *Full Circles: Geographies of Women over the Life Course* (London: Routledge) 107–21.

Putzel, James (1992) *A Captive Land: The Politics of Agrarian Reform in the Philippines* (London/New York: Catholic Institute for International Relations/Monthly Review Press).

Quilodrán, Julieta (1992) 'Peculiarities of Border Marriage Patterns', in John Weeks and Roberto Ham-Chande (eds) *Demographic Dynamics on the US-Mexico Border* (El Paso: University of Texas Press) 89–103.

Quiróz, Teresa; Osorio, Rodolfo; León, Carmen Violeta and Vásquez, Rita (1984) *La Mujer en Costa Rica y su Participación Política-Económica en el Desarrollo del País* (San José: Instituto de Investigaciones Sociales, Universidad de Costa Rica, Avances de Investigación No.51).

Quisumbing, Purificacion (1990) 'Taming the Law', in Marjorie Evasco, Aurora Javate de Dios and Flor Caagusan (eds), *Women's Springbook: Readings on Women and Society* (Fresam Pres: Quezon City) 43–54.

Radcliffe, Sarah (1986) 'Women's Lives and Peasant Livelihood Strategies: A Study of Migration in the Peruvian Andes'. Unpublished PhD thesis (Department of Geography, University of Liverpool).

Radcliffe, Sarah (1992) 'Mountains, Maidens and Migration: Gender and Mobility in Peru', in Sylvia Chant (ed.), *Gender and Migration in Developing Countries* (London: Belhaven) 30–48.

Rahat, Naveed-I (1986) 'Meharabad, a Punjabi Village: Male Out-Migration and Women's Changing Roles', in Frits Selier and Mehtab Karim (eds), *Migration in Pakistan: Themes and Facts* (Lahore: Vanguard) 139–60.

Rakodi, Carole (1991) 'Women's Work or Household Strategies?', *Environment and Urbanisation*, 3:2, 39–45.

Ramirez, Mina (1984) *Understanding Philippine Social Realities Through the Filipino Family: A Phenomenological Approach* (Manila: Asian Social Institute Communication Center).

Ramírez Boza, Mario (1987) *Limitaciones y Obstáculos que Tiene la Mujer de Dos Sectores Populares del Campo para su Integración al Mercado Laboral* (San José:

Instituto de Investigaciones Sociales, Universidad de Costa Rica, Avances de Investigación No.62).

Rasanayagam, Yoga (1993) 'Women as Agents and Beneficiaries of Rural Housing Programmes in Sri Lanka', in Janet Momsen and Vivian Kinnaird (eds), *Different Places, Different Voices: Gender and Development in Africa, Asia and Latin America* (London: Routledge) 146–58.

Republic of the Philippines and the United Nations Children's Fund (UNICEF) (1990) *Situation of Children and Women in the Philippines* (Manila: Republic of the Philippines/UNICEF).

República de Costa Rica (1986) *Código Civil y de la Familia* (San José: Colección Leyes Editorial Porvenir).

Resources for Action (1982) *Women and Shelter in Honduras* (Washington DC: USAID, Office of Housing).

Reuben Soto, Sergio (1986) *Estructuras Familiares de Costa Rica en 1973* (San José: Instituto de Investigaciones Sociales, Unversidad de Costa Rica, Avances de Investigación No.57).

Reyes, Socorro (1992) 'Legislative Agenda on Women's Issues for the New Congress', *Lila: Asia-Pacific Women's Studies Journal*, 2, 45–64.

Roberts, Bryan (1991) 'The Changing Nature of Informal Employment: The Case of Mexico', in Guy Standing and Victor Tokman (eds), *Towards Social Adjustment: Labour Market Issues in Structural Adjustment* (Geneva: Internationa Labour Office) 115–40.

Roberts, Bryan (1994) 'Informal Economy and Family Strategies', *International Journal of Urban and Regional Research*, 18:1, 6–23.

Roberts, Penelope (1991) 'Anthropological Perspectives on the Household', *IDS Bulletin* (Sussex), 22:1, 60–64.

Robertson, Claire (1976) 'Ga Women and Socioeconomic Change in Accra, Ghana', in Nancy Hafkin and Edna Bay (eds), *Women in Africa: Studies in Social and Economic Change* (Stanford: Stanford University Press) 111–33.

Robertson, Claire (1984) *Sharing the Same Bowl: A Socioeconomic History of Women and Class in Accra, Ghana* (Bloomington: Indiana University Press).

Rodman, Hyman (1965) 'Middle-Class Misconceptions about Lower-Class Families', in Hyman Rodman (ed.), *Marriage, Family and Society: A Reader* (New York: Random House) 219–30.

Rodman, Hyman (1971) *Lower-Class Families: The Culture of Poverty in Negro Trinidad* (New York: Oxford University Press).

Rodríguez, Lilia (1993) 'Respuestas de las Mujeres Pobres Frente a la Crisis en el Ecuador', in Zonia Palán, Caroline Moser and Lilia Rodríguez, *La Mujer Frente a las Políticas de Ajuste* (Quito: Centro Ecuatoriano para la Promoción de la Mujer) 45–83.

Rogers, Barbara (1980) *The Domestication of Women: Discrimination in Developing Societies* (London: Tavistock).

Rojas Chaves, Carlos (1986) *Problemas Sociales en América Latina y el Caribe: El Caso de la Mujer Jefe de Hogar* (San José: PANI, Oficina de Planificación).

Roll, Jo (1992) *Lone Parent Families in Europe: The 1992 Report* (London: Family Policy Studies Centre).

Romero, Carmen; Ramírez, Mario and Tanzi, Giannina (1983) 'La Investigación de los Problemas de la Mujer Rural', *Revista de Ciencias Sociales*, 25, 47–58.

Romero, Mayra (1994) 'De la Modernización al Ajuste Estructural: 30 Años de la Revolución Verde', *Revista de Ciencias Sociales*, 63, 109–17.

del Rosario, Virginia O. (1995) 'Mainstreaming Gender Concerns: Aspects of Compliance, Resistance and Negotiation', *IDS Bulletin* (Sussex), 26:3, 103–9.

Rose, Damaris (1993) 'Local Childcare Strategies in Montréal, Quebec: The Mediations of State Policies, Class and Ethnicity in the Life Courses of Families with Young Children', in Cindi Katz and Janice Monk (eds), *Full Circles: Geographies of Women Over the Life Course* (London: Routledge) 188–207.

Rosenhouse, Sandra (1989) *Identifying the Poor: Is 'Headship' a Useful Concept?* (Washington DC: World Bank, LSMS Working Paper No.58).

Rudd, Diane (1989) 'Older Women Living Alone', in Duncan Ironmonger (ed.) *Households Work* (Sydney: Allen and Unwin) 113–28.

Safa, Helen (1980) 'Class Consciousness among Working Class Women in Latin America: Puerto Rico', in June Nash and Helen Safa (eds) *Sex and Class in Latin America* (New York: Bergin) 69–85.

Safa, Helen (1981) 'Runaway Shops and Female Employment: The Search for Cheap Labour', *Signs*, 7.2, 418–33.

Safa, Helen (1983) 'El Empleo Femenino y la Reproducción Social en la Clase Obrera Puertorriqueña', *Estudios Sociológicos* (El Colegio de México), 1:3, 459–86.

Safa, Helen (1990) 'Women and Industrialisation in the Caribbean', in Sharon Stichter and Jane Parpart (eds), *Women, Employment and the Family in the International Division of Labour* (Basingstoke: Macmillan) 72–97.

Safa, Helen (1995) *The Myth of the Male Breadwinner: Women and Industrialisation in the Caribbean* (Boulder, Colorado: Westview Press).

Safa, Helen and Antrobus, Peggy (1992) 'Women and the Economic Crisis in the Caribbean', in Lourdes Benería and Shelley Feldman (eds), *Unequal Burden: Economic Crises, Persistent Poverty and Women's Work* (Boulder, Colorado: Westview Press) 49–82.

Sage, Colin (1993) 'Deconstructing the Household: Women's Roles Under Commodity Relations in Highland Bolivia', in Janet Momsen and Vivian Kinnaird (eds), *Different Places, Different Voices: Gender and Development in Africa, Asia and Latin America* (London: Routledge) 243–55.

Saktanber, Ayse (1994) 'Becoming the "Other" as a Muslim in Turkey: Turkish Women vs Islamist Women', *New Perspectives on Turkey* (Economic and Social History Foundation, Istanbul), 11, 99–134.

Salaff, Janet (1990) 'Women, the Family and the State: Hong Kong, Taiwan and Singapore - Newly Industrialised Countries in Asia', in Sharon Stichter and Jane Parpart (eds), *Women, Employment and the Family in the International Division of Labour* (Basingstoke: Macmillan) 98–136.

Sandoval Lara, Miguel and Arroyo García, Francisco (1990) The Mexican Economy at the end of the Century, *CEPAL Review* (UN, Santiago), 42, 195–209.

Sanjek, Roger (1983) 'Female and Male Domestic Cycles in Urban Africa', in Christine Oppong (ed.), *Female and Male in West Africa* (London: George Allen and Unwin) 330–43.

Saradamoni, K. (1992) 'Introduction', in K. Saradamoni (ed.), *Finding the Household: Methodological and Empirical Issues* (New Delhi: Sage) 17–30.

Sassen-Koob, Saskia (1984) 'From Household to Workplace: Theories and Survey Research on Migrant Women in the Labour Market: Notes on the Incorporation of Women through Immigration and Offshore Production, _International Migration Review_, xviii:4, 1144–67.

Scarnecchia, Tim (1993) 'Access to Housing in Urban and Rural Zimbabwe: Historical Observations on the Nuclear Family', in Hemalata Dandekar (ed.), _Women, Shelter and Development: First and Third World Perspectives_ (Ann Arbor, Michigan: George Wahr Publishing Co.) 295–303.

Schlyter, Ann (1989) _Women Householders and Housing Strategies: The Case of Harare, Zimbabwe_ (Gävle: The National Swedish Institute for Building Research).

Schmink, Marianne (1984) 'Household Economic Strategies', _Latin American Research Review_, 19:3, 87–101.

Schmink, Marianne (1986) 'Women and Urban Industrial Development in Brazil', in June Nash and Helen Safa (eds), _Women and Change in Latin America_ (Massachusetts: Bergin and Garvey) 136–64.

Scott, Alison MacEwen (1990) 'Patterns of Patriarchy in the Peruvian Working Class', in Sharon Stichter and Jane Parpart (eds) _Women, Employment and the Family in the International Division of Labour_ (Basingstoke: Macmillan) 198–220.

Scott, Alison MacEwen (1994) _Divisions and Solidarities: Gender, Class and Employment in Latin America_ (London: Routledge).

Seccombe, Wally (1980) 'Domestic Labour and the Working Class Household', in Bonnie Fox (ed.), _Hidden in the Household: Women's Domestic Labour under Capitalism_ (Toronto: The Women's Press) 25–99.

Segal, Lynne (1995) 'A Feminist Looks at the Family', in John Muncie, Margaret Wetherell, Rudi Dallos and Allan Cochrane (eds), _Understanding the Family_ (London: Sage) 295–316.

Selby, Henry; Lorenzen, Stephen; Murphy, Arthur; Morris, Earl and Winter, Mary (1990) 'La Familia Urbana Mexicana Frente al Crisis', in Guillermo de la Peña, Juan Manuel Durán, Agustín Escobar and Javier García de Alba (eds), _Crisis, Conflicto y Sobrevivencia: Estudios Sobre la Sociedad Urbana en México_ (Guadalajara: Universidad de Guadalajara/CIESAS del Occidente) 369–88.

Selby, Henry; Murphy, Arthur and Lorenzen, Stephen (1990) _The Mexican Urban Household: Organising for Self-Defence_ (Austin: University of Texas Press).

Sempio-Diy, Alicia (1988) _Handbook on the Family Code in the Philippines_ (Quezon City: Joer Printing Services).

Sen, Amartya K. (1987) _Gender and Cooperative Conflicts_ (Helsinki: World Institute for Development Economics Research, Working Paper No.18).

Sen, Amartya K. (1991) 'Gender and Cooperative Conflicts', in Irene Tinker (ed.) _Persistent Inequalities: Women and World Development_ (New York: Oxford University Press) 123–49.

Sen, Kasturi (1994) _Ageing: Debates on Demographic Transition and Social Policy_ (London: Zed).

Sethi, Rama (1993) 'Crossing Oceans: A Cross-cultural Look at Elderly Immigrant Women in the United States and Elderly Women in India', in Hemalata Dandekar (ed.), _Shelter, Women and Development: First and Third World Perspectives_ (Ann Arbor, Michigan: George Wahr Publishing Co.) 408–13.

Sevilla, Judy Carol (1989) 'The Filipino Woman and the Family', in Amaryllis Torres (ed.), _The Filipino Woman in Focus: A Handbook of Reading_ (Bangkok: UNESCO).

Shanthi, K. (1994) 'Growing Incidence of Female Headship: Causes and Cure', _Social Action_ (New Delhi), 44, 17–33.

Shanti, Margaret (1995) 'Hinduism: Caste, Gender and Violence', *Lila: Asia Pacific Women's Studies Journal* (Intitute of Women's Studies, St Scolastica's College, Manila), 5, 17–30.

Shaw, Sandra (1991) 'The Conflicting Experiences of Lone Parenthood', in Michael Hardey and Graham Crow (eds), *Lone Parenthood: Coping with Constraints and Making Opportunities* (Hemel Hempstead: Harvester Wheatsheaf) 143–55.

Sheahan, John (1987) *Patterns of Development in Latin America: Poverty, Repression and Economic Strategy* (Princeton: Princeton University Press).

Sherriff, Farida (1991) 'Shelter and Beyond: The State, Gendered Residential Space and Survival in Tanzania', in Geertje Lycklama à Nijeholt (ed.), *Towards Women's Strategies in the 1990s: Challenging Government and the State* (Houndmills, Basingstoke: Macmillan) 71–96.

Shimuzu, Hiromu (1991) 'Filipino Children in Family and Society: Growing Up in a Many-People Environment', in Department of Sociology-Anthropology (ed.), *SA 21: Selected Readings* (Quezon City: Ateneo de Manila University, Office of Research and Publications) 106–25.

Simms, Margaret C. (1986) 'Black Women who Head Families: An Economic Struggle', in Margaret C. Simms and Julianne Malvaux (eds), *Slipping Through the Cracks: The Status of Black Women* (New Brunswick, New Jersey: Transaction Books) 141–51.

Singh Shekhawat, Prahlad (1989) 'Sati in Rajasthan', in Pramila Dandvate, Ranjana Kumari and Jamila Verghese (eds), *Widows, Abandoned and Destitute Women in India* (London: Sangam Books) 39–48.

Sklair, Leslie (1991) *Sociology of the Global System* (Hemel Hempstead: Harvester Wheatsheaf).

Smith, Joan and Wallerstein, Immanuel (eds) (1992) *Creating and Transforming Households: The Constraints of the World Economy* (Cambridge: Cambridge University Press/Paris: Editions de la Maison des Sciences des Hommes).

Smith, Raymond T. (1956) *The Negro Family in British Guiana* (London: Routledge and Kegan Paul).

Smith, Raymond T. (1988) *Kinship and Class in the West Indies: A Genealogical Study of Jamaica and Guyana* (Cambridge: Cambridge University Press).

Sojo, Ana (1989) 'Social Policies in Costa Rica', *CEPAL Review*, 38. 105–19.

Sojo, Ana (1994) *Política Social en Costa Rica: Reformas Recientes* (San José: FLACSO, Programa de Costa Rica, Cuadernos de Ciencias Sociales No.67).

Solien de Gonzales, Nancie (1960) 'Household and Family in the Caribbean', *Social and Economic Studies*, 9,101–6.

Solien de Gonzales, Nancie (1965) 'The Consanguineal Family and Matrifocality', *American Anthropologist*, 67, 1541–9.

Solien de Gonzales, Nancie (1969) *Black Carib Household Structure: A Study of Migration and Modernisation* (Seattle: University of Washington Press).

Sparr, Pamela (1994a) 'What is Structural Adjustment?', in Pamela Sparr (ed.), *Mortgaging Women's Lives: Feminist Critiques of Structural Adjustment* (London: Zed) 1–12.

Sparr, Pamela (1994b) 'Feminist Critiques of Structural Adjustment', in Pamela Sparr (ed.), *Mortgaging Women's Lives: Feminist Critiques of Structural Adjustment* (London: Zed) 13–39.

Spivak, Gayati Chakravorty (1988) 'Can the Subaltern Speak?', in Cary Nelson and Lawrence Grossburg (eds), *Marxism and the Interpretation of Cultures* (Basingstoke: Macmillan) 271–313.

Srinivasan, Vidya (1987) 'Deserted Wives in the Slums of Madras City — A Pilot Study', *The Indian Journal of Social Work*, XLVIII:3, 287–95.

Stack, Carol (1974) *All Our Kin: Strategies and Survival in a Black Community* (New York: Harper and Row).

Stack, Carol (1993) 'Domestic Networks: "Those You Count On"', in Caroline Brettell and Carolyn Sargent (eds), *Gender in Cross-Cultural Perspective* (Englewood Cliffs, New Jersey: Prentice Hall) 301–10.

Stack, Carol and Burton, Linda (1994) 'Kinscripts: Reflections on Family, Generation and Culture', in Evelyn Nakano Glenn, Grace Chang and Linda Rennie Forcey (eds), *Mothering: Ideology, Experience and Agency* (New York: Routledge) 33–44.

Standing, Guy (1989) 'Global Feminisation through Flexible Labor', *World Development*, 17:7, 1077–95.

Standing, Guy and Tokman, Victor (eds) (1991) *Towards Social Adjustment: Labour Market Issues in Structural Adjustment* (Geneva: International Labour Office).

Staudt, Kathleen (1991) *Managing Development: State, Society and International Contexts* (Newbury Park: Sage).

Starr, June (1993) 'The Legal and Social Transformation of Rural Women in Aegean Turkey', in Caroline Brettell and Carolyn Sargent (eds) *Gender in Cross-Cultural Perspective* (Englewood Cliffs, New Jersey: Prentice Hall) 278–96.

Stewart, Frances (1992) 'Can Adjustment Programmes Incorporate the Interests of Women?', in Haleh Afshar and Carolyne Dennis (eds), *Women and Adjustment Policies in the Third World* (Basingstoke: Macmillan) 13–45.

Stewart, Frances (1995) *Adjustment and Poverty: Options and Choices* (London: Routledge).

St Hilaire, Colette (1992) *Canadian Aid, Women and Development: Re-baptising the Filipina* (London: Catholic Institute for International Relations, Philippine Development Briefing No.3).

Stichter, Sharon (1990) 'Women, Employment and the Family: Current Debates', in Sharon Stichter and Jane Parpart (eds), *Women, Employment and the Family in the International Division of Labour* (Basingstoke: Macmillan) 11–71.

Stivens, Maila (1987) 'Family and State in Malaysian Industrialisation: The Case of Rembau, Negeri Sembilan, Malaysia', in Haleh Afshar (ed.), *Women, State and Ideology: Studies from Africa and Asia* (Basingstoke: Macmillan) 89–110.

Stolcke, Verena (1992) 'The Slavery Period and its Influence on Household Structure and the Family in Jamaica, Cuba and Brazil', in Elza Berquó and Peter Xenos (eds), *Family Systems and Cultural Change* (Oxford: Clarendon Press) 125–42.

Sykes, Roger (1994) 'Older Women and Housing — Prospects for the 1990s', in Rose Gilroy and Roberta Woods (eds), *Housing Women* (London: Routledge) 75–100.

Thomas, J.J. (1995) *Surviving in the City: The Urban Informal Sector in Latin America* (London: Pluto).

Thompson, Linda (1992) 'Feminist Methodology for Family Studies', *Journal of Marriage and the Family*, 54, 3–18.

Thomson, Marilyn (1986) *Women of El Salvador: The Price of Freedom* (London: Zed).

Thorbek, Susanne (1987) *Voices from the City: Women of Bangkok* (London: Zed).

Thorbek, Susanne (1994) *Gender and Slum Culture in Urban Asia* (London: Zed).
Thorner, Alice and Ranadive, Jyoti (1992) 'Working Class Women in an Indian Metropolis: A Household Approach', in K. Saradamoni (ed.), *Finding the Household: Methodological and Empirical Issues* (New Delhi: Sage) 143–62.
Tienda, Marta and Ortega, Sylvia (1982) 'Las Familias Encabezadas por Mujeres y la Formación de Nucleos Extensos: Una Referencia a Perú', in Secretaría de Programación y Presupuesto (SPP) (ed.), *Estudios Sobre la Mujer 1. El Empleo y la Mujer, Bases Teóricas, Metodológicas y Evidencia Empírica* (México DF: SPP).
Tinker, Irene (1990) 'A Context for the Field and for the Book', in Irene Tinker (ed.), *Persistent Inequalities: Women and World Development* (Oxford: Oxford University Press) 3–13.
Tinker, Irene (1993) 'Global Policies Regarding Shelter for Women: Experiences of the UN Centre for Human Settlements', in Hemalata Dandekar (ed.), *Women, Shelter and Development: First and Third World Perspectives* (Ann Arbor, Michigan: George Wahr Publishing Co) 23–32.
Tipple, Graham; Amole, 'Bayo; Korboe, David and Onyeacholem, Helen (1994) 'House and Dwelling, Family and Household: Towards Defining Housing Units in West African Cities', *Third World Planning Review*, 16:4, 429–50.
Todes, Alison and Walker, Norah (1993) 'Women and Housing Policy in South Africa: A Discussion of Durban Case Studies', in Hemalata Dandekar (ed.), *Women, Shelter and Development: First and Third World Perspectives* (Ann Arbor, Michigan: George Wahr Publishing Co) 41–53.
Tonghuthai, Pawadee (1995) 'Asian Women in Manufacturing: New Challenges, Old Problems', in Mihály Simai with Valentine Moghadam and Arvo Kuddo (eds), *Global Employment: An International Investigation into the Future of Work Vol.1* (London: Zed) 167–81.
Townsend, Janet; Arrevillaga Matías, Ursula; Cancino Córdova, Socorro; Pancheco Bonfil, Silvana and Pérez Nasser, Elia (1994) *Voces Femeninas de la Selva* (México DF/Durham:Centro de Estudios de Desarrollo Rural/University of Durham).
Townsend, Janet and Momsen, Janet (1987) 'Towards a Geography of Gender in the Third World', in Janet Momsen and Janet Townsend (eds), *Geography of Gender in the Third World* (London: Hutchinson) 27–81.
Trejos, Rafael A. (1992) 'Desarrollo del Sector Servicios en Costa Rica', in Juan Manuel Villasuso (ed.), *El Nuevo Rostro de Costa Rica* (Heredia: Centro de Estudios Democráticos de América Latina) 493–507.
Trenchard, Esther (1987) 'Rural Women's Work in Sub-Saharan Africa and the Implications for Nutrition', in Janet Momsen and Janet Townsend (eds), *Geography of Gender in the Third World* (London: Hutchinson) 153–72.
Trotz, Alissa (1996) 'Gender, Ethnicity and Familial Ideology in Georgetown, Guyana: Household Structure and Female Labour Force Participation Reconsidered', *European Journal of Development Research*, 8:1.
Ugalde, Juan Gerardo (1989) 'Síndrome de la Mujer Agredida: Síndrome de la Agresión Familiar', *Mujer*, 5, 41–3.
Ulate, Anabelle (1992) 'Aumento de los Exportaciones: Obsesión del Ajuste Estructural', in Juan Manuel Villasuso (ed.), *El Nuevo Rostro de Costa Rica* (Heredia: Centro de Estudios Democráticos de América Latina) 471–92.
United Nations (UN) (1990) *Demographic Yearbook 1988* (New York: UN).

United Nations (UN) (1991) *The World's Women 1970–1990: Trends and Statistics* (New York: UN).

United Nations Development Programme (UNDP) (1994) *Human Development Report 1994* (New York: Oxford University Press).

United Nations Development Programme (UNDP) (1995) *Human Development Report 1995* (New York: Oxford University Press).

United Nations Division for the Advancement of Women (UNDAW) (1991) 'Women and Households in a Changing World', in Eleanora Masini and Susan Stratigos (eds), *Women, Households and Change* (Tokyo: United Nations University Press) 30–52.

Valdeavilla, Ermelita (1995) 'Breakthroughs and Challenges of Making the Philippine Government Work for Gender Equality', *IDS Bulletin* (Sussex), 26:3, 94–101.

Valladares, Licia (1989) 'Family and Child Labour in the Favela'. Paper presented at the International Symposium on Third World Urbanisation, Swedish Council for Research in Humanities and Social Sciences, Stockholm, June.

Varley, Ann (1993a) 'Gender and Housing: The Provision of Accommodation for Young Adults in Three Mexican Cities', *Habitat International*, 17:4, 13–30.

Varley, Ann (1993b) 'Gender, Household Structure and Accommodation for Young Adults in Urban Mexico', in Hemalata Dandekar (ed.), *Shelter, Women and Development: First and Third World Perspectives* (Ann Arbor, Michigan: George Wahr Publishing Co.) 304–19.

Varley, Ann (1994a) 'Housing the Household: Holding the House', in Gareth Jones and Peter Ward (eds), *Methodology for Land and Housing Market Analysis* (London: UCL Press) 120–34.

Varley, Ann (1994b) 'Targeting Female-headed Households: A Progressive Strategy?'. Paper presented at the Symposium 'Gender in Latin America', Annual Conference of Society of Latin American Studies, University of Liverpool, 25–27 March.

Varley, Ann (1995) 'Neither Victims Nor Heroines: Women, Land and Housing in Mexican Cities', *Third World Planning Review* (Special issue on 'Gender and Development'), 17:2, 169–82.

Varley, Ann (1996) 'Women-headed Households: Some More Equal than Others?, *World Development*, 24.

Varma, Rameswari (1993) 'Assessing Rural Development Programmes in India from a Gender Perspective', in Janet Momsen and Vivian Kinnaird (eds), *Different Places, Different Voices: Gender and Development in Africa, Asia and Latin America* (London: Routledge) 120–30.

Vega, Isabel (1992) 'Cambios en los Patrones Organizacionales de la Familia', in Juan Manuel Villasuso (ed.), *El Nuevo Rostro de Costa Rica* (Heredia: Centro de Estudios Democráticos de América Latina) 25–44.

Vellenga, Dorothy D. (1983) 'Who is a Wife? Legal Expressions of Heterosexual Conflicts in Ghana', in Christine Oppong (ed.), *Female and Male in West Africa* (London: George Allen and Unwin) 144–55.

Vera-Sanso, Penny (1994) 'What the Neighbours Say: Gender, Personhood and Power in Two Low-income Settlements of Madras'. Unpublished PhD thesis (Department of Anthropology, Goldsmiths College, University of London).

Vincenzi, Atilio (1991) *Código Civil y Código de la Familia* (San José: Lehmann Editores).

Villariba, Mariya (1993) *Canvasses of Women in the Philippines* (London: Change, International Reports on Women and Society No.7).

Visaria, Pravin and Visaria, Leela (1985) 'Indian Households with Female Heads: Their Incidence, Characteristics and Level of Living', in Devaki Jain and Nirmala Banerjee (eds), *Tyranny of the Household: Investigative Essays on Women's Work* (New Delhi: Shakti Books) 50–83.

Wade, Peter (1993) *Blackness and Race Mixture: The Dynamics of Racial Identity in Colombia* (Baltimore: Johns Hopkins University Press).

Wallerstein, Immanuel and Smith, Joan (1991) 'Households as an Institution of the World Economy', in Rae Lesser Blumberg (ed.), *Gender, Family and the Economy: The Triple Overlap* (Newbury Park: Sage) 225–42.

Wallerstein, Immanuel and Smith, Joan (1992) 'Households as an Institution of the World Economy', in Joan Smith and Immanuel Wallerstein (eds), *Creating and Transforming Households: The Constraints of the World Economy* (Cambridge/Paris: Cambridge University Press/Editions de la Maison des Sciences des Hommes) 3–23.

Walther, Uwe-Jens and Simbriger, Angelika (1996) 'Variety as Normality – Innovative Housing for Single Parent Families: Examples from Germany. An Annotated Bibliography', in Emine Komut (ed.), *The Housing of the 'Others'* (Ankara: Turkish Chamber of Architects).

Watkins, Francis (1994) 'They Save There, We Eat Here: Gender, Houses and Labour Migration in a Pakhtun Village' (University of Edinburgh, Department of Social Anthropology, mimeo).

Ward, Peter (1993) 'Social Welfare Policy and Political Opening in Mexico', *Journal of Latin American Studies*, 25, 613–28.

Weedon, Chris (1987) 'Radical and Revolutionary Feminism', in Frankie Ashton and Gill Whitting (eds), *Feminist Theory and Practical Policies: Shifting the Agenda in the 1980s* (Bristol: University of Bristol, School of Advanced Urban Studies) 6–18.

Weekes-Vagliani, Winifred (1992) 'Structural Adjustment and Gender in the Côte d'Ivoire', in Haleh Afshar and Carolyne Dennis (eds), *Women and Adjustment Policies in the Third World* (Basingstoke: Macmillan) 117–49.

Westwood, Sallie (1984) '"Fear Woman": Property and Modes of Production in Urban Ghana', in Renée Hirschon (ed.), *Women and Property — Women as Property* (London: Croom Helm/New York: St Martins) 140–57.

Wetherell, Margaret (1995) 'Social Structure, Ideology and Family Dynamics: The Case of Parenting', in John Muncie, Margaret Wetherell, Rudi Dallos and Allan Cochrane (eds), *Understanding the Family* (London: Sage) 213–56.

Wieringa, Saskia (1994) 'Women's Interests and Empowerment: Gender Planning Reconsidered', *Development and Change*, 25, 829–48.

White, Sarah (1994) 'Making Men an Issue: Gender Planning for the Other Half', in Mandy MacDonald (ed.), *Gender Planning in Development Agencies: Meeting the Challenge* (Oxford: Oxfam) 98–110.

White, Sarah (1992) *Arguing with the Crocodile: Gender and Class in Bangladesh* (London: Zed).

Wilder, Bill (1995) 'More on Madness: The Case of Malay Divorce'. Paper presented at the 15th annual conference of the Association of Southeast Asian Studies in the United Kingdom, 'Gender and the Sexes in Southeast Asia', University of Durham, 29–31 March.

Wilk, Richard R. and Netting, Robert McC (1984) 'Households: Changing Forms and Functions', in Robert McC Netting, Richard R. Wilk and Eric J. Arnould (eds),

Households: Comparative and Historical Studies of the Domestic Group (Berkeley: University of California Press) 1–28.

Wilkinson, Clive (1987) 'Women, Work and Migration in Lesotho', in Janet Momsen and Janet Townsend (eds), *Geography of Gender in the Third World* (London: Hutchinson) 225–39.

Willis, Katie (1993) 'Women's Work and Social Network Use in Oaxaca City, Mexico', *Bulletin of Latin American Research*, 12:1, 65–82.

Willis, Katie (1994) Women's Work and Social Network Use in Oaxaca City, Mexico. Unpublished DPhil dissertation, Nuffield College, Oxford.

Wilson, Chris and Dyson, Tim (1992) 'Family Systems and Cultural Change: Perspectives from Past and Present', in Elza Berquó and Peter Xenos (eds), *Family Systems and Cultural Change* (Oxford: Clarendon Press) 31–45.

Wilson, Fiona (1991) *Sweaters: Gender, Class and Workshop-based Industry in Mexico* (Basingstoke: Macmillan).

Wilson, Gail (1987) 'Women's Work: The Role of Grandparents in Inter-generational Transfers', *The Sociological Review*, 35–4, 703–20.

Winchester, Hilary (1990) 'Women and Children Last: The Poverty and Marginalisation of One-parent Families', in *Transactions, Institute of British Geographers NS*, 15:1, 70–86.

Wolf, Diane (1990) 'Daughters, Decisions and Domination: An Empirical and Conceptual Critique of Household Strategies', *Development and Change*, 21, 43–74.

Wolf, Diane (1991) 'Female Autonomy, the Family and Industrialisation in Java', in Rae Lesser Blumerg (ed.), *Gender, Family and the Economy: The Triple Overlap* (Newbury Park: Sage) 128–48.

Wolf, Margery (1985) *Revolution Postponed: Women in Contemporary China* (Stanford, California: Stanford University Press).

World Bank (1994) *World Development Report 1994* (New York: Oxford University Press).

World Bank (1995) *Advancing Gender Equality: From Concept to Action* (Washington DC: World Bank).

Wratten, Ellen (1995) 'Conceptualising Urban Poverty', *Environment and Urbanisation*, 7:1, 11–36.

Wyss, Brenda (1990) 'Family Policy in Five Caribbean Countries'. Draft Manuscript available from Nancy Folbre, Department of Economics, University of Massachusetts, Amherst, MA 01003.

Yanagisako, Sylvia Junko (1984) 'Explicating Residence: A Cultural Analysis of Changing Households among Japanese Americans', in Robert McC Netting, Richard R. Wilk and Eric J. Arnould (eds), *Households: Comparative and Historical Studies of the Domestic Group* (Berkeley: University of California Press) 330–52.

Yen, Maria and Keigher, Sharon (1993) 'Shelter Options for Elderly Women: An Overview', in Hemalata Dandekar (ed.), *Women, Shelter and Development: First and Third World Perspectives* (Ann Arbor, Michigan: George Wahr Publishing Co) 374–6.

Young, Kate (1992) 'Household Resource Management', in Lise Østergaard (ed.) *Gender and Development: A Practical Guide* (London: Routledge) 135–64.

Young, Kate (1993) *Planning Development With Women: Making a World of Difference* (Basingstoke: Macmillan).

Young, Michael and Willmott, Peter (1957) *Family and Kinship in East London* (London: Routledge and Kegan Paul).

Young, Mei Ling (1992) 'Analysing Household Histories', in Elza Berquó and Peter Xenos (eds), *Family Systems and Cultural Change* (Oxford: Clarendon Press) 176–200.

Youssef, Nadia (1972) 'Differential Labour Force Participation of Women in Latin American and Middle Eastern Countries', *Social Forces*, 51, 135–53.

Youssef, Nadia and Hetler, Carol (1983) 'Establishing the Economic Condition of Women-headed Households in the Third World: A New Approach', in Mayra Buvinic, Margaret Lycette and William McGreevey (eds), *Women and Poverty in the Third World* (Baltimore: Johns Hopkins University Press) 216–43.

Yudelman, Sally (1989) 'Access and Opportunity for Women in Central America: A Challenge for Peace', in William Ascher and Ann Hubbard (eds), *Central American Recovery and Development: Task Force Report to the International Commission for Central American Recovery and Development* (Durham: Duke University Press) 235–56.

Zinn, Maxine Baca (1989) 'Family, Race, and Poverty in the Eighties', *Signs*, 14:4, 856–74.

Zinn, Maxine Baca (1990) 'Family, Feminism and Race in America', *Gender and Society*, 4:1, 68–82.

Zorrilla-Vazquez, Emilio (1995) 'NAFTA: Reflections and Queries for Policy Design in Mexico', in Michael Hodges (ed.), *The Impact of NAFTA: Economies in Transition* (London: London School of Economics, Centre for Research on the USA) 96–120.

Zosa-Feranil, Imelda (1984) 'Female Employment and the Family: A Case Study of the Bataan Export Processing Zone', in Gavin Jones (ed.), *Women in the Urban and Industrial Labour Force: Southeast and East Asia* (Canberra: Australian National University, Development Studies Center Monograph No.33) 387–403.

Index